PAUL TILLICH'S PHILOSOPHY OF CULTURE, SCIENCE, AND RELIGION

PAUL TILLICH'S PHILOSOPHY OF CULTURE, SCIENCE, AND RELIGION

JAMES LUTHER ADAMS

Harper & Row, Publishers

NEW YORK

To Margaret, the Beloved

Preface

RAPHAEL in his altarpiece, "The Coronation of the Virgin," for the first time in the history of painting took the bold step of combining two previously unrelated iconographic traditions, that of the Assumption and that of the Coronation of the Virgin. Erwin Panofsky in his remarkable study of Dürer has observed that in this painting the celestial and the terrestrial spheres are sharply separated by means of a horizontal band of clouds. Moreover, the Apostles on earth, like those of a Gothic tympanum, are depicted on a straight line, in "isocephalic" fashion.

Dürer, in his "Heller Altarpiece," only a few years later adopted this bold combination—"a miracle on earth and a ceremony in Heaven not meant to be observed by mortal eyes." In doing so he retained in part Raphael's visualization of the distinction between the celestial and the terrestrial spheres. But Dürer in turn also introduced innovation. He strove to connect the two worlds by a device that engenders a sense of dynamic relation between the divine and the human. The separating band of clouds is removed, and the Apostles, instead of being arranged in a straight row, are placed in a semicircle that "opens toward the back, so that the celestial apparition seems to soar from their very midst."

Dürer's painting, precisely in its difference from Raphael's, in some measure offers a visualization of Paul Tillich's conception of the dynamic relation between the divine and the human. In Tillich's view also, the divine appears in the very midst of the human scene; and even there it is not a separate function. But Dürer's painting, like Raphael's and like most visualizations of the divine, tries to spatialize it. In order to avoid this blasphemy, Tillich is wont to speak of the divine as erupting from the depth of existence. Thus he would translate the Dürer analogy in such a way as to reject a separate supranatural realm, in favor of a paradoxical view of the nature and presence of the divine. In any authentic religion man is aware of his finitude and is therefore aware of the infinite; he is aware of being remote or estranged from, and yet also near to, the divine. This paradoxical formulation implies the rejection of the spatialization of the divine. The infinite is to be understood in terms of quality rather than of quantity.

Dürer's altarpiece draws attention to the vertical relation between the divine and the human. In one sense, as we have observed, the image is appropriate. But what of the relation between the vertical and the horizontal? According to a Christian view, the divine offers a summons to man in ongoing history; it brings judgment upon history and transforms it. It impinges upon and informs not only religion in the narrow sense but also the full range of cultural activity—the sciences and the arts and all social and political concerns and forms. This particular relationship between the divine and the human is not the explicit concern of Dürer in the altarpiece. The relation between the vertical and the horizontal has been a characteristic and systematic concern of Tillich. Although he is a teacher of systematic theology, most of his writings—including the three volumes of *Systematic Theology*—try to define the relation between religion and culture.

For an artistic visualization of this aspect of Tillich's outlook one might turn to a picture by Raphael, to the great painting, "The School of Athens," which decorates the wall of the Stanza della Segnatura in the Vatican. Both the vertical and the horizontal dimensions are explicitly taken into account here. On the wall opposite "The School of Athens" is "The Disputá," depicting a dialogue regarding the unity of faith in heaven and earth—a Dantesque vision of light. "The School of Athens" is often wrongly considered to be merely a glorification of the pursuit of knowledge, but it has also a profound religious quality. From recent studies of Raphael and of this painting we have become aware of a *religious* rebirth that is implied by the concept of the Renaissance. Ostensibly, this Raphael masterpiece is a depiction of the philosophers and scientists of ancient Greece, the wall to its right presenting the arts. But behind its conception in the mind of Raphael was a tradition going back through Dante and Giotto to Bonaventura and Francis of Assisi. Vasari even hints that Raphael is a new Francis. Raphael is thus seen to be inspired by a "rebirth" that began with Joachim of Fiore and Francis and Giotto. For this reason "The School of Athens" and "The Disputá" are in certain quarters today given "a Franciscan interpretation." "The Disputá" is of course recognized to be the celestial and "The School of Athens" the terrestrial sphere, and "The School," with its gray tones, is subordinate to "The Disputá" with its "light-ness" that is reminiscent of Dante's Paradise. Moreover, there is here an attempted reconciliation of the conflict between religion and the sciences, a conflict characteristic of the Early Renaissance. The gestures of the central figures of "The School"—Aristotle with his hand extended to the world about him and Plato with his finger pointing heavenward (he "yearns," as Goethe remarks, "to participate once more in the origin from which he sprang"— synthesize heaven and earth.

I cannot refrain from mentioning here the roughly analogous interpretation of Grant Wood's "American Gothic"—that, so far from derogating the provincial American farmer and his wife, the painter intended to suggest a religious (American Gothic) interpretation of the struggle and achievement and sterling character of these two people who actually were his respected friends.

I do not know how Tillich would interpret "The School of Athens" or "American Gothic." We do know that he considers Picasso's "Guernica" "a great Protestant painting." In his view it stresses "the negative-Protestant" interpretation of, and protest against, the predicament of our time. Probably he would see also in many of Dürer's works a recognition of the dark side of the human venture which is not conspicuous in Raphael's synthesis of heaven and earth. Raphael was scarcely an existentialist.

In any event, Tillich's philosophy of culture, science, and religion is part of a lifelong effort to give a religious interpretation of the character and significance (and the perversions) of the various spheres of culture—the spectrum symbolized by "The School of Athens" and the accompanying paintings. No contemporary theologian has made such an extensive effort of this sort as has Tillich; and the spread of his roots is as broad as that of Raphael, indeed it is broader.

The present book, a revision of my 1945 doctoral dissertation at the University of Chicago, is a background study of this aspect of Tillich's writings. It confines attention, however, to his earlier writings (before 1945), most of them in German. The reader must therefore take warning. This book, by ignoring for the most part Tillich's writings of the past two decades, gives an incomplete account. Many of his writings since 1945 deal with and develop the same themes, such as for example his essays collected under the title *Theology of Culture* (1959).

A second warning must be given to the reader. The present background study by no means covers the full range of Tillich's concern for a philosophy of the various spheres and perspectives of cultural life. Little, if anything, will be found here regarding his many writings on social ethics, religious socialism, political theory, psychotherapy, and education. Nor is there much that is substantial here regarding his theology or his writings about church life, past and present. A treatment of these aspects of his outlook would require another volume or two. The reader of the present study, then, must be aware of the fact that what is presented here regarding Tillich's philosophy of culture, science, and religion cannot be properly appreciated apart from its relation to the larger corpus of his writings. It is believed, however, that familiarity with what is treated here can serve as an instructive background for the understanding of his treatment of the other areas and for an understanding of his later writings.

Yet a third warning must be sounded. The reader will encounter a number of references to the writings and outlook of Karl Barth. These references are now "dated," and indication of this fact is given in the text or the footnotes. The situation of the discussion between Tillich and Barth has changed. In Tillich's view, Barth in some respects has come nearer to Tillich's fundamental position about religion and culture, as can be seen in his history of Protestant theology in the nineteenth century and also in his study entitled "The Humanity of God."

There is a certain repetitiousness in the presentation. In the central sections of the book which in turn deal with the philosophy of culture and art, of science, and of religion, some of the basic ideas of Tillich appear and reappear, set forth respectively within the context of the discipline under discussion. Consequently, the reader is not obliged to refer back to earlier chapters. Moreover, variety of formulation and of implication can in this way be observed.

I should add here that recently many of the earlier writings of Tillich have been appearing in a series of volumes, a standard edition of his *Gesammelte Werke,* published by the Evangelisches Verlagswerk in Stuttgart. The reader will find information regarding these items in the bibliography.

I am deeply indebted to Walter F. Bense, until recently the teacher of Theological German at Harvard Divinity School and at present in the Department of Humanities at the University of Massachusetts in Boston. He has given substantial and indispensable assistance not only in reading proofs and verifying the bibliography but also in improving the translation of certain passages from the German.

JAMES LUTHER ADAMS

Harvard Divinity School
July, 1965

Contents

PAUL TILLICH'S PHILOSOPHY OF CULTURE, SCIENCE, AND RELIGION

I

The Need for a
New Language

AMONG contemporary theologians no one has more radically questioned prevailing ideas and practices in the Christian churches, especially among Protestants, than has Paul Tillich. In this respect he scarcely seems typical. For the theologian is not usually thought of as a disturber. When one hears the word "theologian" one is likely to imagine a professional journeyman comfortably ensconced within the securities of a religious institution. Theologians, it is held, by the very nature of their vocation, are engaged in the devising of means whereby "the faithful" may be exhorted to greater fidelity to tradition. They are not expected to serve as gadflies within the church itself, disturbing, attacking the false or irrelevant in church practice. If a theologian does give this appearance, the observer expects that he will turn out to be merely a more subtle, effective stimulus to institutional morale.

Paul Tillich sets forth his criticism of the church precisely as a theologian. For him, protest is an ineradicable element in Protestantism as such, and the first task of the theologian is to proclaim the protest. In his role as disturber within the church Tillich does not, of course, stand alone. Karl Barth, for example, especially in his earliest writings and in his attack upon the "German Christians" of the Third Reich, has secured a reputation as such a disturber. But by the time his second major work was published, Barth's disturbance had quieted down and he had returned to a new form of confessionalism.

Paul Tillich, on the other hand, is acutely aware not only that present-day Protestantism is moribund but also that it is moribund partly because the language of tradition can in our day have little effect upon the believers and still less upon those outside the churches. He holds that the Protestantism to which we are accustomed has almost exhausted itself by becoming identified with the dominant powers of the environment—that is, with a convulsive nationalism and with bourgeois interests. Hence, he believes that a radical protest against the churches is necessary if Protestantism is to fulfill its vocation for our time; indeed, he is convinced that for a long time to come protest must take priority.[1] This protest must include a rejection of outdated terminology and it must issue in the creation of the word that speaks to our present condition, to the distressed condition of our particular time and of our particular churches. Emerson said that if one should cut Montaigne's words they would bleed. Tillich's view is that cutting into conventional religious language is almost like dissecting a corpse. He says that "we no longer have words in which the power-fulness of the word pulsates." But protest against dead words is not enough: Protestant protest must result in Protestant realization, in the word that releases new vitality. New life demands new words—first to slay death and then to summon daring novelty.

The more encrusted the habits of the mass of churchmen and the more rigid the sense of authority attaching to conventional terminology, the more daring will the innovation seem. Innovation with respect to religious language frequently elicits even a sense of shock among the faithful, with the consequence that they make little serious attempt to understand new terms. Indeed, Tillich confesses that in his own life, "the immemorial experience of mankind that new knowledge can be won only through breaking a taboo and that all autonomous thinking is accompanied by a sense of guilt, has been a fundamental experience." The positive effect of this sense of taboo has meant for Tillich that "every step in theological, ethical, and political criticism encountered inhibitions which often could be overcome only after conflicts lasting for years."[2]

If Tillich's attitude toward the language of tradition differs from the attitude of Barth, it offers striking comparison with that of the young Schleiermacher. When Schleiermacher over a century and

---

[1] *Religiöse Verwirklichung* (Berlin: Furche, 1930), p. 44 and note 2. Hereafter abbreviated *Rel. Verw.*

[2] *Interpretation of History*, trans. Rasetzki and Talmey (New York: Charles Scribner's Sons, 1936), p. 23.

a half ago summoned "the cultured despisers of religion" and undertook in the *Addresses* to show them the indispensability and inevitableness of religion, he felt he owed his audience an explanation for the fact that his language was not the language of the theologian. After "confessing" to his hearers that he is a theologian by profession, he says,

> It is a willing confession, but my language would not have betrayed me, nor should the "eulogies" of my colleagues in the profession; what I desire lies so far out of their orbit and would little resemble what they wish to see and hear. . . . I am aware that in all I have to say to you I fully disown my profession, and why should I not therefore confess it like any other misdemeanor?

With greater cause than Schleiermacher, Tillich might well say this of his own language, for, as one of his European critics has observed, "his writings delight the reader in a remarkably untheological, secular way."[3] It is no doubt partially for this reason that Tillich has been sometimes spoken of as an apostle to the Gentiles.

Barth, who says he would be "especially pleased" if his commentary, *The Epistle to the Romans,* should stray into the hands of some who are not theologians, finds it necessary to beg the indulgence of such nontheological readers because they may find his writings difficult to read. In response to his critics who urge that "simplicity is the mark of divinity" he says, "I could not make the book more easily intelligible than the subject itself allows. If I be not mistaken, we theologians serve the layman best when we refuse to have him especially in mind, and when we simply live of our own."[4]

The explanation of the difference between Tillich and Barth here is to be found in the former's conviction that the words of the theologian should be words that speak to our time. In his view, the theologian must not be content with proclamation of the "Word of God" once delivered; he must accept the responsibility and challenge of apologetics. Strict adherence to an "established," "holy" language constitutes a "legalism of the word." Hence Tillich in many of his writings has made a deliberate effort to express himself in "an untheological, profane way." His

[3] Erica Küppers, "Zur Religionsphilosophie Paul Tillichs," *Zwischen den Zeiten,* IX (1931), 123. The passage from Schleiermacher, cited above, is quoted in this article. Translations from German writings, unless otherwise noted, are by the present writer.

[4] Karl Barth, *Epistle to the Romans,* trans. Edwyn C. Hoskyns (London: Oxford University Press, 1933), p. 5.

Religious Situation and scores of his magazine articles published
in Germany and America reveal the intent and the effectiveness of
this effort.

The affinity between Tillich and Schleiermacher in their search
for a new language is by no means a coincidence. They share a
similar intellectual parentage. In certain fundamental ways
Tillich, like Schleiermacher, stems from the great trunk of German classical philosophy. Without giving systematic attention
to further comparisons between Tillich and Schleiermacher, we
should here at the outset recall some of the outstanding features
of German classical philosophy, viewing it particularly as the
background of much of Tillich's work.

The major thrust of German classical philosophy derives in
part from the Renaissance, but (more than the Renaissance) it
presupposes in a positive way the Christian traditions of theology
and philosophy. The German classical school is often spoken of
as speculative, but in addition to being speculative in the popular
sense, these philosophers were speculative in the generic sense
of the term. They aimed to "look" (*speculare*) at the world in a
new way, and yet in doing so to penetrate anew the meaning
of certain old ways. For our purpose it is especially useful to
observe what this school was opposed to and what they viewed
as their own positive effort.

On the one hand the German classical school of Kant, Fichte,
Schleiermacher, Schelling, and Hegel turned against the Enlightenment with its secularizing, skeptical rationalism which issued
in a positivism that did away with the infinite, and also against
the authoritarianism of the Age of the Despots. These philosophers in varying ways attempted to "establish" the infinite without the use of finite categories; they also attempted to grasp the
fundamental qualities of human freedom. In their rejection of
finite categories for understanding man's relation to the infinite,
these philosophers expressed a characteristic concern of the
Romantic movement. They responded to the Faustian impulse,
the striving in restless movement toward the infinite (*Unend-
lichkeitsstreben*), though the "movement" aimed also to relate
the infinite to the finite. On the other hand the German classical
philosophers were opposed to the supernaturalism of Christian
rationalistic orthodoxy and also to the disjunction between
theology and philosophy and between religion and culture.

With respect to these various motifs, the German classical
school was by no means a unitary movement. Nor is it to be
simply identified with philosophical idealism. Indeed, one branch

of the classical school (represented especially by the later Schelling), the branch to which Tillich mainly belongs, radically qualified the philosophical idealism of the earlier developments. Indeed, in the writings of Schelling and Kierkegaard, and also of Feuerbach and Marx, one can see the beginnings of modern existentialism. At the same time these later developments can be understood only in relation to the earlier idealism. As against the earlier idealism we find here the assertion that "being is finite, existence is self-contradictory, and life is ambiguous."

Taking into account the positive and negative aspects of the classical school and viewing it as a broad religious and cultural movement, we may say that German classical philosophy represents, among other things, a *diastasis* (separation) from the Enlightenment and from Christian rationalistic orthodoxy with its supernaturalism. It represents also an effort in the direction of synthesis between historic religious and Christian insight and a new, critical and constructive philosophical theology, a theology that, as with Schleiermacher, aims to explicate distinctive Christian elements and at the same time to recognize some positive relation between Christian faith and religiousness in general.

In the effort to overcome the debilitating disjunction between religion and culture the German classical school attempts to take into account and to give a religious interpretation of all spheres of culture—the sciences, the arts, politics, and even play. Tillich has often pointed out that it is no accident that this effort of German classical philosophy was promoted by men who in many instances were sons of Protestant ministers and who were also disciplined in the *Paideia* of the German humanistic *Gymnasium* with its curriculum of classical studies. (Tillich himself had this combination of upbringing and education.) The dichotomy between secular skepticism and traditional faith played a smaller role in Germany than in France and England. In the German classical school a critical attitude toward the Enlightenment and toward Christian orthodoxy was combined with a positive, creative thrust in the direction of re-conceiving the relations between theology and philosophy and between religion and culture. This outlook conditions both the ultimate orientation and the breadth of concerns of the German classical philosophers, and it also lies behind their search for a new language. In all of these respects Tillich must be considered a scion of the German classical stock. As we shall observe, however, Tillich's outlook is not confined to these perspectives, and thus it is not oriented merely to idealism or existentialism.

The average reader today will probably view the thrust of the German classical philosophy to be somehow alien to American traditions. The American philosophical tradition is generally thought of as empirical (in the line from Bacon through Locke and Hume) rather than as bearing affinity to the German classical school. Yet, there are strains that are more or less directly connected with that school.

Familiarity in the United States with German philosophy and theology considerably antedates the period of the classical school in Germany. The interest in German literature and philosophy, however, gained markedly at the end of the eighteenth century, largely under the influence of the formidable Salem clergyman-scholar, William Bentley (1759-1819). This is a topic with which the present writer would be pleased to deal at length, for his first parish ministry was in the church in Salem, Massachusetts, of which Dr. Bentley was minister from 1783 until his death in 1819. In Bentley's column, beginning in 1794 in the *Salem Gazette* and from 1800 to 1819 in the semi-weekly *Impartial Register,* he provided a "Summary" of news and of what at the time was deemed noteworthy in the theology and philosophy, the natural sciences, the literature and art of Germany. Bentley's learning with respect to German scholarship gave rise in America to the first general scholarly interest in the subject.

Henry A. Pochmann in his copious work on *German Culture in America: Philosophical and Literary Influences 1600-1900* (1957) has fully documented the familiarity in the United States with the writings of the German classical school, showing the growing influence of the school in the nineteenth century and down to the First World War. With varying degrees of understanding all of the major and many of the minor philosophical and theological figures in Germany were known, especially among the Transcendentalists (who, by the way, did not relish this name which was imposed upon them). An explicitly Hegelian movement was established in St. Louis, and in the periodical of this group, *The Journal of Speculative Philosophy* (1867-93), translations and treatments of Kant, Fichte, Schelling, and Hegel appeared. The motto of this magazine was taken from Novalis: "Philosophy can bake no bread, but it can give us God, Freedom and Immortality." In 1873-74 Francis Bowen at Harvard introduced the first collegiate course in German philosophy. In 1884 the Harvard Unitarian theologian Charles Carroll Everett published a critical exposition entitled *Fichte's Science of Knowledge;*

this work of Fichte, we shall see, is fundamental for an understanding of Tillich's philosophy of science. But many translations, as we have observed, were available before this. In 1847 the Unitarian theologian Frederick Henry Hedge, later to be professor of German at Harvard, edited and published a very large volume of translations. James Elliott Cabot, who heard Schelling's lectures in Berlin in 1841, immediately sent to Emerson a manuscript translation of Schelling's *Of Human Freedom,* a writing of considerable significance for Tillich—a writing in which Schelling broke through the previous essentialist idealism to an existentialist dialectic. In the twentieth century German classical philosophy has found distinguished representatives in Josiah Royce and William Ernest Hocking, and also in Borden P. Bowne and Edgar Brightman. John Dewey from his early days lived in the foothills of German idealism.

It is not expedient or necessary to try to characterize the tendencies emanating in America from German classical philosophy. It will suffice to say that in general the role of this philosophy in the nineteenth century in America was quite similar to the role played in Germany. Moreover, in the effort to interpret religious and Christian ideas in relation to the various spheres of culture the Americans, like the Germans of the classical school, recognized the need for a new language.

In Tillich's opinion, the traditional language of theology, despite any value it may possess for the expert, tends to create a gulf not only between the church and the world but also between the theologian and the layman. This traditional language often obscures and even perverts the essential and relevant message of the church, whether it is directed to the churchman or to the outsider. Because of it the characteristic doctrines of Christianity as well as the liturgy and preaching in the churches are at present largely ineffective. The characteristic doctrines of the Reformation, for example, doctrines that "four centuries ago split the European continent asunder and aroused savage and bloody wars," are now "so strange to the modern man that there is scarcely any way available for making them intelligible."[5] By trying again and again to impose upon men as law the religious language of earlier generations, the churches are defeating their own proper ends. Our intellectual and social situation is different from that out of which previous ecclesiastical formulations were born.

[5] *Rel. Verw.* pp. 30-31.

Our age has lost "the presuppositions that the Middle Ages and the Reformation had in common: those of the certainty of God, and with it the certainty of truth and meaning."[6] The modern man has experienced autonomy and he will not surrender it, at least not for long; and it includes a certain sense of autonomy with respect to modes of expression.

Our intellectual and social situation is different also from the situations in which the traditional liturgical language of the church originated. The liturgies of the churches have little to do with our contemporary society, whether we think of the traditional liturgy or of that which has supposedly undergone "liturgical reform." If there is to be any advance in the direction of making liturgy relevant to the common life, Tillich believes it "must be brought to light not with the 'long arm' of the antiquarian but rather with the 'cutting edge' of contemporaneity."[7] It requires "a new understanding of natural and everyday processes in their transcendent meaning."

The same situation obtains with respect to "the word of the preacher, whether it be spoken in the church or out of it, and also . . . the hymns. . . ." Some preachers wrongly imagine that ecclesiastical and biblical language are devices that will of themselves be sufficient. But Tillich, with his acute sense of the gulf between the church and the world, holds that "insofar as our understanding of the words of the Bible requires us to separate ourselves from the here-and-now, from our own contemporaneity, they are not the Word of God." The test of a realistic faith is the objectively powerful word.

Among "the faithful," the traditional language often serves to develop a mentality that is closed to criticism as well as to new light, a mentality that is unconcerned about either the irrelevance or the ineffectiveness of the churches. Indeed, the indifference of "the world"—and even of the lukewarm within the churches— often elicits among churchmen only "a spirit of ill-tempered *hybris*."

Instead of meeting the challenge to speak to the contemporary condition of their hearers, many representatives of the church prefer a sort of intoxicated renunciation of success or effectiveness, a renunciation that is in the end self-destructive. But even the message of the Bible can give no justification for repealing contemporaneity.[8]

6 "Rechtfertigung und Zweifel," *Vorträge der Theologischen Konferenz zu Giessen*, No. 39. (Giessen: Töpelmann, 1924), p. 20.

7 *Rel. Verw.*, p. 85.

8 *Ibid.*

In this passage Tillich is thinking especially of the Barthian opposition to any human attempt to give the Word of God contemporaneity, but the implications are also of general import. "The Word of God," he says, "is any reality by means of which the eternal breaks with unconditioned power into our contemporaneity."[9] It is not a question any longer of "a direct proclamation of the religious truths as they are given in the Bible and the tradition, for all of these things are torn down into the general chaos of doubt and questioning."[10] By ignoring these facts, the churches are actually accelerating and deepening the crisis of modern religion and civilization.[11] They are arousing positive hostility to the message and work of the churches not only among the educated but also among the oppressed groups who are seeking a new meaning in life. "Until the appointed representatives of the Protestant message understand this, their work in the widest circles, and especially among the working classes, will be utterly hopeless."[12] Any attempt to proclaim a religious message without taking this situation into account constitutes culpable blindness. Tillich concludes that we have here "the most urgent need of the church today in the proclaiming of its message: its language is remote from contemporary life and yet it makes a demand upon that life."[13] The churches cannot reasonably expect to make any positive impact upon that life if they are ignorant of it or if they are out of direct touch with it. The chasm represented by the differences in language is, of course, only the linguistic reflection of a chasm in life. The one cannot be closed without closing the other, but we must first find the relevant words that "pulsate with the powerfulness of the word."

The problem is more difficult when we remember that the cohesion of a religious community demands continuity of linguistic usage along with novelty introduced for the sake of achieving contemporaneity. In this connection, it should be emphasized that despite his severely critical attitude toward traditional language, Tillich recognizes the significance of "objective constructions like the confessions of a church, the meaning of which transcends subjective belief or doubt, and which are thus able to support communities in which all tendencies of doubt, criticism and

[9] *Ibid.*
[10] *Ibid.*, p. 38.
[11] *Ibid.*, p. 188.
[12] *Ibid.*, pp. 38 and 275, note 20. Here contemporary literature on the proletariat is cited to show the great distance of the workers from the church.
[13] *Ibid.*, p. 85.

certainty are admitted, provided only that the confessional foundation of the community is given general recognition."[14] Tillich's
attitude toward the deficiencies of traditional language should,
therefore, not be interpreted as favoring an abandonment of all
church confessions or of the historic doctrines of the church. He
does not propose that a general chaos of fresh thought and
language be introduced into church life. As a theologian he hopes
rather to give new relevance to the basic faith of the church,
to give its doctrines, wherever possible, the living meaning implicit and latent within them. He neither wishes nor expects the
new language of a particular theologian to replace the more
slowly changing language of the community. As a matter of fact,
Tillich's attitude is similar to that of most creative theologians.
They have spoken, as it were, in tongues, but they have not aimed
to become ventriloquists for the community. We must bear these
considerations in mind in our whole discussion of Tillich's
criticism of the traditional language of the churches. Otherwise,
we shall fail to understand his true meaning and wrongly suppose
that he wishes to replace a fetishism for traditional language with
a fetishism for novelty. Such a replacement would, of course, be
impossible of achievement. And even if it were possible to achieve,
it would be psychologically and sociologically self-defeating. As
Tillich puts it, "Realization in worship, sermon, and instruction
assumes forms that can be imparted. Ecclesiastical reality, the
reality of the personal religious life, yes, even the prophetic word
itself assumes a sacramental foundation, an abundance from
which they live."[15] The demand for novelty must not be interpreted
as incompatible with these other aspects of a continuing church
fellowship. On the other hand, the latter considerations must not
blind one to the imperative character of the demand for novelty.

The church in its rigid adherence to traditional language always appeals to divine sanctions in order to justify itself. But
however convincing these sanctions may be, the churches that
employ them often actually ignore the fact that the intellectual
situation has changed. They ignore the fact also that language is a
temporal, cultural creation. A vocabulary that in some different
situation in the past served as an effective means of communica-
tion is now a strange idiom, a sort of fossil preserved because of
the falsely pious notion that it is a sacrosanct ark of the covenant
to be touched by human hands only on pain of spiritual death.

[14] *Interpretation of History*, pp. 18-19. These sentiments reflect Tillich's
orientation to the church situation in Europe in 1936.
[15] *Ibid.*, p. 27.

Stubborn adherence to the language of the fathers generally brings about a degeneration into a quasi-priesthood of Scriptures and "sound doctrine." It may be added that this consequence attaches also to much liberal reinterpretation of traditional language, for the reinterpretation often has as little effect as the original. Thus both the liberal and the orthodox churches communicate something that breeds death or false life. And in the outcome the traditional language, in its resistance to any disturbance of creature comfort, must for its continuing viability depend upon an appeal to "conventional, mediocre theology as a protection against a better, though unconventional, theology."[16]

It would be wrong to suppose that, in Tillich's view, the need for disturbance in the church arises merely from its predicament of being tongue-tied. The predicament is, as we have observed, only one aspect of a larger embarrassment, one due to the fact that Protestantism in its present form is reaching its limit. Protestantism is not now adequately equipped to meet the demands of the historical situation. The powerful motives that were effective in certain earlier periods of Christianity are no longer really functioning. It is to no purpose merely to repeat the old ideas in their frayed forms. Nor will it be possible to leap over the gulf between Protestantism and its lost provinces by simply resuming its connection with the Reformation or with some other period regarded as normative.[17]

Protestantism by its very essence and through its inheritance of the substance of Christianity possesses a basis for coping with the situation. Before God, Protestantism must protest against all false securities and undertake a new realization relevant to the present historical situation. If the churches wish to reach the men of today, they must "discover anew the reality which was apprehended in earlier times and which is in essence the same today, and then present it in quite new terms." Only then can they "understand that reality on the basis of what the old words intended."[18] Only then can they break through the "academically petrified problems" and achieve an immediate knowledge of essential reality. "Religious knowledge is knowledge of reality." It is "not primarily the unfolding of a tradition; it is rather a

---

[16] *Protestantisches Prinzip und proletarische Situation* (Bonn: Cohen, 1931), p. 24.
[17] *Rel. Verw.*, p. 47. Protestantism may not "on any point attribute a sort of classical status to the period of the Reformation in a normative sense. It is of the essence of Protestantism that there can be no classical period for it."
[18] *Ibid.*, p. 31.

turning towards reality,"[19] "a penetrating in an ultimate sense into what happens day by day, in labor and industry, in marriage and friendship, in ordinary social intercourse and recreation, in meditation and quiet, and even in sleep."[20]

In this respect, certain secular philosophers of our day are exhibiting more nearly the right attitude than are some theologians. In fact, Tillich's own attempt to discover anew the powerful experiences that lay behind the old religious symbols— now so largely powerless—is, in many ways, similar in purpose, for example, to Martin Heidegger's attempt to discern the original experiences from which the leading conceptions of philosophy have been created. Tillich says:

> Something very tragic tends to happen in all periods of man's spiritual life: truths, once deep and powerful, discovered by the great geniuses with profound suffering and incredible labor, become shallow and superficial when used in daily conversation. How can this happen? It can happen and it unavoidably happens, because there is no depth without the way to depth. Truth without the way to truth is dead; and if it is still used, in detachment, it contributes only to the surface of things.[21]

These words come very near to expressing the sentiments of the existential philosopher Heidegger, though Tillich does not agree with Heidegger's atheistic position.

Other secular philosophies and movements today exhibit the same desire to approach reality directly and to break through the encrustations of impotent traditional conceptions. Thus they "confirm and strengthen what is really at issue in theology itself: a penetration unhampered by the restraints of traditional ways of posing problems and concepts. . . . Our attachment should be to the things themselves and not to mere authority."[22] They also demonstrate that no group of men holds a monopoly on the ability to penetrate reality. This fact leads Tillich to adopt a positive attitude toward secularism in so far as it uncovers depths of being and of history inaccessible to merely traditional ways of thinking and speaking.

Theology must find a new approach to reality. The old method of authority, which appeals to Scripture or church doctrines, breaks down because unavoidable conflicts arise between dogmatic materials and scientific treatment, with the result that either

19 *Ibid.*, p. 58.
20 *Ibid.*, p. 61.
21 "Depth," *Christendom*, IX (1944), 319.
22 *Rel. Verw.*, p. 23.

science is mutilated by authority or authority is undermined by science. In face of this situation Tillich agrees with the modern man who believes that the days of authoritarianism and supernaturalism are numbered; science is here to stay.

Since the time of Schleiermacher, an attempt has been made to devise a second approach by combining his psychological method with modern psychology, sociology, and history of religions. But however important its contributions, Tillich holds that this method is also to be criticized. It "remains enclosed in the subjectivity of religious consciousness and never attains an immediate grasp of the contents intended in the religious act, for it is improper to try to define the referent in terms of the act instead of defining the act in terms of the referent."[23]

His criticism of the second method suggests a third way of approaching reality, the path which Tillich wishes to follow. He calls it the immediate approach through "phenomenological intuition." In this approach, he says, "we turn neither to the authorities nor to religious consciousness, but immediately to the whole of reality, and endeavor to uncover that level of reality which is intended by the religious act."[24] This path is to be distinguished especially from that of rationalism, for it is not possible to reach the substance of religion without experience of the religious act itself. Rationalism not only fails to penetrate the depth of the religious act; it also ends by negating the substance of religion.

We shall have to return later to a discussion of these and other methodologies. Here we are centering attention upon the question of language. And, as we have already indicated, the significant thing to observe is that Tillich attempts in much of his writing to set forth his conception of religion and of reality without resort to the language of tradition. Indeed, in one of the most important expositions of his religious position, the essay entitled "Belief-ful Realism," he sets forth his ideas without making use of conventional "religious" symbols at all.[25] The method of phenomenological intuition insists that the real basis of theological thought is human existence itself and not certain sacrosanct words that have been fixed by the crust of habit or by the traditions of the schools. The methods of the schools derive concepts from con-

---

23 *Ibid.*, p. 128.
24 *Ibid.*, p. 129.
25 Cf. Tillich's discussion of the ability of some poets to use words that "are both symbolic and precise" and that "nevertheless penetrate into the deepest levels of existence." Cf. *Rel. Verw.*, p. 109 and note 17.

cepts instead of from objects. Thus the paradox, the tension, the vitality, the depth and wonder of life are rationalized and lost. Tillich believes that these methods can and must be put aside if the living, concrete, real power of religious symbols is to be allowed to spring forth. The new method must attempt to discover things directly without terminological prejudice.

To be sure, perils attend all attempts to clarify vision or to introduce new language into religious discussions, the perils of the eccentric and the esoteric. But the present theological situation demands that such risks be taken. "Without daring, even frustrated daring, the impasse of the present theology cannot be resolved."[26] The spirit and the intention with which Tillich ventures to escape this impasse can best be indicated by his own characteristic words, words that again reveal the undogmatic theologian:

This unusual method, in which scarcely a word of the religious tradition is used, and for which a painstaking and sensitive intuition of the things nearest to us, the most living things and therefore the most difficult to observe, is demanded—this method is intended only as an attempt that will be followed by other and better ones, so that we may see with *our own* eyes and name with *our own* words that which is not bound to any time or any eye or any word.[27]

What we must see and what we must name is, in the words of the poet, nothing less than "the grandeur of God," the living majesty in "the dearest freshness deep down things." This dearest freshness has been seared with trade, smeared with toil and with the worn-out words which the generations have pressed upon it.

The world is charged with the grandeur of God.
    It will flame out, like shining from shookfoil;
    It gathers to a greatness, like the ooze of oil
Crushed. Why do men then now not reck his rod?
Generations have trod, have trod, have trod;
    And all is seared with trade; bleared, smeared with toil;
    And wears man's smudge and shares man's smell: the soil
Is bare now, nor can foot feel, being shod.

And for all this, nature is never spent;
    There lives the dearest freshness deep down things;
And though the last lights off the black West went
    Oh, morning, at the brown brink eastward, springs—

26 *Interpretation of History*, p. 284.
27 *Rel. Verw.*, p. 141.

Because the Holy Ghost over the bent
World broods with warm breast and with ah! bright wings.[28]

Now, the demand for seeing and naming anew the grandeur
of God would seem, at least at first blush, to be no cause for disturbance in the churches, or in the "world" either, for that matter.
Have not the poets and the liturgies of the ages again and again
seen anew and named the grandeur of God? The answer is that
they have, but that all too often the seeing and naming anew
have caused no disturbance and have brought no new vitality.
If one proposes "to penetrate in an ultimate sense what happens
day by day in labor and industry, in marriage and friendship" and
in all the important concerns of the common life, one proposes
to discover anew something that is seldom suggested, even to the
average believer, by the phrase "the grandeur of God." In Tillich's
view, to be sure, the embarrassment of present-day civilization
and of present-day Christianity must be interpreted in the end as
the result of a loss of the sense of the majesty of God. But in order
to interpret the embarrassment after that fashion, one would have
to give the phrase a meaning it does not often possess in ordinary
parlance. The word "God" has in many quarters lost its potency
and become a trivial breath of tepid air, suitable only for the
hollow men of limbo. For many people, in fact, the word represents only a fantasy, a nonentity. For the unbeliever it suggests,
and for many believers it provides, an escape from reality rather
than a penetration of it. Somehow the believers (as well as the
unbelievers) have failed to penetrate in an ultimate sense what
happens day by day. Belief in the grandeur of God, as ordinarily
understood, is not enough.

These observations only give the greater plausibility to Tillich's
claim that we need to discover and name something anew. It may
well be that even the word "God" has been so much bleared and
seared that it is, for wide circles of men, not even potential with
greatness. At least, Tillich's own writings would seem to indicate
that he believes this is the case, for he has been veritably
ascetic in his sparing use of the word. Indeed, certain theologians
in Germany some years ago charged him with being an atheist.
Early in his career (in 1926) the clergy in Saxony protested
against his appointment to the chair of philosophy in Dresden.
This protest was made because of his prominent work among the

---

[28] "God's Grandeur," *Poems of Gerard Hopkins*, with Notes by Robert
Bridges (London: Humphrey Milford, 2nd ed., 1931), p. 26.

religious socialists and the unbelievers. The fact that he was
known as a religious socialist convinced some conservative Christians that he is surely an atheist. And who would be so bold as
to say that knowledge of the same fact would not elicit a similar
reaction from many Christians and believers in God in other
countries? It would appear that for some people there are matters
of much greater moment than "God" or "the grandeur of God."
If we could discover what these things are we would have discovered what God really is for these "believers." Evidently the
question is: Which God really has the grandeur?

Now, Tillich's writings "delight the reader in a remarkably
untheological, profane way" just because he wishes to get behind
both religion and irreligion, behind theology and "anti-theology,"
to penetrate in an ultimate sense into what happens day by day
in labor and industry, in war and "peace," in church and culture.
For the fulfillment of this end he poses again and again the question: What is man's ultimate concern? Or rather, what should
it be? As we have indicated, he believes that the actual ultimate
concerns of men—and of churches—are to be discovered by
penetrating their very embarrassments; if one can discover what
has caused the embarrassment one may discover what the ultimate concerns have been and also what they should be. In order
to accomplish this purpose, he wishes to ascertain anew the
dearest freshness deep down things and to remove again the
blight that old and uncouth words have wrought upon it.

II

Tillich's Basic Concepts

In order to name with his own words what he has seen, Tillich, convinced of the present ineffectiveness of conventional religious language, inevitably has had to devise a new vocabulary. Obviously, other men have often made the same attempt. They too have "turned directly to reality" with the intention of grasping it in some new and deeper fashion. They too have then returned to the cave with new and wingèd words. What, then, distinguishes Tillich's concepts from those of many other thinkers, and why should they make any special claim upon our attention? The answer is that in turning "directly to reality" Tillich has attempted to see it and name it in the spirit of a radical Protestantism. What he sees and what he names with his own words—the concrete, dynamic, tensional, and tragic qualities, the intimate and the ultimate qualities of experience—he associates with a Protestant interpretation of the nature and meaning of life. In turning directly to reality he wishes to test, and haply to confirm, the validity of Protestant principles as he understands them. Hence there is in his method, as in all critical methods, a constant interplay between reality as immediately experienced and reality as interpreted by historically inherited and tentatively held principles. Indeed, the tentative character of his approach aims to exhibit something of the spirit of science.

Emerson once lamented that it is not possible to utter twenty-four sentences simultaneously. Anyone attempting to give an exposition of Tillich's thought might make the same lament. His philosophy is in its entirety extensive in range and his vocabulary is one that, because of its novelty and obscurity, demands close attention if it is to be understood. Each of his concepts is related to all of the others.

Hence, if we should immediately undertake a comprehensive exposition of his thought, the first part of the exposition would not achieve its full meaning until the end. In order to assist the reader to appreciate the meaning and significance of the matters to be treated as the exposition unfolds, we shall therefore, at the risk of repetitiousness and oversimplification, first list and define briefly his major concepts. Later we shall examine these concepts in greater detail as occasion demands.

Prominent among the concepts is an idea, already mentioned, which runs through all of Tillich's life and thought, namely, the concept of *the present*.[1] This emphasis corresponds to his conviction that Protestantism should in both its protest and its positive realizations be concrete and contemporaneous. It corresponds also to his conviction that the existential element in philosophy involves not only the individual but also the total social situation. Thus religious knowledge includes knowledge of the present. Protestant protest and realization are protest and realization in the present. Only through concern with the present can concern with the future lead to fulfillment. Without concern for the present, irrelevance, disillusionment, futility, and even self-destruction ensue. With it, the ultimate seriousness of a divinely sponsored adventure appears. Hence reform of any kind, whether it be in theology, in liturgy, in religious education, or in social action, must keep its eye on the present total situation if it is to be worthy of being taken seriously as possessing positive significance. Reform that aims merely to restore lost or forgotten treasures of the past is bound to lose contact with the present. Neither Protestant protest nor Protestant realization finds relevant expression in antiquarian restoration, for the demand of history is that of "transforming the past into the future." The demand is that we allow our past and our present to be grasped by, and imbued with, the creative and re-creative power that has worked hitherto and that awaits new reception or release. "The kingdom of heaven is at hand," it is coming, it is drawing near.

But even conceptions so powerful as those of the New Testament may also degenerate into mere antiquarian fossils; or, to

---

[1] In order to assist the reader in identifying the major concepts here discussed, key words will be italicized.

use the figure of Schleiermacher, they may become a monument showing that "a great spirit was once there but is there no longer." One of the paths leading to this sort of impotence is that of abstractionism. Abstractions are indispensable if man is to grasp clearly his situation, but abstractions can deprive him of a vital relation to the contemporary. Like Hartmann, Tillich believes that they may substitute static forms for creative thought (*dynamisches Schöpfungsdenken*). They can serve as a path of escape from reality. A specialized and isolated concern with abstractions may prevent one from taking time and history seriously. By its ascetic attitude toward the concrete present, such specialized concern with abstractions virtually *spatializes* the ultimately meaningful by sending it into exile. It is, as Schopenhauer would put it, a way of giving the polite *congé* to God.

This attitude assumes a great variety of forms. It may take the form of identifying religion with mystical experience above time and space; here the desire for unity leads away from the present and the concrete, the present becoming a vale of illusion. It may take the form of undue regard for abstract philosophic contemplation; again the present is missed and concern with essences (as, e.g., in Husserlian phenomenology) rather than with existence predominates. Or it may take the form of a preference for the "purely spiritual" religion that wishes to avoid controversy concerning "materialistic," this-worldly things; here we have a capital instance of *spatialization*, the limiting of the religious to one sphere, an abstract sphere of "spirit." This type of spatialization is a part of the progeny of the old dichotomy that divorces the secular from the sacred. Or again, it may take the form of devotion to a "Word of God" that relates man only to the past or to the "wholly Other." None of these forms of spatialization helps transform the past into a more meaningful future. In their avowed aloofness from the present they only provide a way of permitting the rest of the world to go by and then of permitting one to go comfortably along with it. Some of these forms of non-contemporaneity are accompanied by a very practical and unabstract trafficking with the contemporary.

Tillich's strictures against abstractionism are by no means confined to a criticism of mystic communions with God, nor to criticism of ivy-towered or spiritualistic liberalism. Insofar as Barthianism involves an abstract escape from reality (with the subterranean support of the status quo), Tillich has radically criticized it. "The repudiation of ethics by dialectical theology," he says, "is the consequence of the view that the universal is necessarily abstract and non-contemporary."[2] This deficiency in Barthianism is, he believes, due partly to the large Kantian influence upon it. Kant's categorical imperative is abstract and untimely, and gives little direct stimulus to face the present concretely. Noting the social implications of Barth's love for the non-contemporary, Tillich again and again pointed out the disastrous consequences of Barthian "neutrality" with respect to immediate social and political issues:

Karl Barth's pessimistic supernaturalism helped to destroy the Religious-Socialist attempts in pre-Hitler Germany to stop Nazism by creating a better social order on the basis of Christian principles. And even when Barth became a fanatical anti-Nazi he showed in his letter to the British Christians that it was not the common fight of people of all religions and creeds against the National-Socialist distortion of humanity that interested him, but the defense of the church as the finger pointing only to heaven and not to earth. . . . He, like all pessimistic supra-naturalists, is not interested in history as such nor in social transformation for the sake of humanity.[3]

We see what a distance there is between Tillich and the outlooks just characterized when we read, "The task of Protestantism is at any given time set by the immediate present; and here 'the present' is viewed as the central concept that integrates all the tensions characteristic of a certain epoch."[4]

But if Protestantism is to fulfill its proper task at any given time, it must in an ultimate sense penetrate *the present* not merely as a concept but also as a reality. It must penetrate the concrete present. It must be practical in the sense that it must deal with the present as it concerns us in the very depth of our being. The word "practical," however, should not be interpreted as "anti-theoretical." Since the influence of Ritschl has been such as to give "practical" an anti-theoretical connotation, it is better to use Kierkegaard's word *"existential."* "Existential is what characterizes our real existence in all its concreteness, in all its accidental elements, in its freedom and responsibility, in its

[2] *Rel. Verw.*, p. 78.

[3] "Trends in Religious Thought That Affect Social Outlook," in *Religion and the World Order,* ed. F. Ernest Johnson (New York: Harper & Brothers, 1944), pp. 24-25. Tillich recognizes today, two decades later, that a new Barth has been emerging. Accordingly, some of the above formulations no longer obtain—in the light, for example, of Barth's more recent stress upon "the humanity of God."

[4] *Rel. Verw.*, p. 54.

failure, and in its separation from its true and essential being."[5]

Always for Tillich religious concern must be a concern about the meaning of life *for us* in our total existence. The spectator attitude is not a religious attitude. Our whole being, in mind and body and spirit, in external relations as well as in the inner life, must be brought face to face with the threat and the support of existence. The fact that Barth, through his supernaturalism and his static confessionalism, has set himself against every theology concerned with "the actual state of reality (*Sein*) and with its transformation" is for Tillich "the most painful and downright disastrous event in recent Protestant theology."[6] Protestantism must come to terms with the distinctive cultural realities of the time, with the arts and the sciences, with the educational, social, economic, and political institutions and trends. Only in and through these concrete manifestations can it make contact with the present, and only through these concrete manifestations can it penetrate in an ultimate sense the characteristic spirit of the age. When it has done so, it may be able to see not only the way in which it is itself entangled in the age but also what manner of protest and realization it must attempt in order to transform the past into the future; and withal, it may also be able to discover the secular forces of protest and realization with which it may in some way join its efforts. It may be able to understand the union of the present with what has gone before, its affirmations and denials of the past, its creative forces pregnant with the future; and most important of all, it may be prepared to discern within and beyond this growth and decay the unconditioned meaning and depth of

[5] "Philosophy and Theology," *Religion in Life*, X (1941), 28; reprinted in *The Protestant Era*, trans. James L. Adams (Chicago: University of Chicago Press, 1948), p. 88. Here we should observe Tillich's characteristically "existential" preoccupation with the concrete as it affects even his shaping of concepts. This concern is one of the reasons for Tillich's dissatisfation with Husserlian phenomenology.

[6] *Rel. Verw.*, pp. 20-21. In this essay of the late Twenties Tillich explicitly applies this same criticism to Barth's doctrine of the *Word* of God: "The recently influential 'theology of the Word' should be careful not to confuse the divine 'Word,' which has appeared as a personal life and is the Gestalt of grace, with the biblical or ecclesiastical word. For Christian theology Jesus as the Christ is the Word (i.e., the divine self-manifestation); and this involves his being (*Sein*) in its totality, to which his deeds and his suffering belong, and not his words alone." *Rel. Verw.*, p. 49. (The translation here represents Tillich's slight revision as it appears in *The Protestant Era*, p. 211.) Karl Barth replies to this criticism in *The Doctrine of the Word of God*, trans. G. T. Thomson (Edinburgh: T. & T. Clark, 1936), p. 156.

past, present, and future.[7] In other words, it may be able to see how "the unconditionally powerful breaks in, revealing itself in the present, in the power of being which appears in the here-and-now."[8] (Some of the expressions just quoted we shall deal with later.) Tillich's concern with the concrete present must be remembered as we continue our survey of the central concepts by means of which he approaches reality and by which he interprets the age. Otherwise the exposition of the concepts will itself seem merely another illustration of escape from contemporaneity and into abstraction.

Since his concept of the present and its connection with the existential attitude is so fundamental for Tillich's outlook, it may be well to indicate here the intellectual ancestry of these ideas. Kierkegaard is, of course, the principal ancestor of contemporary existential philosophy, and especially significant is his resistance to the rationalistic dialectic in which Hegel's love of the complete system finds expression. But Kierkegaard's main concern was with the individual's "existential" confrontation with ultimate reality. Tillich shares this concern, but he is also interested in other metaphysical aspects of the reaction against Hegel and in the social aspects of the reaction against Hegelianism. The metaphysical aspect is to be seen in his great interest in Schelling's overcoming of idealism understood as the replacement of a negative philosophy of mere possibilities by a positive philosophy as well as in Schelling's qualification of the philosophy of identity in terms of a self-seeking, self-isolating freedom issuing in the consciousness of guilt. (Tillich's first two dissertations dealt with Schelling.) Schopenhauer's analysis of the individual life process represents for Tillich also a reaction against Hegelian panlogism and an anticipation of the interpretation of existence as life (in the later *Lebensphilosophie*). The social aspects of the reaction against Hegelianism may be symbolized by the names of Feuerbach and Marx. "Feuerbach's materialism," says Tillich, "is another expression of the emphasis on existence—a word used by him against Hegel."[9] But Marx goes even farther in his reaction against Hegel, in effect transferring the Kierkegaardian concern with inward tensions of the individual to a concern with the outward tensions of social process. Tillich accordingly combines the interest in the

[7] *The Religious Situation*, trans. H. Richard Niebuhr (New York: Henry Holt and Co., 1932), pp. 4-7.

[8] *Rel. Verw.*, p. 81.

[9] "Kierkegaard in English," *American-Scandinavian Review*, XXX (1942), 256.

present with the existential outlook, through his passionate concern with the total social situation in its present crisis.[10]

Tillich believes that despite the vaunted claims of American empiricism and positivism to provide, as it were, a corrective to Hegelian abstractionism, these "characteristically American" philosophies in their turn need the correction of a genuine existentialism that takes individual "ultimate concerns" and social actualities seriously. Tillich's emphasis on *Existenz* and the Present are so directly related to his attitude toward Anglo-American thought that we should quote at length Tillich's views on the latter:

Although the empiricistic and positivistic trend of the Anglo-Saxon mind has prevented the domination of a speculative system, the question of existential and objective truth is by no means solved by them. American theology still . . . confuses systems of ethical abstractions or metaphysical possibilities with ethical and religious existence before God. It has not yet accepted existential materialism as the great corrective to the Christian-bourgeois idealism. And contemporary philosophy has either—as logical positivism—extinguished every trace of existential passion and interest within philosophical thought or it has—as metaphysical naturalism—removed the individual "existing" man who stands between the infinite and the finite and never can be understood as a part of the whole of natural objectivity. And even pragmatism which is more closely related to existential thinking than the two other groups—because it acknowledges the fragmentary and dynamic character of truth—has surrendered itself as "instrumentalism" to the objective process of nature and society, producing means for ends which are finite and, consequently, not a matter of infinite, passionate concern.[11]

This paragraph introduces ideas that are not directly germane to our discussion at this point, ideas that will have to be dealt with later, but the context and implications of Tillich's concern with *Existenz* and the Present are brought sharply into relief by the whole passage.

If the concept of *the Present* is the central concept that integrates the tensions characteristic of an epoch, the concept of *decision* is the idea that integrates the tensions of an individual or a group as it confronts the present. The manner in which the past is transformed into the future depends upon the kind of

[10] For an extensive survey of the main stages and themes in the development of existential philosophy, see Tillich's essay "Existential Philosophy," *Journal of the History of Ideas,* V (1944), 44-70.

[11] "Kierkegaard in English," pp. 256-57.

decision with which man meets the present. And if that decision is to take time by the forelock, it must be *daring* decision, for there are in this world no guarantees of success in man's rendezvous with time. "The act of daring is an act that pushes ahead into the uncertain, an act that renounces securities and risks assured possessions."[12] This leap into the uncertain future is unavoidable. The difference between men appears when they make decisions. "There are those who really dare, who aim the bow sharply and shoot the arrow of their deed into dark distances; and there are those who aim too short, in the secret hope of being able to remain on the firm ground of the secure path."[13] To be sure, man faces always the possibility of going amiss; and he has a sense of guilt when he does go amiss. Yet the very possibility of making daring decisions belongs to man alone. No other creature can miss the mark through the violation of universal norms. Existence is given to other creatures immediately, but man is not something merely identical with his immediate existence. The very fact that in man existence rises above itself is the occasion for peril and opportunity. It is the ground for what Pascal calls the misery and the greatness of man. And it is the ground for decision.

Let us examine more closely the nature of decision. In his immediate existence man is in a state of *cleavage*, or inner contradiction, as is shown by two things.[14] First, every man raises a question about his existence: Is it true existence? In doing so, he implies that he does not possess the thing he raises the question about. Moreover, by asking he shows that he is in some fashion free from existence. On the other hand, in seeking an answer to the question, he can miss getting the answer. And whatever answer he gets, he will remain in a state of cleavage. This suggests the second consideration. Every man makes a demand upon existence. The presupposition is that the thing demanded is not present: there is a contradiction between existence as it is and as it should be. In man life rises above itself; the immediacy of the life-process is broken through the fact that freedom enters on the stage. In a sense, man is unfree in possessing freedom, for to rise above the immediacy of existence is to lose it; and he cannot regain it. Any attempt to return to the mere life-process

12 "Predigt zum Semesterschluss vor der Theologenschaft der Universität Marburg," *Neuwerk*, VIII, No. 11 (1927), 469.

13 *Ibid.*, p. 470.

14 The following analysis of decision and its relation to "the present" is based primarily upon the article "Gegenwart und Religion," *Neuwerk*, XI, No. 1 (1929), 2-11, and upon *Rel. Verw.*, chap. i.

contradicts the *fate* of man. He cannot return to the subhuman level. By way of summary then: Man *must* raise the question as to the character of true existence, and he *must* make a demand. "He cannot escape this *fate*, the fate of being man. If he did not wish to raise a question, his not doing it would itself be an answer to a question. If he did not choose to make a demand, his not making it would be obedience to a demand. Man always acts even when inaction is the burden of his action."[15] He must dare to make decisions, and this necessity brings anxiety, the anxiety that may pervert his freedom. We turn then to a description of man's *freedom* and of his *perversion* of that freedom.

Man is a living subject, "a Gestalt, a totality of interdependent relations in which no part can be isolated as long as the living process goes on."[16] Within himself he is the dynamic unity of reason and power, of intellectual universality and vital individuality. On the other hand, he "has a world which is at once unitary and infinite," a world "set over against himself, from which he is separated and to which he belongs at the same time. . . . Being between himself and his world, man is free from both of them even while he is bound to both of them."[17]

In the relations between this living subject, this Gestalt, and its world, there are various levels and degrees of *freedom*. Man can transcend any given situation; thus he can imagine and realize something new. He has the moral freedom to transcend himself "in the direction of complete unity of universality and individuality." This is the freedom "to receive unconditional demands," and it is a freedom fraught with high seriousness. He has cultural freedom, the freedom to create with purpose, to represent the world and himself with symbols. And he has freedom from his own freedom, the freedom to play. This freedom is the "playful" counterpart of the seriousness of moral freedom.

But man's power of self-determination is not unlimited. "The new which is created by man is dependent on the given which he finds—on himself as well as on his world. Man does not exist by himself alone nor does his world."[18] Although he possesses a freedom from himself and his world, he participates in the primary creativity on which both he and his world depend. When he uses his freedom to act against freedom, he decides against

[15] *Rel. Verw.*, p. 32.
[16] "The Conception of Man in Existential Philosophy," *Journal of Religion*, XIX (1939), 202. Cf. also *Rel. Verw.*, p. 168.
[17] "The Conception of Man in Existential Philosophy," p. 205.
[18] *Ibid.*, p. 209.

his essential nature. Thus he perverts his freedom into servitude; it is transformed and becomes tragic and sinful. "Freedom can maintain itself only insofar as it chooses the content, the norms, and the values in which our essential nature, including our freedom, expresses itself."[19]

The possibility of the surrender of freedom arises not out of necessity but out of the freedom to forget that one is finite. Nor is this possibility the result of reversion to the animal level; it comes from "stepping too high." This is the tragic perversion of freedom, the attempt of man to make his finiteness infinite. "The individual thinking to make himself universal instead of subjecting himself to the universal is the tragic individual."[20]

This tragic servitude to the infinite desires of the self often has actually the opposite effect from that intended: it separates the self from "the infinity of universality," and it leads to the destruction of the self and its world. Thus man is brought into the realm of necessity, a necessity that is both transcendent and immanent. It would be wrong, however, to suppose that necessity operates only after the perversion of freedom. Necessity is present even in the exercise of freedom, for man lives in history, and the forms and limits of freedom are partially determined by the human past, by material factors, and by the social environment. The creature that is free stands under the fate of unfreedom. Nevertheless, his freedom remains undestroyed. The creativity is always primary, for everything depends upon it. This is the case even though the outcome of tragic servitude is a destructive one. Indeed, the destructive tendency may itself prepare the way for new creation.

The possibilities of the perversion of freedom exist on all levels of freedom, and no change in the social environment can secure man against the realization of these possibilities. Only the complete loss of freedom can do that. For this reason human freedom will always be human peril.

The ability to transcend any given situation implies the possibility of losing one's self in the infinity of transcending one's self. Technical freedom may become technical servitude if the means become ends in themselves. Moral freedom may become moral servitude if the individual self, in order to preserve itself, resists the demand coming from the other and loses personality and community. Cultural freedom can become cultural servitude if it finds expression in the will-to-power or the will to draw the totality of one's world

19 *Ibid.*, p. 208.
20 *Ibid.*, p. 210.

into the limitations of one's individual self. Freedom to play may become the surrender of one's own freedom, thus wasting one's self and one's world.[21]

Just because human freedom is human peril, man characteristically suffers anxiety—the anxiety of "not actualizing all possibilities and the anxiety of leaping from possibility into actuality. Man is afraid not to use this freedom and yet he is afraid to use it." Anxiety gives rise to temptation, which appears on all levels of freedom. Here again decision, and daring decision, is demanded.

The human situation with respect to freedom and necessity can be described also in terms of freedom and *fate*. Freedom is always entangled in fate, which involves three things. First, fate is related to freedom: where there is no freedom there is no fate, and where there is no fate there is no freedom. A merely physical object that is conditioned in all ways is entirely without fate because it is wholly bound to necessity. On the other hand, anyone whose freedom is absolute, whose freedom is not jeopardized by an ever intruding necessity, has no fate. Second, all freedom is subjected to necessity: no being has unconditional power over itself; and when it acts as though it did have, it is driven by inexhaustible desire from one illusion to another until it encounters resistance and penalty. Third, freedom and fate do not appear separately and alternately; they interpenetrate each other in every event: every man's character and every civilization's character are the result of creative freedom but they are also "conditioned by events that in their origin go back to past generations, back to much earlier manifestations of the continuing and living fabric of humanity." Thus they are, as we have already indicated, conditioned by national, economic, and geographic factors, and also by unconscious vitalities and tensions. These factors always affect philosophy and theology as well as other human endeavors. Man is thrown into existence at a particular time and place in unity with all other beings. Yet he feels himself responsible for his existence in the context of his unity with, and differentiation from, all other beings. Hence human existence is always comprised of both the fated (or given) fact and the responsible act; freedom and necessity, fate and guilt presuppose each other and they cannot be separated.[22]

[21] *Ibid.*, p. 208.

[22] This paragraph is based upon the formulations set forth in "Philosophie und Schicksal," *Kant-Studien*, XXXIV (1929), 302 ff. (and also upon certain theses in the mimeographed outlines of "Systematic Theology," Third

In the teeth of this tension or polarity between freedom and fate, between fate and guilt, between spirituality and vitality, between reason and the will-to-power, or reason and pleasure, man must decide. But, as Tillich understands it, decision is not merely decision between surface alternatives of existence. It possesses a dimension of *depth*. To speak of depth, of the depths, the ground, the abyss, is for Tillich highly characteristic. Instead of looking up and away from reality he prefers to look down through it. In his view the metaphors of height, so widely familiar in religious usage, are today unconvincing. They suggest what Henry Churchill King used to call "the seeming unreality of the spiritual life." This seeming unreality attaches to any religion that makes a business of looking to the heights and of averting the eye from the ground and abyss underneath.

Although depth is a dimension of space, it is employed as a symbol for a spiritual quality.[23] Like most of our religious symbols, it reminds us of our finitude and our bondage to things that are visible. We are and we remain "tied to sense" even when we deal with things spiritual. But in religious usage the word has also another connotation, as is suggested by the familiar texts, "The Spirit searcheth all things, even the deep things of God. . . . Out of the depth have I cried unto thee, O God."

There are two meanings of "depth" when considered in the religious sense. It is either the opposite of shallow or the opposite of high. "Truth is deep and not shallow. Suffering is depth and not height. Both are deep, the light of truth and the darkness of suffering. There is depth in God and there is a depth out of which the psalmist cried to God." We think of truth as deep, and we think of suffering as deep. We use the same spatial symbol for both of them, because the search for truth and the experiences of disappointment and suffering drive us to dig deeper than the surface of things.

Science makes its great contributions when it penetrates the surfaces. Penetration into the depth of things has let loose earthquakes in the history of science, as, for example, when Copernicus questioned the sun's appearance of revolving around a stationary earth or when Einstein questioned the assumption that there is

---

Part, a preliminary draft for the private use of students only). This essay appears in English translation in *The Protestant Era*, pp. 3-15.

[23] The following paragraphs are based primarily on the article "Depth," *Christendom*, IX (Summer, 1944), 317-25. As with the theosophical writers upon whom Tillich depends, "depth" is not to be interpreted in a spatial sense. It symbolizes, rather, the inmost character of reality.

an absolute point from which the observer can look at the motion of things. The early Greek philosophers likewise penetrated beneath the surfaces when they questioned "being" itself, asking why "there is something and not nothing" (Schelling's formulation).

Depth psychology has led us from the surfaces of consciousness into the subconscious. Here again an earthquake has ensued, and men have not yet been able to regain equilibrium, for, deep as the probings have been, depth psychology cannot alone strike a supporting depth. "It *can* help us to find the way into our depth, although it can *not* give the final help because it cannot guide into the deepest ground of our being and of all being, the depth of life itself."

All of these questionings have been daring ventures. And so must our questionings be if we wish to delve beneath the surface of ourselves and of the opinions we take for granted. This is a painful process. Usually we prefer to wait and let the depths erupt beneath us. We are not prone to search in the depths unless an earthquake brings us disillusion concerning the surfaces. Then self-knowledge is itself shaken and disrupted. The only substitute for an earthquake is that we travel steadily and voluntarily the road into the depths of being and into the depths of our own being. It is a hard road.

But we have to penetrate to the depths not only of self and of being. Depth must be seen in *the present*. There are depths in the common life; there is a depth in history. Here again earthquakes occur when men look beneath the surface. Marx set off an earthquake in social life and thought when he questioned whether there is an intellectual and moral history independent of its economic and social basis. A sociology of depth arose, showing us the support and especially the eruption from below. But earthquakes are necessary in the social life too before most of us can see the depths. In history we live as much on the surface as we do in our individual lives. The noise of shallow waters prevents us from listening to the sounds out of the depth, to the sounds of what really happens at the base of our social structure, in the longing hunger and oppression of the masses. "We have believed that we were living in a period of unavoidable progress to greater humanity. But in the depth of our social structure the forces of destruction have already gathered strength." We have become weak in our strength; the improved means and tools of life have been turned into the means and tools of self-destruction. Therefore, within the community a rebellion against the surface has started. Yet many people still want to return to the "normalcy" of the old surfaces. They want to escape from the depth of the present into the shelter of an illusory security.

It is natural that men should shun the depths. In the depths of being and history they find a threat to human existence and to accepted values. They find suffering there. They discover not only the depths of emptiness, as Thomas Müntzer called it, or the depth of humanity, as Marx called it, but also the chthonic depth, which in religious language is often called the dwelling place of the evil forces, of the demonic powers, of death and hell. It is through these depths that men must go if they are to find the depth of truth and of being.

The German people have been "possessed" by these morbid and destructive depths. They are the prime example in modern history of a people that did not know how to plumb to the depths that would lead, through suffering, to hope and joy; they did not know how to pierce the surfaces of nationality and reach the creative depths.

Tillich raises the question as to why the German people were thus caught by the evil, the demonic depths of destruction. His answer to the question should be quoted at length, for it bears not only upon the contemporary "German problem" but also upon the contemporary religious problem (and the problem of language) with which he is concerned. In answering the question, he reminds us of a beautiful ancient myth:

> When the soul leaves the body it has to traverse many spheres where demonic forces rule. And only the soul which knows the right and powerful word can continue its way to the ultimate depth of the divine ground. No soul can avoid these tests. If we look at the struggle of the saints of all times, of the prophets and reformers, of the great creators in all realms, we recognize that the myth tells the truth. Everybody has to face the deep things in life. Danger is no excuse. He has to conquer the danger. He has to know the liberating word. The German people and many people in all nations have not known this word, and so they were caught by the evil forces of the depth and missed the ultimate, saving depth.[24]

Nowhere in Tillich's writings do we find a more illuminating discussion of the relation between the Word and the penetration into the depths of the human condition. Here is expressed the significance of the task of discovering "the dearest freshness deep down things" and of naming the saving word that pulsates with the powerfulness of the depths.

[24] *Ibid.*, p. 323.

This significance resides in the fact that willy-nilly our every pattern of decision possesses a dimension of depth. Decision involves not merely a choice between surface alternatives. To be sure, it may be made with reference to surfaces alone, but the surfaces only thinly conceal the supporting and disrupting powers, the ground and abyss of the depths. The disrupting powers have become a darkness visible in the convulsions of the twentieth century, as they break open the surfaces. Fate and decision have wrought us woe. In our time we have seen the disruptive depths of decision not only in the German parade of death down into the demonic depths. All over the planet modern capitalism, nationalism, communism, and racism have been taking the same path. These depths are the abyss of destruction.

But those who know the depth of what has happened should not rest on this level where all seems hopeless. Here there is danger of despair and cynicism. We must dig deeper—into the ground of our historical life to the *ultimate* depth of history, to the depth of the supporting creative powers. This depth Tillich calls "the infinite and inexhaustible ground of being." It is the depth that is the ground of hope. It is the dynamic source of all creative decision. The way to it leads beyond woe to joy, for the end of the way to the depth is joy. Nietzsche, the depth philosopher, knew this even though he was "a man who in his passionate striving for the depth was caught by destructive forces and did not know the word to conquer them." Nietzsche, the philosopher of joyous suffering, glimpsed the deepest depth, the dearest freshness deep down things, when he wrote, "The world is deep, and deeper than the day could read. Deep is its woe. Joy deeper still than grief can be. Woe says: Hence, Go! But joys all want eternity. Want deep, profound eternity." Commenting on these words Tillich says:

This is the message of all religions: the Kingdom of God is peace and joy. This is the message of Christianity. . . . But eternal joy is not to be reached by living on the surface. It is reached by breaking through the surface, by penetrating into the deep things of ourselves, our world, and God. At every moment in which we reach the last depth of our lives we can experience the joy that has eternity in it, the hope which cannot be destroyed and the truth on which life and the world are built.[25]

Thus we find in the depths of being and history not only the threat to human existence and to human values. We find not only

[25] *Ibid.*, p. 325.

suffering there but also the purifying fire through which we pass in order to reach the depth of truth. Tillich is, then, a philosopher of tragedy, but he is also a philosopher of joy; and for him the "deeper" of these is joy. This fact must be borne in mind when Tillich speaks of the creative and destructive depths as the infinite and inexhaustible ground and abyss of all being.

We see now what is meant by the assertion that decision possesses a dimension of depth. It means that true decision possesses the depth of a spiritual attitude oriented to the ultimate, the infinite and inexhaustible ground and abyss, the dynamically supporting and threatening *Apeiron*.[26] The perversion of freedom ensues when decision involves only decision for the infinity of one's own desire; when vital power is made to predominate over rational mutuality; when man attempts to place himself at the depth or the center of being rather than relate himself to it; when man, who is dependent upon the primal "given" creativity of being, sets up his own creaturely and conditioned character as unconditioned. It appears, in short, when he tries to make his own finiteness infinite. This is to court disaster in the jaws of the abyss; it is to incur the wrath of the abyss, to invite demonic possession. Thus the depth dimension of decision may be the tragic dimension. But that is not all, for there is an alternative. It is decision in the true dimension of depth, *decision for the Unconditioned*.

This brings us to the central concept of Tillich's philosophy of religion, a concept that also bears upon his whole social philosophy and his interpretation of Protestantism. But before taking up this difficult concept, we should say a further word

[26] We use the word of Anaximander here in order to bring into relief both the infinitely creative and the tragically destructive aspects of Tillich's conception of ground and abyss, the absolute Something and the absolute Nothing. "Abyss" carries a double connotation: inexhaustible, restless, positive dynamic and threatening, disruptive dynamic. The concepts "ground" and "abyss" stem from Jacob Boehme. As we shall observe again and again, Boehme is a major source for certain crucial elements in Tillich's outlook. Here it is Boehme's insight that "Yes and No are in all things." For an indication of Tillich's appreciation for the voluntaristic mysticism and dialectic of Jacob Boehme see his Preface to J. J. Stoudt, *Sunrise to Eternity* (University of Pennsylvania Press, 1957). Here Tillich says, "If Protestant theology wants to penetrate the ontological implications of the Christian symbols, it would do well to use the ideas of Boehme more than those of Aristotle. In contrast to Aristotle with his orientation to the *actus purus*, Boehme tried to describe in metaphysical-psychological symbols the *living* God in whom the roots of every life must be sought" (pp. 7-8).

concerning the idea of depth as it appears in Tillich's life and thought. More consideration must also be given to the setting in which the concept of "the Unconditioned" appears.

It is reported by Tillich's colleagues that one of his favorite retreats has always been a seat on the rocks above the edge of the ocean. No doubt one reason for this attraction is, so to speak, philosophical. For him the ocean possesses a metaphysical *frisson*. In the waves can be seen the motion of the depths disturbing the face of the waters. Here is the symbol of the infinite bordering on the finite and of the infinite depths touching the finite surfaces.

In Tillich's own autobiographical sketch, these and other aspects of the dimension of depth are referred to in a felicitous, personal way. After mentioning his early love of nature, "great memories and strong longings interlaced with landscapes, with the soil and the weather, with corn fields and the smell of autumnal potato foliage, with the forms of clouds, with wind, flowers, and woods," he writes:

Most important, however, was the fact that from my eighth year onward annually I spent some weeks, later even months, by the seaside. The experience of the infinite bordering upon the finite, as one has it by the sea, responded to my tendency toward the border and supplied my imagination with a symbol from which feeling could win substance and thinking productivity. It is likely that my development of the theory of the human border-situation in *Religiöse Verwirklichung* ("Religious Realization") and its more anthropological formulation in lectures at Yale University, might not have turned out as it did without that experience of nature. But there is also another element in the contemplation of the sea: the dynamic, the aggression upon the land in its tranquil finiteness, the ecstatic quality of gales and waves. Thus the theory of the "Dynamic Mass" in my essay "Masse und Geist" ("The Mass and the Spirit") was conceived under the immediate impression of the agitated sea. Also for the doctrine of the Unconditioned as both ground and abyss of dynamic truth, and of the religious essence as the eruption of the eternal into finiteness, the sea supplied the imaginative element needed for these thoughts. It was Nietzsche who said that no idea could be true unless it was thought in the open air. Obedient to the saying, many of my ideas have been conceived in the open and even much of my writing has been done among trees or on the seaside.[27]

[27] *The Interpretation of History*, trans. Rasetzki and Talmey (New York: Charles Scribner's Sons, 1936), pp. 7-8. Since a number of the themes of the present discussion are imaginatively expressed in it, the author's "meditation" on Water is appended at the end of the chapter. This "meditation"

In this passage certain of the motifs we have already discussed are evident, but here the dynamic, tensional character of Tillich's life and thought is especially brought to the fore through his use of the concept of the border. In his autobiographical sketch Tillich speaks of living on the boundary between various possibilities of existence. Now the notion of the *border-situation* is given a different turn, a "deeper" metaphysical interpretation, and it is related to the central Tillichian concept of the *Unconditioned*.[28]

Before giving even a general definition of these concepts we should make note of their bearing on two corresponding problems of philosophy and religion, namely, the problems posed on the one hand by ecclesiastical or political absolutism and on the other by historical and ethical relativism. Our exposition will seem to "take the longest way home," but it is only by this way that we can see the problem situation out of which the concepts emerge.

Martin Luther once said that humanity is like a drunken sailor riding horseback. At one moment the sailor jogs up and comes down almost falling off the horse on one side; at the next moment he jogs up and comes down almost falling into the mud on the other side. This sort of drunkenness has frequently been displayed in modern times as men have recovered themselves from the tyranny of absolutism only at the next jog of history to fall into the slough of relativism. At the one extreme, men absolutize a particular point of view, endowing it with final validity; at the other they question whether any position has a validity beyond the fact that it satisfies desire.

We need not here enter a detailed discussion of the tangled problems suggested by the correlative terms "relative-absolute." It will suffice if we say that Tillich found satisfaction in neither of the main solutions with which he was presented. On the one hand, he saw in the inflated claims of the churches to possess

---

shows that the references to water in the passage quoted above are by no means accidental.

[28] *The Interpretation of History*, pp. 3-73. Tillich speaks of his life as being lived on the boundaries between city and country, between social classes, between reality and imagination, theory and practice, heteronomy and autonomy, theology and philosophy, church and society, religion and culture, Lutheranism and socialism, idealism and Marxism, home and alien land.

It should be observed here that in his later writings Tillich does not use the substantive form, "the Unconditioned." He tends to use instead the existential formulation, "object of unconditional concern." If the substantive form appears, he speaks of "being itself," "ground of being," "power of being."

the absolute something as unacceptable as the equally inflated claims of the prevailing economic and political philosophies of "liberal" capitalism. Such boisterous complacency must, in his view, be punctured. In their varying ways all claimed to have domesticated the absolute. In short, they asserted that salvation was firmly in their possession. Science, or rather scientism, was itself making similarly self-regarding ordinances. On the other hand, complete relativism could not be accepted. If it were, all claims to truth or value could only be adjudged illusory along with the vaunted claims of absolutism. In either case, the meaning of human existence was in question.

In face of this spiritual and philosophical embarrassment, German idealism had ventured a solution. It had maintained that its "system of meaningful categories portrays reality as a whole" and thus provides the next step beyond religion and other mythological fumblings. According to it, reality is the appearance of essence refracted dialectically but fulfilled in cultural synthesis reaching ever greater richness. This optimistic philosophy evidently strongly appealed to Tillich in his youth, though the later Schelling's departure from idealism had already impressed him as early as 1910. Tillich came to hold, with Schelling, Kierkegaard, and Marx, that idealism itself represents "a definite and limited relation to reality" and that reality is a contradiction of essence. This fact was especially evident in the imminent breakdown of the social system idealism had supported or condoned. Idealistic synthesis has no place for real evil and destruction. It seeks only the support of existence and ignores the threat, the abyss of being and meaning. Moreover, its subjection of everything to the purely rational form deprives it of a sense of the positive vitality and dynamic of reality. Hence it degenerates into formalism, and its view of the basic meaning of life becomes a relative, conditioned meaning. Tillich therefore felt the demand for a transcendent meaning that would invade and break through the system of pure forms. He came to view the idealistic synthesis as a form of spatialization of the infinite, as an imprisonment of the infinite in the finiteness of a static, self-assured understanding that serves as a sanction for a crumbling social system. Such a spatialization, he decided, fails to recognize the depth of our being, the infinite and inexhaustible ground and abyss of meaning. It fails also to recognize the socially and historically conditioned character of human thinking.

Tillich's concepts of the boundary-situation and of the Unconditioned cannot be understood apart from a recognition of his inner drive to overcome the idealistic synthesis that provides a comfortable cushion not only for formalistic rationalism but also for those who are terribly at ease in Zion, for those who do not see the guilt of the human condition, for those who find in idealistic metaphysics a divine sanction for accepting conservative and decaying bourgeois ethics and for interpreting evil as merely a dialectical necessity and therefore as good. The reasons for his turning against idealism in these respects are set forth succinctly in the following passage:

The catastrophe which idealism had suffered in the nineteenth century had been too terrible for anyone to invite its recurrence. . . . It cannot see the true religious situation, the situation of time in the presence of eternity, it seeks to evade the judgment under which the temporal stands before the eternal. Its forms, to be sure, are open to the reception of living content, it restores to the state and even to logic their primordial and essential holiness, but it rests content then with these sanctified forms; it does not penetrate to the absolutely transcendent, to that which lies beyond even the most sacred form, whether it be called the church or state; it does not see the abyss which opens before every time and every present. . . . War and revolution have revealed depths of reality which idealism cannot master.[29]

In the light of his view, then, that both absolutism and idealism make unwarranted claims for themselves and end by becoming illustrations of historical relativism, and in the light of his view that relativism cannot be overcome without a more adequate apprehension of something standing beyond the relative, we must understand his conceptions of the boundary-situation and of the Unconditioned. The one provides a limiting principle, the other a supporting principle. The two would seem to lead in opposite directions, yet they actually aim at the same goal. "The one is the way of most radical apprehension of the Protestant principle as a proclamation of the 'human boundary-situation,' the other is that of decided affirmation of the presence of the Unconditioned-Beyond, the 'speaking' or expression of a 'form (*Gestalt*) of grace.' "[30]

The metaphysical concept of the "human boundary-situation" as the limit of human possibility—in distinction from the idea of the border as a line between contrasting possibilities of existence—has been used also by a number of other theologians and some secular philosophers, especially by Kierkegaard, Barth, and

[29] *The Religious Situation*, pp. 43-44.
[30] *Rel. Verw.*, p. 15.

Jaspers. It is also anticipated after a fashion by Nietzsche's idea of the self-surpassing character of human nature. In general, we may say that its use is the trademark of existential philosophy and theology.

The concept of the Unconditioned, as the ultimate that is presupposed by all meaning, being, and value (conditioning and supporting them), is a composite concept. In Tillich's usage it draws upon and modifies the ontological and axiological concepts of Greek and modern thought, from Anaximander and Parmenides to Spinoza and Kant, though in its modified form it aims to give expression to the Jewish-Christian idea of the majesty and unspeakable richness of the divine.

These concepts of the boundary-situation and of the Unconditioned are proposed as demand and expectation—demand in face of the eternal, in face of the infinite and inexhaustible ground and abyss of being, and expectation in the sense of anticipating the possible realization of the true meaning of life.

The boundary-situation is encountered as an aspect of both this demand and this expectation. On the one hand, man finds support in the human and cosmic situation; on the other, he confronts a threat to meaningful existence. In short, he finds himself suspended over the "depth" of the infinite and inexhaustible ground and abyss of being. The boundary-situation is the boundary between support and threat. Or as Tillich puts it, "The boundary of human activity is encountered when human possibility reaches its absolute limit, when human existence is confronted by unconditional threat. . . . This border-situation of man is possible because man stands above his mere existence, because he is in his immediate existence in a state of cleavage." Thus man, in transcending mere existence, possesses a freedom to say Yes or No to existence. But his very freedom becomes the occasion for a radical threat to his existence. The fate of having to make decisions is the profoundest disturbance of our existence. This inescapable freedom is a threat to us because of the consequences that follow from our decisions, especially when the decisions are seen in the pattern of the totality and meaning of the human situation. When his decisions are seen in their relation to this pattern, man knows that he does not fulfill the demand for the right existence, and that he possesses no guarantee of fulfillment. "Wherever this situation is experienced in its unconditioned and inescapable character, the human border-situation is encountered. The point at which nothingness threatens us unconditionally, is the boundary line of all human activity, the human boundary-situation."[31] Protestantism had its very origin in the proclamation of this boundary-situation, and accordingly it denies security to all human possessions including religion and the church. Recognition of the limit and of the threat that attach to religion itself is a necessary implication of the Reformation doctrine of justification by faith.

Men are, then, confronted with the questions: Where does one find the threat to human existence? And where does one find its support? The major differences among men—that is, among their ultimate orientations—depend upon the differences between the answers they give to these questions.

Tillich holds that the fate of unfreedom arises out of the opposition between freedom and existence, but that the ultimate support comes from something beyond their opposition. The support depends upon something we do not produce at all; it is the power of being that is the core of all creativity. This primary creativity is expressed even in the threat to human existence. Anything that exists must in some fashion participate in the basic "given" creativity, and anything that completely violates the conditions of creativity will not exist at all.

The forms of expression which threat and support may take fall into two principal groups; there are those which aim to be absolutely nothing other than an expression of threat and support, and those more indirect forms which have no explicit sense of ultimate threat and support. The first are religious forms, the second are cultural. This does not mean that religious forms are not a part of the culture. It means rather that the religious forms are by intention religious, and the cultural forms are not so by intention, though they are so in actuality (or in substance). Every expression is, then, an explicit or tacit expression of the human situation in its ultimate dimension.

---

[31] *Ibid.*, p. 32. For a telling presentation of the unconditional seriousness of the boundary-situation, see Kierkegaard's parable of the King's coachman in *Judge for Yourself,* reported by W. Lowrie, *Kierkegaard* (London: Oxford University Press, 1938), pp. 480 ff. Compare these typical sentences from Karl Barth: "The mature and well-balanced man, standing firmly with both feet on the earth, who has never been lamed and broken and half-blinded by the scandal of his life, is as such the existentially godless man" (*Epistle to the Romans,* trans. Edwyn C. Hoskyns [London: Oxford University Press, 1933], p. 235). "The frontier of religion is the line of death which separates flesh from spirit, time from eternity, human possibility from the possibility of God" (*ibid.,* p. 258). These sentences show Barth's conception of the boundary. As we shall see presently, Tillich does not draw the border line in precisely this way.

Now there are sundry and devious methods whereby man attempts to conceal from himself the disturbance and the insecurity of all forms, whether religious or cultural. The ambiguous character of the human situation "can be covered over or weakened by our relying upon truth that we have already achieved or upon demands already fulfilled, thus evading the unconditioned threat. This is a possibility that is always present; and in one way or another all of us try to make this escape."[32]

Depth psychologists have revealed the tortuous processes of rationalization whereby men conceal from themselves their own insecurity and attempt to compensate by projecting a false security. Depth sociology has disclosed analogous concealments in social life, rationalizations that take the form of ideology, smoke screens that mask the actual situation of being confronted by demand and threat. One finds similar attempts at concealment in "religion." Indeed, most religions may be classified according to their modes of concealment. Hence religion may be a deception and a snare. Tillich would agree with the young Barth before his retreat into the concealments of confessionalism, the Barth who said, "Religion, then, so far from dissolving men existentially, so far from rolling them and pressing them against the wall, so far from overwhelming them and transforming them, acts upon them like a drug which has been extremely skilfully administered."[33] At least, he would agree if this Barthian protest against "religion" did not lead to a new form of concealment in supernaturalism.[34] Another form of concealment is to be discerned, as we have seen, in philosophical idealism.

Absolute seriousness with respect to the boundary-situation is found only where men scorn the possibility of escape, only where men renounce the illusory possibility of escape by submergence in the life-process, in intellectual or cultural activity, in mysticism and asceticism, in strenuous works of piety, in the guarantees of the church, of "sound doctrine," and of the "Word of God," in

---

[32] *Rel. Verw.*, p. 32.

[33] Barth, *op. cit.*, p. 236.

[34] Commenting on Barth's early assertion that Tillich's struggle against "The Grand Inquisitor" of guaranteed and enforced securities is no longer necessary today, the latter observed in 1935 that "the development of the German Confessional Church in the last two years has proved that it is necessary. The Grand Inquisitor is about to enter the Confessional Church, and strictly speaking with a strong but tight-fitting armor of Barthian supranaturalism" (*Interpretation of History*, p. 26). From Tillich's point of view, Barth represented here a form of concealment of the boundary-situation comparable to that provided by Roman Catholicism.

the sacraments of the nation, the tribe, or the economic and social system. The modern man believes he has in principle made these renunciations. As a matter of fact, however, he has in wide areas of life either explicitly or tacitly renounced the renunciation and has attempted to "escape from freedom" into one or another guaranteed temporal security.

Insofar as the modern man takes seriously the border-situation, he is able to understand the radical element in Protestantism, its doctrine of justification by faith and its prophetic protest. On the other hand, insofar as Protestantism forgets that it stands in the boundary-situation it forfeits its own character and becomes a weakened imitation of Catholicism. As a consequence it elicits protest from those in religious and secular groups who are aware of the boundary. The very moment it ceases to hold itself in question, it is brought into question by those who have understood and in some fashion have accepted its original principle.

But if Protestantism, in recognizing the boundary-situation, only insists upon the ambiguity of all human securities and of all human (and "religious") forms, it serves merely to relativize all knowledge and conduct. Its message becomes nothing more than a stentorian "No" to all human endeavor, nothing more than a proclamation of the threat to human existence. The doctrine of the majesty of God becomes the basis for a complete devaluation of his creatures. In this fashion the boundary is really dissolved, for one confronts only a No; the Yes to concrete decision is not heard.

This sort of interpretation creates a spiritual vacuum so far as active participation in the contemporary life of society and culture is concerned. Barth himself helped to bring about such a vacuum by restricting attention to the demand that the church resist the attempt of the National Socialist state to subject it to state policy. Only after the advent of World War II and the German invasion of Czechoslovakia did he deign to make a political decision; and even then the decision was made only in the name of the church's right to proclaim the gospel.

Into the spiritual vacuum created by this aversion to concrete social and political decision the German Christians rushed with their idol of German Christianity. Indeed, Emanuel Hirsch perverted Tillichian doctrine into obedience to "the sovereign of history" speaking through Adolf Hitler. Here again the boundary was dissolved; the German Christian could hear only the Yes.

In order to avoid these errors of interpretation, the concept of the boundary-situation must be understood in relation to the concept of the *Unconditioned* and its corollaries, the ideas of "the form of grace" and the *Kairos*.

Tillich has nowhere written a systematic essay on the concept of the Unconditioned. This is unfortunate, for his many and scattered references to it make for great difficulty in securing a consistent and synoptic view of it. The difficulty is increased by the fact that Tillich's language is obscure and by the fact also that Tillich has not remained consistent in his definitions. Here we shall adumbrate only its main features, basing the synthetic definition upon formulations drawn from various periods in his development.

The concept is variously referred to as the unconditioned transcendent, the unconditionally real, the unconditionally powerful, the unconditionally personal, the unconditionally perfect, the inaccessible holy, the eternal, the unconditional demand, and the unconditional meaning.

In Tillich's view, "it would not be worthwhile to speak at all of the fact that all sorts of things, ideas or feelings or deeds, move out of the past into the future . . . if all this were nothing but a moving, a flowing, a becoming and decaying without ultimate meaning or final importance."[35] It is really worthy of serious concern and decision only if something transcends the process of mere becoming, the mere transition from past to future. There must be something that "supports the times but is not subject to them."

The direction of consciousness toward unconditioned meaning is a necessary function that constitutes the reality of meaning. The prius of every individual apprehension of meaning is the unconditioned meaning itself, the prius of every *form* of meaning is the direction toward the unconditioned form, and the prius of every content of meaning is the unconditioned import. It is senseless to ask whether there is an unconditioned meaning, for the very question presupposes an ultimate meaning. It is also senseless to ask whether the Unconditional "exists," for if it were something established in the temporal order it would no longer be the Unconditional; moreover, it would be some object the "existence" of which would be susceptible—at least theoretically —of proof. But the Unconditioned cannot be proved. It can only

[35] *The Religious Situation*, p. 7.

be pointed to as the meaning that is the foundation of all meaning-fulfillment.[36]

The above formulations appear relatively early in Tillich's writings (1923). Almost twenty years later, he says that direction toward the Unconditioned is a matter of decision and *faith*, of orienting ourselves to a creative reality, a transcendent order that informs but also contradicts the order to which we belong. It involves receiving this transcendent reality as a gift, an unconditional power that grasps us and gives to the passing fact and decision an unconditional seriousness and meaning.[37] It confronts us as the depth of our life, as the source of our being, as our ultimate concern. We take it seriously and without reservation. Only the person who can in complete seriousness say that there is nothing to be taken seriously and without reservation is lacking in faith; only such a person is a real atheist. And anyone who attempts to take seriously the mere surface appearances possesses no principle of selection; if he possesses a principle of selection he has already questioned the surfaces and is started on the path into the depths. In the path leading to the depths one will, as we have seen, be driven either to the demonic depths and their threat or to the deeper depth—the infinite and inexhaustible ground and abyss. He who has been grasped by the experience of the unconditioned meaning of life is a man of faith, whether he calls himself atheist or not. And conversely, the person who has not known this depth of life is an atheist, whether he calls himself religious or not.

It must not be supposed that religion is "the only phenomenon which bears witness to the ultimate." "In some periods it is not even the most important of the witnesses or the most effective in expression and symbolism."[38] Every time has something within it which drives it beyond itself to a reality, a meaning underlying all time and all existent forms. In every time there is a paradoxical taking up of the unconditioned meaning into the forms of time. "That which is not existential form becomes an existing form." There are therefore within every time two tendencies

---

[36] *Das System der Wissenschaften* (Göttingen: Vandenhoeck und Ruprecht, 1923), p. 130. The unconditioned meaning should not be interpreted as being some ethereal or purely spiritual reality. As will be indicated later, it is inherent in the nature of being to strive for meaning-fulfillment. Hence the term "meaning" involves something ontological as well as axiological.

[37] "'Faith' in the Jewish-Christian Tradition," *Christendom*, VII (1942), 525-26.

[38] *The Religious Situation*, p. 9.

moving in opposite directions, the one toward that which is not in time but beyond it and beneath it, the other a tendency to give a name and a local habitation to this depth which is beneath time.

We find self-transcendence in every time, openness to the eternal, a hallowing of time; but upon the other hand we see the appropriation of the eternal, the self-sufficiency of time, the secularization of the holy. There is a movement to and fro between self-transcendence and self-sufficiency, between the desire to be a mere vessel and the desire to be the content, between turning towards the eternal and the turning towards the self. In this action and reaction we discern the religious situation of every present at its profoundest level.[39]

Hence in a general sense we may say that every period has an unconscious, self-evident faith lying at a deeper level than the apparent antithesis of belief and unbelief, both of which arise out of it and are rooted in it. Religion and every cultural or spiritual phenomenon of a period express its sense of eternal import. Accordingly, religion may be defined as the relatedness to this ultimate depth and meaning and power. It is the relatedness to what is of ultimate concern, to what may be taken seriously without reservation. The Unconditioned is the symbol of this ultimate concern; it is that to which all genuine religious symbols, including the word "God," point when they are alive.

Remembering that Tillich has said that the concepts of the boundary-situation and of the Unconditioned seem to lead in opposite directions but actually aim at the same goal, we may now in a definition of religion bring together what is the essence of the experience of the boundary-situation and of the experience of the Unconditioned:

Religion is an experience of the Unconditioned and that means an experience of absolute reality on the ground of the experience of absolute nothingness; it will experience the nothingness of all existing things, the nothingness of values, the nothingness of the personal life; where this experience has led to the absolute, radical No, there it shifts into an equally absolute experience of reality, into a radical Yes. It is not a question of a new reality beside or above things; that would be only a thing of a higher order that would again fall under the No. Rather, right through things there forces itself upon us that reality which is at the same time the No and the Yes over things; it is not an existing thing, it is not the substance, the totality of the existing order; it is, if we may use a mystical formula, the Super-existing, that which is at the same time the abso-

[39] *Ibid.*, p. 11.

lute Nothing and the absolute Something. But the predicate "is" conceals the real situation, for it is not a question of an existent reality, it is rather a meaning-reality: the ultimate, the deepest, all-shattering and ever newly creating meaning-reality.[40]

From beyond the boundary, then, there proceeds a Yes as well as a No. The Yes affirms the positive meaningfulness of "the stream of events hastening out of the past into the future." The No negates the claim to finality. Here in this early writing of Tillich we find the formulations basic to all his writings—formulations that aim to give expression to the Christian doctrines of creation and of justification by faith.

As we have seen, Tillich's view is that reality is infinitely power-ful and dynamic. The deepest "depth" is the depth in which we confront the infinite and inexhaustible ground and abyss of all being and meaning. Man may not identify himself or any of his creations with this depth; he is not self-existent, he is separated from the depth by "the boundary." Hence no existing form of real-ity, no temporal manifestation of the ground of being and mean-ing is unambiguous. When we properly describe or evaluate re-ligiously any temporal reality, whether it be a human person, a human institution, a religious doctrine or symbol, a cultural crea-tion, we must see that it is partial, it is subject to criticism, it can lose its powerfulness, it is conditioned. Hence, although it has a dimension of depth, every temporal reality has an absolute limit; it stands in the boundary-situation.

Accordingly, the concept of the Unconditioned is to be under-stood first as a limiting concept, as a qualification of everything in the temporo-spatial, the conditioned order.[41] Many of the philosophical concepts historically employed to refer to the abso-lute include this negative implication. We may think of the Greek notion of pure form, of the One, Substance, the Good, the In-finite, the Absolute. All of these concepts imply a "distance" be-tween the individuated forms and the ultimate unity. The word "absolute," for example, means that which is separated, that

---

[40] "Ueber die Idee einer Theologie der Kultur," in *Religionsphilosophie der Kultur* (*Berlin: Reuther und Reichard*, 1919), p. 35. The second edition (1921, p. 35) reads a little differently: "Religion is relatedness to the Un-conditioned. Through existing realities, through values, through the personal life there becomes evident the meaning of unconditional reality, before which every particular thing and the totality of all particulars, before which every value and the system of values, before which personality and community are shattered in their own self-sufficient being and value."

[41] Later on we shall consider the historical sources of the term.

which is absolved. All of these concepts, however, seem to suggest a separate sphere of pure form or being.

Tillich chooses the word "Unconditioned" in order to express the negative implication but also in order to avoid the spatialized conception of another order of being. The term is a neutral one, implying neither a dualistic nor a monistic world view. In recent years Tillich (in his lectures) has spoken of this limiting aspect of the Unconditioned as the negative Unconditioned. The latter formulation underlines the awareness that the absolute cannot be "located" or "domesticated" in the temporal, contingent order, that the inexhaustible ground cannot be compressed into any form, or even into a name. It aims to point to the ultimate and not to express it. So much for the negative Unconditioned.[42]

Now, the Unconditioned is a constitutive as well as a regulative concept. It connotes the participation of everything ontic in an ontological structure of being. This does not mean that the conditioned order is to be explained by some other extrapolated order. The Unconditioned may not properly be spoken of as "existing"; it is a reality but it is not, as such, a part of the existential order. Rather, it is that which is presupposed in any meaningful order of thought or being. It is a necessity of the human mind, for no mind can think nothingness. It is presupposed even when one merely asks whether the unconditionally meaningful is a reality. It is the symbol of the depth of things, "the basis of the being of things whereby 'being' is taken absolutely, transcendently, as the expression of the secret into which thinking cannot penetrate, because as something existing it is itself based on it."[43] In other words, it is "the Unconditioned of being." Like Schelling's *Unvordenkliche*, it is that which all thinking and all being must presuppose and it is also ultimately inaccessible to thought. It is a symbol of that which does not lend itself to intellectual realization, a symbol of the inner transcendence of things. But the symbolic character of the Unconditioned as pointing to what is anterior to and inaccessible to all thought does not deprive it of reality or of amenability to human apprehension; it

[42] The terms "negative Unconditioned" and "positive Unconditioned" do not appear in Tillich's early writings. His use of them in his lectures at Union Theological Seminary reflects the result of his working out in detail his conception of the method of "correlation" between philosophy and theology. According to this view, philosophy leads only to the radical question of the negative Unconditioned: "Why is there something and not nothing?" He holds that the question can be answered only by the Christian revelation.

[43] *Interpretation of History*, p. 83.

lifts the reality out of the conditioned into the unconditioned sphere, concerning which we can speak only in symbols. Indeed, any attempt to speak unsymbolically (i.e., literally) of the Un-conditioned is an attempt to erect a Tower of Babel to reach the infinite. It is to commit blasphemy. It is to rob the Unconditioned of its unconditionality.[44] An analogous blasphemy is committed when the word "God" becomes a literal representation of a "highest Being." The word "God" properly understood does not refer to a "thing." If it did, God would be one thing among others, one thing "existing" alongside other things. He would be spatialized and conditioned. The word "God" is a symbol for the unconditioned transcendent. "The unconditioned transcendent surpasses every possible conception of a being, including even the conception of a Supreme Being."[45] The religious act, when genuine, annihilates any such materialization. When God or when the Unconditioned is made into a "thing," it becomes a contradiction in terms and an absurdity. By definition there can be no unconditioned being. The demand for belief in such a "thing" quite properly leads to atheism. Hence, "it is the religious function of atheism ever to remind us that the religious act has to do with the unconditioned transcendent, and that the representations of the Unconditioned are not objects concerning whose existence or non-existence a dis-cussion would be possible."[46]

Supernaturalism characteristically and inevitably elicits this "atheistic" protest. Its "tendency to go beyond the natural sphere into the supernatural, in order to be grasped there by the un-conditionally powerful, binds the latter to one definite and limited sphere and thus deprives it of its unconditioned power." Hence criticism of supernaturalism might be said to be the beginning of all criticism. Even if it leads to atheism, the latter is more appropriate to "the majesty of the unconditionally powerful than a theism that fetters it to one supernatural sphere of being"[47] or to a realm of pure miracle.

Tillich is unambiguous in his hostility to this sort of super-naturalism, and the point should be stressed. One must, he says, always struggle against any attempt to put God *outside* of nature

<hr>

[44] "Religionsphilosophie," in Max Dessoir (ed.), *Die Philosophie in ihren Einzelgebieten* (Berlin: Ullstein, 1925), p. 798.

[45] *Rel. Verw.*, p. 102. In his later writings Tillich says the Unconditioned is not God. We shall return to this point.

[46] *Ibid.*

[47] *Ibid.*, p. 86.

or of anything. "The unconditioned character of the Divine . . . destroys the 'side-by-side' theology even if it appears in the disguise of a 'super.' "[48] He views this spatialization of the Unconditioned, which is accomplished by supernaturalist materializations or objectivations of the divine, as the blasphemous devitalization and trivialization of the divine power and majesty.

Such reduction of the Unconditioned is often implicit in the supernaturalist conception of God as a personal being.

The concept of a "personal God" interfering with natural events or being "an independent cause of natural events" makes God a natural object beside other objects, an object amongst objects, a being amongst beings, maybe the highest, but anyhow *a* being. This, indeed, is the destruction, not only of the physical system, but even more the destruction of any meaningful idea of God. It is the impure mixture of mythological elements (which are justified in their place, namely in the concrete religious life) and of rational elements (which are justified in their place, namely in the theological interpretation of religious experience). No criticism of this distorted idea of God can be sharp enough.[49]

Supernaturalism represents also an escape from "the present." Indeed, Tillich finds more genuine religion among those who understandingly repudiate supernaturalism than in those who turn their backs on time and history in the name of the eternal.

The person who is fully aware of the significance of the here-and-now and who feels himself to be separated by a deep gulf from the "religious" person who holds this sort of theology, is often more fully aware of the unconditioned power and majesty of God than is the "religious" person who believes that in his communion with God he has God in his possession. The latter is unaware of the fact that he really possesses nothing but his own piety and that his piety is unrelated to the here-and-now.[50]

Such a person has put his piety in the place of the infinite and inexhaustible ground and abyss of being and meaning and history. There is no way in which man can by piety control the uncondi-

---

[48] Cf. Tillich's review of H. N. Wieman and W. M. Horton, *The Growth of Religion*, in *Journal of Religion*, XX (1940), 69 ff. In this review Tillich questions the propriety of describing Wieman's point of view as "naturalistic" and implies that Wieman has wrongly described Tillich as a "supernaturalist."

[49] "The Idea of the Personal God," *Union Review*, II (1940), 9.

[50] *Rel. Verw.*, p. 86. As in other instances, this passage is rendered differently in Tillich's revised version of the essay in *The Protestant Era* (p. 82).

tioned powerful; it grasps us when and where it will. Yet one must prepare for it by taking seriously the here-and-now.

The concept of the Unconditioned, as we have indicated, is constitutive in a different sense from that attaching to "existence." The unconditioned transcendent is that which gives being to existence, as the transcendent power of being. Because of it both the world and the mind have what Tillich, following the Neo-Platonists, calls an ecstatic character.

The world and all beings point to some unconditioned in which they participate and from which they are separated at the same time. The world has—to use an unusual term—an "ecstatic" character approachable by the human mind, which shares this character. Not a transcendent world but the transcending character of our world must be taught. I do not know whether this is neo-supernaturalism or neo-naturalism, and I do not think the question of the name is very important.[51]

The ecstatic character of reality is described as faith in "the paradoxical immanence of the transcendent." These formulations accent the view that all existent realities are on the periphery of reality and yet are related to its center, its inviolable core. Here is one of the meanings of the doctrine of Providence. Later on Tillich calls this aspect of the Unconditioned "the positive Unconditioned."

The positive Unconditioned is, then, the creative power that is manifest in, but never exhausts itself in, the manifold creaturely events and thoughts and deeds of the temporal order. It is paradoxically present, for it is both operative within existence and beyond the border, in the depths. Belief in its reality (and not in its "existence") is a matter of faith, of a faith that is inextricable from a continuance of meaningful living, either for an individual or for a culture. Belief in its reality is ecstatic in the sense that it involves being grasped "ecstatically" by a dynamic power beyond one's self and being thereby imbued with transcendent joy and enthusiasm.

Any enhancement of one's own power by another power is at the moment of union ecstatic. Ecstasy operates in such a way as to break through the given fixed form of an individual existence. Only by means of ecstasy is a grasping of the essential power of reality possible; it is also the only means of grasping even the essence of the contemporary.[52]

[51] Tillich's review of Wieman and Horton, *Growth of Religion*, pp. 71-72.
[52] *Rel. Verw.*, p. 83. Cf. Kierkegaard's association of "passion" with the moment in which the individual "realizes existentially a unity of the infinite

The third meaning of the concept of the Unconditioned, Tillich calls the "Unconditioned of value." All cultural creations and human nature itself can be understood and evaluated only in relation to universal norms. In confronting these norms man stands at the boundary; he recognizes the demand implicit within the norms as unconditional demand. No one can escape or deny the unconditional demands of logic and of mathematical propositions except by lying, and even the lie is conditioned by the unconditional demand it denies. The same unconditionality attaches to moral freedom, which is recognized as in some sense superior to everything else, as worthy of ultimate concern; it attaches also to the categorical imperative of ethical behavior. And with respect to the norms of truth as well as of the good, there is presupposed a harmony between the demands and the essential structure of being. Thus in confronting the limited character of our existence, in confronting the ambiguous events of the temporal order, in confronting the normative demands of truth, goodness, and beauty, we find a qualification which we intuit in reality itself, the qualification of the conditioned by the Unconditioned.

If the Unconditioned qualifies all meaning and value, it cannot be properly interpreted as one part of existence or as one meaning among others or as one value among others. It is presupposed by all of these concerns. It is even presupposed when one asks whether there is any ultimate or unconditioned concern. But this presupposition does not mean that the Unconditioned is something separate from existence. Such a conception would make it precisely one thing alongside others. It is a *qualification* of existence and meaning and value.

Hence we may be grasped by the Unconditioned only in and through and beyond vitality, in and through and beyond form and valid rationality. Yet, it "speaks" and it expresses itself only through form. This is a paradoxical idea, for it implies that the creation of and the breaking through a form is itself a form. But paradox is necessary if we are to express the immanence of the transcendent. "To come into being means to come into form. . . . At the same time, however, there dwells in everything the inner inexhaustibility of being . . . the will toward breaking through its

---

and the finite which transcends existence. . . . In passion the existing subject is rendered infinite in the eternity of the imaginative representation, and yet he is at the same time most definitely himself." *Concluding Unscientific Postscript,* trans. David F. Swenson (Princeton: Princeton University Press, 1941), p. 176.

own limited form."[53] This inner inexhaustibility of being, when it expresses the Unconditioned, becomes a *form of grace*. It is a *form* or *Gestalt* in the sense that it is a dynamic form-creating tendency, it is perceptible in the present, and it appears through the medium of a form of existence. It is a form of *grace* if it pulsates with a transcendent meaning and if it carries with it a protest against the identification of its particular form with the Unconditioned. In other words, it is an "ecstatic" form of being, open to the infinite—as judgment and as anticipation of fulfillment—and to the incursion of the new form. It bespeaks both the divine Yes and the divine No. This conception is manifestly a sort of ideal type, for the perfect form of grace never appears. Fate is an ingredient of every action, not only in the sense that fulfillment is always ambiguous, but also in the sense that man cannot control it or induce it, he can only prepare for it through the "ecstatic" operation of faith.

The violation or frustration of the form of grace appears in a variety of ways. It may appear in the distortion, the sin, of arrogant self-inflation. (Of this we shall speak presently.) Or it may appear where there is a spirit of *self-sufficient finitude*, the ethos of pure *secularism*. In its truncated orientation, self-sufficient finitude is to be contrasted with the form of grace: it is tangible in the present but it ignores the protest against self-identification with the Unconditioned because it imagines it is immune to such distortion. And yet, it had its origin in protest against this very distortion.

But the seeds of death are in secularism. It does not stand

---

[53] *Rel. Verw.*, pp. 84-85. Two central ideas of Tillich are to be observed here, the idea of infinity and the concept of Gestalt (form). Infinity is not something spatial. Nor is it equivalent to limitlessness or endlessness. Hegel rightly calls that "bad infinity." It is to be understood qualitatively, not quantitatively, in terms of "the inexhaustible depths," "the inner inexhaustibility of being."

We should understand the concept of Gestalt in relation to this idea of infinity. Gestalt is a living structure in which the whole determines the special effects within an open or dynamic dialectic of necessity and freedom. As a living whole a Gestalt is rooted in the inner inexhaustibility of being.

The concept of Gestalt appears again and again in the history of Western thought from Plato and Aristotle through Bruno, Leibnitz, Kant, Goethe, and Schelling to contemporary Gestalt psychology. It is employed by Tillich in the interpretation of all aspects of life, in the interpretation of nature, the sciences, art and religion. In the treatment of his philosophy of science we shall observe in some detail his use of the term in the analysis of "the Gestalt sciences." Here he speaks also of a "cosmic Gestalt." So much does the idea of Gestalt appear in Tillich's writings that one might call him a Gestalt philosopher or theologian.

still. It moves either towards emptiness or towards the acceptance of false infinites. In the first instance it is on the path leading to lassitude. In the second, it is on the path leading towards the *demonic*. The self-sufficient entity attempts to capsule the inexhaustibility of being within itself. It identifies itself with the Unconditioned. This arrogant self-sufficiency results in the eruption of the abyss and in destruction. The demonic cannot be understood, however, unless one realizes that it has positive significance. *Demonry* appears when the urge for form-creation, by stepping too high, drives on toward self-inflation and form-destruction. Hence it combines meaningful and meaningless elements, with the latter becoming predominant through the violation of universal norms. Neither element normally obtains complete sway in this world of ambiguity. If the meaningless element predominates to the point of complete disintegration, the demonic becomes *satanic*. The concept of the demonic, properly understood, combines destructive and creative elements. Because the concept of the demonic characterizes a reality from which even the secular sphere cannot withdraw, a sphere in which either positive or negative "ecstatic" decision is demanded, the concept prevents secularism from maintaining the appearance of being merely a two-dimensional surface phenomenon. Here then the false sense of immunity mentioned above is dispelled. Secularism is shown to have its demonic dimensions of depth, its connection with the destructive abyss of being. On the other hand, we must remember that demonry is not confined to secularism. It appears in its most deceptive form in "religion." Any religion that spatializes the absolute in a book, in an infallible doctrine, or in a sacramental system is a demonry, and it is all the more deceptive just because it appeals to "divine" sanctions. Some "religions" combine a number of demonries in one system, drawing together into one idol a sacred book, a sacred tradition, a sacred hierarchy, and even a sacred social system. By virtue of this combination, "Roman Catholicism is the most potent system of religious demonry."[54]

There are various forms of resistance to demonry. One of the most common is simply another demonry. This sort of conflict Tillich calls the struggle between polytheisms. It may be a conflict between hallowed spatializations of blood and soil. Or it may be a conflict between an established demonry and a newly emerging rival, as, for example, between capitalism and communism. Thus do extremes breed extremes and demonries breed demonries, ever delaying the appearance of true forms of grace.

[54] *Interpretation of History*, p. 24.

(In essential respects this interpretation which relates the
demonic to the spatializations and conflicts of polytheism, it
should be noted, stems from Boehme's view of the demonic,
as developed further by Schelling.)

But resistance to the demonic takes other forms. There may
arise rational and prophetic protests, explicitly religious or only
tacitly so. In either event, they represent a new awareness of
relatedness to the Unconditioned, an appearance of the *divine*.
They may appear from within religious groups or from without,
among the "atheists" and the secularists. Hence the form of grace
as well as its distortion may appear either within religious institutions or outside and against them. Its essential character is
not altered by the locus of the appearance. Barth recognizes the
ubiquity of distortion, though not of the forms of grace, when he
says, "Smoke from the fire of Zeus may penetrate farther than
other fumes, it may display greater variety, but it does not differ
in kind."[55] For Tillich, both the protests and the forms of grace
in "secularism" are often more effective than so-called "religious"
protest; certainly, they are more soundly religious than the self-
styled religious institution or personality which is actually demonic. For this reason Tillich speaks of the secularism that in
actuality recognizes the boundary-situation, and that is, in reality
if not in word aware of the Unconditioned, as a *Protestant secularism* and as a concealed form of grace. Protestant secularism may
conceal within itself a latent protest against itself. Hence it may
be attacked, not only from the outside, but also from its own
depths.[56]

There are, then, different types of "religion" and different types
of "secularism." Both religion and secularism may manifest truly
religious forms of grace and truly demonic forms of distortion.
The churches have no monopoly on the forms of grace, and
secularism has no monopoly on self-sufficient finitude.

The ambivalent character of secularism as well as of "religion"
is to be understood in terms of the threefold distinction between
autonomy, heteronomy, and *theonomy.* We have seen that true
religion is defined as relatedness to the Unconditioned. Culture,
on the other hand, is defined as relatedness to the conditioned
forms of meaning and their fulfillment. The fulfillment of cultural effort occurs only when culture in all its forms gives expression to the unconditioned meaning. But culture as such—
in contrast to religion—actually relates itself to the conditioned

55 *Op. cit.,* p. 236.
56 *Rel. Verw.,* p. 16.

forms and their unity without giving heed to the unconditioned meaning. The attitude here represented is called "autonomy."

In every autonomy, that is, in every secular culture there is a dual element: the "nomos," the form or "law" which is supposed to be radically carried out in accord with the unconditioned demand for meaning, and the "autos," the self-assertion of the conditioned, which in the finding of a form loses the unconditioned meaning. Autonomy is therefore always at the same time obedience and contradiction to the Unconditioned. It is obedience in so far as it subjects itself to the unconditioned demand for meaning; it is contradiction in so far as it denies the unconditioned meaning itself. Autonomous culture is, as the myth puts it, always at the same time *hybris* and a gift of God.[57]

But autonomy is unable to maintain itself; by inward necessity it comes to its own limit. For Tillich the great historical proof of the inability of autonomy to create a world with any content from within itself is seen in "the development of Greek philosophy from the first appearance of rational autonomy up to its decline into skepticism and probabilism and its inversion into the 'new archaicism' of late antiquity."[58] The modern history of autonomy has pursued the same course, ending in the emptiness of present-day capitalism.

Yet at the outset autonomy serves a noble purpose. It arises as a protest against submission to "divine" and secular absolutes (or false infinites). The cultural expression of autonomy is classicism or humanism, which "is the attempt of man to rely upon himself, to find in his own existence the fulfillment of its meaning."[59] At first humanism carries residues of religious orientation. Confronted by heteronomy, which garbs a portion of human-religious reality in the unconditioned validity of the divine, it raises protest. "A reality such as a book, a person, a community, an institution, or doctrine, claims absolute authority and lays claim to submission of every other kind of reality, life, and doctrine. . . . But that this claim is established by a finite, historical reality, is the root of all heteronomy and of all demonry."[60] In

[57] "Religionsphilosophie," p. 801. For a discussion of some of the eighteenth- and nineteenth-century sources of the concepts autonomy, heteronomy, and theonomy see the article by the present writer, "What Kind of Religion Has a Place in Higher Education?" *Journal of Bible and Religion,* XIII (1945), 184-92. Kant, Rothe, and Troeltsch are the principal figures who contribute to this typology of authority.

[58] *Interpretation of History,* p. 23.

[59] *Rel. Verw.,* p. 195.

[60] *Interpretation of History,* pp. 25-26.

face of this arrogant claim of heteronomy, in face of this demonic unity of the transcendent and the destructive, humanism considers itself "a defense against the destructive incursion of the Beyond Being into being. Its religious background is precisely that of fighting the religious demonry and trying to protect human nature as such."[61]

But the great failure of autonomy is that in destroying the heteronomous demonry it also loses contact with the depths of being and becomes shallow; it overcomes heteronomy but at the same time it tears itself loose from the divine. Thus revolutionary humanism is followed by classical humanism and this in turn by romantic humanism. Romantic humanism observes the religious background fading away and attempts to restore it by reviving religious forms out of the past. But it does not succeed in bringing the religious background into the foreground. "And since it remains a background, it fades away. The self-sufficient human creature absorbs, as it were, the transcendent into itself and thus destroys it as transcendent. The awareness of the threat to human existence is lost and with it the awareness of the support."[62]

Autonomy and heteronomy both fail to cope with the fundamental theological problem: "the relation of the absolute, which is assumed in the idea of God, and of the relative, which belongs to human religion."[63] They both become empty because in opposite ways the unconditioned meaning is lost. They both subsist on theonomy and fall to pieces as soon as the theonomous synthesis has entirely disappeared. This is the synthesis in which the boundary-situation and relatedness to the Unconditioned appear together, the synthesis that emerges when the recognition of the unconditioned demand for meaning is joined with autonomous consciousness of form. Only when these elements are together can persuasion and creativity subsist.

Theonomy is that attitude which at the same time is form-creative and related to the Unconditioned. It signifies the situation in which "autonomous forms are imbued with a transcendent import supporting and breaking through them."[64] But again, theonomy may become an abstraction and lose its existential relevance. In order to achieve relevance it must combine a sense

---

[61] *Rel. Verw.*, p. 196.
[62] *Ibid.*, p. 197.
[63] *Interpretation of History*, p. 25.
[64] *Rel. Verw.*, p. 16.

of the universal with a sense of the demands of a particular situation. It must combine *Logos* with *Kairos*. Man cannot with impunity think timelessly. Heteronomy attempts to do so by claiming finality for one form. Autonomy attempts to do so by claiming the self-sufficiency of a particular set of cultural norms. But time demands new decisions, new ways of giving expression to the unconditioned meaning. The term *Kairos*, taken from the New Testament and meaning "the fullness of time," expresses the fact that every moment approaches men as fate and as the demand for decision. Hence it expresses the fact that "at a special time special tasks are demanded."[65] In the *Nicomachean Ethics*, Aristotle defines *Kairos* as "the good in the category of time." Tillich connects this concept with the idea of grace. If a special moment of time is good for the fulfillment of something, this moment is its *Kairos* and it may look toward fulfillment through "ecstatic" decision. In the fullness of time a new decision must be made in order to give the unconditioned meaning vital, "timely" expression. *Kairos* is, then, the concept relating the Unconditioned to the present. A corpus of unchanging commandments, however necessary, is not adequate alone for the achievement of relevance in a changing world. The Unconditioned always remains transcendent; "but it appears as a judgment to a given form of society and as a norm of a coming one." There must be an actual living obedience which is grasped by the Unconditioned and which recognizes what is timely (*Kairos*) and what is untimely. Only in the *Kairos* may one escape the toils of spatialization, for the *Kairos* demands time-thinking rather than space-thinking. This insight becomes decisive not only for Tillich's philosophy of history but also for his theory of truth.

Truth is not statically apprehended, as is attempted by both Catholicism and classicism, but rather it is apprehended dynamically. . . . The truth stands in fate just as does existence. The truth of every religious realization is its standing in the depth of historical fate, its standing in the Kairos, in the transcendentally shattered present. The dynamic truth is the living, moving element of all that is here thought and said. It is an expression of the boundary-situation, and also for each of these ideas and concepts. None of them can be separated from the dynamics of cognition. Each of them is justified in so far—and only in so far—as it is an adequate expression of our Present, of our Kairos.[66]

[65] *Ibid.*, p. 57.
[66] *Ibid.*, pp. 18-19.

What Tillich calls "the inner infinity of everything existing," applies, then, to truth as well as to being, to thought, value, and meaning, and to history.

Repeatedly in the foregoing discussion we have mentioned the idea of *meaning*. We have reserved until the end the treatment of this concept, for it is the most comprehensive and characteristic of all of Tillich's concepts. We shall encounter it again and again in the ensuing chapters, where ample occasion will appear for concrete illustration of its meaning and importance. Here we must be content with a sketch of its main features and implications.

In recent literature the concept of meaning has been employed most frequently in the discussion of semantics[67] and in the discussion of the Husserlian philosophy of phenomenology.[68] Tillich's interest in meaning has to do with the problem of the meaning of life. In this sense, meaning is the characteristic concern of the human spirit, and hence it is, for Tillich, the foundation of his whole system.[69] In making the problem of the meaning of life central, Tillich is again showing his concern with the direct confrontation of life in the spirit of existential philosophy. Here the question is not *how* to live but *why* live. In using the concept of meaning he employs a category of philosophical thought which had become familiar not only among writers of the existential school, such as Heidegger and Jaspers, Barth and Brunner, but also among those of the idealistic and Neo-Kantian tradition, such as Dilthey, Brentano, Rickert, Windelband, Eucken, Troeltsch, Hartmann, and Husserl, and among writers like Oswald

[67] Here the concept of meaning has received its principal denotations from the formulations devised by such writers as Rudolf Carnap, I. A. Richards, and Charles W. Morris. In these formulations the center of attention has been directed to a consideration of "the meaning of meaning" in the psychological sense involved when we say that a person in using a term may "mean" some object or state of affairs or may "mean" some other term which has its place in some system of signs and symbols. Other meanings may attach also to the term "meaning," such as are involved in the "emotive" functioning of words. These aspects of meaning are treated by Tillich in his discussion of religious symbols (to be dealt with later).

[68] Here the term "meaning" is used to refer to a concept in the sphere of pure logic. Meaning has to do with "meaning-giving acts" of the mind, acts which it is held involve the apprehension of ideal unities or essences. "Meaning" is that in which and through which a person experiences an object or a thing. As we shall observe later, Tillich's use of the term "meaning" and his conception of "essence" have been partially, if also negatively, conditioned by phenomenology, but Tillich's primary concern is of a different sort from that which is characteristic in phenomenology.

[69] *Interpretation of History*, p. 38.

Spengler and Theodor Lessing. One finds repeated references to "meaning," in the general sense, in the writings of Barth and Brunner, especially in Barth's commentary on *The Epistle to the Romans* and *The Word of God and the Word of Man,* and in Brunner's *Die Mystik und das Wort* and *Philosophy of Religion.*[70] But the last-named writers do not give the term systematic attention. Tillich sharpens and clarifies the concept by relating it to his whole philosophy of spirit and being.

Spirit (*Geist*) is the concept that denotes the dynamic power of creativity in man. It is not to be identified with reason or with creative intellect; it is rather in between the two. It unites elements of the universal, the rational, the existent, the creative, and the individual. It is best understood when we see it in its relation to more basic concepts. It is dependent on thought and being. Spirit is the self-determination of thought in the realm of existence.

It is not possible to grasp the essence of spirit without grasping metalogically the two basic elements of knowledge [thought and being]. The essence of spirit, its internal tension, its dynamic character, flow from the infinite contradiction between thought and being. In the logistic analysis of mind the being-element is usually neglected while the psychological analysis neglects the thought-element. Both neglect the tension of these elements. However, spirit is not a thought-form just as it is not a form of being. In spite of its dependence upon both, spirit is a separate and particular form. Spirit is the form of thought in the existential dimension. (*Geist ist Form des seiendes Denken.*)[71]

When thought confronts being and apprehends it, thought is realized as a form of being, as a dependent, limited, immediate form. But in the activity of spirit thought frees itself from its dependence, its immediacy; it stands over against all forms of being and posits the unconditional character of its claim; it stands over being as validity. Therefore the complete separation of something existing from the immediate bondage of its finite

[70] It is not unlikely that Brunner's *Philosophy of Religion* (London: Ivor Nicholson and Watson, 1937) reflects the influence of Tillich in this respect. The concept of meaning is used by Brunner in far more than a casual way. See especially pp. 24, 26, 40, 44, 45, 48, 59, 62-64, 74, 78, 80, 87. For Reinhold Niebuhr's conception of "the totality of things conceived as a realm of meaning" see his essay "Religion and Action," *Religion and the Modern World* (Philadelphia: University of Pennsylvania Press, 1941), pp. 89-108.

[71] *Das System der Wissenschaften,* p. 90. In the ensuing chapters we shall see that this view of spirit, thought and being determines the structure of Tillich's theology of culture and of his system of the sciences.

form is the presupposition of the realization of spirit. Thus freedom is the presupposition of spirit. Only to the free, individual
form is an unconditional demand possible. Only on the basis of
freedom can something valid be realized. The spirit is real only
in that realm where validities, subject exclusively to their laws of
meaning, are grasped in individual forms which, as such, are
subject to their own structural laws. Therefore, every spiritual act
is an act of stepping beyond the boundaries of that which has immediacy of form. It is an act of stepping beyond but not of ex-
ploding. For by its very nature the spirit-bearing form realizes in
itself something that does not originate in it, namely, the valid.

In its characteristic activity spirit goes beyond the validities
of pure thought (logic and mathematics). Spirit is present only
if something existing comes under the claim of validity, only if
the unconditional claim is somehow absorbed into being. This
is the bond between spirit and being which panlogism overlooks
just as psychologism overlooks the freedom of spirit from being.
But spirit is not bound to the universal; it is something absolutely
particular, individual, though it can take up the universal within
itself. Whatever it takes up, however, receives the peculiar shape
that happens to correspond to its individuality. Thus spirit receives concreteness and fullness, an individuality and infinity
that can be suggested only by the "ecstatic" word "grace."

Spirit is, in short, creative in the realm of meaning. Although
spirit is not divorced from the realm of causality, it is characteristically oriented to the realm of meaning, where individuality
expresses itself by living in and beyond reality, by accommodating
itself to the nature of being but by also giving to being a novel
expression. The realm of meaning then presupposes thought and
existence but goes beyond both into the realm of the creative
and into the realm where the meaning of life is experienced and
realized in some new form.[72]

Every spiritual act is, therefore, an individual meaningful act
fusing thought and being. It is an individual meaning-fulfilling
act. Considered in its cultural context, the reality in which the
spirit—or the spirit-bearing form—lives and creates is meaningful reality. This meaningful reality represents the creative unity
of thought, being, and intuited meaning. Thus it represents the
unity of intention toward the universal and the realization of
creative individuality. Where the universal is ignored, the purely

---

[72] *Ibid.*, pp. 90 ff. and 101 ff. The view of individuality set forth here is a
restatement of certain aspects of conceptions that appear in the writings of
Dilthey and Troeltsch.

arbitrary results; where the creative individuality is ignored, pure abstraction or formalism is the consequence.

Now, in Tillich's view, the theory of the structure of meaningful spiritual reality is the primary concern of philosophy, and the theory of the principles and elements of meaning is its first task. Remembering that meaning is possible only in the life of spirit (as described), we may now turn our attention to a closer definition of meaning. Tillich's theory of the elements of meaning brings together various motifs that have already been presented:

There are three elements in every awareness of meaning. First, an awareness of the context of meaning in which every separate meaning stands and without which it would be meaningless. Second, an awareness of the meaningfulness of the context of meaning and thus of every particular meaning, i.e. the consciousness of an *unconditioned* meaning which is present in every particular meaning. Third, an awareness of the demand under which a particular meaning stands, to fulfil the unconditioned meaning.[73]

This means that an awareness of the totality of meanings in the world is not enough.

Even the totality of meaning need not be meaningful, but could disappear like every particular meaning in the abyss of meaninglessness, if the presupposition of an unconditioned meaningfulness were not alive in every act of meaning. This unconditionedness of meaning is itself, however, not a meaning, it is rather the ground of meaning.[74]

The nature of ultimate meaning can be understood only in relation to the form and content of the spiritual act. Every spiritual act has a form, a content, and an import. The form is glimpsed in the multitude of theoretical and practical activities of the spirit, scientific and aesthetic, juridical and social. The content is the objective element in its simple character (*Sosein*); the content is raised by the form into the cultural-spiritual sphere. The import, or meaning, is the substance that gives the form and its content significance. "One can therefore say: the import is grasped and brought to expression in a content by means of a form. The content is the accidental, the import the essential, the form the mediative element."[75] The import is the meaningfulness giving every particular meaning its reality and power; it is the ground for an inner infinity of meaningfulness. This brings us back to

[73] "Religionsphilosophie," p. 789.
[74] *Ibid.*
[75] "Ueber die Idee einer Theologie der Kultur," pp. 38-39.

the depth, the infinite and inexhaustible ground and abyss of meaning. Or, if we consider the phenomenal aspect of the situation, it brings us back to the *Gestalt* of grace in which the unconditioned meaning is expressed and in which the claim to exhaust it is renounced.

In summary, then, we may say that meaning is understood as a *Gestalt* in which the dynamic depths of being are expressed and existence rises above itself into that creative realm made up of value, being, and import, all together pulsating with the powerfulness and holiness of the divine.[76] Or in fewer words, meaning is the combining of value and reality in creative individuality.

The possibilities of meaning are infinite in variety. Yet certain types may be discriminated in terms of form and import. Three major types of meaningful creation result—two represented by the two poles and a third in the middle. The first is "the typically secular and formal cultural creation," the second is "the typically religious cultural creation in which the import predominates," and the third is the type in which form and import find equilibrium in classicism.[77] Other typologies will be presented in due course. Perhaps the most important of the typologies of meaning is that suggested by the tripartite distinction already discussed, namely, autonomy, heteronomy, and theonomy. Although a certain amount of repetition will be involved, we quote Tillich's article on "Theonomie," for it sums up much that he has written on meaning and import and gives typical illustrations of the forms of meaning and of its distortion. In the quotation it will be observed that a description of the highest type of meaning is identical with the definition of theonomy and that this in turn is the attitude requisite for the appearance of a form of grace, a living structure pointing beyond itself.

Theonomy, originally signifying a law or validity with divine sanction in contrast to the law emanating from the self or autonomy, has in contemporary discussion acquired a more definite meaning. It is sharply distinguished from heteronomy, i.e., from the shattering of autonomously validated forms of human thought and action by a law alien and external to the spirit. Theonomy is in contrast to heteronomy an imbuing of autonomous forms with transcendent import. It originates not through the renunciation of autonomy, as

[76] Later we shall see that this definition of meaning presupposes Tillich's overcoming of realism and idealism in belief-ful or self-transcending realism; it is in turn a presupposition for his Logos Christology.
[77] "Ueber die Idee einer Theologie der Kultur," p. 39.

does, for example, the Roman Catholic idea of authority, but only through the deepening of autonomy in itself to the point where it transcends itself. The transcending of the autonomous forms in culture and society, their being impressed or imbued by a principle supporting and at the same time breaking through them but not shattering them: that is theonomy. In this sense the early and in part still the high Middle Ages is a theonomous period, while at the end of the Middle Ages the autonomous principles became independent and in contrast to this development the church set up resistance by becoming heteronomous. The struggle for the idea of tolerance on the soil of capitalistic society destroys the political power of heteronomy and gives to the autonomous principles a possibility of free development. But autonomy left to its own devices leads to increasing emptiness and—since there cannot be a vacuum even in the spiritual realm—it finally becomes imbued with demonically destructive forces. The insight into this whole complex of cultural development has led to the demand for a new theonomy.[78]

Here we have presented to us an outline of the history of modern culture, as well as a typology of the forms and degrees of meaning. Here also we come to the conclusion of our survey of the basic concepts employed by Tillich. We shall later undertake to expound the "meaning" of the present historical situation as Tillich interprets it, but we give here some anticipation of his analysis by quoting the remaining sentences of his definition of theonomy:

The concept of theonomy plays a decisive role in religious socialism. But politically opposed groups also take a positive attitude toward what is meant by the concept. The danger of romantic misinterpretation of theonomy can be overcome only if the autonomous principles are not brought into question from without but are rather driven from within to the point where their dependence upon a transcendent ground—an abyss—becomes evident. Not romantic return to past theonomous eras, but rather advance by means of an inner struggle with autonomy to a new cultural and social life imbued with transcendent import: that is what the demand of theonomy implies.

The succeeding chapters will explore the implications of the concepts described above as they bear upon the multiform aspects of the human condition and especially as they relate to Tillich's philosophy of culture, his philosophy of science, and his philosophy of religion.

[78] "Theonomie," *Die Religion in Geschichte und Gegenwart*, ed. Hermann Gunkel *et al.* (Tübingen: Mohr, 1931), Vol. V.

APPENDIX

WATER*

PAUL TILLICH

It was in the earliest Greek philosophers that the human spirit first asked the question of the nature of all things. And the first answer given to the question was: Water. In the saying attributed to Thales "But the Best of all things is Water," we find that peculiar combination of primitive mythical overtone and rational abstraction which characterizes all pre-Socratic thought. It is therefore incorrect to interpret the "Water" of Thales and the "Air" and "Fire" of the other nature philosophers as objects in the sense of modern natural science. Such objects appear only after philosophy has undergone further development; they do not appear at the beginning. It has been said rightly that the "Water" of Thales is a "metaphysical" water; that is, in water the *archē*, principle of all being, is envisaged. It is not as if the *archē* were something behind the water, but that water for Thales had the quality of being more than mere water as such, namely, the principle of all being.

In the biblical story of creation water has a double significance. The water of chaos over which the spirit of Yahweh hovers is a different water from that which is present after His separation of the land from the seas on the second day of creation. In the water of the primeval chaos sea and land are still undivided. The waters above and below the firmament, divided on the second day of creation, and the waters "gathered into one place" on the third day, are the opposite of the dry land. Nevertheless even this water which has been given its limits still has chaotic qualities. It is the place of the beast of chaos mentioned in the book of Job.

The relation between water and chaos is in the background of the story of the Flood. The Flood is the threat that again all will be engulfed by chaos; and the rainbow of the Noah story is the symbol of the certainty that form forever will be able to stand against chaos.

The half-demonic character of water comes out clearly in the

* Wilhelm Stählin (ed.), *Das Gottesjahr 1932* (Kassel: Bärenreiter, 1931), pp. 65-68; an annual volume of meditations published for the Berneuchen Group. (Translated by J. L. Adams and Mrs. George W. W. Brewster.) See p. 33, n. 27, *supra*.

remarkable passage in the book of Revelation, where the visionary is shown the "sea of glass, which is like crystal" (4:6). The sea is there, but it has become transparent, and anything that has become transparent has lost its mythical-demonic character. In the final vision (21:1) the demonic character of the sea is expressed with greater sharpness. It is said that the sea is no more. It has so much of the chaotic or the demonic in it that it is not susceptible to the eschatological transformation, and it disappears.

But water also receives an absolutely positive valuation in the Bible, as the source or stream that refreshes all living things and makes the earth fruitful. Therefore it is the element which has been taken up into form and has been ordered by it. In the "water of life" as in the rivers of Paradise nothing demonic remains.

We see the relationship of water to chaos and form again in the rite of baptism. Here also it has a double meaning. The water takes back what it formed from itself (immersion), and gives forth something new from itself (rebirth). This double relationship of chaos to the individual appears in the first original sentence of Greek philosophy we possess, Anaximander's great fragment: "And into that source from which the things arise that are they must pass away, according to necessity; for they must pay the penalty and make atonement to one another for their injustice according to the decree of Time." The principle from which they receive their birth Anaximander calls "the Infinite," but it has entirely the qualities that water has for Thales. Out of chaos we come and into chaos we return, bound by the tragic decree of our guilt. Similarly, yet in quite another way, in baptism the same man who is taken back by water comes forth from water again, although now he is a different man. This is a necessary transformation, since his first birth led to "injustice" (*adikia*, according to Anaximander and frequently, the New Testament). So the chaos force of water is expressed in its power to swallow up in death and bring to birth again.

Water receives a special depth of significance from the fact that man, like many other living beings, is enveloped in the amniotic fluid of the mother's body, so that in the strictest sense his birth is an issuing from water. In the Gospel of John the conversation between Jesus and Nicodemus alludes to this. Jesus has just said: "Unless one is born anew, he cannot see the Kingdom of God." Nicodemus asks if a man can enter a second time into his mother's womb and be born, and Jesus replies that one must be born of water and the Spirit if he is to enter the Kingdom of God. Here we can see also an emergence from chaos into form.

Today these things are pointed to again by psychoanalysts. We know how much the pre-natal situation affects the development of the child, and how a more negative or a more positive situation may have some effect in differences of type in man. There is a type related to the motherly, the encompassing, the flowing, the chaotic, in contrast to a type related to the masculine, the free, the firm and the formed. In the two types the response to water, sea, clouds, and the like, is quite different. Perhaps in the one there arises a positive, in the other a negative reference to the mother's womb. The first type can change more easily because its form is less established; the second must destroy form in order to be able to plunge into the water of rebirth. The second type is rarer but more radical. This contrast is decisive, too, for the typology of religion and piety.

The purifying power of water is also known to us, through its capacity to take into itself and destroy what is in a state of corruption and uncleanness. Here we remember the Nietzsche saying: one must be a sea if one is to absorb a foul river without becoming foul oneself. The "negating" power of water is at the same time its power to purify.

Under these circumstances it must be made clear that the reference to "plain (simple) water" in Luther's Catechism is not adequate for a description of the sacramental situation. Luther stood in necessary opposition to a sacramental magic that connected saving effects with the sacramental use of water as such. His opposite assertion was the complete profanization and removal of the potency of water as such. But there is no "as such" in this sense; rather, there are various correlations of understanding in which different levels of being are opened up. Hence we must ask if the spiritual situation that created the sacraments did not have access to sacramental elements that have been lost to us and can only be re-discovered by the roundabout ways of mythology and psychoanalysis. If we can obtain access to these elements today, we shall understand that water is not contingently and externally symbolic, but has reached sacramental significance by its own intrinsic power of being.

III

The Theology of Culture and Art

IN that classic of spiritual direction *Letters to a Young Poet*, Rainer Maria Rilke writes, reflecting on the beauties of Rome, the Eternal City:

Waters unendingly full of life go over the old aqueducts into the great city and dance in the many squares over white stone basins and spread out in wide spacious pools and rush by day and heighten the sound of their rushing in the night that is large and starry here and soft with winds. And gardens are here, unforgettable avenues and stairs, stairs devised by Michelangelo, stairs that are built on the model of downward-gliding water—broadly bringing forth step out of step in their fall like wave out of wave. Through such impressions one collects oneself, comes to oneself again from amid so much that is pretentious, that talks and chatters (and how talkative it is!), and learns slowly to know the very few things in which the eternal endures that one can love and the solitary in which one can quietly take part. . . . Seek the depth of things.[1]

No words could better reveal the ruling interest of Tillich's thought—learning to know the things in which the eternal endures. Although it has been attached to a wide range of concerns —science and technology, philosophy and religion, art and social theory—this interest seems first to have become explicit in his study and enjoyment of art. We can therefore better understand

[1] Rainer Maria Rilke, *Letters to a Poet*, trans. M. D. Herter Norton (New York: W. W. Norton & Co., 1934), pp. 42-43.

Tillich's thought—and also some of his characteristic categories
—if we observe the early development of his interest in art.

In his autobiographical sketch he tells us that his father, a
Protestant minister in a small trans-Elbian town, not only maintained the musical traditions of the evangelical pastor's house-
hold but also tried his hand at composing. The son was not himself inclined to the study of music. His first warm interest in art
seems to have been in the field of literature, and he tells of his
early intoxication with the plays of Shakespeare and with Schelling's philosophy of nature. He asserts that his "instinctive sympathy" for German existential philosophy undoubtedly goes back
to the excitement created in him by the reading of *Hamlet*, a play
that he calls "this most precious work of secular literature viewed
existentially." He was never in his youth greatly attracted to the
writings of Goethe. The German poet's works, he says, "seem to
me to express too little of the 'border-situation.' " As he grew older
he turned his attention to the other arts, especially architecture
and painting. The study of painting was for him an experience of
decisive importance. Eventually he came into intimate association
with the practicing artists of his generation. The most widely
read book of his earlier period, *The Religious Situation,* was
dedicated to an artist friend.

Tillich's knowledge and appreciation of art are, so to speak, the
jewels he found in the adversity of four years of military service
as a chaplain during the First World War. In his years at the front
he determined to find respite from the bludgeonings of war by
devoting his leisure to the study of art. He says that from his
"pleasure in the poor reproductions that were obtainable at the
military bookstores in the fields, there grew a systematic study of
the history of art." Out of this study "came the experience of art,
chief of all that first experience, like a revelation, of a picture by
Botticelli" when he went to Berlin on his last furlough of the war.
A little later the early Christian art of Italy made "an overwhelming impression" upon him. "What no amount of study of
church history had brought," he says, "was accomplished by the
mosaics in ancient Roman basilicas."

For Tillich the proper enjoyment of works of art "makes them
the expression of the most beatific form of human freedom." They
reveal what the inmost character of a spiritual situation is,
whether that situation be a particular historical one or the human
condition in general. Art "does this more immediately and directly
than do science and philosophy, for it is less burdened by objec-

tive considerations. Its symbols have something of a revelatory character while scientific conceptualization must suppress the symbolic in favor of objective adequacy."[2]

The enjoyment of art is not merely an aesthetic experience in the narrow sense of the term. Nor is its function, strictly speaking, either theoretical or practical. If it were theoretical, its aim would be that of *Theoria*, the pure apprehension of the essence of things. If it were practical, its aim would be to represent ethical ideals in tangible form. The touchstone of art is its force of expression, not the ideal nature of what is expressed. Although theoretical and practical apprehensions of the human situation have a definite relevance for art, its function is to be distinguished from theirs. Art fulfills a more basic (*fundierte*) theoretical function in the life of spirit. "The existential import of things which it strives to grasp is the revelation of pure being, of the unconditioned import in the particular form of things." "It's immediate task is not that of apprehending essence but that of expressing meaning."[3] This broader or deeper aspect of the aesthetic experience is brought into relief in the passage from Rilke quoted above. Tillich, in speaking of Michelangelo's masterpieces in the Sistine Chapel in Rome, uses words quite similar to those of Rilke. "Some eternal meaning," he says, "gives greatness to these pictures." This eternal meaning is not to be identified with the subject matter. The material element, the content of the pictures, is not decisive for its expression. Something less tangible gives the dimension of depth.

Interestingly enough, Tillich's comment on Rilke's own art explicitly suggests what the metaphysical *frisson*—the philosophical and religious significance—of art is. Speaking of Rilke's late poetry he says,

> Its profound psychoanalytic realism, *the mystical fulness, the form charged with metaphysical import*, all that made this poetry the expression of what in the concepts of my philosophy of religion I could seize only abstractly. To me and to my wife, who made poetry accessible to me, these poems became a book of devotion to be taken up again and again.[4]

[2] *The Religious Situation*, trans. H. Richard Niebuhr (New York: Henry Holt and Co., 1932), pp. 53-54.

[3] *Ibid.*, p. 53, and *Das System der Wissenschaften* (Göttingen: Vandenhoeck und Ruprecht, 1923), pp. 126-28.

[4] *The Interpretation of History*, trans. Rasetzki and Talmey (New York: Charles Scribner's Sons, 1936), p. 17. Cf. also *The Religious Situation*, pp. 65 ff., for further discussion of Rilke and of other artists. (Italics mine.)

Something of the same metaphysical import in art also engendered in Tillich an enthusiasm for the novels of Franz Kafka, the explorer of the Kierkegaardian boundary-situation.

In the comment on Rilke's poetry we find two of the basic categories of Tillich's philosophy of religion and of his theology of culture, namely, form and import (or meaning). In the previous chapter we have given a general definition of these concepts. Of special interest here is their place in his theology of culture. But before their role can be properly understood, certain general considerations respecting the nature of culture must be presented at some length.

These can best be introduced by referring to Tillich's comments on certain particular paintings:

If any one, being impressed by the mosaics of Ravenna or the ceiling paintings of the Sistine Chapel, or by the portraits of the older Rembrandt, should be asked whether his experience was religious or cultural, he would find the answer difficult to give.[5]

In answer to the question Tillich replies:

Perhaps it would be correct to say that his experience was cultural as to form, and religious as to substance. It is cultural because it is not attached to specific ritual activity; and religious, because it evokes questioning as to the absolute or the limits of human existence. This is equally true of painting, of music and poetry, of philosophy and science. And that which is valid in the intuition and knowledge of the world is equally valid in the practical shaping of law and custom, in morality and education, in community and state. Wherever human existence in thought or action becomes a subject of doubts and questions, wherever unconditioned meaning becomes visible in works which have only conditioned meaning in themselves, there culture is religious. Through the experience of the substantially religious character of culture, I was led to the border of culture and religion, which I have never deserted.[6]

Thus we are brought again to the characteristically Tillichian idea of living on the border—this time the border between culture and religion.

From this border Tillich early developed his theology of culture and of art. The outlines of his theology of culture were set forth in his 1919 lecture "Ueber die Idee einer Theologie der Kultur," the first work he published after the First World War. The lecture begins by stressing the basic difference between the experimental

[5] *The Interpretation of History*, p. 49.
[6] *Ibid.*

or empirical sciences and the cultural sciences. In the former, he says, reality is the measure of correctness, and reality is one. As between two contradictory points of view only one can be correct, or both can be false. In the latter, the point of view of the investigator belongs to the material itself. In the sphere of the cultural sciences man is at the same time the subject and the object of investigation. The point of view not only determines what one studies and how one interprets cultural or spiritual creations; it also creates them. Here the alternative of "correct" or "false" loses its relevance, for the attitudes of mind in face of reality vary greatly. A Gothic and a Baroque aesthetic, a Catholic and a modern Protestant theology, a Romantic and a Puritan ethic cannot be characterized as simply correct or false. For this reason it is also impossible to create universal concepts of cultural ideas which are useful. Universal concepts are inadequate for the understanding of such manifold individual creations and outlooks. What religion or art is, is not to be learned by means of abstraction. Abstraction obliterates the essential element, the concrete forms. Every universal concept of the cultural sciences is either unusable or a concealed norm-concept. It is either a description of something that does not exist or an expression of a point of view. It is a worthless shell or it is a creation.

The point of view is expressed by the individual; but if it is more than individual arbitrariness, if it is a creation, it is at the same time—in greater or lesser degree—the creation of the group in which the individual stands; and since this group and its peculiar spirituality (*Geistigkeit*) do not exist without the cultural groups that surround it and the creations of the past on which they depend, the most individual standpoint is deeply embedded in the soil of the objective Spirit, the mother-soil of every cultural creation. From it the concrete standpoint derives the universal forms of spiritual or cultural activity, while it finds its own limitation through the ever narrower circles and historical permanencies of concrete spirituality (seen from the perspective of the larger soil), until in creative self-affirmation it develops the new individual and inimitable synthesis of universal form and concrete content.[7]

The cultural sciences take their shape accordingly. First there is the philosophy of culture, which is oriented to the universal forms, the a priori of all culture; second there is the philosophy of history of cultural values and the typology of cultural creations, which together form a transition from the universal forms

[7] "Ueber die Idee einer Theologie der Kultur," *Religionsphilosophie der Kultur* (Berlin: Reuther und Reichard, 2nd ed., 1921), p. 30.

through the multiplicity of concrete manifestations to a third level, an individual standpoint; third, then, there is normative cultural science, which gives the concrete standpoint a systematic expression. The same trilogy of cultural sciences is required for the various fields of spiritual interest, such as art, ethics, and the philosophy of religion. Hence theology is viewed as a concretely normative science of religion requiring the preliminary findings of a philosophy of religion and also of a "construction" of the history of religion.[8]

Considering the philosophy of history of cultural creations as possessing a transitional status, there are, then, two basic forms of cultural science. Their differences may be understood most easily through examples. We may distinguish, for example, between moral philosophy, which asks, "What is the ethical?" and ethics, which asks, "What is ethical?" The former sets forth a universal concept of what the ethical is; the latter develops, from the general concept of what the ethical is, a normative system of what is ethical. So also may we distinguish between the philosophy of art and aesthetics, or between philosophy of religion and theology. Theology is therefore a concretely normative science of religion.

Tillich undercuts the conventional objection that theology cannot be a science of religion insofar as it deals with the purely speculative questions concerning a transcendental object, God, or insofar as it claims to present a supernatural revelation. In his view, theology does not properly deal with these things. Theology is not a science of a particular object alongside others. God is no "object" alongside other objects. Kant's *Critique of Pure Reason* made an end of such a "science," and in doing so it assisted in bringing theology down from the heavens to the earth. Nor is theology a presentation of a particular complex of revelation. This notion of revelation presupposes a supernatural, authoritarian concept, a concept of revelation which has been disposed of by the insights of the history of religions and by the logical and religious criticism of abstract supernaturalism.

The task of theology is to outline a normative system of religion. Tillich's summary of the general principles that should guide the formation of such a normative system should be presented in his own words:

The task of theology is to outline a normative system from the point of view of a concrete standpoint and on the basis of the cate-

[8] Here the influence of Dilthey and especially of Troeltsch is to be discerned.

gories of the philosophy of religion, the individual standpoint being intimately related to the confessional and the universally religious-historical and the cultural-historical standpoint in general. This is not a hidden rationalism, for it involves the recognition of the concrete religious standpoint, and it is no indirect or concealed supranaturalism, as is to be found still in our History of Religion School, for it implies that on the basis of a philosophy of history all authoritarian limitations upon the individual standpoint are broken. It is oriented to Nietzsche's conception of "the creative" on the soil of Hegel's "objective-historical Spirit."[9]

Just as there may be a theology related to philosophy of religion, so may there be a theology of culture related to philosophy of culture. In each pair of disciplines the relationships are mutual, for each is oriented to the other. "Every philosophical concept is empty which is not conceived at the same time as a norm-concept having a concrete basis." The difference between the philosophical and the theological discipline is not, however, to be found here. The difference is rather one of direction. Philosophy is concerned with the universal, the a priori, the categorical, and always on the basis of the broadest empiricism and in systematic connection with other values and concepts. The normative sciences are concerned with the particular, with the material, elements, and with what is supposed to be valid (in the respective systems of the various cultural sciences).

This mutuality of relationship may be viewed as a sort of dialectic:

From the power of the concrete, creative realization, the highest universal concept acquires its material and also comprehensive vitality; and from the all-embracing amplitude of a highest universal concept, the normative system derives its objective scientific significance. In every useful universal concept there lies concealed a norm concept, and in every creative norm-concept there lies concealed a universal concept. This is the dialectic of systematic cultural science.[10]

The question now arises as to how the normative science of religion can at the same time be a normative cultural science. The answer has been already suggested. Religion is not a special sphere alongside other spheres, and theology does not have as its object one "being" alongside other beings. Tillich indicates the consequences of this view when he explains his answer to the question whether the experience of viewing (or creating) Michelangelo's paintings is religious or cultural:

[9] "Ueber die Idee einer Theologie der Kultur," p. 31.
[10] *Ibid.*, p. 32.

Religion cannot relinquish the absolute, and therefore universal, claim which is expressed in the idea of God. It cannot permit itself to be forced into a special realm of culture or to a place beside it. Under such an interpretation, as is frequently given by Liberalism, religion becomes superfluous and disappears, for the system of culture is completed and closed in itself without religion. On the other hand, culture has a claim upon religion, which it cannot surrender without surrendering its autonomy, and thus also, itself. It must decide upon the forms, in which every content, including the "absolute" one, expresses itself. It cannot permit truth and justice to be destroyed in the name of the religious absolute. As the substance of culture is religion, so the form of religion is culture.[11]

This view of the relation between religion and culture immediately raises the question: If the substance of culture is religious and the form of religion is culture, what is the fundamental difference between religion and culture? Tillich answers:

There is only this difference, that in religion the substance which is the unconditioned source and abyss of meaning is designated, and the cultural forms serve as symbols for it; whereas in culture the form (which is the unconditioned meaning) becomes perceptible only indirectly throughout the autonomous form. The highest stage of culture is attained where human existence, in complete and autonomous form, is comprehended in its finitude and in its quest after the Infinite. And conversely, religion in its highest form must include the autonomous form within itself, the "Logos," as the Ancient Church termed it.[12]

Clearly, Tillich's view of the relation between religion and culture is markedly different from any view that might be associated with Christian orthodoxy. It is also to be contrasted with the Barthian idea, which completely discredits religion as such, not to speak of culture.[13] Authoritarianism and obscurantism of either the orthodox or the Barthian variety are repudiated. So also is Biblicism of the authoritarian type.

Particularly emphatic is Tillich in his repudiation of the conventional conceptions of the nature of systematic theology and

[11] *The Interpretation of History,* p. 50.
[12] *Ibid.*
[13] These differences are presented in detail in the essay "Die Ueberwindung des Religionsbegriffs in der Religionsphilosophie," *Kant-Studien,* XXVII (1922), 446-69. Accordingly, Barth's attitude toward both culture and religion is characterized as undialectical. Cf. "Kritisches und positives Paradox. Eine Auseinandersetzung mit Karl Barth und Friedrich Gogarten," *Theologische Blätter,* II (1923), 263-69; and "What Is Wrong with the 'Dialectic' Theology?" *Journal of Religion,* XV (1935), 127-45.

of theological ethics. Where the claim is made that theology—with its divisions into apologetics, dogmatics, and ethics—is a peculiar discipline possessing complete independence, the necessary implication is that there is a double standard of truth: one standard for culture and another for theology. The same view holds for theological ethics. Of course, one can say that philosophical ethics is concerned with the *nature* of ethics and not with its norm. Then the two are distinguished as moral philosophy and normative ethics. But this answer does not justify normative ethics' becoming theological ethics. Or one can say that the ethical life must be concrete, that there must be a standpoint which is not only the standpoint of an individual, that the moral life is rooted in a concrete ethical community with historical connections, and that this community is the church. But this answer would be correct only where there is an ecclesiastically guided culture, that is, where science and art and the social life are under the control of the church. In modern society such a situation no longer exists. The Protestant churches have long ago given up the claim to control the culture in this fashion. As soon as the church recognizes a secular culture in principle, there can no longer be a theological ethic any more than a theological logic, aesthetics, or sociology. Indeed, there is just as little place for an (in principle) theological ethics, aesthetics, science, or theory of society as there is for a German or Aryan or capitalist ethics or science or theory of society. What is demanded is a theonomous ethics that deepens and qualifies autonomous ethics.

Tillich therefore concludes that what was originally intended by theological ethics can find its expression only in a theology of culture which is related not just to ethics but also to all cultural functions. This view has certain important implications which should be spelled out here.

Some philosophers, psychologists, and theologians have associated religion with a special psychic function. Their view is untenable. "Neither the Hegelian conception which assigns religion to the theoretical sphere, nor the Kantian which assigns it to the practical sphere, nor the view of Schleiermacher which assigns it to feeling, has been able to maintain itself."[14] When properly understood, the view of Schleiermacher comes nearest to the truth, for it implies an overcoming of the subject-object cleavage in an undifferentiated mystical interpretation of all reality. But feeling as usually interpreted accompanies all cultural experience without giving it a necessarily religious quality. Feel-

[14] "Ueber die Idee einer Theologie der Kultur," p. 33.

ing is no more the distinguishing characteristic of religion than it is of art.[15] If, however, a definite, particular feeling is meant, then with this definiteness a theoretical or practical element is necessarily implied. Thus religion is not feeling, but rather a direction of the spirit, involving the practical, the theoretical, and the feeling sphere, all bound together in a complex unity. Rudolf Otto overlooked this fact when he made the holy a separate category, the "Wholly Other." If the holy is essentially only the Wholly Other in the sense of the "*mysterium tremendum et fascinosum*," an aesthetic attitude with regard to it is possible through which it is put into the service of subjective emotional excitement. "Only when its essential apprehension stands under the Unconditioned of validity, is the danger of aestheticizing mysticism overcome."[16] Such a view as that of Otto, Tillich says, splits the consciousness and thus prevents *us* as total human personalities from experiencing the holy.

Conversely, no cultural manifestation stands outside the holy sphere, for as soon as a cultural creation is formed, it carries within itself the implicit recognition of the holy as the unconditionally valid. And although a rational system may forget the ecstatic element residing in the unconditioned element of the valid, nevertheless the truth in all *ratio* lives from this. On the other hand, the holy can be grasped in no way except through forms that carry in themselves the consciousness of validity. Man is man not only through his religious "head" but also through his "body"—the culture-form—and the one does not appear without the other. This does not mean that the *mysterium* cannot be apprehended by means of a purely theoretical function. Indeed, it is by means of such apprehension that the holy permeates and bursts through the limits of form, inciting new realization in a higher ecstatic form. Obviously, however, it is not the form itself that is holy, but rather the Unconditioned that bursts forth into the form and at the same time breaks through every form it assumes. The rational cultural forms are thus not only rational. In each of them—and all the more so the farther removed we are from mere formalism—the *mysterium* of "the ground" is present. Early Greek humanism and Renaissance Christian humanism offer striking examples. Every form is on the one side superficial and transitory and on the other an expression of the

[15] *Das System der Wissenschaften*, p. 127.

[16] Tillich holds that Otto failed to express the essential relation that obtains between the *mysterium* and the rational forms. Cf. "Die Kategorie des 'Heiligen' bei Rudolf Otto," *Theologische Blätter*, IV (1923), 11.

ground out of which it rises and into which it recedes. The same thing holds for the totality of all forms as well as for every particular form.

Yet, although all forms are somehow related to the ground of all meaning and being, it is possible to classify them with respect to function.

If we now—according to what is in my opinion the most correct classification—divide the total range of cultural functions into (a) those functions through which the spirit perceives the object, i.e., intellectual and aesthetic functions bound together as *theoretical* functions in the sense of *Theorie*, contemplation or intuition, and (b) those functions through which the spirit aims to penetrate or permeate the object, to impose form upon it, the functions of individual and social ethics (including law and community organization), i.e., the *practical* functions, then the result for religion is that it can become operative only in relation to a theoretical or a practical attitude or procedure.[17]

Moreover, each function of religion (or culture) must itself be understood dialectically. In its actual operation no one of these functions can be viewed as unambiguously religious. "The religious potency, that is, a certain quality of the consciousness, is to be distinguished from the religious act (that is, an independent theoretical or practical process) which contains that quality."

But a further classification is necessary. Some functions are explicitly religious and others are considered merely cultural. It is through the combining of the religious principle and cultural function that a specifically religious culture-sphere arises—as, for example, "religious" cognition: myth, or dogma; a sphere of religious aesthetics: cultus; a religious shaping of the person: consecration; a religious social form: the church, with its special law and its special community ethics. Hence we may distinguish between specifically religious spheres and those which are not explicitly so, though we must remember that only in connection with extra-religious cultural functions does the religious principle find incarnation. On the other hand, the religious element constitutes no principle alongside others in the life of the mind: the character of absoluteness in the religious consciousness would break through any such limits or bounds. "Rather, the religious [element] is relevant to *all* provinces of the mind."[18]

The fact, however, that we can distinguish between the explicitly religious and the cultural spheres complicates the prob-

[17] "Ueber die Idee einer Theologie der Kultur," p. 34.
[18] *Ibid.*

lem of definition. As we have noted, there is in every province of the spiritual life a special area, a special sphere, from which explicit religion exerts its influence. In connection with this specialization some of the great conflicts of the modern era have taken place, the conflicts between church and state, between the religious community and the society, between art and the cultus-form, between science and dogma. Of course, no conflict was possible so long as the various cultural functions were held fast in heteronomy by authoritarian religion. But this situation was changed just as soon as the several cultural functions carried through their struggle for autonomy without reservations. What then becomes of religion? Is it on the side of authoritarianism or on the side of the struggle for autonomy?

Certainly, we have to say that so long as there is beside science a dogma, or alongside society a "community," or alongside the state a church that claims certain definite inviolable spheres for itself, the autonomy and unity of the spiritual life is threatened. Indeed, it may be destroyed. In such a situation there arises, as we have said, a double truth, a double morality, a double law, one-half of which is not rooted in the validity upon which cultural functions depend but rather is born out of an alien validity allegedly provided by "religion."

This dualism of "side by side" must under all circumstances be resolved. It is intolerable as soon as it comes into the consciousness, for when taken seriously it destroys the consciousness. It is Manichean in principle, and like Manicheanism it induces schizophrenia in the human psyche and in the community. The reader will recall that a similar dichotomy is found when religion is interpreted as oriented to a supernatural sphere alongside temporospatial existence. In this dichotomy God becomes one being among other beings, and is thus spatialized. According to Tillich, neither religion nor culture nor God may be justifiably spatialized.

The preservation of the religious principle and of cultural autonomy—that is, the protection against spatialization—can be achieved only on the basis of a more comprehensive concept of religion than is implicit in the struggles between science and dogma or between ecclesiasticism and statism. The definition of religion which Tillich gives in his early lecture on the theology of culture is so important for his later development and also for an understanding of his theory of culture and art that it should be quoted again at length:

Religion is directedness toward the Unconditioned and that means an experience of absolute reality on the ground of the experience of

absolute nothingness; it will experience the nothingness of all existing
things, the nothingness of values, the nothingness of the personal life;
where this experience has led to the absolute, radical No, there it
shifts into an equally absolute experience of reality, into a radical Yes.
It is not a question of a new reality beside or above things; that would
be only a thing of a higher order that would again fall under the No.
Rather, right through things there forces itself upon us that reality
which is at the same time the No and the Yes over things; it is not an
existing thing, it is not the substance, the totality of the existing
order; it is, if we may use a mystical formula, the Super-existing, that
which is at the same time the absolute Nothing and the absolute
Something. But the predicate "is" conceals the real situation, for it is
not a question of an existent reality, it is rather a meaning-reality, the
ultimate, the deepest, all-shattering and ever newly creating meaning-
reality.[19]

There is therefore no proper place for a special religious cognition and no place for special religious spheres (in the literal
sense) as distinguished from special cultural spheres. (There
may of course be spheres in which the religious function is made
explicit.) The conflict between culture as such and religion as
such and the conflict between science and dogma are overcome.
In principle the autonomy of science is thoroughly protected and
with it the autonomy of other cultural spheres and functions.
Every heteronomy is made impossible, and instead science and
culture along with "religion" are placed under the theonomy of
the paradoxical religious experience of confronting threat and
support. The same principles hold for ethics. There can no longer
be a personal or social ethic in some special way protected by
religious sanctions, with another ethic standing alongside as a
secular ethic. This would again constitute spatialization. Ethics
must be autonomous; it must be free from and unencumbered
by religious heteronomy. But if it is not to be spatialized it must
in its depth be theonomous. The possibilities of conflict between
culture and religion are in principle precluded when they are
confronted with the demand of the Unconditioned. The specifically religious and cultural spheres are superseded.[20]

We are now ready to consider more fully the basic categories
of Tillich's theology of culture (which he derives from his study
of art), namely, the categories of form, content, and import. As
we have noted in the preceding chapter, any painting will have

---

[19] *Ibid.*, p. 35.
[20] For an application of these principles to the various spheres of culture,
see Tillich's statement of "A Basic Policy," *The Protestant,* IV, No. 5
(April-May, 1942), 16-19.

form, it will have subject matter, and if it has "greatness" it will point beyond itself to an eternal meaning or import. This fact provides a basis for certain analogies between the concepts of art and of religion. As Joachim Konrad has pointed out, analogies of this sort fall into two classifications: the analogies that involve the element of expression and those that involve the element of validity.[21] If we adopt this classification we may say that Tillich views the concepts of form and content as belonging in the first type of analogy and the concept of import as belonging in the second. For anything to exist it must have form, and every form treats some subject matter. But within and beyond both form and content there is a meaning.[22] Here the form and the content are not to be understood as opposites. Rather they both stand at one pole, while at the other stands the import or meaning. The content is here of least significance. The form can lose its necessary relation to the content because the content may recede in significance before the predominant abundance of the import. In this way the form acquires the quality of being detached from the content; it may stand in immediate relation to the import. It becomes a form in a paradoxical sense, since it expresses the import and yet allows itself to be shattered by it. In the import, then, appears that ultimate reference which is called religious. From it there proceeds the Yes and the No over things.

Within these contexts reside infinite possibilities of variation, both with respect to relation between form, content, and import, and with respect to the relative significance of the Yes and the No. According to the major variations the typologies of art and of culture may be devised—typologies such as the formal-cultural (impressionism and realism), the import-predominant or religious (romanticism and expressionism), and the balance between form and import (classicism). Another typology can be devised which concerns types of meaning—the typology of autonomous and theonomous, for example. The autonomy of cultural functions has to do with their form; theonomy has to do with their import,

---

[21] Cf. Kurt Leese's discussion of Konrad's book, *Religion und Kunst* (Tübingen: Mohr, 1929), in *Zeitschrift für Theologie und Kirche*, XII (1931), 460-61.

[22] It should be noted in passing that the distinction between form and import employed by Tillich appears also in Hegel's "Vorlesungen über die Aesthetik," *Werke* (Berlin: Duncker und Humblot, 1843), X, Part II, 229 ff. It is doubtful that Tillich was consciously influenced by Hegel in the use of the terms, for he never mentions his indebtedness to Hegel in this respect.

that is, with the reality that presents itself in the form and in the "material" employed by the form. Since any material may in principle be amenable to form, we may disregard it for the moment. The point that must be stressed is this: the more the form, the more the autonomy; the more the import, the more the theonomy. Yet the one cannot exist without the other; a form that expresses nothing or forms nothing is as unintelligible as an import that stands in no form. Hence the relation of form to import must be thought of as a line. One end signifies the pure form, and the other signifies the pure import. On the line, however, both are always in unity. Wherever the import becomes predominant the form is shown to be inadequate, and it is broken through by an exuberant abundance which it cannot hold. Indeed, this exuberance and this shattering of the form is itself a form. Tillich expresses the relationships by the use of a telling metaphor:

> If we imagine the import (or ultimate meaning) to be the sun, and form the orbit of a planet, then for every form of culture there is proximity to and distance from the sun or the import. If on the one hand it is the power of the sun which is revealed in the nearness to the sun it is on the other hand the peculiar power in the movement of the planets which is expressed in the distance from the sun; and yet, it is the sun itself which supports both nearness and distance. Thus there are styles in which the domination of import over form stands out as sharply as does the specific movement of form in others; and yet both the style dominated by import and the style dominated by form, are as style an expression of the import. This peculiar dialectic makes it possible for us, in a narrow sense, to discuss style. Were it not a fact that in the very essence of the style in and for itself there is a relation to the religious function, it would be beyond comprehension how the relation could ever enter in. Conversely, if within this sphere the antithesis of an import-dominated style and a form-dominated style were not operative, no particular religious style could come into prominence.[23]

We now see what is meant by Tillich's statement, quoted earlier, that "the existential content of things which art strives to grasp is the revelation of pure being, of the unconditioned import in the particular forms of things." The total direction of

---

[23] "Religiöser Stil und religiöser Stoff in der bildenden Kunst," *Das neue Deutschland*, IX (1921), 155. In this essay Tillich classifies various schools of painting into the types here mentioned. But he also introduces other means of classification, especially the classification according to concern with subjective or objective spirituality (e.g., impressionism and expressionism on the one hand and realism on the other).

aesthetic apprehension depends ultimately upon the way in which reality is interpreted in its essential character. In short, it depends upon a fundamental metaphysical attitude.

The import is not this or that individual psychological element, nor is it biographical or sociological or national. All of these factors are co-determinative. They provide the subjective possibilities of the style, just as the forms determine the objective possibilities. But a possible basis is not a real basis. The essence of the import lies beneath all these subjective factors. It is a certain attitude toward reality. It is an interpretation of ultimate meaning, the most profound apprehension of reality. It is the functioning of the Unconditioned which supports every conditioned experience, colors it and prevents it from plunging into the void of nothingness.[24]

The influence of the metaphysical attitude upon the aesthetic form is the *style*. In other words, style is the general determination of the aesthetic forms according to the way in which the import is grasped. This is true for the style of a period, of a school, of an individual, or even of a single work of art. Hence just as science depends upon metaphysics because of the implications of science for the nature of thought and being, so aesthetics is dependent upon metaphysics because of the implications of aesthetic creation for the nature of form and import. Art without metaphysics is without style. It is either abstract formalism or formless arbitrariness.[25]

Hence art stands on the border between religion and culture, facing the religious "object" (the unconditioned import), glancing at it, or turning away from it to the form. This is the line from theonomy to autonomy. The material used by the given artist is of no special significance. What matters is the relation between form and import. A picture of an apple may convey the metaphysical attitude of theonomy; on the other hand, a picture of Jesus may convey nothing but distance from the sun of import. In other words, the religious styles give a religious quality to every material with which they deal, and, conversely, unreligious styles relatively —never absolutely—make all their material unreligious, profane, and self-enclosed.

It is therefore not justifiable to make a sharp distinction between religion and culture. Religion is always assuming cultural form, and culture is always (like a planet) near to and distant from the ultimate source (and abyss) of meaning.

[24] *Ibid.*, p. 155.
[25] *Das System der Wissenschaften*, p. 128.

As a matter of fact it is possible to see in a still-life by Cézanne, an animal picture by Marc, a landscape by Schmidt-Rottluff, and an erotic picture by Nolde, the direct revelation of an absolute reality in these relative things. The world-import, experienced in the artist's religious ecstasy, shines through the things; they have become "holy" objects.[26]

"It is not an exaggeration to ascribe more of the quality of sacredness to a still-life by Cézanne or a tree by van Gogh than to a picture of Jesus by Uhde."[27] This observation should not, however, lead us to ignore the fact that certain materials are by tradition more readily amenable than others to the religious style of treatment or that profane material offers something for the religious style to overcome.

Now, it is the task of a theology of culture to investigate and describe the process whereby meaning or an ultimate import is expressed in all spheres and creations of culture. But it does not, as a theology of culture, view these creations from the standpoint of form; that would be the task of the relevant cultural science. Its concern is with the import.

We have assigned to theology the task of bringing to systematic expression a concrete religious point of view, on the basis of a universal formation of concepts (the philosophy of religion) and by means of an arrangement presupposing a philosophy of history.

The task of the theology of culture corresponds to this. It undertakes a universal religious analysis of all cultural creations, it sets forth a philosophy of history and a typological scheme of the great cultural creations from the viewpoint of the religious import realized in them, and it creates on the basis of its concrete religious standpoint the ideal sketch of a religiously imbued culture. There is therefore a threefold task for the theology of culture, corresponding to the threefold character of systematic cultural sciences in general and to the systematic science of religion in particular: (1) A general (universal) religious analysis of culture; (2) A religious typology and a philosophy of cultural history; (3) A concrete religious systematization of culture.[28]

With respect to the first task of the theology of culture, two things are to be observed. First, although the religious analysis of culture is primarily concerned with import, it must also take form

[26] "Religiöser Stil und religiöser Stoff in der bildenden Kunst," p. 156.
[27] *The Religious Situation*, p. 57. Cf. the sharp words of criticism directed by Tillich against some of the so-called religious art in the Berlin exhibition for which he delivered the opening address: "Kult und Form," *Die Form*, V (1930), 582-83.
[28] "Ueber die Idee einer Theologie der Kultur," p. 38.

into account. The content (as defined earlier) may be a matter of indifference, but the import is expressed through form though it bursts or shatters the form. Thus the form may become something detached and free-swaying, standing in immediate relation to the import through which the religious reality appears with its No and Yes over things. This first observation leads to the second: the relation of the No and the Yes are to be discerned by the theologian of culture. Moreover, the power with which the one or the other is given expression is to be noted. In both of these respects the possibilities are infinite.

The nature of the second task of the theologian of culture has already been suggested, namely, the construction of a typology and a philosophy of history of cultural values. In this task the culture-theologian concerns himself with the various relations between form and import. We have mentioned three of the major possibilities on the "line" from form to import—the secular, the classical, and the religious. But again the possibilities are infinite, allowing for many intermediary stages and transitions. If this theory of types is related to the present and the past in some systematic fashion, there arises a philosophy of history of cultural values. We shall presently discover some examples of it in Tillich's own discussions of the history of culture.

In his third task the theologian of culture attempts to apply his own concrete theological standpoint, criticizing and approving autonomous productions of culture, and with the available material he outlines a religious culture system. He may also go beyond the available material to show the direction in which he envisages the fulfillment of a truly religious culture system. But in no case does he become himself the creator. He indicates the presence or absence of import in the actual expressions, and points to possible fulfillments.

He can show the relationships that lead from one phenomenon of the culture to another, through the substantial unity of the import expressed in them; he can thereby help to bring about the unity of the culture from the point of view of the import, thus accomplishing something analogous to what the philosopher does from the point of view of pure forms, the categories.[29]

It would be wrong, however, to suppose that the task of the theologian of culture is merely analytical. After making the religious analysis of culture with a view to determining the

[29] *Ibid.*, p. 40.

(religious) import of the different cultural productions and functions, the culture-theologian undertakes the synthetic task of setting forth a normative, systematic outline of a religiously imbued culture. The synthesis not only brings together the different cultural functions but also overcomes the culture-destroying contradiction between religion and culture. It does so through the sketching of a religio-cultural system "in which in place of the opposition between science and dogma there appears a science religious in itself, in place of the distinction between art and the form of the cultus there appears an art religious in itself, in place of the dualism of state and church a state-form religious in itself, etc. Only with this breadth of goal is the task of the theology of culture to be conceived."[30]

This description of the synthetic task of the theologian of culture is of primary significance for an understanding of Tillich's idea of the kind of society to be striven for, namely, the theonomous society. Frequently he refers to the high Middle Ages as having closely approximated this idea. He thinks that our society could move in the same direction by adopting religious socialism, though in 1926 he did not think this movement had much promise of success in the Protestant churches of Germany.[31]

We shall not pause here to show how Tillich (in his early lecture) applies his conception of the functions of the culture-theologian. A few casual observations must suffice. We shall later discuss in detail Tillich's comments on modern art. Here it should be noted that in his writings of the early Twenties, Tillich shows himself markedly affected by expressionism. Indeed, it may well be that the relative insignificance he attaches to content in his discussion of the categories is largely due to this influence. One might suppose that his repeated references to the No and the Yes over things reflect the influence of Barth's dialectical theology, but Tillich's writings in the early twenties give little explicit evidence of this influence. Schelling and Hegel and expressionism seem to be much more significant—Schelling because of his concern with mystical unity with "the terrible," and with the consciousness of guilt; Hegel because of his dialectic and his concern with the philosophy of art; expressionism because

---

[30] *Ibid.*, p. 41. As will become clear later, these formulations are not to be interpreted as precluding the necessity of special religious spheres in the culture. Tillich does not suggest (with Richard Rothe) that the task of the church is to eliminate itself by imbuing the whole culture with religion.

[31] *The Religious Situation,* p. 174.

in its productions content is of little importance and because a form-bursting, pulsating No seems to emanate from them.

The No pulsating within expressionist painting seems to imply for Tillich a repudiation not only of capitalist culture but also of Neo-Kantian secularism. In the latter he sees the predominance— and the deadening power—of form. As against the Neo-Kantians he looks back to Hegel with his grasping of the No and the Yes, yet in Hegel he finds an overoptimistic predominance of the Yes and misses the experience of terror more profoundly felt by Schelling and Schopenhauer. But the Neo-Kantians, in his view, have lost contact with any ultimate Yes or No.

In Nietzsche's philosophy he finds a supreme modern example of theology of culture, especially in the criticism of individual ethics. Despite Nietzsche's anti-Christian orientation, his criticism of moralism is rated as second only to that offered by Jesus and Luther. The Yes and the No receive powerful expression in this philosopher, who "could be called the anti-moralist par excellence, as Luther had to be stigmatized as the greatest libertine by all whose personal thought proceeds in the categories of virtue and reward."[32] Some of Tillich's expressions in this discussion suggest a sort of Nietzschean upper-middle-class Bohemianism as well as a religious antinomianism. Throughout Tillich's writings one finds reminiscences of these early moods. Indeed, it is always well to remember, when one is inclined—like some of his American critics—to censure him for the ethical irrelevance of his doctrine of the Unconditioned, that he is not here to be classed with Karl Barth and his ascetic attitude toward nature and spirit but rather with Nietzsche's conception of "the creative" beyond good and evil.

Something analogous to this attitude is to be found in his treatment—as culture-theologian—of social ethics. Here he praises "the newly emerging mysticism of love," which theonomously breaks through the autonomy of formal ethics without falling back into the heteronomy of a specifically religious community of love. Referring to the idealistic socialists and communists, to Tolstoi's interpretation of the Sermon on the Mount, and to the poetry of Rilke and Werfel, he finds in his contemporaries a new appreciation of the fact that the content of love "flows over the narrow cup" of Kantian formalism in an inexhaustible stream.

The world as it is, split into individual creatures, is negated and experienced as an empty, unreal shell. Whoever bases his thought

[32] "Ueber die Idee einer Theologie der Kultur," pp. 43-44.

merely on the individual can never achieve love, for love stands beyond the individual. Whoever bases his thought merely on purpose or design does not know what love is, for love is pure experience of being, or reality. Whoever wishes to set a limit or a condition upon love, does not know that it is universal, cosmic, for the very reason that it affirms and embraces everything real as real.[33]

From these few quotations the reader can get an impression of what Tillich meant at this time by the Yes to social ethics. His demand for a theology of culture on the basis of socialism indicates also the meaning of the Yes and the No.

The same spirit pervades his application of his theology of culture to the discussion of the state. The power-state or utility-state is characterized in Nietzschean terms as "the coldest of all monstrosities." Nor is the situation improved "when this abstract, autonomous state is decked out with all functions of the culture, as with Hegel, and becomes God on earth, for now the spirit itself becomes a thing of power or utility." The autonomous state is broken through by theonomy in the state that is erected out of the cultural communities in the state, which, in the sense of the theology of culture, is to be characterized as a "church." This state is described as

the universal human community constructed from the cultural communities and carrying within itself all cultural functions and carrying in itself their religious import, whose teachers are the great creative philosophers, whose priests are the artists, whose prophets are the seers of a new ethic of personality and community, whose bishops are the leaders to new goals of the community, whose deacons and almoners are the guides and re-creators of the economic process. Business and industry can break through their mere autonomy and self-sufficiency (finding their end in themselves) to the import of religious love-mysticism which does not produce for production but rather for the sake of man and yet does not curtail the process of production heteronomously but rather guides it theonomously as the universal form of a previous specifically ecclesiastical almonry which is on socialistic soil superseded along with the concept of the poor.[34]

So much for certain examples of the way Tillich applies his theology of culture in the criticism of culture. Some of the formulations we have cited here are strongly romantic in character. We should observe, however, that after the rise of Nazism and again after the Second World War, Tillich spoke of certain of

[33] *Ibid.*, p. 45.
[34] *Ibid.*, pp. 45-46.

his views of the Twenties as utopian. We turn now to the question of the relation between the theologian of culture and the church-theologian.

What becomes of the specifically religious culture, of dogma, cultus, consecration, fellowship, and the church? What place is there for a special sphere of the holy?

The answer depends upon the relationship of polarity that obtains between the secular and the religious element of the culture line: they are *realiter* never distinguished from one another, but they are distinguished *in abstracto,* and this distinction is the expression of a psychological necessity of the most general sort. We are again and again compelled to separate in our consciousness things that are really intertwined, so that something may be experienced. In order that we may experience in culture the religious values, in order that we may develop a theology of culture, in order that we may distinguish and designate the religious elements, a specifically religious culture must take the lead. In order that we may conceive of a state as a church, of art as a cultus, of science as a theory of faith, the church, cultus, and dogma must be there previously, and not only that. In order that we may experience the holy in any way distinguished from the secular, we must bring it into relief and concentrate it into a special sphere of cognition, of worship, of love, of organization. The secular pole of culture, exact science, formal aesthetics, formal ethics, the merely political and the merely economic element makes absolute claims upon us if the opposite pole does not hold a balance against them; a universal secularization, a profanation of life would be inevitable if a sphere of the holy did not constitute itself in opposition and contradiction. This contradiction is insurmountable so long as form and content must be distinguished, so long as we are compelled to live in the sphere of reflection and not of intuition; it belongs to the deepest tragic contradictions of cultural life. It is, however, the greatness of the development of the recent centuries that it has taught us to penetrate through this contradiction and deprive it of its real fundamental significance; hence it has lost its ultimate sharpness.[35]

Tillich's exposition begins with a discussion of the element of meaning or import as it appears within a culture. He then shows how, for the sake of the presentation and the enhancing of the religious qualities of a culture, a specifically religious culture-sphere emerges, not as a sphere with independent logical but rather with "teleological dignity." For the church-theologian this sphere is available as an expression of a definite religious concreteness. It is not now created out of the culture but rather has its independent history that reaches back far behind that of

[35] *Ibid.,* pp. 47-48.

most cultural creations. It has developed its own forms, each with its own history, an independence and continuity in spite of all influences from the autonomous culture-forms.

Now there are three possible attitudes which the church-theologian can adopt toward culture. He can subsume culture under the concept of "the world" and contrast it with the kingdom of God which is realized in the church. This is a typically Catholic attitude and does not permit the development of culture-theology. He can, secondly, take the attitude of Old Protestantism, in which supernatural revelation is retained as the absolute science. This view has been shattered by the Enlightenment.

It is the task of the contemporary and future Protestant theology to find the third position. This position should distinguish between the religious principle and religious culture, between religious potentiality and actuality; it should assign absoluteness to the religious principle alone, that is, to no single element of religious culture however firmly established historically. On the other hand, it will not only abstractly conceive its religious principle; it will also seek to bring it to actualization. It will be oriented to past as well as to future, conserving and selecting. Tillich would here accept the admonition of Schleiermacher, "The Reformation must continue," as the watchword. This means not revolution but reformation, for the substance of the concrete standpoint must be retained, and the new realizations of form in all spheres must adapt themselves to the old.

The attitudes of the theologian of culture may be compared with those of the church-theologian. According to Tillich, the theologian of culture does not have to take the precautions that the church-theologian does, for he stands free in the living movement of the culture, open to every form and also to every new spirit. Although he, like the church-theologian, is nourished in the soil of a concrete and definite tradition, he is at all times ready to extend it, to alter it: he has no special interest in ecclesiastical (or churchly) continuity. This last characterization seems scarcely essential, for the theologian of culture might conceivably possess an interest in the extension or alteration of a culture only in certain directions consistent with his theology; that is, he might conceivably, and for that matter at his best, be interested in maintaining a cultural continuity analogous to that which appears in a church tradition. Indeed, it is difficult for the present writer to see why the church-theologian should necessarily favor the conserving tendencies and the theologian of culture should be naturally disposed to favor novelty and discontinuity. In any event, Tillich recognizes that the theologian of culture (as he has described him) stands at a disadvantage because "he is in danger of becoming a religious-fad prophet of a cultural development insecure in itself and disunited."

The contrasts between the tasks of the theologian of culture and the church-theologian place them in a relationship of mutual complementarity, best achieved through the uniting of the functions in one person. Yet this doing of double duty is not necessarily desirable under all circumstances, for the "division of labor" may be conducive to the freer development of both types. Somewhat inconsistently with the above description of the theologian of culture—as not interested in continuity—Tillich comments:

> At all events, a real opposition is no longer possible at the present moment, where the theologian of culture recognizes the necessity of the concrete standpoint in its continuity, and the church-theologian recognizes the relativity of every concrete form in face of the exclusive absoluteness of the religious principle itself.[36]

This does not mean, however, that the ideal of the theologian of culture involves the abrogation of the polarity between the sacred and the secular; in the world of reflection and abstraction that is impossible. But, as indicated earlier, it does look toward the society in which a unified meaning (or import), an immediate spiritual substance, will imbue the whole cultural movement and thereby make it an expression of an all-embracing religious spirit whose continuity will be one with the continuity of the culture itself. When this occurs, the opposition between the theologian of culture and the church-theologian will be superseded, for it is only the expression of a culture divided in its orientation to meaning and import.[37]

Yet, even in a "new, unified culture" the treatment of the predominantly religious elements in the culture would be entrusted to the theologian—and that on the soil of a specifically

---

[36] *Ibid.*, p. 50.

[37] Because Tillich in his lecture on the idea of a theology of culture has spoken in such seemingly Utopian fashion about a future time in which the tensions between church and culture are to be reduced (in a new, unified culture), and because Tillich looks to socialism to provide the social structure for the new theonomous society, Hans von Soden very sharply criticizes him in his essay "Kirchentheologie und Kulturtheologie," *Zeitschrift für Theologie und Kirche*, II (1921), 468-77. Von Soden's discussion concerning the legalistic (in contrast to the epistemological) significance of doctrine as well as concerning the sacramental (in contrast to the aesthetic) significance of cultus is of less pertinence to the main purpose of Tillich in this work.

religious community. This religious community would not be essentially different from the rest of the cultural community. In fact, the church would be the *ecclesiola* in the *ecclesia* of the cultural community in general.

The church is in a fashion the circle that is *idealiter* commissioned to remove from chance the religious elements in the cultural community through the creation of a specifically religious sphere, to bring them together, to concentrate them, theoretically and practically, and thereby to make them into a powerful, indeed into the most powerful, cultural factor supporting everything else.[38]

This sort of situation is to be sharply contrasted with the prevailing situation of our own day. The isolation of the German church and of the theological faculty from culture and from the other faculties has contributed to the fragmentation of society. The theologians have aggravated the predicament by continuing the tradition of viewing theology as a "scientific knowledge of God in the sense of a special object beside others" and by conceiving of it as "a presentation of a definite, limited confession with authoritative claims." But if religion is understood as concerned with the ultimate meaning of all life and if theology is defined as a normative science, they take on a central, unifying significance. Indeed, theology might then be properly called again the queen of the sciences, and its first task would be the development of a theology of culture. Only by the adoption of some such program can the secularization, the emptying, the fragmentation of culture be overcome. Such a restoration of religion and theology to the center of interest has promise of success, Tillich thinks. "It will be victorious, for religion is, as Hegel says, the beginning and end of everything, and likewise it is also the center that enlivens, inspires, ensouls everything."[39]

As we shall observe in the next chapter, Tillich's later writings do not retain the distinction between "culture-theology" and "church-theology." Yet he has given in his early works, especially in the lecture on "The Idea of a Theology of Culture," certain of the basic principles that persist throughout all his writings. Especially significant are his conceptions of form and content and import, and also his interpretation of the nature of religion and of culture and of the relations between them. He seems, too, to retain the notion that the ideal society would be one in which the whole culture is theonomously imbued and in which this

[38] "Ueber die Idee einer Theologie der Kultur," pp. 50-51.
[39] *Ibid.*, p. 52.

orientation would receive spontaneous—and, of course, non-authoritarian—expression. On the other hand, we should repeat here that later on Tillich came to view this optimism of his early period as utopian.

In his systematic discussions he has applied these principles to the cultural criticism of science, of ethics, of politics, of religion and the churches, and of art. Here we confine our attention to his observations on artistic creations and on the technical aspects of modern culture. We shall present these observations at considerable length in order to show that Tillich's theology of culture is not concerned with mere abstractions but involves rather an attempt to penetrate concrete realities, and to understand them in terms of their import, in terms of the ultimate Yes and No, and in terms of the border-situation.

One of Tillich's most extensive discussions of particular works of art is to be found in his *Masse und Geist,* published in 1922—a study of different types of mass movements in modern society. In his comments on the paintings of the various periods of modern civilization we see how style affects the treatment of form, content, and import—in short, how style and religious orientation are related. "Painting," he says, "is a mute revealer and yet to the interpreting spirit it often speaks more clearly than the word that conveys a concept." *Masse und Geist* begins by setting forth a typology of masses and it partially accomplishes this purpose by sketching the principal characteristic treatments of masses to be found in paintings of the various periods of modern social development.

Tillich first examines early Gothic paintings of masses. In a "Carrying the Cross" portraying a crowd of followers, in a "Birth of Christ" with its shepherds and kings, or in a typical secular picture of a battle, he finds the crowd fully dominated by the overwhelming idea that it represents, whether it be the idea of the following, or of adoring worship, or of the battle. "All individuality is suppressed: *one* expression of the face, *one* bearing of the head, *one* body and vestment line, *one* strength of light make them all equal to each other. And none is given prominence."[40] Two-dimensional space unites the crowd to a *corpus mysticum* which is imbued with the transcendent life of a supranatural idea of cosmic scope. Three-dimensional space, which accentuates the individuality of persons, is not used. Even the

[40] This quotation and others in our exposition are taken from *Masse und Geist* (Berlin and Frankfurt a. M.: Verlag der Arbeitsgemeinschaft, 1922), pp. 5 ff.

leader receives little individual characterization. He is simply the center of gravity of the picture; he is larger than the others and more richly attired. The inner mysticism which imbues the crowd is centered in him; he is the mediator of the revelation, the representative of the supranatural idea that pervades the whole picture. A picture of this sort shows that its figures live in a time in which neither personality nor masses are detached independent realities. All are carried by "universalia" in the sense of philosophical realism (or of what is today called idealism). "A hierarchy of realistic, substantial common conceptions, beginning with the highest, the divinity, is the real world. In this hierarchy, which comprises also the social life of the time, everyone has his appointed place." In short, we have here the mystical conception of the masses.

A late Gothic or an early Renaissance picture, for example in Holland or Germany, conveys a different idea of the meaning of life and of the *meaning* of the masses in the period. A new style is emerging. A "Mockery," a "Peasants' Feast," or a "Person Being Taken Prisoner" shows that a great change has taken place since the earlier pictures were painted. The individual has been discovered, and nature plays a more prominent role. The former mystical masses have been dissolved into single, highly realistically conceived individuals. The use of the third dimension provides the opportunity to show that the individuals have found their natural space. The picture-space is deepened in perspective to an infinite world-space. The earlier "common feeling" is lost. Now the picture is comprised of units of unorganic details. The leader has lost his central position. Even Christ has become one figure among many in the crowd. Other figures may stand in front of him, he may be surrounded, or he may even be at the side of the picture. Other figures, even the figure of the hireling who strikes him or of the soldier whose ear is being cut off, are just as important as he. The mystical mass of the earlier period has become a conglomeration of separately depicted, and interesting, individuals. Yet there is a sort of unity pervading the picture. It is no longer the unity of the supranatural idea. Nor is it the common human nature. The latter is not permitted by the nominalism of the period. Rather, the nature of each individual, the psychological homogeneity, provides a unity despite hatred, pain, and desire. This unity is not from above but from below; hence the new unity of desire represents, so to speak, the unity of distortion. The leader has become the agitator. In other words, the picture shows that medieval society is decomposing. Supranaturalism is receding before the newly discovered naturalism. The realism of the idea is destroyed by nominalism. The particular is coming to the throne. It is the time of social revolution, the harbinger of the Peasants' Revolt. In short, we have here the realistic masses in place of the mystical masses.

Tillich then proceeds to discuss the art of the baroque period and to show how it reflects the shift of interest to the inner personal convictions of faith and to an urban and aristocratic society.

Of more immediate interest to us is his discussion of the schools of impressionist and expressionist painting. Impressionism is the style of the individualistic middle classes of the nineteenth century. Monet and Degas see every individual subordinated to the primacy of nature—not of nature in the metaphysical meaning but rather of nature in its surfaces. The inner life and dynamic of the baroque period are gone. In their place, light unites men and things, a light that illumines the surfaces. Everything, including the factories and the masses of the proletariat, is a study in light, a piece of the surface of nature. Every object provides only a vision for the moment, interesting, piquant, but fundamentally a piece of the landscape which is to be conquered and given form. The masses and the individual are treated alike. Both are formal problems for the artist. The form, which has become the highest technique and rationality, is all. Here then is expressed the epoch of perfect technology, the age when the metropolis is the decisive social form. The masses are there but not in their intrinsic power. They are only on the surface like everything else. They are, like nature, an object of formal technology. They are only objects and not subjects. They are the object of agitation and education, the object of social welfare and of—disdain. The age finds its meaning in surfaces. It is the age of the technological masses, the age in which the masses are an object of impression and of technology.

But before the end of the nineteenth century a spirit of revolt has begun to appear, revolt in the name of a deeper meaning in life. The revolt, however, did not appear among the "religious" leaders or artists. In philosophy it is best exemplified by Nietzsche; in social thought, by Karl Marx. But these men are only preparing the way for the new spirit. Its prophetic utterance pointing the way to new depths of meaning is given by the painter. Things begin to exhibit a new power. To be sure, things seem in outward form to be more disintegrated than they were with the impressionists. But this is not decay; it is the path to a new basis, a new depth. Thus with expressionism a new mysticism enters, a new inner experience of things; a fundamentally different metaphysical attitude creates a new style. As presented in this new style, the individuals are similar to each other. A dull something presses down upon the masses, a new two-dimensional space deprives them of individuality. Again the two-dimensional space suggests a metaphysical unity. The masses at one moment seem to be pressed down to animality, but to a metaphysical animality, an animality characterized by loss of redemption. At another moment they are lifted above humanity to an ecstatic height. The masses have again become a subject. To be sure, they have no leader, but their suffering is the prelude to new birth. The leader will be born from the depths of the burning desire of the masses. This is the period of the First World War, of the outbreak of the Russian soul-chaos, and of the Communist martyrs.

At the conclusion of the survey, then, the end is united with the beginning: new mystical masses are appearing. This time the mysticism is not supranatural and guided from above; it is now immanent and breaking out of the depths of the soul, yet remaining within the reality of this world. This is the age of an immanent mysticism.

With such an interpretation of art, and especially of expressionism, it was a natural step for Tillich to develop the theology of art and of culture which we have already described. Indeed, his concepts of form and import as applied to painting and to culture in general seem to have been derived especially from his reflection on expressionism. Many of the expressionists had themselves claimed to be moved by a strong religious passion. They frequently appealed to *Weltanschauung* in order to explain the meaning of their pictures; some even referred to the Bible.

It is clear, first, that here the content has become in the highest degree without significance, the content, that is, in the sense of the outer actuality of things and processes. Nature is stripped of its appearance, one sees her by going to her roots. At the bottom of everything living, however, there dwells the terrible, says Schelling, and this terror seizes upon us from the pictures of the expressionists, who want to do more than destroy the form for the sake of the throbbing life (as Simmel thinks). But what is taking place is this: a form-bursting religious import is struggling for form. This is a paradox most people find unintelligible and annoying. There also is a terror here that seems to me to be deepened by a sense of guilt, not in the properly ethical sense but rather in the cosmic sense, the guilt of mere existence. The solution, however, is the merging of one individual existence into another, the obliteration of harsh individualism, the mysticism of love, of becoming one with all the living.

Thus, a No and a Yes come to expression in great depth in this art. But the No, the form-destroying element, seems to me to have the upper hand throughout, even though this is not the intention of the artist, for in him there pulsates a passionate will to a new, uncon-ditional Yes.[41]

What applies to painting applies also to the other arts and to culture in general. The bursting forth of a religious import can occur within culture as well as within the explicitly religious sphere. In fact, the past half-century gives us more examples of its bursting forth in secular culture than in religious circles or even in so-called religious art.

In an address delivered at the opening of an art exhibition in Berlin in 1930, Tillich stresses the vitality of current "secular" art and the moribundity of "religious art." After defining religion as "the experience of being grasped unconditionally and inescapably by that which is the supporting ground and the consuming abyss of our existence," as "a shattering and transforming eruption of that which is more than our existence and which is therefore alone able to give to our existence depth, seriousness, import and meaning," he argues again that this depth and seriousness cannot be thought of as one thing alongside other things, but must rather be thought of as intrinsic in all things. Hence he says the art forms appropriate for purposes of worship are not forms alongside other forms. All activity in its depth and seriousness is worship-ful. The whole of life is the service and worship of God. Accord-ingly, he sets up three prerequisites for religious art: It must be determined by the daily life, by *our* particular contemporary situa-tion, and by reality. In explaining the last prerequisite he says something that has quite direct bearing on the conception of culture and of art we have been dealing with, something that indicates the source of vitality and the source of enervation in both religion and culture:

Everything has its own powerfulness, a radiance, an abundance of reality. . . . The powerfulness of things is their objectiveness, and this criterion is to be applied with greater stringency where it is a question of creating new forms for worship; that is, where it is a question of creating these forms out of the true and ultimate, objective powerfulness. Whoever attempts to create art forms for religion should know that a cross is no opportunity for decorative embellish-ments, that a chalice is a drinking vessel whose meaning and power

41 "Ueber die Idee einer Theologie der Kultur," pp. 41-42.

is its use as such, that we no longer as in former times see the power of writing in its magical radiance but rather in its clarity, in its inner appropriateness to that which it expresses, in its capacity to communicate ideas.[42]

This means that the creator of religious art, like any other artist, has the demand of truth placed upon him. It is a demand that may be responded to by a secularist as well as by a religious person. Religion has no monopoly on the way of depth into truth and reality. Indeed, at times it seems to be excluded from that way.

It is a judgment upon religion, that it—the supposed witness to truth as such—is always shamed by the sincerity of those who stand far away from it, who remain entirely removed from its cultus and myth. These people must for their own sincerity's sake remain aloof, so long as religious art is not an art expressing truth and reality. It is at the same time both characteristic and disgraceful for our religious situation that in this Exposition the secular objects alone are entirely penetrating and impressive, the things that are presented as expressly not for use in the cultus. A simple bowl even in the ultimate religious sense shames almost all the things that are assembled here as objects for the cultus. There are, to be sure, some items here which show creative power for purposes of public worship, and we are grateful to those who have broken new paths. But almost without exception these items are frustrated by the old, false understanding of worship as a special sphere alongside the breadth and the reality of daily life. Almost always the cultus is removed from the present and thereby deprived of its ultimate seriousness. We are grateful that the Art Association has taken up the struggle for a new, contemporary, real art form, that it has taken up the struggle for an art that has the power of witness. In the sign of this struggle we open the Exposition.[43]

One of the primary reasons for the divorce of religion from life is the fact that religion in its institutional forms and expressions has become a sort of cultural residue, it has not maintained a vital relation to the driving tendencies of the age. We live in a technical age, that is, in an age where technology has become decisive not only for creative expression but also for the expression and the frustration of meaning. In fact, modern technology has appeared in the nations of the West with the suddenness and power characteristic of a natural catastrophe. The people of our period—including the religious people—have submitted to technology without understanding what has been happening. The

[42] "Kult und Form," p. 582.
[43] *Ibid.*, pp. 582-83.

path of technology has presented new possibilities and new dangers far beyond those of the previous history of humanity. It pulls the whole of humanity in its direction, even the reluctant Asia. Europe herself is pulled along by the younger, more rapidly advancing America. Hence certain world perspectives have been opened up which demand recognition. If we are to live in the present we must ask the meaning of the new technology. And this demand requires that we first come to a clear understanding of the definition of technology. Only after we have defined technology in its *logos* can we comprehend its power as a *mythos* in our life.[44] Since the development of technology is related to art as *technē* and is also itself another index to the changing meaning of existence in the mind and life of the West, we should give it some attention here.

First Tillich's definition of technology must be considered. Since "technical" activity is the adjustment of means to purpose, technology is present wherever purposes are realized. Hence it is universally operative in nature and history. It is to be associated with the Greek word *teúchein*, "to succeed." Wherever anything is successful through the use of suitable means we have technology.

Whereas in nature every means serves a purpose and every purpose is also a means, in spiritual or cultural activity a purpose is posited and then the means for its fulfillment are sought. Spirit creates forms, technical forms, for the achievement of posited purposes. In the realm of spirit there are three kinds of technology.

1. The technology of development. Here the spirit appropriates some living form, biological, psychological, or social, and attempts to protect it from destruction with a view to assisting in its development. With respect to the plant, the animal, or the human body, it assists the process of breeding, feeding, and healing. This kind of technology covers a wide range of technical activity from agriculture to medicine. With respect to the psychic form, it aims at healing or education, here covering the range from psychotherapy to pedagogy. With respect to the social organism, it helps to unfold the social functions of nutrition and defense, as for example in economic or in military concerns, in traffic and communications, in public administration, criminology, and hygiene, in social work and education. Other factors are present in these areas besides "developmental technology," but the

---

44 The following discussion is based on Tillich's lecture, "Logos und Mythos in der Technik," delivered at the celebration of the ninety-ninth anniversary of the founding of the Technische Hochschule in Dresden and published in *Logos*, XVI (1927), 356-65.

characteristic common element is the development of something within the life process, in its own terms.

2. The technology of realization. This type of technique offers the spirit the possibility of coming into existence in its highest reaches. In music it is the instrument, in the graphic arts it is the material, in science and poetry it is the printed word that makes possible the objectification or realization of spirit, a process that in turn transforms the spirit itself. Here technology affects the spirit directly and provides new forms of actualization. Most recently the moving picture and the radio have offered a technical possibility of a new form of art.

3. The technology of transformation. This type creates structures determined by the posited purpose and by that alone; it uses a material for a purpose completely alien to it. It is the type usually referred to by the word technology. It has created the technical epoch to which we belong. It does not aim at the development of a given form nor does it aim directly at the realization of spirit. It destroys vital connections within things. It fells a tree and transforms it into wood for technical use. It blasts rocks and transforms them into "technical" building stones. It changes the surface of the earth to make roads and canals. It presses the resisting iron into arbitrary forms according to human purpose. Consequently, it creates the technical structure, a structure that has only a teleological character. When the structure loses its relation to this purpose it no longer has its "technical" existence. A machine that is worn out does exist, to be sure, but it has sunk back into the chemical sphere from which the "transforming technology" had raised it. Because of the predominance of the posited purpose, this type of technology is characterized by complete rationality. This implies the perfect relation of the whole and the parts, the elimination of the superfluous, the achievement of a perfect inner necessity. It implies also an absolute adjustment to natural laws. And it implies economy of means. The necessity of complete rationality here should not, however, cause us to neglect the large role of insight or intuition involved in all creations from the wheel to the steam turbine engine.

So remarkable are the results of these technical activities of man that the machine, the most characteristic creation of technology, assumes a sort of life and beauty of its own. It compels men to delight in it and admire it as well as to adjust themselves to it, eliciting at times the sense of its demonic power and at other times inspiring a relation to it similar to the relation to something alive. Thus the machine becomes a symbol for immense possibility, unlimited in contrast to handicraft production and, with respect to present possibilities of prediction, limited only by the raw materials and by the forces stored up in nature.

Now we are ready to consider the relation of technology to

other spiritual domains. Technology is the outstanding, convincing test of the truth of science. Moreover, the progress of science depends on technology. The Greek mind valued pure science as superior to applied science. Its passion for knowledge led it to search for pure unchanging being. Modern Western man since the Renaissance is more interested in shaping existence. Hence the passion for knowledge expresses itself more characteristically in applied science. In the future, it may be hoped, these two tendencies will unite to create a scientific attitude that combines interest in "being" with interest in "existence," that combines human insight with the capacity for technical transformation.

But what of the relation between technology and art? This is the question we have been leading up to. We have spoken already of the inner beauty of the well-constructed technical device or structure, a beauty manifesting itself with increasing impressiveness in the development of many modern creations, as, for example, the railway train or the automobile. This is, of course, not precisely the beauty of "pure art"; it represents a special category—which we may call "technical beauty."

But there are closer connections between technology and art. The most remarkable examples are architecture and clothes. Here we enter more deeply into the domain of spirit, the domain in which the essential meanings of life are discovered or expressed. Here the forms adopted and the materials used serve to express the totality of the life of spirit which they serve.

Let us examine architecture from this point of view. A house is not merely "a dwelling machine" but an ambiguous structure in which rational purposes have to be combined with inner symbolic power for the life of its inhabitants.

When Tillich interprets the meaning of domestic architecture he exhibits in a most original and stimulating way his capacity to combine general philosophical considerations with concrete realities. Indeed, his application of the theology of culture to an interpretation of domestic architecture brings into play a number of his characteristic theological and philosophical concepts and relates them to the things nearest to us, the concrete things of our daily life. Theology of culture *must* do this, he says, "for in the nearest things to us, in that which concerns our daily life, in the apparently trivial thing something metaphysical really hides. The here-and-now is the place where our existence must find an interpretation if it is to find one at all."[45]

[45] The ensuing paragraphs on domestic architecture are based on an address delivered at the dedication of a house, "Das Wohnen, der Raum, und

Certainly, the dwelling-house is something near to us. Moreover, it represents an important aspect of the togetherness of human life by providing the first and most immediate relationship which man has to space. In the dwelling-house man creates for himself the space that is *his* space. Only on the basis of his space can he advance into space in general, into infinite space. We should therefore have some definite idea of its significance for the meaning of human existence. "Our having of space and our creating of space" demands interpretation. A strong architectonic desire in the artist has created these spaces, and he has accomplished his purpose on the basis of an important idea. The accomplishment deserves to be intellectually apprehended and organized in its proper context of reference.

It should be said in passing that the architectonic desire of the artist, referred to by Tillich, is something he shares. Just as in his "Address of Dedication" one observes in Tillich the impulse always to form an architectonic structure, so one may observe it also in his whole system of thought. One is reminded of Goethe's famous characterization of the philosophy of Aristotle in which he compares it to a pyramid. Tillich's thought, as can most readily be observed in his *System of the Sciences*, also possesses a pyramidal quality. Goethe contrasts the philosophy of Plato with that of Aristotle by comparing it to a flame. The present writer asks indulgence if he dwells for a moment on these comparisons and recalls to the reader that Raphael, in "The School of Athens," depicts Plato as pointing his finger heavenward whereas Aristotle has his hand spread out over the earth. It would be correct to say that Tillich's philosophy combines several of these features; permitted a little poetic license, one could say that his architectonic impulse might be represented by the pyramid and his "ecstatic" orientation might be symbolized by either the flame or the sign to look "beyond." This brings us back to our immediate concern —space. Since man's standing in space is always also a standing in time—indeed, since space and time go together and struggle with each other—Tillich will lead the discussion on to a consideration of time and to the limits of all creation of space. In short, after having conceived space architectonically he will point beyond it. Here again we discover a border-situation.

Space is not easy to describe. It is no thing; it is also no receptacle in which things exist. It is rather, says Tillich, the manner in which the living being comes to existence. Space

die Zeit," published in *Die Form*, VIII, No. 1 (January 1933), 11-12. The editor of the magazine describes Tillich as an architect!

must be understood in relation to power: it reveals the power of the living thing to create space for itself.

There is, then, no space per se. There are as many kinds of space as there are forms of existence. Everything, including the human being, may be described according to the way in which it is related to space. Hence the various levels of existence reveal different kinds of space. Tillich discriminates four types of space:

1. First, there is the inorganic type of space in which things exist alongside each other. One thing impinges upon another through pressure and impact, from the outside. There is here no inner unity of space. Each thing fills a certain space, it stands by itself maintaining itself and warding off everything else. This is to be observed in the impenetrability of the walls of a house. We have here, then, the character of the inorganic, its quality of occupying space and of confronting other spaces. This quality may be found in widest ranges, reaching from nature to the highest forms of arranging space.

2. This rigid discreteness of space is dissolved in the space of the organic order, "vegetative space." Space is here raised to the level of unfolding or development. Each space extends beyond itself, providing a self-extension which yet never becomes a separation. There is here a unity, a "sympathy" that binds all aspects of unfolding organic existence. Space is as it were concentrated on one point, and yet again unfolded into breadth or latitude. The life process of growth illustrates an interpenetration of things standing alongside each other. But these spaces standing alongside each other are not the spaces of the inorganic order. They are rather the spaces which living things create.

3. The next level of space is that of movement, the space of the animal sphere. The occupying of space and the unfolding of space remain, but movement is now added. The animal anticipates the remote space towards which it moves. It breaks through the vegetative bondage to the soil, it advances into spaces that do not limit it immediately. At the same time, however, the counterpole develops in the animal, the longing for its own limited space, the space of the nest or the lair. Accordingly, the higher animal is thrown into space through birth, that is, by being pushed out of the originally supporting and limiting space of the mother's womb. In the longing for the nest or the den is expressed the impulse to turn back to the encompassing, supporting space.

4. On the next, the human level, all the above forms of space are at man's disposal. But beyond them he advances in a twofold direction, one external and the other internal.

a) Man externally overcomes the limited movement-space to which the animal, even the wide-ranging animal, remains bound. Man breaks through every space limitation and creates for himself infinite space, according to the power of his being. Space in itself is neither finite nor infinite. To speak of space, either infinite or finite, as a thing is to speak nonsense. Space is infinite, because the human way of creating space breaks through every finite limit. Space is finite because man at times sets up a limited space in which he remains and from which he advances into the infinite. Finitude and infinitude of space represent, then, a polarity in which the powerfulness of human existence comes to expression. It is the polarity within which man creates space and, in doing so, expresses his characteristic quality.

b) Along with this external projection there is an inner projection. Man is the creature that is content with nothing that is given. He pushes out beyond to something that he posits as a task or goal. He is not content with what is, but rather has a vision of what should be. He sketches out and shapes above the world he finds, a second world that he creates. He consciously and creatively gives shape to the space that is supposed to be his space. Here the polarity already observed in the animal sphere comes into play on a new level. In man this polarity is decisive for his shaping of space. On the one hand there is the desire to limit himself as much as possible from infinite space, to make the house into a den, the mother-womb. Moreover, he takes up into this defined or delimited space the images of plant and animal existence. Thus in the forms and colors of furniture and of walls he draws these other spaces into his own space. On the other hand there is a desire to detach himself from limited space and relate himself to infinite space. Thus he takes nothing in but that which is necessarily connected with the *meaning* of the dwelling. He opens himself to the space of the world and to all forms that remain out there, and yet like light and wind they stream into his limited space. Here we have the impulse not to go back into the den or into the mother-womb, but rather the impulse to move out into the infinite.

This polarity of man's spaces affects his whole life as well as his shaping of the human dwelling. There is a sacredness attaching to both poles. On the one hand, space has the character of the supporting element in existence, the support of the originally limiting space, the soil. The house-gods are the gods of the soil upon which the house stands; and, often enough, blood is shed and sacrifices are made for them. In this respect the dwelling house resembles the bondage to the soil characteristic of existence. But not only is one's own house the locus of the delimitation of space. So also are the neighbor's house, the city in which the house stands, the landscape, the nation and its soil. And all of these share in the sacredness of the space which supports our existence.

The exclusive preoccupation with the supporting soil leads to a demonic exaltation of one's own blood and soil. This is the characteristic pathos of National Socialism.[46]

On the other hand, the space-creating power of man goes beyond such limits and seeks to transform the earth into the unified dwelling place of humanity. In doing so it detaches itself from every special soil. But at this point, human space-creation becomes the creation of ever-growing spaces for living. It becomes the creation of space in the progress of time. And time becomes powerful over space. This aspect of man's outreach becomes the characteristic element of prophetism, prefigured in the myth of Abraham, who detached himself from any particular soil and went out not knowing whither he went. Abraham is the symbol of time overcoming space.[47]

The relation of space to time may be interpreted in terms of the various spaces. The mere occupying of space has no other relation to time than that it endures in time. The relation of vegetative space to time is more inward in character. Plant life goes through cycles of youth, maturity, and old age. In the animal sphere the future is anticipated and the past echoes after. In the inner consciousness of the animal both expectation and memory converge to create the threefold character of time, as involving past, present, and future. In man, finally, time becomes infinite, as does space. Man anticipates the future in unlimited remoteness. The coming millions of years represent for him just as little the end of time as the past millions of years represent the beginning. Man transcends every form, even every form that creates space. He transcends these forms in his impulse towards novelty. And in the new the limit of all his spaces and of his creations of space is broken through. He arrives at the boundary between time and eternity. (Observe here again the concept of the border-situation.)

But time cannot dissolve space. Time wins the present only in space. In the present and only in the present do time and space unite. Whoever has space has the present, and whoever has found no space is still without a living space; he moves towards the future in order to get out of it, to create for himself a present. But even if he has a space—that is, if he has found the present— time drives him on. The power of the human being to create time-

---

[46] This theme is developed in *Sozialistische Entscheidung* (Potsdam: Alfred Protte, 1933).

[47] This idea, which in another context takes form in the concept of *Kairos*, is appropriated from the young Hegel. Cf. Herman Nohl (ed.), *Hegels theologische Jugendschriften* (Tübingen: Mohr, 1907), pp. 368 ff.

space for itself drives it on into the future, for the future is the mode through which time becomes time. To create time—that is, to create the future—is to break loose from the present, to transcend space. Man must again and again leave the space that surrounds him. He does so for the sake of time, for the sake of the future. He begins this process by being born, by leaving the mother-womb. Hence the command to Abraham to go out from his established space into an unknown future is symbolic of human existence in general. It is symbolic also of the spiritual and social struggles of our time, for today the deepest cause of struggle is the fact that the gods, the powers of limited spaces, resist being uprooted to grow into a more encompassing space, into a space for humanity and into a future in which human existence may fulfill itself anew. This struggle of our day seems to have awakened and irritated the demons of the soil, and they show a terrible, a savage energy of resistance. They have renewed the struggle between space and time, the struggle against their unity in a fulfilled present.

We see then that the dwelling, the house, the home, provides a present in a limited space. Every house is a fulfillment of human desire to create space, of the longing for the present. Thus every house carries within it a danger, the danger that sacrifices will be offered there to the divinities of a limited space, that sacrifices will be made which do not belong to the house-god. The dwelling house and its surroundings, therefore, may be taken as a symbol for the task of man to create spaces in which the tension is maintained between the desire to limit or define one's self in the creation of space (to protect one's self from the all-absorbing infinity of space) and the desire to advance beyond the limited space into the infinite space (to advance beyond the supporting and at the same time cramping space of the den). They symbolize for us the task of overcoming space by time.

We have expounded at length Tillich's theory of domestic architecture in order to illustrate his manner of performing the function of the theologian of culture. In this particular instance the various levels of space and the relation of space to time—as exemplified in the dwelling house—become aspects of meaning and of the frustration of meaning. Indeed as we shall see, Tillich makes of the window—which encloses a space but also lets in infinite space—a symbol of the human boundary-situation.

This discussion of the meaning of domestic architecture is of a very general character, as is appropriate for the theology of culture. The reader may wonder whether Tillich, the culture-theologian, would be able to carry his method over to the interpretation of particular styles of domestic architecture. The answer is that he does do so in his discussion of the different types of city in the history of man. We shall give some indication of his thought in this area presently.

But before proceeding thereto, we would remind the reader that the discussion of domestic architecture was introduced in order to show the relation between technology and art. The confining of attention to the practical art of architecture does not imply, however, that there is no relation between technology and "pure art."

Pure art is often distinguished from practical art by asserting that it is without didactic purpose. This assertion is true in the strict sense. But we have already seen that in Tillich's view pure art has a purpose in a broader sense: it expresses the meaning of life, and by relating the ultimate meaning to a particular epoch and a particular technology it expresses a style. As we have observed, the relation between art and meaning involves no merely aesthetic experience. It presupposes a fundamental metaphysical attitude toward life and existence. This fact will become clear if we now examine Tillich's interpretation of contemporary life as expressed in modern technology and in the revolt of the artist against the meaninglessness of an urban, capitalist society.

The motive of technology is production. Every technology is driven by economic necessity. To be sure, other factors are involved; the intrinsic impulse may be a purely "technical" creative will. But this impulse seldom operates alone. Usually it has economic roots. And no economy has ever given such incitement as the capitalistic economy. Yet capitalism provides also a hindrance to technology. It has obscured technology by the shadows of its own depravity. In innumerable instances it has stood in the way of rational perfection or of new creations, precisely because of the interest of the economic power groups. It has even prevented the machine's achieving its purpose completely, namely, the purpose of liberating people from the curse of mechanical work. The capitalistic economy compels the machine to use its boundless possibilities for production of goods that have no inner spiritual necessity, that stimulate needs in an artificial way purely for the sake of profit, and that satisfy them very poorly, again because of the greed for profit.

The machine itself, however, is neutral. It can be used for good or for evil purposes. The charge against technology that it is the source of our woes is false. Technology is neutral. It offers means, not ends. Just because it offers means it offers possibilities, and possibility offers temptation. Technology is not to be repealed. Our sorry plight today is due to the fact that we tolerate the capitalistic economy, which, from the point of view of human fulfillment, abuses technology.

The inmost "pathos" and drive of the true technician is his awareness of the fact that through him a new form comes into existence. What was hidden in the lap of creative possibilities becomes a reality through him. By controlling nature, the human being is liberated from many mechanical functions. Technology can redeem man from pain, from the dull oppression of the daily vicissitudes of life, from the defenselessness of the human creature in the face of nature. Technology can even make men free from the bounds that space and time set to human community. Through it the idea of one humanity can be realized.

But technology can bring also a new *emptiness of meaning*. Through technology nature has lost something of its intrinsic freshness and abundance. It is "dominated." Hence power has in wide areas taken the place of *Eros* uniting man to man. Technology with its surface rationality has cut us off from the deeper vitalities. In some quarters men have wanted to destroy the machine. But this is not the solution. The path of spirit is forward. It is not long content with the phantoms of romantic nostalgia for the past. We must recognize that technology is a creative, so to speak, redemptive thing; but we must recognize also that it is a demonic, enslaving, and destructive thing. It is like nature and spirit—it is ambiguous. Hence technology must itself be "redeemed." We can see what this means only if we become aware of precisely what the threat and the promise of technology are, what technology involves for the life of the modern city, by recognizing what it entails in the metaphysical sense—by observing, in short, what it *means*. In order to discern the meaning of the modern city, we must envisage it not only as a material object but also as a symbol of a kind of existence.[48] If we do this from the point of view of the theology of culture, we shall discover that the city symbolizes the character of human existence and that the modern technological city symbolizes the character of human existence in a particular historical situation.

In every human soul as it confronts the world there is a sense

---

[48] The following paragraphs are based on an article, "Die technische Stadt als Symbol," written for the opening of the annual technological exhibition in Dresden and published in the *Dresdner Neueste Nachrichten,* No. 115 (May 17, 1928), p. 5.

of the portentous. Not that we are confronted by portentous
things alone. But those things that *are* portentous are changing
symbols of a primeval feeling of the portentous which man has in
face of existence itself. Our existence, our being here at all, our
being in the world, is the really portentous fact for us; it is
the sense of the unfamiliar, the strange, the threatening, the sense
of not being at home in the world, even when there are no special
threats. In fact it is just when there is no special threat that we
feel the strangeness, for when we are threatened by anything
positive we defend ourselves, and the very defending of ourselves
deprives the thing of its menace. When we cannot defend ourselves just because there is nothing that opposes us in a tangible
way, then the portentous appears in its real power. Here again
we find the boundary-situation.

To escape the portentous, man tries to make himself at home
in existence. He tries to dispel the strange, the threatening element. As we have noticed already, the dwelling-house symbolizes
this effort, as do also its predecessors, the cave and the tent. The
house has a purpose to serve, and with reference to this purpose
it is formed and transformed. But the house has also a symbolic
value: through it a part of existence is made homelike, rendered
familiar. The portentousness of infinite space which wants to
absorb us is kept away by the limited space in which we can find
our existence. At the same time, the portentousness of complete
limitation—the limitation of the cave, of the labyrinth, of narrowness (with which the fear is connected)—is mitigated through
a relation to infinite space represented by the window, the balcony,
the tower, the court, and the garden. Hence we may say that between the portentousness of the unlimited and that of the entirely
limited there is the "hominess of the house." The outlook on life
determines which of the two poles will predominate: the modern
house, with its transformation of the wall into a window, with
the interpenetration of the infinite and the limited space, and with
the elevation of the foundation above the soil, is a symbol of the
modern outlook and of its fear of the narrowness of the cave.

The house is the "cell" of the city, and like the house the city is
also a symbol of the primeval flight from the portentous. The
isolated peasant of Lower Saxony, in the hominess of his house,
defies the portentousness of the open spaces that surround him
and banish him to solitude. Here we have a symbol and at the
same time a cause of his peculiarly defiant personality. The towns-
man of the Middle Ages draws into a narrow space in order to
escape the portentousness of the wide, open spaces. Only in the

projection of the tower does he break through the narrow spaces
of his dwelling, but the projection is upward into the beyond
and not into the breadth of existence. We feel the homelike,
enclosed character of medieval towns but we feel also the threat
of their narrow, cavelike streets. One thinks, for example, of
Meyrink's portrayal of the Jewish ghetto in Prague. The modern
city, by contrast, is wide and bright. The spacious, lighted streets
and the squares of our large cities are symbols of the overcoming
of narrowness without the admission of the infinitely spacious.
(The typical suburb has neither the narrowness nor the spacious-
ness of the inner city, and through the portentousness of its
"desolation" it pushes back into the center.)

Just as the dwelling-house and the city are the means of
adaptation to human existence, so all technology is an overcoming
of the portentousness in things. The bare knowing, the classifying,
of things by means of laws and general interrelationships represents a repression of their demonic depths, of their incompre-
hensibility, of their strangeness, their threat to human existence.
Coming to know the world is always a becoming at home in the
world too, and the history of science is also a story of the victory
over the portentous. This victory, however, is always achieved by
means of technology. As we have observed earlier, technology not
only is the great means of experiment that tests scientific knowledge but also brings science into the service of human purposes.
Moreover, anything that is completely determined by its purpose
has become completely fathomed by knowledge. It conceals no
longer a threatening depth, no shattering, unpredictable reality. It
is subject to the law the knowledge of which is its basis; it is
calculable in each of its parts and elements.

Through the unity of technology and science man has subjected
the earth to his own will. He has, as it were, made the whole
earth into his dwelling, as the Utopians of the Renaissance fore-
told. Indeed, the man of the Renaissance saw as the future consequence of the revolution in astronomy the making of the earth
into the home of man, the appropriation of it, the making it
familiar, the depriving it of its portentousness. The earth had
become a star like every other stellar object. But the divine was
now not nearer to the stars than to the earthly sphere, as was
believed in Greek antiquity and in the Middle Ages. Today man
need not long for the stars. He lives on a star himself and must
shape it into his dwelling in the infinite cosmos. The means is
technical "magic," of which man is capable because he stands
in the focus of all spheres of being. This was the demand of

Renaissance philosophy, and it is the desire of the technical age to fulfill the demand.

Of all the creations of the technical age the technological city is the most powerful symbol. It unites the idea of the domination of existence with that of becoming at home in the world. In the technological city there appears in immediate, concentrated form something that in its effects embraces the whole earth: the earth as the "dwelling of mankind," the mastering of all the powers of reality, the victory over the portentous, the strange, the threatening elements in existence.

All of this comes to expression in the various aspects of the technological city. In each aspect is represented an enormous appropriation of latent resources. In each characteristic element of the technological city there is a liberation of man from enormous burdens of mechanical work. Each is a symbol of the liberation of the world from the demons. Each is a creation of a new and often wonderful form of being. "The technical house, the technical city, the earth ruled by the technical city, all together making the earth into the dwelling house of mankind: that is the symbol of our age, of the age of the fulfillment of the technical Utopia, of the era in which man becomes at home on earth, the age of the appropriation and transformation of the earth by man."

But simultaneously with this advance, the technological city has also become a symbol of the very thing that is questionable in our age. With technology there has come not only fulfillment but a new portentousness, a new threat that cannot be banished by science and technology. Indeed, it has been brought about by science and technology. Like the machine, technology has a sort of life of its own. The more powerful and the more complicated the technical structures are, the more they gain a life of their own —a life independent of man; the more difficult it is to control them, the more they become a threat even for the technicians. Hence we now find ourselves in a paradoxical situation. What with the technical structure's possessing a life of its own, a new threat has appeared in the very midst of that which is best known to us, the technical structure adapted perfectly to a purpose. This threatening element of technology will grow in direct proportion to the degree to which the whole earth becomes a "technological city" and a technical house.

Another paradox inheres in the new situation, or rather a contradiction. Because of scientific knowledge the technology has lost its threatening character. But it has nevertheless not become really familiar. The technical house and the technical city remain strange. In the very process of acquiring a life of its own the technical thing has been deprived of a life of its own. It lacks an inner vitality and warmth, with the consequence that no *Eros* can now unite it with our own life. It has become rigid and it makes us become rigid. It has no inner vitality and it makes us lose our own inner vitality. Our relation to the soil, to the living earth, has been destroyed. The hewn or artificial stone separates us from it. The house of iron and concrete separates us from the cosmic forces, more than do loam, wood, and brick. Water is shut up in pipes, fire in wires. Animals are separated from or deprived of their vital forces. Trees and plants are made technically useful for urbanite "recreation." Hence a certain strangeness remains or has been introduced into modern life, and that in spite of our apparent knowledge and mastery, and it increases to the degree of being insurmountable in the large city. With this appearance of strangeness in the mechanized world of things, then, a new portentousness appears, a horror of the rigid world that serves us and that cannot talk as a living thing to a living thing. And there come moments when—mostly out of false romanticism and sometimes in true despair—we should like to rush back into all the portentousness of earlier times just in order to escape the menace of the strangeness that arises from the subjugated world of things. (National Socialism with its doctrines of the sacred blood and soil made precisely this appeal.)

We can describe the situation in another way. We may say that we ourselves are deprived of our vitality and that we have become rigid and mechanical in the service of that which we have made rigid and mechanical. This embarrassment is one that concerns us all, but especially those who are most fully brought into the service of the technical city, those who nowhere find a compensation for the loss of vitality, who, it is true, exercise a fabulous domination over things but yet are dominated themselves, stunted in their vital and intellectual life, namely, the proletariat. And here rises a new threat, the threat of a humanity bowed down by a sense of emptiness, condemned to be the slaves of the servant of man. The threat becomes still more threatening through the fact that it gains its strength from the insecure, the ignored, the unintegrated status of the proletariat. All of this fosters a fear of life. Of course the basic reason for the situation is the demonry of the economic process, which has long since slipped from the control of mankind. Again there rises from the technical city a new, portentous shadow, which makes dubious all the splendor and makes one wonder how long it can continue as it is.

These threats pose a deep question: the question concerning the meaning for life of all such technical domination; the question as to the meaning of the "well-furnished house, the earth." We do not dwell in order to dwell. We dwell in order to live. But if our whole life is in the service of the dwelling, in the service of the technical city, to what purpose is our life? The technical city does not give an answer to that question. It *asks* the question.

In short, the technological city provides a symbol for opposite social realities: it is a symbol of the peculiar power of the modern age and it is a symbol of the dubiousness of the very existence brought into being by this power.

It is in connection with this questionable aspect of the modern technical age that we must understand the painting of the past century. Naturalism and impressionism were really a product of the capitalist temper of a technological society. The self-enclosed aspect of the new society with its technology came to expression in these forms of painting. Their forms

are the perfect forms of self-sufficient finitude, in naturalism on the side of the object, in impressionsionism on the side of the subject. . . . nowhere does one break through to the eternal, to the unconditioned content [import] of reality which lies beyond the antithesis of subject and object. An undertone of quiet, naturalistic metaphysics accompanies everything, it is true, but it is the metaphysics of a finitude which postulates its own absoluteness.[49]

We have already referred to the revolt that appeared against this interpretation of the meaning of life. Tillich sees it best expressed in the painting of such artists as Cézanne, van Gogh, and the expressionists. In his view, Cézanne "battled with the form" that depicted self-sufficient finitude and "restored to things their real metaphysical meaning." Van Gogh "revealed the creative dynamic in light and color," and the Scandinavian Munch "showed the cosmic dread present in nature and mankind." These tendencies cannot possibly be understood aright except in their relation to the new technological capitalism and in their relation to the metaphysical import which in their judgment had been hidden by capitalism with its self-sufficient finitude. Hence "expressionism proper arose with a revolutionary consciousness and with revolutionary force. The individual forms of things were dissolved, not in favor of subjective impressions but in favor of

[49] *The Religious Situation,* pp. 54-55.

objective metaphysical expression. The abyss of Being was to be evoked in lines, colors, and plastic forms."[50]

The revolt on the part of expressionism must be interpreted not only as a revolt against capitalism but also as a revolt against the religious art of capitalism. At its best this religious art depicted an ideal, finite reality, but the reference to the eternal was never successfully expressed. The reason has already been suggested in our discussion of the technological city. "The religious art of capitalist society reduces the traditional religious symbols to the level of middle-class morality and robs them of their transcendence and their sacramental character."[51] Expressionism would have none of this.

Here again we discover the relative insignificance of the content (or material) of a painting in comparison to the metaphysical import. We observe also how deceptive are the distinctions between secular and sacred. Expressionism wished to reveal a mystical, religious character in reality, but in face of the brummagem capitalist art of the period it could not utilize the recognized religious material. Some of the artists turned back to "older, primitive and exotic forms in which the inner expressive force of reality was still to be found untamed." Cubism and futurism made a more direct protest against the prevailing forms and modes of capitalist culture. "The dissolution of the natural forms of things took on a geometric character." The planes, lines, and cubes acquired an almost mystical quality. "The self-sufficient form of existence was broken through." No reference is to be found here to a transcendental order of "religion"; rather, a transcendental reference *in* things to that which lies *beyond* them is expressed. All natural objects are qualified by the transcendental reference. Expressionism attempted to express this metaphysical or mystical attitude quite apart from the choice of subjects. Indeed, when it used religious subjects it was peculiarly unsuccessful. It could not derive inspiration from the old symbols, nor could it give new meaning to them.

What Tillich has to say concerning expressionism's inability to use explicitly religious materials is significant for his whole theology of culture:

This process [of failing to make successful use of religious subjects] is highly characteristic of the contemporary religious situation.

---

[50] *Ibid.*, p. 55.
[51] *Ibid.*, p. 57.

It indicates how the continuity of the religious tradition has been broken by capitalist culture and how the modern religious consciousness must find itself again, without the aid of any definite symbolism, in a pure, mystical immediacy. But this may be done by means of any symbol.[52]

Tillich believes that the very vehemence of protest in the capitalist society against these new art forms may be taken as evidence of the vitality and relevance of the attack. The expressionists deprived things of their independence; they made a break with the accepted values and especially with the "self-sufficient finitude" of a complacent capitalist culture. Though in feeble accents, eternity was proclaiming its "No" against the time.

This proclamation as conveyed by the expressionists was largely negative. But it was followed by a new realism which seemed at first to restore confidence in capitalist traditions but was actually a more mighty opponent, "carrying the battle into the camp of the enemy and employing his own best weapons against him."[53] In this new realism, as, for example, in the work of George Grosz and Otto Dix, a new metaphysical import was expressed and *also* a new and positive evaluation of the subjects was presented.

The relation between expressionism and the new realism is one upon which Tillich has placed great emphasis. Indeed, this course of development in painting became for him the symbol of a trend toward what he calls "belief-ful realism." We should quote his evaluation of these trends in art.

Something remarkable had happened: In one of the most powerfully expressive areas of culture a radical revolution had turned against the realism of the nineteenth century. This revolution was directed with equal force against both conventional, idealistic realism and unconventional, critical realism as well as against the subjectively impressionist school. Things were envisaged in their cosmic meaning and in their depths. Their outer form was shattered in order to reveal their inner significance. A metaphysical glow of color was laid over the gray of the real world. Bold hopes for the resurgence of myth and cultus were awakened. Moreover, the revolution in all the other areas of culture and society seemed to confirm the genuineness of these artistic insights.[54]

Here he is speaking of expressionism. Now let us note his comments on the new realism:

[52] *Ibid.*, pp. 57-58.
[53] *Ibid.*, p. 59.
[54] *Rel. Verw.*, p. 65.

It was about the year 1922 that there suddenly appeared certain works the extraordinary artistic power of which was immediately evident, and yet they could by no means be considered a part of the earlier movement. A critical realism of demonic power made that earlier artistry that sought to include the cosmic and metaphysical dimensions, appear romantic, arbitrary, and extravagant. Although at the beginning a certain revolutionary tendency, a tendency toward caricature and cynicism, was associated with this realism, this tendency gradually disappeared and there arose a demand for a simple, unsophisticated awareness of things. Thus the new realism emerged and revealed an astonishing vitality; it carried with it even its critics, including those who had been most deeply affected by expressionism and who now even abandoned it, though often not without an inner struggle. . . . They could accept it because the new realism was really a new movement that had assimilated the strongest motifs of expressionism. The empirical reality of things again became the object of attention but this time not for its own sake. Despite this empirical approach things were nevertheless viewed as an expression of an objective value, an expression of the inner power of things.[55]

Tillich goes on to point out some of the deficiencies of the new realism but he believes that art was here unconsciously moving towards a belief-ful realism. Art was discovering the inner infinity of things—the infinite and inexhaustible ground and abyss, the Yes and the No of being and meaning.

We have now given enough illustrations of Tillich's application of his culture-theology to make possible an understandable recapitulation of his conception of its nature and functions. The task of theology of culture is to develop a systematic sketch of the nature of a religiously imbued culture; it is, in short, a normative cultural science. In order to accomplish his purpose the culture-theologian must have first a general religious conception of the nature of actual cultural creations; he must have also a philosophy of cultural history and a typology of cultural creations. We may simplify the characterization of these cultural sciences if we use Tillich's central concept of meaning as the basis for unity and distinction. The three disciplines could, in terms of the concept of meaning, be characterized as (1) a theory of the principle of meaning; (2) a theory of the material of meaning—philosophy of history and typology of cultural creations; and (3) a theory of the norm of meaning.[56] Throughout, the primary concern of the

[55] *Ibid.*, pp. 65 f.

[56] This tripartite division corresponds to the construction of systematic cultural sciences set forth by Troeltsch, *Der Historismus und seine Ueberwindung* (Berlin: Rolf Heise, 1924), p. 28.

culture-theologian is the import that is realized or pointed to in cultural creations. He leaves the question of the appropriateness of forms to others. He attempts to show in a general way the direction in which he sees the fulfillment or frustration of meaning.

One point to be stressed is that cultural creation is never arbitrary creation; it is historical creation. In order to understand cultural creation Tillich develops his theory of the principles of meaning which present the functions and categories of the various spheres of meaning. The study of the historical creations themselves has for its purpose the exhibition of how the principles of meaning are realized concretely. But cultural creation is also related to norms of meaning. Therefore the study of cultural history pushes on towards the explication of a particular normative attitude or position. Indeed, the study of the principles of meaning and of the history of culture has some norm, explicit or concealed, as its constant presupposition. All three disciplines are inwardly related. They can never be completely separated from each other. Only together do they form the normative cultural science. Even the explication of the principles of meaning presupposes some norm that is inherited from or has grown out of cultural history. Hence the three disciplines may be separated only for purposes of division of labor; they constantly illustrate a many-sided interdependence. Yet the three disciplines do not coincide. Each has its special task.

By this conception of the nature of cultural science Tillich aims to avoid the abstract rationalistic approach. The principles of meaning, as with Troeltsch, are based upon immanent experience; they contain within themselves the wealth of concrete reality. Yet they are so formulated as to leave the way open for novelty of creation. Thus the study of cultural history and the study of the norms of culture aim to provide a creative understanding of meaning. They are to be understood as possessing the concreteness and particularity of an individual spiritual creation. The study is always directed toward the "unity of essential form," but it is never more than the concrete synthesis of an individual system, a creative synthesis beyond which historical developments may pass, and in face of which the ungraspable Unconditioned of being and value must be seen as tangential. The norms of meaning are therefore not held to be a priori. If they were so considered, "there would emerge the absolutization of an individual standpoint or a rationalizing of the spirit," which hinders the individual creative capacity of the mind.

With such a view of the theology of culture as this, in which the normative science of theology is integrally related to principles of meaning and to the history of culture as understood by the systematizer, it is extremely difficult to determine whether the theology is a historical theology related to a specifically Christian tradition or is a norm merely posited by the culture-theologian and used to explicate and justify certain aspects of a historical tradition.

Tillich himself attempts to combine in his writings the functions of the theologian of culture and of the Christian theologian. The culture of which he is a theologian has itself been partially nourished by Judeo-Christian influences.[57] But according to his interpretation of the nature of the religious principle, neither the culture nor the Christian church may be identified in its actuality with the religious principle. Hence he is not bound to any tradition as an immanent reality. He interprets and criticizes the culture and the churches in the light of certain principles that have grown out of his own creative selection and out of his apprehension of the ultimately meaningful—an apprehension that is conditioned by radical Protestantism. These *motifs* are elaborated in his *Systematic Theology,* a work that lies beyond the scope of the present discussion. We now turn to a consideration of his system of the sciences and of his philosophy of religion.

[57] The Christian elements in Western culture as interpreted by Tillich are discussed in his essay "Kirche und humanistische Gesellschaft," *Neuwerk,* XIII (1931), 4-18.

IV

The System of
the Sciences

OTTO PIPER has said of Tillich that "among the postwar theologians [in Germany] he has had the clearest view of the impossibility of expressing Protestant faith with the usual theological methods."[1] Karl Barth could also rightly claim to have shown an awareness of the necessity for unusual methods in the presentation of the Protestant faith. But whereas Barth virtually separated theology from the other concerns of culture—at least until after the rise of National Socialism—Tillich has attempted to bring it into closer relation to them in both a theoretical and a practical sense. Tillich's theoretical attempt has been presented in a general way in the preceding chapter. It would be difficult to imagine Barth's writing in a systematic way on the subjects dealt with in that chapter. Clearly, the "Protestant faith" of Tillich is in certain fundamental ways different from that of Karl Barth, in both the theoretical and the practical dimensions Tillich's more practical efforts have been expressed in the religious-socialist movement, a subject beyond the scope of the present study.

With respect to the differences between Barth and Tillich, it is instructive to observe that although both of them were nurtured in German classical philosophy, this philosophy has positively influenced the thought of the two men in quite different ways. Barth and those closest to him have repeatedly expressed

[1] *Recent Developments in German Protestantism* (London: Student Christian Movement Press, 1934), p. 136.

their approval of Kant's emphasis on a universal categorical imperative. Emil Brunner has spoken of the critical philosophy as "the penitent attitude in the language of the philosopher." Tillich has adopted the idea of an unconditional imperative but he believes that in Kantianism the imperative has become an abstraction, incapable of being satisfactorily related to the ever-recurrent Kairos. In his view, the rationalistic moralism and the abstract universalism of Kantian ethics have served to give an abstract, "untimely" character to Barthianism; indeed, they have contributed to prevent Barthianism, which claims to be "critical" of all culture, from achieving relevance to a particular "crisis" in terms of careful social and institutional analysis. As against Brunner's view, Tillich questions whether any particular philosophy by nature stands nearer to faith than any other. "Idealism," he says, "has in principle no position of superiority from the point of view of faith, indeed it possesses peculiar dangers—corresponding to the dangers of other viewpoints."[2]

For his own part, Tillich has maintained—in contrast to Barth —an interest that is characteristic of idealism since Hegel, the interest in the philosophy of culture. As we have seen, this interest was largely motivated by the desire to achieve a unifying philosophy of meaning. Concern with meaning is not peculiar to Tillich. Indeed, he holds that it is the characteristic concern of philosophy in our age. The interest of philosophical idealism in this problem is neither accidental nor peculiar to it. It is an expression of the principal demand of reflective thought as it confronts the disruptions and embarrassments characteristic of a particular time. That demand cannot be met merely by an appeal to a universal categorical imperative. Meaning and demand must be related to a concrete situation.

So closely is philosophy connected with the concerns of a specific time that the essence of philosophy as well as the doctrines of any particular philosophy are in some fundamental way bound to, or are an expression of, a historical situation. Philosophy stands in fate, and its concerns and doctrines in any one age demonstrate this fact in one way or another. The philosophy of the Greeks, with the background of the world of the Homeric gods expressive of the Apollonian mentality, exalted "seeing" (*Schau*) as the perfection of human existence. In Hellenistic philosophy pure theory became the basis of a rational ethos, or it was imbued with religious ecstasy. In the Middle Ages the

[2] "Christentum und Idealismus," a review-article in *Theologische Blätter*, VI (1927), 31.

"vision" (*Schau*) remained the goal of religion—the vision of the divine in its pure transcendence. The religious doctrines themselves were presented as philosophy: though based on revelation, they attempted to answer the radical, i.e., the philosophical, question. In the modern period philosophy became a means of shaping the world according to autonomous utilitarian ends. With the crisis of modern bourgeois culture, the interest in the patterning of the world has been replaced by a concern for *meaning* which is characteristic of certain dynamic philosophies of recent decades.[3] Especially significant among these are the existential philosophies of the past century and the philosophies of culture and meaning set forth by certain Neo-Kantians. Wilhelm Dilthey, Heinrich Rickert, Nicolai Hartmann, and Ernst Troeltsch may be taken as typical figures in the recent development of the philosophy of culture and of meaning. They and others like them have expressed the special concern of our age—an age threatened with meaninglessness.

In face of this concern with the meaning of our present historical existence, Barth and Brunner, despite their limited preferences for Kantian philosophy, have repudiated idealism as a philosophy of meaning. Indeed, they in varying ways have tended to separate theology from philosophy. Tillich, on the other hand, has believed that a philosophy of meaning can be achieved only by bringing the autonomous and questioning attitude of philosophy into vital relation with the theonomous and integrating attitude of theology. As we have seen, however, this does not mean that any particular philosophy is necessarily to be preferred as a point of departure toward theonomy.[4] A truly theonomous philosophy of meaning should attempt to penetrate beneath or beyond all culture and all philosophies to a basic import of meaning.

Theonomous philosophy does not signify a decision for a definite philosophy compatible with, or suited to, faith. There is no such philosophy. Rather, theonomy signifies a making visible of the inner transcendence of existence itself, regardless of whether epistemological reasons drive one to interpret this idealistically or realistically, spiritualistically, vitalistically, or materialistically. Theonomy struggles only against that philosophy which wishes fundamentally to evade

[3] "Philosophie," *Die Religion in Geschichte und Gegenwart*, ed. Hermann Gunkel *et al.* (Tübingen: Mohr, 1930), 2nd ed., IV, 1198-1204. Accordingly, history has become *the* problem of our period. Cf. *Review of Religion*, III (1938-39), 255-64.

[4] This idea is stressed in Tillich's article, "All Things to All Men," *Union Review*, VI, No. 3 (1945), 3-4.

this shattering, in which existence and the concepts of existence stand for faith. . . . It should not identify itself with any special philosophical solution, and yet this does not rule out that one's own philosophical position will be discernible in the kind of solution that is proposed.[5]

What is demanded is that one acquire a principle of meaning which relates cultural phenomena to one another as well as to the Ultimate. By this principle of meaning all cultural phenomena should be interrelated and given positive significance, and not, as with Barth, be merely brought into crisis.

Every life that goes beyond the immediacy of the purely biological, psychological, and sociological is meaningful life. . . . In every meaning there lies the silent presupposition of the meaningfulness of the whole, the unity of all possible meanings, i.e., faith in the meaning of life itself. . . . Meaning is always a system of meanings.[6]

This system of meanings is not understood if one speaks only of the "Wholly Other." "Meaning stands with meaning in a context of meaning, and conviction stands with conviction in a context of conviction. An incompatible standing alongside another incompatible is in truth an antagonism, a disruption of meaing, a destruction of conviction."[7]

Tillich sees this sort of disruption of meaning and destruction of conviction in the theory of double truth of the late Middle Ages.[8] (The medieval theonomous attitude envisaged the eternal as a unifying realm of meaning manifest in all the multitude of struggles and searchings characteristic of the time.) He sees a similar disruption of the unity of meaning in the "side-by-side" metaphysics of orthodox supernaturalism of the eighteenth century, a metaphysics that spatializes the infinite as a realm of being and meaning existing "above" the finite order.[9] He sees it again in Ritschlianism, which renounces metaphysics and "travels to an island" of ethical rationalism around which "the ocean of remaining reality is left to the winds of secularism and chaos." This moralistic isolation of theology "incurs perhaps the heaviest

[5] "Christentum und Idealismus," p. 31.

[6] *The Interpretation of History*, trans. Rasetzki and Talmey (New York: Charles Scribner's Sons, 1936), pp. 221-22.

[7] *Das System der Wissenschaften* (Göttingen: Vandenhoeck und Ruprecht, 1923), p. 122.

[8] "Die Theologie als Wissenschaft," *Vossische Zeitung*, No. 521 (October 30, 1921).

[9] *Der Begriff des Uebernatürlichen*, . . . *dargestellt an der supranaturalistischen Theologie vor Schleiermacher* (Königsberg: Madrasch, 1915).

loss" by neglecting the Augustinian idea that "God is truth" as well as love.[10] He sees the disruption of meaning in marked degree in our own day in the outcome of Barthianism, which, despite its laudatory intention to magnify the majesty of God, makes a cleavage between theology and culture, and between theology and science—a cleavage virtually depriving both culture and science of positive significance.[11] Indeed, it also deprives religion of any positive significance for culture and science by giving it the function of pointing only to a Beyond from which there proceeds only an eternal No upon all culture and human science. As Kurt Leese has observed, this "consigning of the world to the devil in the name of God" carries little persuasion for the modern man.[12] Tillich goes farther than this in his criticism of Barth and declares that he virtually denies the Christian doctrine of creation. "It is not permissible," he says, "to interpret creation only negatively."[13]

Otto Piper's reference to Tillich's "view of the impossibility of expressing Protestant faith with the usual theological methods" acquires concrete significance when we observe that Tillich's first full-sized book after the First World War was not concerned *directly* with theology or religion. Indeed, the terms "God" and "Word of God" seldom appear in it at all. Yet, the book is one in which a theologian attempts to overcome the disruption of meaning incident to the separation of theology from other concerns. It is a book on *The System of the Sciences*, a subject on which only one other theologian of the twentieth century has written at length, namely, the British F. R. Tennant. To be sure, many other theologians have been concerned with the nature and significance of science, but, aside from Tillich and Tennant, none has produced a full-length study of the objects and methods of all the major sciences.

Although Tillich's interest was at first in the cultural sciences, this study pushed him more and more to raise questions concerning the relations between all the sciences. These questions were posed as a result of the encroachments of positivism from the direction of the natural sciences and of historicism from the direction of studies in historical methodology. These pressures

[10] "Albrecht Ritschl," *Theologische Blätter*, I (1922), 52.

[11] "Denker der Zeit: Karl Barth," *Vossische Zeitung*, No. 32; *Das Unterhaltungsblatt*, No. 16 (January 20, 1926), p. 1.

[12] "Das System der Wissenschaften," *Christliche Welt*, XL (1926), 318.

[13] "Denker der Zeit: Karl Barth," *Vossische Zeitung*, No. 32; *Das Unterhaltungsblatt*, No. 16 (January 20, 1926), p. 2.

had the effect of questioning the fundamental legitimacy of theology as such; even where this query was not raised an equally devastating challenge was posed in the name of the relativity of all knowledge. These questions, combined with the desire for a unifying philosophy of meaning, served to whet his interest in the all-embracing problem of the classification of the sciences. One could not, of course, find a more comprehensive or complicated way of testing the validity of one's philosophy of meaning. Indeed, the book which was the outcome of Tillich's attack upon this problem was so extensive in scope and so elaborate in execution that only two theologians would venture to criticize it in print in the first six years after its publication.[14]

In the Foreword to *Das System der Wissenschaften* Tillich gives the following explanation of his attempt to classify the sciences:

> It became more and more clear to me that a system of the sciences is not only the goal but also the starting point of all knowledge. Only the most radical empiricism can dispute that. For the radical empiricist there can be no system at all. But whoever wishes to develop a fully critical and self-conscious attitude toward scientific knowledge—and that is a necessity not only for the worker in the cultural sciences—must be aware of the scientist's place in the totality of knowledge, both in regard to the material he deals with and in regard to the methods employed. For all science functions in the service of the one truth, and science collapses if it loses the sense of the connection with the whole.[15]

Clearly, he wished to overcome the disruption of meaning and conviction which had been brought about by the fragmentation of life and of the sciences and by the enervating struggle between religion and science and between theological truth and other forms of truth. In other words, he wished to develop further his theology of culture by setting forth a system of all the sciences.

[14] Emanuel Hirsch, editor of *Theologische Literaturzeitung*, confesses to embarrassment because he had been unable to secure a review of the book. Several theologians accepted the book for review but later returned it to the editor with apologies for their inability to review it. Cf. E. Hirsch's review of Tillich's "Religionsphilosophie," *Theologische Literaturzeitung*, LI (1926), 97. Kurt Leese, a friend of Tillich, published an expository review of the book in *Christliche Welt*, XL (1926), 317-25, 371-75. G. Wobbermin, six years after its publication, set forth some criticisms of *Das System* in his *Richtlinien evangelischer Theologie* (Göttingen: Vandenhoeck und Ruprecht, 1929), pp. 54-61. The two critical reviews by theologians were by August Dell and Friedrich Büchsel. Cf. Bibliography for other references to brief reviews.

[15] *Das System der Wissenschaften*, p. v.

If the service of truth was to possess the dimension of depth it would have to be truth that would at the same time take all the sciences into account and give them an ultimate—that is, a theological—orientation. Such a goal inevitably raised certain questions: "How is theology, together with its several offsprings, related to the other sciences? What is outstanding in its method?"[16] So far as theology was concerned, then, the problem was to "win for it a legitimate place in the totality of knowledge." If this unity and this totality were to be achieved it would not be sufficient merely to arrange and classify facts and meanings. It would be necessary to discern a principle that would inform the total structure of thought and reality. Such a principle, Tillich felt, would unavoidably have to be on the one hand an intuition into the character of reality and on the other the expression of a basic attitude toward human life itself.

In approaching the problem Tillich was confronted with the necessity of coming to terms with the intellectual struggle of his generation for a new *Weltanschauung*, a struggle made necessary partially by what Nietzsche had called the "crisis in science." This crisis occurred mainly because of the failure of science to offer guidance and criticism in the development of cultural aims. As a reaction to the crisis there had arisen a new interest in the differences of aim and method between the natural sciences and the cultural sciences. Although the understanding of these differences could no longer be in terms of the differences suggested by Schelling's philosophy of nature and Hegel's philosophy of history, the problems posed by the fact of a fundamental difference between philosophy of nature and philosophy of history had to be faced. A *Weltanschauung* relevant to the cultural needs of the generation could not be created by further development of natural-scientific interests. Especially inadequate were the methods of a mathematical or rationalistic naturalism deriving either from the Enlightenment or from nineteenth-century positivism. A philosophical treatment of history and culture was therefore required as a supplement or perhaps even as a substitute for the earlier philosophical treatment of *natural* science which, as Troeltsch observed, had aroused interest since the time of Galileo and Descartes.[17] These new problems had received the attention of such philosophers as Nietzsche and Dilthey, but with the First World War their urgency became more widely

16 *The Interpretation of History*, p. 38.

17 Ernst Troeltsch, *Der Historismus und seine Probleme* (Tübingen: Mohr, 1922), p. 11.

recognized, especially among thinkers like Windelband, Hartmann, and Troeltsch. With Tillich also the problems of the philosophy of culture became urgent during and after the war, as is evident from the fact that his first publication after the war was his essay "On the Idea of a Theology of Culture." Although Tillich seldom mentions Spengler's *Decline of the West*, it is clear that for him as well as for many others this book gave powerful expression to the sense of crisis not only in Western culture but also in the search for unity of aim and meaning in historical experience in general. Certainly, the interpretations of history from the point of view of orthodox Christianity in its several varieties could not meet the pressing intellectual and social issues. And the interpretation of history in Karl Barth's *Römerbrief*, published at about the same time as Spengler's *Decline of the West*, did not come to terms directly with the general cultural crisis; indeed, it virtually ignored the *social* crisis and it showed no positive interest in the intellectual problems relating to the methods of the sciences. As we have observed, Barthianism, despite its valuable first emphasis, appeared to Tillich to contribute to a disruption of meaning.

If theology was to play a relevant role in the situation it would not only have to describe and justify a place for itself among the imperative scientific concerns; it would also have to confront the issues disputed by the natural and the cultural sciences. Hence, Tillich's concern with the problem of the system of the sciences was not merely academic. It was not motivated by any mere love for system. Rather, it represented an attempt to take seriously the total religious and cultural situation with a view to establishing an orientation for the various intellectual and scientific disciplines that engage the attention of the principal bearers of the culture.

We should observe that in confronting this problem Tillich encounters one of the most comprehensive questions that has engaged the interest of the philosophers, theologians, and scientists of the West, the question as to the way in which to give order to all knowledge in accord with the order of the world, and thus to classify all of the sciences in terms of the data and of the methods appropriate for dealing with these data. Indeed, the problem has become so vast in the twentieth century that most philosophers and scientists are unwilling today to attempt to deal with it. In making the attempt Tillich shows himself to be a scion of the German classical philosophers who were bent on reuniting theology and philosophy and the sciences.

Any fully adequate treatment of Tillich's attempt at construct-ing a system of the sciences would require us to "place" Tillich's system in its proper context in the history of the subject. Tillich does not himself provide this larger frame of reference. Such a task belongs to the history of philosophy and of the sciences. Here one would have to classify the principal conceptions of system which have been proposed or which have prevailed since the times of Plato and Aristotle. The Middle Ages and the Renais-sance produced a plethora of systems. The medieval and the modern university has been organized in terms of these systems of the classification of the sciences. This concern is symbolized by the terms, *studium generale* and *studium universale*. In this connection it is worth recalling that in the Middle Ages there was a legend that Julius Caesar transferred the *studium* from Greece, through Alexandria to Rome, and that Charlemagne brought it on to Paris. This peregrination was correlated with the transfer of the *sacerdotum* from Jerusalem to Rome, and with that of the *imperium* from Rome to the North. A later symboliza-tion of the *studium* is to be found in two pictures by Raphael in the Vatican, *The School of Athens* and the *Disputá*. But Raphael is really looking backward. The major revolutions that inaugurate the modern era are symbolized by the names of Copernicus and Bacon, and then later that of Kant, the inaugurator of the "new Copernican revolution."

Every system of the sciences is of course an explication of a fundamental view of existence, of man and his world. This fact becomes evident if we only list the names of the framers of the outstanding systems of the sciences of the modern period, such as Copernicus, Bacon, Descartes, Leibnitz, Kant, the French Encyclopedists, Hegel, and Comte. A whole family of systems of the sciences is to be found in the German classical school. Kant, Fichte, Schelling, Schleiermacher, and Hegel, for example, were concerned with the problem. Samuel Taylor Coleridge, by the way, attempted to devise a system in accord with Schelling's distinction between reason and understanding. The American nineteenth-century proponents of German classical philosophies gave no little attention to the problem of the system of the sciences, and especially to the systems proposed by Fichte, Schelling and Hegel. For Tillich the *Enzyklopaedie* of Hegel was a major source of stimulus. But, as we shall see, Tillich adopts and adapts a general pattern proposed by Fichte, a pattern that enables him to set forth the implications of his own critical realism. Tillich was stimulated also by the discussion of the differences between, and the respective methods of, the natural and the cultural sciences, discussions carried on by Dilthey and also by the neo-Kantians. But before dealing with these patterns we must take note of a fundamental insight that informs Tillich's whole effort, an insight that possesses special significance with respect to his intention to devise a system of the sciences which will give a significant place to theology.

Having already developed the outlines of a theology of culture, Tillich in *The System of the Sciences* approaches the general problem of the system with the apparatus already constructed. Although a multitude of problems that were not explicitly dealt with in his essay on the theology of culture now present themselves, the distinction between form and import again serves as a *Leitmotif* for the whole study. Again also, the distinction between form and content is of far less significance than the distinction between form and import. For Tillich, there is implicit within and there breaks through the formal system of the sciences at every moment something that is not merely formal, something that qualifies the form and that qualifies the material within the form. As we have seen, he calls this the import or meaning. It is the ultimate meaning and substantial metaphysical power present within and beyond all forms as well as beyond the indispensable integrating concept of science which gives expression to the nature of all finite and limited objects.

The philosophy of meaning is therefore decisive for his philosophy of science as well as for his philosophy of culture. The tripartite division of the disciplines of the cultural sciences of meaning also reappears. Indeed, many of the major concepts we have already set forth in a preliminary way are brought into play in his system of the sciences just as they are employed also in his conception of Protestantism, in his philosophy of history, and in his religious socialism. With these facts in mind, we turn now to examine his conception of science and of the system of the sciences.

The volume on the system of the sciences, covering as it does all the disciplines that attempt to give order to thought and to existence, cannot be dealt with here in its entirety. It is a book of almost two hundred pages, it is written in a compact, closely knit style, and it takes into account a multitude of considerations involved in the discussion of the various sciences in their relations to one another as a part of a system. One thing will become immediately evident, namely, that the study gives ample scope to Tillich's characteristically architectonic habit of mind. We shall have to limit our discussion here to the main outlines of the system. We cannot, of course, give even a cursory exposition of his treatment of all the sciences. Instead, we shall have to give special attention to the main principles of the methodology and to the philosophical and theological aspects of the treatment.

The task of setting forth a system of the sciences is itself a scientific task. In Tillich's discussion, the consideration of this task of classification appears in the place assigned to it in the system, namely, in the discussion of the cultural sciences. But what is the nature of science itself? This question is discussed again and again in other writings of Tillich. Before undertaking the exposition of his classification of the sciences, we should therefore secure a clear idea of his conception of the scientific attitude as such. This is imperative if one is fully to understand his scientific purpose in devising a system of the sciences.

As Tillich sees it, science is one of the many ways of confronting the world and the self. Viewed historically, it belongs temporally to the latest and geographically to the most limited way of confronting the world. Indeed, science presupposes a human attitude that is only seldom purely realized. The presupposition of science is that through it one confronts the world and the self and yet at the same time retains the "attitude of distance," that is, an attitude of detachment. It implies negatively that there is some element of deception involved in the attitude of pure immediacy, and it implies positively that something dependable can be arrived at by the scientific attitude of distance. This positive implication is, however, a matter of faith; it is the faith that precedes all science and that is itself not grounded scientifically, even though it may find confirmation in innumerable instances.

The knowledge sought by science is, then, to be distinguished from the knowledge of immediacy. In the Greek view of science, the object sought was a world of essences beyond, or within, or behind the immediate world of perishing objects. In the modern view, what is sought is a set of descriptive laws that discriminate order within the immediately encountered world and that help one to control that world.

But the attitude of objectivity can itself lead to deception. The more science holds fast to its object by remaining "outside" it, the poorer it is in the quality of its scientific understanding. A tension arises between the attitude of immediacy and the attitude of distance. It then becomes clear that both attitudes give rise to knowledge and that both have characteristic limitations.

The tension and the limitations become evident wherever tension exists between "science and life" or between "science and religion." Tensions again and again bring about a crisis within science itself, contributing to its enlargement and sometimes affecting the whole culture. Nietzsche rightly predicted such a crisis when he foresaw the dissatisfaction that would be felt against any science that is a self-sufficient reality alien or irrelevant to the deepest concerns of the culture. Marx illumined the crisis of science when he demanded that it be connected with a social and political *changing* of the social structure. With Nietzsche this attack upon the autarchy of science involved a doubt as to the authority of science; with Marx it gave rise to a new dogmatism in favor of an allegedly Marxist science.[18]

These recurring tensions indicate the necessity for something more than objectivity in science. The attitude needed may on its subjective side be called passion or conviction, the existential attitude. Where man feels himself and his whole existence at stake he recognizes that knowledge involves decision and not merely objective reflection *about* things. This element of "decision" is reminiscent of what Kierkegaard called "subjectivity," though in Tillich's usage this view of the self and the world stems from Fichte. The human spirit is a creative, dynamic expression of individuality envisaging and co-creating the new. Tillich uses the term *Geist* (spirit) to bring together these various constituents of knowledge, namely, reason, passion, conviction, decision, creativity. (Hence the term *Geisteswissenschaft* should be understood to be concerned with the individual creations of *Geist*.) In terms of epistemology this one thing needful beyond objectivity may be characterized as "understanding": it penetrates to the "inside" of an object and thus feels the pulse of a dynamic reality in both object and subject. In terms of metaphysics, this one thing needful is the recognition of the identity of the structure of the spirit and of the world, the recognition that the categories of the mind fit also the structure of the world. The world is not a box. As Fichte insisted, it is always related to ourselves. Indeed, if the essential structure of the world and the essential structure of the self are not the same structure, we have no possibility of reasoning or speaking. The structure of the world and the spirit come to perception in the mind. Remembering that the dynamic aspects of knowledge and reality (referred to above) must also be included in the Tillichian theory of knowledge, we may quote

[18] "Wissenschaft," *Die Religion in Geschichte und Gegenwart,* ed. Hermann Gunkel *et al.* (Tübingen: Mohr, 1931), 2nd ed., V, 1985-87.

here a significant statement indicating his indebtedness to Kantianism:

> I do not believe that I can ever unlearn what I learned there. Above all I am indebted to Kantian criticism, which showed me that the question of the possibility of scientific knowledge cannot be answered by pointing to the realm of things. The point of procedure of every analysis of experience and every concept of a system of reality must be a point where subject and object are at one and the same place. . . . I am an idealist if idealism means the assertion of the identity of thinking and being as the principle of truth.[19]

This principle, as we shall see, is decisive for his classification of the sciences. We shall observe also, however, that other German classical philosophers, for example Fichte and Schelling, provide certain motifs—motifs that sometimes are more existentialist than idealistic.

The attacks upon science show that science cannot escape the radical questioning emanating from an epistemological and a metaphysical position. Indeed, they show that science itself willy-nilly presupposes some fundamental attitude toward the ultimates. In face of these ultimates the "objective" attitude reveals itself as insufficient. But this does not mean that one must turn simply to the attitude of immediacy. Science, culture, and religion—and life itself—must in their depth be understood as having a relationship to something that is prior to them all. From the point of view of historical development as well as from the point of view of principle, the prius of science is an attitude that is not "scientific" in character, an attitude that is either autonomous or theonomous according to the ultimate orientation.

If a thing is known only when it "occupies a necessary place within a frame of reference," then science and the classification of the sciences also can be understood only when they are placed within a coherent frame of reference. For science is itself a *fact*, and a changing fact. Every single science is, like philosophy and religion, a historical phenomenon that sprang up from some causes. Since it has its existence in history, it is subject to change with regard to both its objects and its methods. "One can rightly interpret science, therefore, as a historical reality; one can observe its evolution, one can write a history of every science, and a history of the sciences." One can write a history of the classification of the sciences and of the philosophy of science. "One can also write a psychology and a sociology, indeed, even a biology

[19] *The Interpretation of History*, p. 60.

of science. In each of these ways the sciences would be arranged in a coherent frame of reference; they would, in short, become an object of knowledge."[20] The task of the classification of sciences is, then, the task of again and again placing it in a comprehensive frame of reference.

For the reasons just suggested, one must recognize that no final system of the sciences can ever be constructed. "The inner infinity of everything existing"—and in this formulation from Schelling we find an adumbration of an important aspect of Tillich's epistemology and metaphysics—prevents one from ever completing such a structure. Yet some intellectual system is necessary and attainable for each epoch, a system in which men become critically aware of the domain controlled by the mind, of the objects in this domain and of the methods whereby control is brought about.

The power and action of the mind reveal themselves not so much in the extent and detail of its knowledge as in the organizing power of the mind to give unity to all this knowledge. And although the subject matter remains a strange, inexhaustible ocean, yet the form is the mind's own peculiar sphere, and the mind must again and again revive its consciousness of this fact after periods of attention to subject matter, and each time in a more rich and more penetrating way than before.[21]

Two other important motives for attempting a classification of the sciences should be mentioned. First, the system of the sciences is necessary in order that the conflicts between different methods may be either resolved or accepted. Only in this way can the destructive imperialism of the several sciences be held in check. Thus the theory of the system of the sciences is a perennial task, the task of giving expression to the living and ever changing scientific attitude of a period. Again we see that the classification of the sciences is no merely formal, scholastic undertaking. Second, the very process of classifying the sciences enables the mind to acquire the power of establishing concepts in a critical way and of understanding their ultimate significance. This also is a perennial task, especially needful if dogmatism and obscurantism are to be avoided.

With respect to the last-mentioned motive Tillich approaches the idealistic outlook again, for he believes the significance of the system of the sciences may in large degree be understood

[20] *Das System der Wissenschaften*, p. 1.
[21] *Ibid.*, p. 2.

in the light of a Kantian epistemology. That is, if the categories of objects are envisaged as the basic functions of consciousness,

then the system of the sciences becomes the expression of the system of the functions of the mind, and the structure of the mind becomes evident through the different directions in which science finds its objects and delimits them. Through the structure that obtains in the realm of objects we see at the same time the structure that obtains in the realm of the subject.[22]

This consideration suggests another aspect of the problem of method mentioned above. The philosopher of science is confronted on the one hand by certain objects and on the other by methods through which the mind apprehends these objects. The relations between methods and objects must be determined. Indeed, the most important task of the system of the sciences is to be found here, for it is by no means true that a definite method corresponds to every object—a method that would be adapted to it and only to it; the same method strives to grasp a variety of objects, and different methods can be applied to the same object; in fact, closer investigation shows that the difference between object and method is a blurred one. These are the questions confronted by the system of the sciences, which must indeed be a system "according to objects and methods."[23]

But the system of the sciences is not merely a study of "data and methods." It is, as already indicated, an attempt to understand the sciences in terms of a comprehensive frame of reference. However close Tillich may be to Kant in certain aspects of his epistemology, he goes beyond the confines of idealistic philosophy for his comprehensive frame of reference. As we shall see, this larger framework serves also to qualify the idealistic character of Tillich's epistemology.

Two aspects of Tillich's transcending of idealism and of his criticism of it should be mentioned here. First, he rejects the idealists' claim that "their system of meaningful categories portrays reality as a whole." Instead, he asserts that it should be viewed "as an expression of a definite and limited relation to reality." He has in mind here not only the intellectualistic and rationalistic tendency of idealism (of which we shall speak later). Its philosophy of identity with its concept of essence is unacceptable. Following the later Schelling, Tillich holds that "reality is not only the appearance of essence, but also the con-

22 *Ibid.*, p. 3.
23 A reference to the subtitle of the book.

tradiction of it, and that, above all, human existence is the expression of the contradiction of its essence." (Here again we see a breakthrough from idealism to existentialism.) Moreover, our thinking is itself "a part of our existence and shares the fate that human existence contradicts its true nature."[24]

Second, the idealists' notion that their system of meaningful categories portrays reality as a whole must be rejected for another reason. For Tillich, both mind and world are through the dimension of depth related to the inexhaustible ground and abyss. Thus the dimension of depth as well as the contradiction of essence implies that both mind and its objects are to be understood in terms of a living principle that informs, but does not exhaust itself in, the phenomena—including the system of sciences. Without some such living principle any system of the sciences will end in mere formalism. But with the intuition of this living principle a system of the sciences can become an expression of an ultimate intuition of reality, of a fundamental attitude toward life. Again, as in his philosophy of culture, a form-creating and form-bursting power is believed to pulsate through the whole of reality and even through the system of the sciences.

An import constantly breaks (and shines) through the formal system of the sciences, an import that is metaphysical; that is, it is something that is beyond every particular form and beyond the totality of forms and therefore can never be a form beside other forms as it would be in a false metaphysics. The metaphysical is the living power, the meaning, the blood of the system. In this sense, but only in this sense, is the formal system of the sciences metaphysical.[25]

In Tillich's view, this recognition of an import that constantly breaks through and shines through the formal system of the sciences represents again the transcending of idealism which was

[24] *The Interpretation of History*, p. 61.

[25] *Das System der Wissenschaften*, p. 4. These formulations are reminiscent of Schelling's conception of "archetypal knowing" as set forth in his *Vorlesungen ueber die Methode des akademischen Studiums* of 1803 (Eng. tr. from 2nd ed., 1813, Ella S. Morgan, *Journal of Speculative Philosophy* [St. Louis, Mo.], XI [1877], 92-100, 160-77, 225-44, 363-70; XII [1887], 205-213; XIII [1879], 190-98, 310-19). A characteristic formulation appears in the First Lecture: "Only knowing in its totality can be a complete reflex of that original knowing, but each single knowing and each particular science is included as an organic part of this whole, and hence all knowing which is not mediately or immediately, no matter through how many intermediate members, related to the archetypal knowing, is without reality or meaning" (*op. cit.*, XI, 96-97).

accomplished by Schelling when in *The Ages of the World* (begun in 1811) he rejected the Hegelian dialectic in favor of a new realism, that is, in favor of an existential dialectic. Moreover, something of "the import that breaks and shines through the formal system of the sciences" is to be observed already in Schelling's *Lectures on the Methods of the Academic Disciplines* (1803). In the First Lecture, Schelling finds the presupposition of all science to be "the essential unity of the unconditioned ideal and the unconditioned real."

Taking all of the factors mentioned into account, we see then that the Tillichian system of the sciences is concerned with the relations between mind and its objects, with the creative functioning of the human spirit (in what are called the cultural sciences), with the methods appropriate to these respective spheres, and finally with an ultimate intuition into reality which qualifies the mind and its objects as well as the human spirit in its characteristic creative productions. In all these areas the system of the sciences is a construction "according to objects and methods." It aims on the one hand to search for a unity in all knowledge and on the other to determine the relations between objects and methods.

We have already referred to Tillich's dependence upon, and criticism of, Kantian idealism. Turning to the consideration of what he calls "the idea of knowledge" in its relation to the classification of the sciences we become aware immediately of his dependence not only upon Schelling's conception of "archetypal knowing" but also upon Fichte's doctrine of knowledge. This is evident not only in what Tillich calls the "idea of knowledge" but also in *the tripartite division of concepts* which determines the whole classification of the system of the sciences and is derived from that "idea of knowledge." It is a source of difficulty that Tillich makes only one (somewhat casual) reference to Fichte: hence the reader is left with the problem of discriminating his dependence upon Fichte. The fact that Fichte never showed much interest in the particular sciences to which his doctrine of knowledge is supposed to apply does, however, simplify the problem.

But what is this Fichtean "idea of knowledge" and what is the corresponding classification of concepts? The answer to these questions will disclose basic principles of the system of the sciences.

According to Tillich, every system of the sciences takes its beginning or its point of departure from a "principle" that can be no other than the "idea of knowledge" itself—a principle that is the essence of science. In his view there are different types of knowledge appropriate for the component elements of reality and culture, that is, for the realms of thought, existence, and spirit. Frequently this fact has been neglected, for the classification has proceeded less from a strictly systematic interest than from the practical necessity of creating a general view of the various domains of investigation and from the desire to work out a division of labor. The division of the faculties in the university generally obscures the actual connection between the sciences and the unity of the sciences which undergirds them all. The only way to overcome the confusion is to grasp the idea of knowledge itself.

What, then, is the essence of knowledge? In every act of knowledge there are two aspects: the act as such and that toward which it is directed, the thinking and that which is intended or thought. "If we call the act by which consciousness, in the interest of objective understanding, directs itself at something, 'thinking,' and if we call that to which it is directed 'existence,' we discriminate two basic elements as thinking and being or existing."[26] In such a description of the act of knowing neither the psychological process of thinking nor the idea of a particular existing thing is directly involved. Here we are concerned with the original elements of knowing and with their mutual relatedness—elements that must be grasped immediately.[27]

Tillich describes the relations between thinking and existence in such a fashion as to adumbrate the characteristic features of the three main types of science—that is, of the science of thinking, the science of existence (or empirical science), and the science of spirit (or cultural science):

[26] *Ibid.*, p. 5.

[27] Repeatedly Tillich uses the concept of "the act." "the act of knowing," "the act of thought," "the spiritual act," "the act of self-intuition," "the theoretical act," "the political act," "the meaning-giving act," "the norm-giving act," "the act of perception," "the act of re-creative historical understanding" are examples. This concept of "the act" would seem to be appropiated from Husserl. The context of the discussion shows, however, that Tillich's use of it and his epistemology in general are different from Husserl's. Tillich interprets mind, spirit, concept, and reality in a dynamic, paradoxical way (as will be seen when we deal with his metalogical method). Moreover, phenomenology as a basic science is rejected from the "system." Tillich seems, however, to have been permanently influenced by it in his general method of *examining* concepts. Indeed, often he gives a phenomenological analysis of a concept and then reinterprets or rephrases the meaning of this "essence" without discussing the truth question raised by the original concept.

1. Thought posits (or recognizes) existence as that which is grasped or conceived, as that which determines or gives content to thinking.
2. Existence is striven for by thought as that which is alien, elusive to intellectual conception, resistant to thought.
3. Thinking becomes aware of itself in the act of thinking; it is directed toward itself and thus becomes a part of existence.[28]

The first proposition Tillich calls the principle of absolute thinking. According to it, existence is that which determines thought. The second he calls the principle of absolute existence. According to it, existence is the "opposite" of thinking. The third he calls the principle of spirit. According to it, thinking is itself being. All of these formulations stem from the Fichtean doctrine of knowledge, but they qualify it in the direction of realism.

Since these three principles determine the general classification of the sciences, we must examine Tillich's exposition of them in detail.

1. *The principle of absolute thinking.* Thinking tries to assimilate every object, whether it be a part of nature, a historical person, an emotion, or a social force, into the sphere of complete consciousness. It is helped by concepts, laws, and frames of reference, in terms of which it interprets the thing. But these concepts, laws, and frames of reference are the creations of thinking, which provide the object of a major type of science, the science of thinking. In the sciences of thinking, knowledge is directed toward thinking insofar as the latter is viewed apart from every definite content. That is, it is directed toward the universal forms to which every content must accommodate itself just because they are the forms of thought itself. But the sciences of thought must always take into account the possibility of a connection with being. Otherwise a pure logism—panlogism—will result. The sciences of thought as such are logic and mathematics. Through them the forms become established under which all existence may be thought. In the forming of concepts the aim of knowledge is always the apprehending of existence. But there is a peculiar paradox involved in the character and function of the thought-sciences. They are directed toward that which exists and yet does not exist. That is, they are concerned with the concept of validity. Thus the thought-form stands over against all reality both as a forming agent and as a demand. Thought-forms are dependent upon definition, they grow out of intuition, and they possess a sort of axiomatic certainty which other kinds

[28] *Das System der Wissenschaften*, p. 6.

of knowledge lack. In other words, they have an intrinsic validity that cannot be dissolved by explaining logic in terms of psychology or of metaphysics. Logic and mathematics are purely formal sciences and their subordination to epistemology, psychology, metaphysics, or the practical techniques for thinking must end in the abolition of thought itself. Without the axiomatic certainty of the principle of identity in logic, it is not possible even to discuss the problems posed by the radical empiricist or the psychologist.

2. *The principle of absolute existence.* Thinking—which seeks and creates unity and universality—looks upon existence as something particular and individual, as that which is strange, contradictory, elusive, as that which lies beyond every pure thought-process. Existence, as such, is not in the realm of validity. It is the absolutely given. On this givenness all panlogism is shattered, for existence points to the depth and creative power of all reality—an "other." The tension between thought and existence, between the unity of "thought" and the alienness of "existence," comes to full expression in the "real," or empirical, sciences. Thought which is self-sufficient in the thought-sciences reaches out beyond itself in the empirical sciences. It gives itself to existence or yields to it, of course within the limits of the forms inhering in thought itself. "The manner in which thought acts in the sciences of thought is through the self-intuition of its pure forms," but "in the empirical sciences the other, the object, is grasped."[29] As we shall see presently, the principle of absolute existence determines a second group of sciences, the empirical sciences of being. Here it should be noted that Tillich does not consider the objections to his idealistic theory of the "forms inherent in thought itself." This fact shows that on this side he has been little affected by the traditions of empiricism. It shows also that he has overlooked the view that different types of logic and mathematics may be posited. We have already indicated the answer he gives to objections here in the name of empiricism.

3. *The principle of spirit.* Thought can be directed not only toward its own pure forms and not only toward a pre-given existence; it can also project itself creatively into the existential order. This is not to say merely that thought, as such, is a part of being in the sense that it exists and possesses intrinsic principles of validity. Thought has the power to produce something in and through the existential order; it has the power to "become" a part of "the other," that is, of existence. And having

[29] *Ibid.,* p. 8.

"become" so, it can observe itself while it thinks, and it can observe and evaluate the result of its creative effort in the existential order. Thus it makes itself into an object among other objects. It considers itself subject to all the conditions and determinations that apply to existence—that is, to the conditions and determinations that thought has classified as existence. "If now we ask where this aspect of thought (which is considered a form of existence) is to be found, we can only answer: in the inner core of the conscious being, and so far as men are concerned it is above all in the cultural life of humanity."[30]

The third and last group of sciences is therefore concerned with this object. These are the cultural or normative sciences. These *Geisteswissenschaften* have as their object spiritual creations like science and art, law and society, philosophy and theology, ethos and metaphysics. Attempts have been made to merge the cultural sciences with one or both of the other groups— for example, with psychology as an empirical science or with logic as a science of thought. The attempt to merge them with the empirical sciences must always be unsuccessful: science, art, law, and similar disciplines are productive and normative. Thus the cultural sciences involve the sphere of existence, but they raise the claim of validity. They express a basic function that is not derivable from the sphere of existence. On the other hand, the attempt to merge the cultural sciences with the thought-sciences has also been made and is likewise unsuccessful.

In this case it is overlooked that the characteristic feature of cultural life is precisely the meaningful link that ties it to existence, that in every act of real cultural life not merely a logical form is realized but that an irrational datum which at first is estranged from everything logical breaks forth uniting itself with the logical and thus becoming spirit, yet it never becomes merely a thought-form. Logism of all kinds neglects the irrationally creative character possessed by cultural life by virtue of the fact that its content is "being." The creative element mentioned above is indeed the peculiar element by which the cultural process is distinguished from mere existence as well as from a mere thought-form. If we call the creative element the normative element in the cultural life, we must posit the cultural or normative sciences as a third group of sciences.[31]

Thus the concept of spirit presupposes the basic elements of knowledge, thought and existence, but in spite of its dependence

[30] *Ibid.*, p. 7.
[31] *Ibid.*, pp. 8-9.

upon them it is a synthetic form not reducible to either of them. The norms of the cultural sciences are not a priori and pre-given. They "are born in the creative process of spirit; only through it do they have reality."[32] "Spirit is only present where existence is impregnated with the unconditional demand that gives it validity."[33] (As with Fichte, both decision and valid demand are involved.) Here the creative spirit brings together individuality and infinity, concreteness and universality, as, for example, in art and in those activities that give form to life in community. This synthetic character of the cultural sciences demands a method appropriate to it. Tillich calls this the metalogical method. The classification of the sciences must itself depend upon such a method, for a system of sciences can be established only in connection with the cultural sciences.

At this point we should note that the metaphysical power already spoken of as permeating both thought and existence comes to its fullest expression in the cultural sphere. When fully understood, culture and the cultural sciences point beyond thought and existence and also beyond themselves to a theonomous ultimate. For the naïve materialist the ultimate principle is a material world of things which is self-sufficient and self-enclosed. For panlogism the ultimate principle is the rational structure of the mind. But for Tillich the ultimate principle that unites thought and existence and that transcends them both is "the unconditionally real," the power of being and the support and threat of meaning. The "unconditionally real" is never to be caught (or capsuled) and given complete tangibility; it is never to be "fixed" within any form, nor is it to be identified with the totality of all thought-forms, nor is it ever exhausted by any form of existence or by all forms of existence together. It is both within and beyond all forms of thought and existence. Here we encounter the idea derived from Nicolas of Cusa, Fichte, and Schelling: the infinite is not a level of being; it is something qualitative, present in every finite entity. One is reminded also of Luther's word that God is completely present in every grain of sand.

By these formulations Tillich, like these predecessors, intends to break through a self-contained idealism to something that is nevertheless not simply a traditional realism. It is rather what he calls "belief-ful realism." Yet there is a sort of (idealistic) dialectic involving thesis, antithesis, and synthesis,

[32] *Ibid.*, p. 100.
[33] *Ibid.*, p. 91.

which in its formal aspects corresponds both to Fichte's doctrine of knowledge and to his tripartite division of reality into thought and existence caught up in the act of creative freedom. As with Fichte, the synthesis points to an open, creatively rational, "individual" spirit.

Referring to the three divisions of reality which must, in his view, constitute the synthesis and also determine the classification of the sciences, Tillich says:

There are three basic concepts to which this kind of knowledge that observes itself has led us: pure thinking, pure being, and spirit [*Geist*] as living thought, considered as a part of being. These concepts recur in a variety of formulations over and over again in the history of philosophy, at their sharpest perhaps in Fichte's doctrine of knowledge which can be understood only if it is conceived not as a fantastic metaphysical speculation but rather as living knowledge observing itself. Here we find ourselves confronted by a sort of inner necessity that must again and again lead to really similar formulations. This inner necessity justifies our making these three factors the basis of the system of the sciences: (a) the pure thinking act, (b) the thing which is referred to by this act, which (just because of this) is something that goes beyond the act of thought, and (c) finally, the actual process in which thought comes to conscious existence—in short, the trinity of thought, existence, and spirit.[34]

We have now considered "the idea of knowledge" presupposed in Tillich's system of the sciences, and we have observed how closely it is related to the conception that is presented in Fichte's *Wissenschaftslehre* and that gives rise to the dialectic of thesis, antithesis, and synthesis. This dialectic provides the formal pattern in terms of which Tillich's system of the sciences is articulated. The "idea of knowledge" is not so much an epistemology as a "system" of reality. One may compare with this the view of John Dewey that experience is not something subjective; rather, the world and experience are *someone's*. Nor is "the world" an objective entity. As the existentialist says, It is *my* world. One is reminded here of Heidegger's statement that "world" is a term always correlative with having a world.

In the light of this Fichtean "idea of knowledge" the tripartite division of the sciences is presented as follows:

I. The Sciences of Thinking
II. The Empirical Sciences
III. The Cultural or Normative Sciences

[34] *Ibid.*, p. 7. This is the one time that Tillich mentions Fichte in this book.

The first main group is constituted by logic and mathematics.[35] The second is divided into three subgroups:

1. The law sciences—mathematical physics, mechanics and dynamics, chemistry and mineralogy
2. The Gestalt sciences
   a. The organic sciences—biology, psychology, sociology
   b. The technical sciences—transforming technology and developmental technology
3. The sequence sciences—political history, biography, history of civilization, anthropology, ethnology, philology

The third group includes as disciplines: in its theoretical series, epistemology, aesthetics, and metaphysics; and in its practical series, jurisprudence, political science, and ethics.

These are the subdivisions of the cultural sciences. Since they deal with norms and meanings, their elements as well as their objects must be classified.

The elements of the cultural sciences are presented in terms of the theory of meaning and are given a tripartite classification: the theory of the *principles* of meaning—philosophy, including the philosophy of religion; the theory of the *material* of meaning—the history of thought from the point of view of the principles of meaning; the *normative system* of meanings—systematics.[36] These disciplines deal in the first instance with general considerations, but, in addition, the several cultural sciences are also subject to the same threefold division. With the exception of theology, the cultural sciences may be autonomous or theonomous in attitude; theology can properly be only theonomous. Systematic theology is the theonomous theory of the norms of meaning—theonomous systematics. Although it is rooted in the living confessions of a church community, it is directed toward the Unconditioned and toward universal norms.

[35] It should be said in passing that the inclusion of mathematics on a rank with logic reveals what we shall find again, namely, the constraint exercised by a speculative construction. Mathematics enjoys a much narrower province in connection with the sciences of the other two groups than does logic. For example, the cultural sciences do not accommodate themselves to the axioms of geometry.

[36] This classification, it will be recalled from the previous chapter, was set forth in Tillich's essay "Ueber die Idee einer Theologie der Kultur," in G. Radbruch and Paul Tillich, *Religionsphilosophie der Kultur* (Berlin: Reuther und Reichard, 1919). It is interesting to observe that this classification is proposed also by Ernst Troeltsch in *Christian Thought: Its History and Application* (London: University of London Press, 1923), p. 81. The latter work appeared in its German edition in 1924.

It does not stand alongside the other sciences; rather, it possesses relevance for all spheres and disciplines of the cultural sciences. Here is the typical Tillichian repeal of disruption.

We cannot here set forth more than a cursory summary of Tillich's detailed and elaborate discussion of the objects and methods of the various sciences. An adequate discussion of his treatment of the sciences and their methods would itself require a volume. We shall confine attention to certain of the key ideas, an understanding of which will serve as a preparation for the later consideration of Tillich's theory of knowledge and of religion.

We have already considered Tillich's exposition of the thought-sciences. The classification of the empirical sciences must now be given attention. In the sphere of the sciences of thinking the antagonism between thought and existence does not become actual. Thought remains confined to itself. Yet the forms are established under which all existence must be conceived. They are not yet applied to actual existence. When thought is directed to existence, it confronts the "other." The *tension* between thought and actuality appears. The "other" which resists the unity of thought is "the manifoldness of the individual." Thought never succeeds in subduing the particular, the individual. Pure existence is "the abyss of cognition." Yet the particular impresses itself upon thought. Because of the tension between thought and existence, the empirical sciences are constrained to devise an endless number of finite forms. This "living opposition between thought and existence" is "the principle of the empirical sciences."

Now, the empirical sciences are those in which the act of thought is directed towards existence with a view to *describing* it correctly. Accordingly, this concept of empirical science is by no means identical with the concept of natural science as it appears in the prevailing system of the sciences. It is much more comprehensive. The group of empirical sciences falls into three subgroups, determined by the elements of law, of Gestalt, and of sequence. The fundamental category of these sciences is causality. The three groups are related to three spheres of reality: the physical, the organic-technical, and historical reality.

When thought attempts to reduce "the manifoldness of the individual," it employs the concept of law. Whereas propositions or axioms are decisive for the sciences of thought, laws become decisive for the empirical sciences. But propositions and laws are alike in one respect: both tend to neglect the particular. They are distinguished from each other by the fact that the sciences of thought do not refer to the particular but only provide pure forms infinitely (!) remote from every particular reality, whereas the empirical sciences seek to grasp the individual in terms of law. The latter are called by Tillich "the law sciences." They constitute the first division of the empirical sciences and include mathematical physics, mechanics, dynamics, chemistry, and mineralogy.

To be distinguished from "law" is that sort of concept which, although fitting the particular into a frame of reference, does not obliterate the individual but rather attempts to bring it into relief. Here the individual is not absorbed into the universal; it is arranged in a framework of temporal succession. This frame of reference is signified by the concept of succession or sequence.[37] Obviously, the concept of time is important here. The concept of law, to be sure, implies a time-relation, insofar as the effect of the law takes place in time. But in the sphere of law time is, so to speak, only a dimension of space. It has no sort of creative power.

It is the essence of time to be a category of the new, of development, of history, of the individual, the existential (*des Seinshaften*). Space is to time what thought is to existence. Where time is decisive, where it is thus not merely a space-dimension, but rather a form of the creative, there existence eludes the domination of thought. The law-relation is replaced by the sequence-relation. Space is replaced by time.[38]

Here, as in all the empirical sciences, objects are observed in a causal context, for every historical moment is conditioned by the totality of previous moments. In the physical law-sphere causality is quantitative and stands under the law of equivalence—there is no more in the effect than in the cause; in the historical sphere causality is qualitative and productive—"in the effect there is something new as over against the cause," and in this context there is a meaning-succession. History is the sphere of the "creative, positing something new."[39] The study of history requires research, empathy, and imaginative presentation, yet the discipline belongs fundamentally among the empirical sciences, for a newly discovered document, for example, could destroy the most careful construction. By this mode of classification Tillich separates history from the cultural sciences, with which it has usually been

---

[37] According to Troeltsch, it was Xénopol who differentiated between *les faits de répétition* and *les faits de succession*. He compares this distinction to that of Bergson between *temps* and *durée réelle*. Cf. Ernst Troeltsch, *Der Historismus und seine Probleme*, p. 24, note 11.

[38] *Das System der Wissenschaften*, p. 23.

[39] *Ibid.*, pp. 33, 76-77.

placed. History is not in itself a normative science; it is the foundation of "cultural history" (*Geistesgeschichte*) and thus a presupposition of the cultural sciences.[40] Accordingly, Tillich includes in the sequence-sciences political history, biography, history of civilization, anthropology, ethnology, and philology. Where these disciplines are oriented to some principle of meaning with a view to discriminating norms, they become a part of the cultural history (*Geistesgeschichte*), classified as a cultural science.

But the concept of law and that of sequence presuppose another concept. Taken alone, they are abstractions. If the living and particular reality is to be grasped, the concept of Gestalt is indispensable. It contains both of the others, for every Gestalt is a particular as well as a universal. Every Gestalt by its individual character distinguishes itself from every other and is at the same time, by virtue of the laws of Gestalt, normative for all similar structures (*Gestalten*).

The peculiar quality of the Gestalt over against laws and sequences depends upon this two-fold character of the Gestalt. Law and sequence each realizes one of the two aspects of the Gestalt. The law-sciences and the sequence-sciences grasp either the universal or the particular processes that do not belong to a complete form. Their subject-matter represents incomplete or open *Gestalten* (a chemical process, a historical series). The relations that they establish are, so to speak, linear: they come out of the infinite and go into the infinite. The interrelation of *Gestalten*, on the other hand, is circular: it presents a complete system. Every concept of Gestalt is at the same time a law and a link in a series of sequences. The more comprehensive a Gestalt concept is, the nearer it comes to a universal concept of law. The cosmic Gestalt concept would be at the same time the cosmic law.[41]

We see then that the concept of Gestalt aims to overcome the antagonism between the individualizing and the generalizing formation of concepts.[42] The physical sciences (the sciences of law) and the historical sciences (the sciences of sequence) really depend upon the sciences of Gestalt; they are distinguished by their differences of emphasis upon the general or the individual. But *Gestalten* are to be found in all three divisions, that is, in

---

[40] *Ibid.*, pp. 75, 80 ff.

[41] *Ibid.*, pp. 23-24.

[42] This distinction was formulated and emphasized by Heinrich Rickert in *Die Grenzen der naturwissenschaftlichen Begriffsbildung*, 2nd ed. (Tübingen: Mohr, 1913). Tillich asserts that Rickert never overcame the antagonism between time and space in his treatment of the formation of concepts.

the sciences of law, in the organic-technical sciences, and in the sequence-sciences. In all three realms elements of the other two are to be found. This is the explanation for the imperialism of the methods: each method strives for universality and for exclusive application to the other sciences. But it must be insisted that each method has its definite limits. In the physical sciences one does not find complete *Gestalten*, though there are elements of structure. In the historical sciences one does not find genuine *Gestalten*, for they are destined to be broken by time. Accordingly, the method of the law-sciences cannot receive adequate application in history, nor can the method of the sequence-sciences find adequate application in physics. Tillich calls the method most appropriate for a given realm "the autogenous method"; he calls the method that invades a partially alien territory because it has some relevance there a "heterogenous method." "The whole profusion of the system of the sciences and also the necessity for the classification of the sciences to mark out the limits of the methods are based upon this distinction."[43] As we have seen, the classification must be oriented to the distinction between the individualizing and the universalizing tendencies.

A multitude of problems is involved in this area of the sciences of Gestalt. It must suffice here to record that these sciences are divided into two groups, the organic and the technical. In the organic sciences are included biology, psychology, and sociology. The task of sociology is characterized by the author as that of distinguishing the constant forms and the variable contents of social life. In the technical sciences are included transforming and developing technology (discussed in the previous chapter), the latter being constituted by biological, psychological, and sociological technology.

Worthy of note is Tillich's emphasis upon the significance of the *concept* of Gestalt. We have observed already the importance of this concept for the empirical sciences. Later on in *The System of the Sciences* Tillich applies the concept to the dynamic structure of personality and community; indeed, one of his most frequently recurring phrases is "the spirit-bearing Gestalt"— which may be individual or social. He points out that the concept of Gestalt as employed in the empirical sciences may be speculatively transformed and then transferred for application in the areas of *Weltanschauung* and metaphysics, where it appears as "the *idea* of a cosmic Gestalt." Cosmic Gestalt is not an object of experience, as are the other conceptions. It is only assumed; it

[43] *Das System der Wissenschaften*, p. 27.

is not a datum. It can be realized only through the infinite sequence of new creations; in other words, the Gestalt is broken by history. Hence, the idea of a universal spirit-bearing Gestalt is "the highest metaphysical symbol,—but it is a symbol."[44] In "The Philosophy of Religion" the idea of cosmic Gestalt is related to the mystical principle of the macrocosm's being reflected in the microcosm. In this same work Tillich also develops one of his most characteristic concepts, "the Gestalt of grace," which relates the *Gestalten* to theonomy and meaning. Wherever the concept appears it serves to preclude every "static world-picture" and to establish a "dynamic world-picture."[45]

This brief survey of the problems dealt with in Tillich's discussion of the sciences of thought and the empirical sciences is, when drawn from the context of the detailed discussion, perhaps scarcely profitable. It serves, however, to indicate the compactness and the complexity, if not the actual wealth, of material in the volume. It can serve also as a preparation for the understanding of Tillich's treatment of the cultural sciences and especially of philosophy and theology. We consider next the cultural sciences, the sciences of the spirit (*Geist*), the *Geisteswissenschaften*.

The cultural or "spiritual" sciences have to do with "spiritual acts." Indeed, they are themselves constituted by the spiritual act. We have already set forth some of Tillich's characterizations of the nature of spirit. Here it will be necessary to mention again only some of its main features. In the spiritual act, elements of thought and existence achieve form as a cultural creation. Here the key word is "creation." In the sphere of the sciences of thought the object of knowledge is *found,* in the empirical sciences it is *discovered,* in the technical sciences, *invented,* and in the cultural sciences, *created.* The spiritual creation emanates from "the inner core of the conscious being," the individual, creative "spirit-bearing Gestalt." In the spiritual act no single psychic function but rather the whole soul, with its capacity for thinking, feeling, and willing, functions in the creation of something new. Every spiritual Gestalt is something particular, something individual. This individual spirit is able to free itself from bondage to reality; it is able to exercise freedom of spirit. Yet in so doing it

<hr/>

[44] *Ibid.,* p. 80.
[45] See pp. 20, 59-60, *ibid.,* for other discussions of the concept of Gestalt in its universal significance. Tillich discusses briefly the role of the concept in the philosophies of Plato, Bruno, Leibnitz, Schelling, and Fechner, and in idealistic epistemology.

confronts something that does not originate in it, namely, something claiming validity. Thus the spiritual individual exhibits the creative self-determination of thought, positing universal norms and yet shaping existence in some individual way. (All of these features of the spiritual act, it will be recalled, are set forth or adumbrated by Fichte.)

The character of "spiritual" or cultural creation reflects the aspects of spirit just described. Creation is an "original positing" —a fact, Tillich says, that has been widely neglected. The creative character of existence is symbolized by the myths of the ancient cosmogonies. Rationalism has dissipated this concept of creation by explaining everything in terms of law, equivalent causality, or evolution. If we are to understand the creations of the individual spirit-bearing Gestalt, we must recapture something of the dynamic conception of "original" creation.[46]

Every creation has a twofold nature: it contains an element of existence through which it becomes an "original positing," and it contains an element of thought through which the creation is determined, through which it becomes a "formed positing." Thus "existence" is the principle of original positing while "thought" is the principle of form, of the unconditionally valid. "Because in every creation existence and thought are one, every creation is at the same time individual and universal. Creation is the individual realization of the universal."[47] The more individual and at the same time universal something is, the more explicit and clear is its creative character. Thus the highest form of the creative element is the spirit-bearing Gestalt.

In order to appreciate the rich character of the spirit-bearing Gestalt we must recall (from our discussion of the empirical sciences) that the inorganic sphere in a preliminary fashion exhibits this organic combination of the universal and the individual. Out of the organic sphere emerge forms or structures possessing a higher type of Gestalt. Indeed, the organic sphere even anticipates the freedom of the realm of spirit.[48] Although biology, psychology, and sociology methodically make use of the concept of Gestalt, they tend to construct abstractions or rational laws that eliminate the full individuality of biological, psychological, and social-individual structures of concrete life.[49] Al-

[46] We omit here a discussion of Tillich's counterconcept, "the exhaustion of substance."

[47] *Das System der Wissenschaften*, p. 92.

[48] Contrast Reinhold Niebuhr's view as analyzed by F. de W. Bolman, "A Theology of the Non-natural," *Review of Religion*, VIII (1944), 254-67.

[49] *Das System der Wissenschaften*, pp. 35, 46 ff.

though the dialectical relation between universality and particularity is to be found in the subhuman sphere and in certain material aspects of the human historical sphere, the *Gestalten* of these spheres are not yet creative in the full sense. Freedom and the highest manifestation of the creative power appear in the realm of spirit where meaning is realized. This meaning cannot be deduced from a structural law and is not a structural law but rather is a unique, valid meaning. Here productive causality —in contrast to equivalent causality—reaches "unconditioned realization."[50] Now operative in the realm of spirit, time, which corresponds to particular historical being and to creation of meaning, overcomes space, which corresponds to thought, to the fixed, rational form, to the law that obliterates all individual elements. With the emergence of Gestalt into the dimension of time, the living import of meaning becomes the substance of every genuine realization.[51] Thus in genuine realization in the realm of spirit, all of reality, from the elemental sphere of the physical through the Gestalt spheres of the biological and the social, and through the sequence spheres of the historical, to the meaning sphere of the cultural, becomes concentrated in the spiritual or cultural individual-universal creation. Hence we see that Tillich's conception of spirit, creatively taking up thought and existence for the shaping of existence, brings the whole of reality to a focus in the original creative activity of the spirit-bearing Gestalt—individual or social—which is rooted in the finite and the relative but beyond them is open to the infinite and the unconditioned meaning-reality. All existence "hankers" after this sort of fulfillment.[52]

The realization of meaning is an infinite process of spirit in history, wherein both the infinity of being and the infinity of thought are manifest. This infinite movement depends upon the dialectic of thought and existence, which operates as an inner tension, as the "dynamic" of spirit. But, as we have already noted,

[50] *Ibid.*, p. 77.

[51] It will be recalled that the concept of time, like the concept of Gestalt, was dealt with also in the discussion of the empirical sciences.

[52] In this context the following sentence from *The Interpretation of History*, p. 61, is to be understood: "It cannot be denied that a correspondence exists between the human spirit and reality, which is probably best expressed in the concept of 'meaning,' and which led Hegel to talk of the unity of the objective with the subjective spirit in an absolute spirit." The entire discussion of meaning, spirit, and the Unconditioned can be interpreted in terms of the relations between subject and object, and also of the transcending of subject and object.

beyond thought and existence there is an even more significant, propelling element, the living import or meaning. Every spiritual act is "somehow" related to this meaning, is "somehow" confronted by the claim of the Unconditioned. In response to this claim, the spirit-bearing Gestalt effects the meaning-giving, or rather the meaning-fulfilling, act.

This does not mean that a reality, meaningless in itself, would become meaningful through the acts of the spirit-bearing *Gestalten*. The meaning-giving acts are rather acts of fulfilment of meaning. The meaning that dwells within all forms of the existing comes to itself in the spiritual act. Meaning realizes itself in the spiritual. All existence is subject to the law of the unconditioned form, but only in spirit is the Unconditioned grasped as unconditioned, as validity. In spirit the meaning of being fulfils itself.[53]

The meaning-fulfilling act may be directed in two ways. Insofar as spiritual creation is directed toward the Unconditioned as import, it stands under the principle of the unconditionally real. Insofar as it strives for pure form, it stands under the principle of the unconditionally valid and is therefore subordinate to the unconditioned form. The first direction is called theonomy; the second, autonomy. The whole problem of the classification of norms and spheres of meaning is affected by these differences. Before we discuss these matters, however, we must take up the problem of method in the cultural sciences.

We have noted already that beyond the dialectic of thought and existence Tillich apprehends a living import or meaning. This complex requires a method of scientific inquiry appropriate to it. Now, since existence cannot be understood except in terms of thought, the dynamic "idea of knowledge" is decisive for dealing with the infinity of thought and existence. On the other hand, the presence of meaning gives to existence and thought their living power for spirit. All three of these spheres—the spheres of thought and existence, and that of import—are involved in the life of spirit; indeed, they cannot be separated except by abstraction. Hence, the understanding of cultural creations involves two principles, one epistemological and the other metaphysical.

The question now arises as to how these two principles can be united, the ultimate epistemological self-intuition (the "idea of knowledge") and the ultimate metaphysical principle (the

[53] *Das System der Wissenschaften*, p. 102.

intuition of "the living power of the meaning, the life-blood of the system"). The uniting point is in the concept of the metalogical: "logical to suit the thought forms, metalogical to suit the actual meaning or import."[54] This method is the method of the cultural sciences.

But it is more than the method of the cultural sciences. It is more than a mere method for securing knowledge.[55] It is Tillich's characteristic and distinguishing attitude as he confronts reality in its depth and power and meaning. It is, so to speak, the correlate of his ultimate intuition into reality, and thus it gives to his whole system its orientation and character.

The metalogical method aims to be appropriate for a dynamic conception of thought and existence as they are taken up by spirit and transformed into a fulfillment of meaning. It aims to prevent their being thought of as only logical categories. It sees something in the logical that remains beyond all particular forms of thought and all particular realizations. It views existence as "living import," which it attempts to grasp through all forms as "the unconditionally real." The essence of the method consists, then, in the fact that it intuits (*hineinschaut*) the irrational aspect of existence of the various functions—epistemological, aesthetic, ethical, religious, and so on—into the logical form, the thought-form. Thus it avoids the error of panlogism (which rationalizes all existence) without falling into the mire of alogistic arbitrariness (which destroys all form). Existence acquires a metaphysical import; it is no longer the mere "object" of epistemological observation. Through the metalogical method, accordingly, being is defined as "the principle of the unconditionally real" and thought as "the principle of the unconditionally valid."[56] Both principles are operative in the spiritual act—though only by intention and through inchoate realization, for the spirit-bearing Gestalt never fully realizes the unconditioned

[54] *Ibid.*, p. 9. Here again we observe the categories of Rickert and Troeltsch.

[55] Tillich distinguishes between his use of metalogic and Troeltsch's by saying, "Troeltsch applies the concept of metalogic in his *Historismus* to what I call 'the goal of knowledge' [the manner of forming concepts]. The connection between the theory of the goals of knowledge and the theory of metalogical categories is obvious. Yet, it seems to me more correct to apply the concept of metalogic not to a subdivision of the theory of method but rather to the type of method itself." *Ibid.*, p. 114.

[56] See p. 10, *ibid*. "'Thought' becomes the expression for the rational, form-creating, form-supporting element; 'being' becomes the expression for the irrational, living, infinite element, for the depth and creative power of everything real."

form and import. Kurt Leese has given an instructive comparison of Tillich's principle with that of other types of philosophy:

> For the atomists being is a material thing-world. For logism it is the limit which is always pushed further back by the progressive determinations of thought. For Fichte it is the limit which the Ego itself posits, in order to spur to restless activity with the thorn of its opposition, that is, to stimulate ever and again the consciousness of duty. For Tillich it is "the unconditionally real giving substantial power to all forms."[57]

This unconditioned meaning-reality bestows reality and meaning on every individual form, and every spiritual meaning-fulfillment bears in itself the *Eros* for the unconditioned meaning. Thus the realizations of the spiritual act become the locus of the paradoxical immanence of the transcendent.

The metalogical method is, then, the method and the attitude whereby the element of "greatness" can be discerned in a world in which some thinkers find only an eternal flux of relativism and in which others find only the recurrence of static forms. By means of metalogic Tillich aims on the one hand to avoid relativism and alogism and on the other to avoid absolutism and logism.

Perhaps we can best understand Tillich's concept of metalogic if we examine in further detail what he means to reject. We shall in this way also bring into relief the religious basis of his whole "system." One could scarcely find a more revealing statement of Tillich's conception of the task that lay before him, and thus of the purpose of metalogic, than appears in his essay on Ernst Troeltsch.[58] This whole essay is as much a self-exposition of Tillich as it is an appreciation and criticism of Troeltsch. The fact that it touches upon most of the major concerns of Tillich's writings indicates on the one hand the importance of Troeltsch as an influence upon Tillich and on the other the significance of Troeltsch as the point from which Tillich may be said to begin his own reflection in this area of thought. Both aspects of the relation of Tillich to Troeltsch may perhaps be inferred from the fact that Tillich dedicated *The System of the Sciences* to Troeltsch.

When Tillich says that "the motivating energy of this powerful

[57] Kurt Leese, "Das System der Wissenschaften," *Christliche Welt*, XL (1926), 322.

[58] "Ernst Troeltsch," *Kant-Studien*, XXIX (1924), 351-58. All of the passages quoted in the discussion of Troeltsch here are taken from this same essay.

intellect" issued from "the tension between the absolute and
the relative," he expresses one of the major tensions of his own
thought and experience. And when he speaks of the "discord in
his [Troeltsch's] destiny" which "placed him between theology
as the symbol of his desire for the absolute and philosophy as
the expression of the conditionality and infinity of all perception," he points to a border on which he has himself lived. But
Tillich believes Troeltsch was never able to resolve the tensions
in the way in which he hoped to, for in the struggle over the
contradiction between the absolute and the relative "the pre-
ponderance lay on the side of the relative." "It was not for external reasons alone that he abandoned theology." Not that his
passage from theology to philosophy was simply a passage from
the absolute to the relative. "The opposite would be more correct." His actual intention was to move from the false absolute
to the genuine. But in his striving for standards Troeltsch attached himself to that wing of Kantianism which moved in the
direction of scientific methodology in accord with the value
philosophy of Windelband and Rickert. In Tillich's view, it is an
illusion to suppose that a philosophy of values can provide an
island safe from the ravages of naturalism.

Compared with the endless shifting of natural and psychological
phenomena, this appeared to be a secure domain of absolute worth,
and there the union of the absolute and the relative elements in the
contemplation of culture and religion appeared to be attained. . . .
Whereas, however, for Windelband the sacred is the one-ness of the
intellectual functions, Troeltsch, under the influence of Schleiermacher
and Ritschl, searches for a special function for religion, a "religious
a priori," according to his now famous, though mistakenly formulated,
phrase. What is meant is clear: That which is valid is contrasted with
the merely actual, and that which is peculiarly religious is contrasted
with the merely cultural. . . . We look in vain for a clear, meaningful
characterization of the religious a priori. If religion is made a function
alongside other functions, its inherent claim to unconditionality remains unrealized, and no adequate, meaningful definition can be
found for it. And if religion is evaluated primarily as an intellectual
function, it is true that a formal consciousness of value can be secured,
but the claim to transcendence in a superformal sense remains unrealized. This means that in both cases the Unconditioned is sacrificed
to the conditioned.[59]

As a consequence of Troeltsch's inability to grasp the "actual import of meaning" in, and in contrast to, the thought-forms, his
conception of the divine appears exclusively "as the basis and

[59] *Ibid.*, pp. 352-53.

meaning of cultural life, but never as a breaking through the cultural." This same bondage to the given forms and its consequent missing of the living power and import of being is to be seen again in Troeltsch's later orientation to Europeanism. From Tillich's point of view, Troeltsch's notion of a creative synthesis in terms of Europeanism has the dynamic quality of reality but it lacks the dimension of depth, and it remains in essence relativistic. Moreover, by remaining within the confines of idealism it fails to overcome the tension between thought and existence. Thus, however much it may be commended for its superiority to a naturalistic view hostile to any genuine concept of spirit, it remains rationalistic. All of these criticisms suggest by negative implication Tillich's view of the role of a theonomous metaphysics.

These considerations have a direct bearing upon the methodology of the social sciences. Tillich's conception of metalogic aims to join together thought-forms (which are universal in scope) with the actuality of an all-embracing, pulsating import of meaning. For him,

mere logism will not grasp the actual meaning or import, and alogism will not achieve the thought-form. The first leads to formalism, the second to arbitrariness. The first must do violence to all sciences by forcing upon them a formal logical pattern, the second is incapable of accomplishing a well-rounded and intrinsically necessary structure. The method of systematic classification of the sciences must, therefore, contain both elements.[60]

The purpose of metalogic can be understood also by noting that it aims to avoid the splitting of reality into the opposites of form and matter, or into a formalistic conception of mind and a naturalistic conception of nature hostile to mind. Thus it intends to overcome both naturalism and rationalistic idealism by intuiting within actuality a living import of meaning and by breaking through the forms of thought to a supporting, transcending meaning.

This is only possible, however, if being is not only conceived as a logical category but is also perceived as an actual living import. The approach to being proceeds through the aesthetic, ethical, social, religious functions as well as through the logical. For each of these functions being is something different, and yet in all these functions it is the same being that underlies them, the unconditionally real which gives import to all forms. The question is now that of making

[60] *Das System der Wissenschaften*, p. 9.

these (metalogical) approaches to being accessible to logical thinking, to find forms that, without losing their logical correctness, will grasp and give expression to the being that imbues the logical forms and that is apprehended in all these functions. We call this method "metalogical" by way of analogy to the word "metaphysical."[61]

By overcoming logistic rationalism this metalogical method achieves the dynamic quality appropriate for a living universe. It is indispensable if one is to apprehend the actual import of existence by penetrating the living mobility of form, which in spite of all movement does not break away from logical unity.

In this connection, we should note Tillich's attitude toward Hegel, one of the most impressive and influential of the encyclopedists who attempted a philosophical classification of the sciences. Tillich speaks of his dialectic as "the last great system-creating method." In his view Hegel's dialectic was in its inception dynamic, but in the end it lost its openness and flexibility.

Its defect was that the logical element in it engulfed the metalogical and the dynamic, and that at a certain point of the logical and temporal development the dynamic element was abolished. Thought wished to subject being completely; but being cannot be subjected, neither in part nor as a whole; it is inwardly infinite and possesses inexhaustible creative power. The metalogical method is always also a dynamic method.[62]

Here we see again the decisive significance of Tillich's conception of meaning: it purports to bring into relief the element that unites and transcends the ideal and real aspects of existence. Another way of stating the difference between Tillich and Hegel is suggested by a characterization of Hegel made by Richard Kroner. The panlogism of Hegel, he says, consists in the relentlessness of his thought.[63] Tillich renounces this relentlessness when he says:

The deepest comprehension of being involves a conscious renunciation of the attempt to grasp pure being; this is not a simple, naive renunciation, but a fully conscious renunciation engendered by the failure of the supreme struggle for form, a renunciation that bursts

[61] *Ibid.*, p. 10.
[62] *Ibid.* This criticism of Hegel is set forth at length in Tillich's address "Hegel," delivered on the one hundredth anniversary of his death, published in the *Sammlung gemeinverständlicher Vorträge und Schriften aus dem Gebiet der Theologie und Religionsgeschichte* (Tübingen: Mohr, 1932).
[63] R. Kroner, *Von Kant bis Hegel* (Tübingen: Mohr, 1924), II, 268. Quoted by Kurt Leese, *loc. cit.*, p. 374.

through the form; indeed, the form of this renunciation is itself precisely the bursting through the form.[64]

What bursts through the form is the living import. Hence we may say that, whereas the synthetic *idea* is basic for the Hegelian system, the synthetic, dynamic form-creating, form-bursting reality and meaning is basic for the Tillichian open system. We say "open" because the Tillichian synthesis is always confronted by the abyss and ground of meaning, the No and the Yes, the threat and the support, the infinite and inexhaustible depths.

Tillich's attitude toward Kant involves somewhat similar considerations. In his view, certain elements of the critical philosophy are to be retained insofar as they illumine the nature of value and insofar as they reject the validity of explaining existence by constructing a world behind the world—an explanation that is no explanation and that also disrupts meaning. Yet Kantianism lacks a dynamic logic that can relate itself to the Kairos, it lacks an *attrait* for the concrete.[65] It logicizes spirit, and everything real becomes rationalized. Moreover, it misses the positive import of being, for it considers any claim regarding it to be metaphysical hypostatizing. The bestowal of meaning (*Sinngebung*) is therefore viewed as a subjective act of giving logical forms to a reality that is formless in itself. In other words, Kantianism overlooks the striving of the real towards spiritual meaning. It loses the unity of subject and object, of being and validity, which is given in creative penetration into meaning. "Pure criticism is thus unable to satisfy the postulate of philosophy, namely, that it is a theory of the principles of meaning."[66]

Implicit in the criticism directed by Tillich at Hegelianism and Kantianism is his appropriation of motifs drawn from other philosophers who in his view represent a more dynamic conception of reality and of spirit. Chief among these are Boehme, Schelling, and Nietzsche; we have already mentioned Fichte again and again. Tillich characterizes this line as a subdominant tendency in Western thought—a tendency that criticizes the rationalism and logism of the main line of modern philosophy.[67] Boehme's theosophy represents for Tillich the modern fountainhead of that dynamic, voluntaristic outlook on the world which

[64] *Das System der Wissenschaften*, p. 74.
[65] As noted earlier, Tillich criticizes Karl Barth for taking over this abstractionism from Kant.
[66] *Das System der Wissenschaften*, p. 115.
[67] We shall find occasion in the next chapter to deal with this subdominant tendency in greater detail.

interprets it as an emanation of tensions between the universal will and the particular (*eigene*) will—tensions rising from an ultimate ground and abyss. This dialectical, dynamic philosophy reappears in the later Schelling's "positive" theory of potencies and in his doctrine of freedom. According to Schelling, the rational, "negative" conception of God is inadequate, for it extends only to the form; it does not touch the real. Hence God is to be conceived as act, as will, as something over and above the rational conception of the divine. Tillich gives a dynamic accent to Schelling's conception of *das unvordenkliche Sein*, a reality or will anterior to and inaccessible to thought. The Tillichian concept of the unconditionally real and the unconditionally valid presupposes a form-creating, form-bursting reality and meaning. Nietzsche's emphasis on "creative spirit" with its criticism of convention and its affirmation of original creating is assimilated by Tillich into the same framework.

To these tendencies in European philosophy should be added the Neo-Platonic "ecstatic" orientation to the One beyond all existence and the accompanying "negative theology." Dionysius speaks of God as nameless, beyond the highest name one can give Him. He is beyond God, if God is spoken of as a divine being. He is "unspeakable Darkness." This "abysmal" One is the source and substance of all being. Tillich's emphasis upon the sense of participation in and separation from the unconditionally real and the unconditionally valid, his insistence upon the idea that the ultimate defies conception, that the forms drawn from the autonomous order must be used symbolically and paradoxically when applied to the theonomous order, are implications of a revised version of Neo-Platonic "ecstatic" and negative theology, with a positive emphasis reminiscent of Nicolas of Cusa.

If now we summarize the elements of earlier philosophy which are represented in Tillich's metalogic, we can say that it represents (with the qualifications made above) the critical-rational-transcendental line from Kant to Hegel, and the existential-creative line from Jacob Boehme, Fichte, and Schelling through Nietzsche, with their concepts of ground and abyss, of freedom, and of creative spirit;[68] and behind both of these lines of thought is Neo-Platonism with its "ecstatic" and "negative theology."

Drawing together Tillich's idealistic principle of the identity

[68] Cf. Leese, *loc. cit.*, p. 374. See also Leese's Von *Jakob Boehme zu Schelling* (Erfurt: Kurt Stenger, 1927) and *Die Krisis und Wende des christlichen Geistes* (Berlin: Junker und Dünnhaupt, 1932).

of thought and existence, his view of the tension and contradiction between essence and existence, his "ecstatic" theory of meaning, and his theory of the spirit-bearing Gestalt, we see that in metalogic he envisages a dialectic of the universal and the particular, the absolute and the relative, the creative and the fateful, the ground and the abyss. In the individuations of cultural life, the principle of life, of creation, of Gestalt, of form and the eruption of form, come to purest realization.[69] By metalogic the rational, shaping, structural, form-bearing elements and the irrational, living, infinite element, the depth and the creative power of all reality, are brought into dynamic and mutual relationship.[70] Through the metalogical method Tillich apprehends the "unconditioned content within the conditioned forms." This is the method "which in the philosophy of the Renaissance has been called the apprehension of the *coincidentia oppositorum*."[71] In other words, Tillich's philosophy is a philosophy of paradox: it affirms the paradoxical immanence of the transcendent.

From the description of the method of the cultural sciences we turn now to a discussion of the tasks of the cultural sciences and to the problem of classification. The task of the cultural sciences is to discriminate the interlacing elements of the fulfillment of meaning in the various spheres of meaning. The achievement of this task is a spiritual act. Hence, like the spiritual act, it is creative. As we have seen, every act of knowledge contains a universal and an individual element. Naturally, the universal element prevails to the extent to which the object of knowledge approaches the universal, the pure thought-form. Consequently, the universal element prevails most in the thought-sciences. On the other hand, the individual element prevails where the object is the least capable of being grasped by thought-forms—that is, in the cultural sciences.

Cultural science exhibits another peculiarity. It does not deal with a given object which it can observe objectively with "the attitude of distance" alone. Cultural science always shares in the positing of the object which it wishes to know. It is not only re-creative like the study of history; it is co-creative, productive. There is in the creative act of the analyst of culture a combination of self-awareness, of concern with the universal

[69] *Das System der Wissenschaften*, pp. 92-93.
[70] *Ibid.*, p. 30.
[71] *Ibid.*, p. 133. The reference is, no doubt, to Nicolas of Cusa.

and the valid, and of concern with creating living, existential meaning-relationships. "Cultural science is productive, that is, it is always at the same time the *prius* and the *posterius* of the spiritual creation. It lives on the creations which it helps to create. . . . It is a systematic form of thinking that determines itself.[72]

The cultural sciences are not only productive but also normative. Norms are, so to speak, the laws of cultural creation. The norms must, of course, correspond to the various cultural activities. The philosophy of science provides norms for scientific work; the theory of art furnishes the norms of aesthetic appreciation; political and juridical theory supplies norms for legal and social action; and metaphysics, ethics, and theology offer norms for the theoretical and the practical disciplines and also for the autonomous and the theonomous attitude in face of the Unconditioned. This definition is, however, scarcely sufficient. These norms are not comparable to those of the thought-sciences. They are not "found" but "created." They are born in the creative process of spirit.

They have reality only through the spirit. They do not rest in an ideal sphere as do the pure forms of the sciences of thought; nor do they have immediate reality as have the structures of the empirical sciences. They have the peculiar reality which the creative process of the spirit bestows upon them.[73]

In view of the fact that Tillich holds that every spiritual act is the establishing of norms and that cultural science is normative insofar as it shares productively in the act, it will be well to present here his careful formulations:

The norms stem from spiritual creation, and spiritual creation conforms to them. They are individual when they are posited by the creative process and they represent the universal when creation is directed toward them. The universal itself, however, does not exist. All spiritual creation and shaping is directed toward the unconditionality of pure form, yet the unconditional itself is not a form. It is the Eros of the spirit which turns to the spirit; it is the longing desire of all conditioned forms for the Unconditioned. And it is not obedience to law, to a system of concrete norms that are more or less recognized, more or less realized. The normative character is thus not an addition to the spiritual creations, but is essential to them. It characterizes their nature, their existence as spirit, as the self-determination of thinking within existence.[74]

[72] *Ibid.*, p. 99.
[73] *Ibid.*, p. 100.
[74] *Ibid.*

In other words, the norms live in the realization of meaning. They continuously raise new objects toward fulfillment of meaning. If we wish to describe this process in traditional religious language we may say: All things strive towards God because they have their origin in him.

These norms are not "subjective." The term "value" suggests subjectivity; hence it may be well avoided. The norms are strivings in the direction of the unconditionally valid and the unconditionally real. The word "value" accents the reference to the subject, a secondary characteristic of the norm. Spirit is primarily validity, truth, norm. There are numerous *values*—biological values, psychological values, economic values, and so on. Spiritual values, however, are oriented to the Unconditioned. Without this qualification the definition of spirit as value is misleading.

The accent on direction toward the Unconditioned is apparent also in Tillich's view of the central or characteristic concept of the cultural sciences, the concept of meaning. In the sciences of thought, the concepts of "form" and "construction" are characteristic; in the empirical sciences, the concept of Gestalt. In whatever sphere it appears, the Gestalt is related to other realities; it absorbs or penetrates them to form a whole. In the pre-spiritual *Gestalten* this process is accomplished immediately and is subject to the structural laws of the empirical sciences. But in the spirit-bearing Gestalt the claim of the Unconditioned supervenes. The relationships are raised from the sphere of existence to that of *meaning*. The meaning inherent in all the forms of existence is realized in the spiritual act. All existence is subject to the law of the unconditioned form, but only in spirit is the Unconditioned grasped as unconditioned, as validity. In the spiritual act the meaning of existence fulfills itself.[75]

Now, the fulfillment of meaning requires a certain unity of spiritual acts. This unity is called a "system." A system is a unique, creative perception of meaning. "It is not a thought-form about which propositions could be made and it is not an existential form about which laws could be formulated. It is a position that has no other existential ground than the spiritual

[75] The similarity to the Hegelian conception of the unfolding of the absolute idea is striking, but it must be recalled from our discussion in Chapter II that Tillich repudiates not only the idea of *Entfaltung* but also the idea that man realizes the absolute. As we shall see in the next chapter, the attempt or the claim to realize the absolute is characterized as "demonic."

act by which it is posited."[76] Explicitly or implicitly, every statement set forth by cultural science is directed toward the system,
and methodologically the endeavor of cultural science is ever
the forming of a system. The concept of meaning is therefore also
a concept of system. Thus the establishment of norms is the attempt to subject creation to the unity of a valid principle.

The meaning-system rests upon the tension between two elements, namely, the principle of meaning and the material in
which meaning is expressed, and through these it is directed toward norms. (Here is the Fichtean pattern again.) Accordingly,
the cultural sciences in each of the areas require the three divisions mentioned earlier: the theory of the principles of meaning,
the theory of the material of meaning, and the theory of the
normative system of meanings. The last-named discipline requires as a prerequisite the first two. The first is the task of
philosophy, the second is the task of the history of thought, and
the third is the task of forming a normative meaning-system
(systematics). We shall discuss these disciplines presently, but
first we must take into account Tillich's classifications of types of
meaning.

In every spiritual act the orientation is toward the unconditioned meaning. Yet one may concentrate attention upon the
forms or upon the import: if upon the forms, the attitude is
autonomous; if upon the import, the attitude is theonomous. On
the basis of this twofold distinction, the cultural sciences have
the task of positing norms for the giving of meaning in accordance with the autonomous or the theonomous attitude. The
construction of the system is decisively determined by this distinction.

The contrast between the autonomous and the theonomous attitude
is directly effective only in those spiritual functions that are directed
toward the Unconditioned, that is, in metaphysics and ethics. There
are autonomous metaphysics and autonomous ethics, and theonomous
metaphysics and theonomous ethics. In other areas of meaning,
on the other hand, this distinction is effective only insofar as these
domains are dependent upon metaphysics and ethics. Considered in
themselves they are always autonomous, that is, they are always
directed toward the valid forms. Therefore no analogous theonomous
forms correspond to autonomous science, aesthetics, jurisprudence,
political science, etc. Consequently, we develop the system of the
cultural sciences within the autonomous sphere and then examine

[76] *Das System der Wissenschaften,* p. 102.

the influence of the theonomous attitude upon the individual areas of meaning.[77]

The presupposition of the distinction and the relation between autonomy and theonomy is the assumption that religion is not one sphere of meaning alongside others but an attitude in all spheres.

The principles for the arrangement of the cultural sciences have now been suggested. The first is the theory of the *elements* of every cultural science: philosophy (the principle of meaning), the history of thought, and the systematic classification of norms. The second is the twofold character of the spiritual *attitude:* autonomy and theonomy. In the center of the arrangement, however, stands the grouping of the spiritual domains and the cultural sciences corresponding to them. Only in these *objects* of the cultural sciences do the *elements* and the spiritual *attitudes* receive their content.

The grouping of the various areas corresponds, of course, to the functions of the spirit-bearing *Gestalten.* As a consequence, the attempt has been made by some thinkers to classify the spiritual domains in accord with the capacities of the soul—for example, thought, volition, and feeling. This tripartite arrangement is implicit in Kant's philosophy. But such an arrangement cannot be carried out because the grouping of the psychic functions is quite uncertain. Moreover, it is difficult to assign special domains to the psychic functions, especially as regards art and religion. Furthermore, as has been pointed out, *all* the psychic capacities take part in every spiritual act.

A preferable principle of classification is to be found in the meaning-fulfilling acts of every spirit-bearing Gestalt. The Gestalt may either assimilate reality in a theoretical thought-determination or project itself into reality in the realization of a meaningful existential relation. In the first case it acts theoretically, in the second case, practically. "The division of the subjects of the cultural sciences into a theoretical and a practical series rests on the fundamental act of the spirit-bearing Gestalt in its duality: the relating of itself to the universality of thought and of being."[78]

Within each of these series, the theoretical and the practical,

[77] *Ibid.,* p. 106. In connection with the reference here to ethics it should be observed that it is defined as "the science of ethos, i.e., of the active realization of the Unconditioned," a paradoxical concept, just as it is in the sphere of knowledge of the Unconditioned, *Ibid.,* pp. 145-46.

[78] *Ibid.,* p. 108.

another type of classification is possible. The spiritual act may be directed toward the individual form and the individual existence; or it may be directed toward the Unconditioned, which underlies all individual forms and existences. The latter, being the foundation of the individual meaning-fulfillment, is called a foundation-establishing or supporting function, and the former is called a supported function. Supported functions may again be classified in a twofold way. They may be directed toward the forms in which the theoretical and practical relationships present themselves, or toward the import which these forms express. This distinction applies to the theoretical as well as to the practical sphere. It corresponds to the distinction between autonomy and theonomy.

From these principles is derived the following arrangement of the areas of meaning:

In the theoretical sphere the supported function, determined as to its form, is *Epistemology*, the supported function, determined as to its import, is *Aesthetics*, while the supporting function of both is *Metaphysics*.

In the practical sphere the supported function, determined as to its form, is *Jurisprudence*, the supported function determined as to it import is *Political Science*, while the supporting function of both is *Ethics*.[79]

These definitions and distinctions cannot be discussed further here, nor can the treatment of the various domains of meaning. It must suffice to say that many penetrating and fruitful suggestions are made in the compact section of the book dealing with these sciences.[80] Indeed, one may find here precise formulations of the meanings of many concepts employed in Tillich's later writings concerning both the theoretical and the practical spheres. We now bring our exposition to a close by discussing the more comprehensive concerns of philosophy, metaphysics, and theology.[81]

[79] *Ibid.*, p. 108.

[80] We have discussed some of this material in the previous chapter, especially material dealing with art and technology and community.

[81] Among the many aspects of methodology which we have omitted, the following should be at least mentioned. The differences between description, understanding, and construction figure in the classification of the sciences with respect to the goal of knowledge—the formation of concepts. The differences between self-evidence, probability, and conviction are taken into account in classification according to degrees of knowledge. Quantity and quality also figure in the classification according to types of knowledge. Differences in the latter respect affect differences in connec-

Philosophy is the theory of the principles of meaning, that is, of the meaning-giving functions and categories. The functions are those intellectual acts by which the independent areas of meaning are demarcated; the categories are the forms by which objects are constituted within the areas of meaning. Other tasks have been given to philosophy during its history, but it is for Tillich's purpose deemed advisable to assign them to other, specialized disciplines. The functions may be treated in general or they may be treated in relation to particular areas. The general treatment is called philosophy. The particular treatment deals with the cultural sciences representing the supported functions and presents a theory of the principle of meaning of science as philosophy of science, of art as philosophy of art, of law as philosophy of law, and so on. Every area of meaning possesses its own categories; there are epistemological, aesthetic, juridical, social-ethical, and metaphysical categories. There are also the theonomous and the autonomous categories. When philosophy achieves its highest function it becomes theonomous; it has the task of establishing the relation between theonomy and autonomy, both in general and with respect to the particular meaning-functions and categories. The highest task of theonomous philosophy is to assert its independence and show its unity with autonomous philosophy. The less it succeeds in this, the more it works within the cultural conflict and the more it becomes a philosophy of a special function. For example, it may become philosophy of religion as opposed to philosophy of culture. Philosophy of religion is frequently only an expression of a conflict between autonomy and theonomy. Religion is then conceived as one function among others, and this leads either to the rational dissolution of religion or the heteronomous destruction of culture. Philosophy of religion has a right to exist only as a theonomous theory of the principle of meaning, which does not stand beside or above autonomy, but rather furnishes it with the *one* right theory of the principle of meaning. The ultimate goal of philosophy of religion is self-annihilation in favor of a theonomous philosophy that carries autonomy within itself as an equally justified element. In any event, philosophy—or philosophy of religion—has the task of dealing with the theory of the principle of meaning, and to this end it employs the metalogical method already described.

The materials of meaning are found in the concrete reali-

tion with the theory of causation. In different types of Gestalt, for example, equivalent causality and productive causality come into play in varying combinations.

ties of history. Indeed, history may be described as the locus of individual-creative fulfillments of meaning. Only from history can the new creations be born. Every spirit-bearing Gestalt, the psychological as well as the social Gestalt, is determined with regard to its creative possibilities by the historical point of view which it assumes. In cultural history the material is seen from the viewpoint of the principle of meaning apart from interest in spatio-temporal relations. On the basis of the understanding of the materials of meaning found in cultural history, the theory of norms (systematics) is developed. In other words, cultural history is pursued in the service of systematic classification, in the service, that is, of the theory of norms. But the three disciplines—theory of meaning-principle, theory of the material of meaning, and theory of the norms of meaning—are interdependent. It would be wrong to say that philosophy is rational, cultural history is empirical, and the theory of norms is individual and creative, with the assumption that they are to be neatly divided. All three are creative, or, to put it in other words, cultural science is creative, but in philosophy it is more "critical," in cultural history more receptive, and in systematic classification of norms more productive. We have now discussed the first two of these disciplines. Before taking up the problem of the concrete theory of norms (systematics) we should give some attention to metaphysics

It will be recalled that spiritual acts are classified as theoretical and practical. Tillich deals in detail with the whole series of theoretical and practical sciences. Of primary concern to us are the theoretical sciences. In the previous chapter and at the beginning of the present chapter we have given some indication of his views on the supported functions, aesthetics and epistemology. We shall discuss now the supporting function of these disciplines —metaphysics.

As a theory concerned with the supporting function, metaphysics has the task of "demonstrating" that the direction of consciousness toward the Unconditioned is a necessary function constituting the meaning-reality.

It has to show that the prius of each individual grasping of meaning is the unconditioned meaning itself, that the prius of each meaning-form is the direction toward the unconditioned form, and finally that the prius of each meaning-import is the unconditioned import. Thus the concept of the Unconditioned stands in the center of metaphysics. Metaphysics is the will to grasp the Unconditioned.[82]

[82] *Das System der Wissenschaften*, p. 130.

When Tillich says that metaphysics demonstrates that direction toward the Unconditioned is a necessary function, he does not mean that it proves the existence of the Unconditioned. As indicated earlier, the question whether the Unconditioned "exists" is a nonsense question, for the category of existence here is irrelevant, and besides, the Unconditioned is presupposed as a meaning-relationship when the question is asked. Metaphysics grasps this meaning-relationship without reference to the supported functions, epistemology and aesthetics, and it should not be confused with them. It is an independent bestowal of meaning that has nothing directly to do with the scientific or aesthetic apprehension of the world.[83]

This independence of metaphysics presents its characteristic problem of expression. It has no other means of expression at its disposal than those which scientific and aesthetic apprehension offer. The same thing holds for ethos, the supporting function in the practical cultural sciences. Here we find the best example, in the theoretical sphere, of the tension between autonomy and theonomy. This tension, as we have seen, is grounded in the dialectic of thought and existence. The autonomous spiritual attitude is directed toward the validity of the form, that is, toward thought. The theonomous spiritual attitude is directed toward the import. Both directions are possible in all functions of meaning and cannot be separated from each other for the forming of independent meaning-functions. They carry the dialectical tension in which the supporting and the supported spheres of meaning stand to each other and which expresses itself in the mutual relationship of these two. Now, the point is that the supporting meaning-functions require a form of expression. Since the Unconditioned can never be immediately apprehended or realized—and since it does not "exist"—there cannot be for the supporting meaning-functions, metaphysics and ethos, any forms of their own in which they can immediately express the Unconditioned. Metaphysics must utilize the forms of expression of scientific and aesthetic perception. Likewise, if ethos seeks to realize the Unconditioned, it can do so only in conditioned practical efforts at shaping existence, in rational forms

[83] This does not mean that metaphysics has no connection with science. Wherever the existential element manifests itself over against the rational forms, impulses to metaphysics are given. Kant is therefore right in refusing to classify metaphysics as a science, but he is wrong when this refusal becomes an absolute rejection. "No 'spiritual' attitude can exist without metaphysics." (*Ibid.*, p. 129.)

of law and community. Hence, metaphysics and ethos make use of the conditioned, supported forms, but they use them symbolically—they "intend" the Unconditioned. In their direction toward the Unconditioned they transcend the finite forms: the Unconditioned can never, properly speaking, be drawn directly into the sphere of the conditioned.

For the metaphysics of belief-ful realism, the Unconditioned can neither become an object of theoretical knowledge beside other objects nor be realized as a concrete reality through the shaping of finite existential relations. Therefore the conditioned forms can be used as expressions for the unconditioned meaning only in a paradoxical way. Just as belief-ful or self-transcending realism asserts the coincidence of opposites, the paradoxical immanence of the transcendent, so the expression forms of metaphysics and ethos can be interpreted only paradoxically. A corresponding dependence of the supported functions upon the supporting function obtains; where the sense of this dependence is lost, self-sufficient autonomy ensues and opens the way to heteronomy or to the exhaustion of the substance of meaning. Metaphysics itself can travel this devil's toboggan slide; it can become autonomous (secularly rational), or it can become heteronomous, or it can become empty. When it claims "scientific" validity for concepts, it becomes autonomous. When it claims absolute authority for the forms of expression, it becomes heteronomous. When it is concerned only with the forms, it becomes empty; indeed, it is no longer metaphysics. Thus the proper relationship is the maintenance of the tension between theonomy and autonomy, the former not annulling but rather deepening and fulfilling the latter, the latter providing the conditioned forms of, and the inner assent to, the former. But just because of this requirement, metaphysics cannot be a "science." It is an independent theory of the ground of meaning.

On the foundation of the elements of meaning the system of metaphysical symbols is erected. This task presents three main problems.

There are three basic questions that must be confronted by every metaphysics: first, the question of the relation of the Unconditioned to the existential order (*das Seiende*); second, the question of the relation between the Unconditioned and the creative cultural process (*der schöpferische Geistprozess*); third, the question of the unity of meaning between the existential process (*Seinsprozess*) and the cultural process. These three questions, however, are not existential questions (*Seinsfragen*), but questions of meaning (*Sinnfragen*).

Genuine metaphysics is meaning-metaphysics (*Sinnmetaphysik*).—
The first question is answered by ontology (*Seinsmetaphysik oder
Ontologie*). Its task is to show how existence in its totality, as a
universal Gestalt, is a symbol for the unconditional meaning. It
must focus attention, in a constructive and critical manner, on those
aspects of reality which most perfectly express the unconditioned
meaning, the ultimate unity of the elements of meaning. It is not
the task of ontology, accordingly, to discern some "being" (*ein Seiendes*) behind the empirical phenomena; its task is rather to represent
the structure of all being (*den Aufbau alles Seienden*), and its unity,
as the expression of pure meaning.—To the contrast between the
idea of universal Gestalt and the idea of universal history, which we
have encountered in the sphere of the empirical sciences, corresponds
the difference between ontology and the metaphysics of history. The
metaphysics of history is the interpretation of the meaning of the
cultural process from the perspective of the unconditional meaning.
Its task is not to discern some mystical spirit-substance behind history; rather, it is to see the revelation of unconditional meaning in
an interpretation of the meaning of the historical evolution.— Ontology and the metaphysics of history come together in the contemplation of universal evolution (*des universalen Prozesses*), in which
even the contrast between intended meaning and fulfilled meaning is
transcended. Only their unity creates the ultimate, highest symbol for
the Unconditioned, the ideal unity of the elements of meaning, which
is simultaneously the goal and the ground of all being and becoming.
In this metaphysics of the absolute idea the system of metaphysics
reaches its culmination.[84]

Metaphysics could be designated as the theory of the world-view
(*Weltanschauungslehre*). The "world-view" would here denote
the union of the theoretical and the practical stance toward the
Unconditioned of metaphysics and ethics; that is, it would denote
the fundamental act of the spirit (*Geist*). Perhaps it would be
more satisfactory, however, to speak of the "intellectual disposition" (*Geisteshaltung*) in the case of the psychic Gestalt, and of
"intellectual situation" (*Geisteslage*) in the case of a social Gestalt,
when the unity of metaphysics and ethics is intended.[85]

Reminding us that the concepts employed by metaphysics are
symbol-concepts and that they are therefore to be interpreted
paradoxically, Tillich sums up his position by saying:

The goal of metaphysical knowledge is the unity of the concept
of being and the concept of meaning; that is, a system that is at the
same time a universal Gestalt and a universal framework of meaning. The approach of metaphysical knowledge is the unity of the ap-

[84] *Ibid.*, p. 132.
[85] *Ibid.*, pp. 132-33.

prehension of form and import, of the scientific and the aesthetic
view, of the perception of being and the understanding of meaning.
The method of metaphysical knowledge is the contemplation of the
unconditioned import in the conditioned forms, which in the philosophy of the Renaissance was designated as the contemplation of the
coincidentia oppositorum. . . . Thus concepts like "intellectual contemplation," "pure intuition," the grasping of the "absolute identity"
and of the "paradox", etc. are expressions for the method of coincidence.[86]

In short, we have arrived again at the principal assumption of
metalogic, the paradoxical immanence of the transcendent.

Owing to the symbolic character of metaphysical concepts,
metaphysics is described as "the mythical will to apprehend the
Unconditioned."[87] Indeed, the most immediate form of theonomous apprehension is the formation of myths, which precedes the
emergence of autonomous science. The most rational form is
metaphysics. It uses the symbols which an autonomous science
transmits to it. But in every myth, so long as it is more than
mere fantasy, there resides also an autonomous element, a will
to conceptual apprehension of being and meaning; and in every
metaphysics, so long as it is more than a theory of pure form,
there resides a "mythical" theonomous element—"the mythical
will to apprehend the Unconditioned." Myth and metaphysics
stand therefore under the same dialectic as being and thinking,
as import and form. The synthesis of the two may take various
forms. It may be a heteronomous dogma. But the more desirable
synthesis produces a metaphysical symbolism creatively adapted
on the one hand to the theonomous attitude and on the other
to the autonomous concept-material. Where this synthesis is successful we have theonomous metaphysics—the metaphysics that
imbues autonomous forms with a theonomous attitude.

Theonomous systematic theology performs its function also
at the point of tension between autonomy and theonomy and at
the point of the ever incipient incursion of heteronomy. Like
metaphysics, then, theology is directed toward the Unconditioned, and its role is not restricted to one area. In their orientation to the Unconditioned, metaphysics and theology find a
common bond. But, unlike metaphysics, theology draws its forms
in the first instance directly from a living community—a church.

[86] *Das System der Wissenschaften,* p. 133.

[87] This extended meaning of the term "myth" is discussed at length
in the essay on "The Religious Symbol," *Religiöse Verwirklichung,* 2nd ed.
(Berlin: Furche, 1930), pp. 88-109. For English translation see *Journal of
Liberal Religion,* II (1940), 13-33, and *Daedalus,* 87, No. 3 (1958), 3-21.

Nevertheless, as in metaphysics, the truth question is decisive, for theology is also directed toward the universal, the unconditionally valid.

The dominant position of theology in the Middle Ages is to be understood in terms of the relationship between autonomous and theonomous disciplines. Theology was identical with theonomous systematics, and until the high Middle Ages it continued to include autonomy. Only with the decline of the medieval spirit did this unity disintegrate. Theonomy became heteronomous while autonomy became rational. Theology became a special science alongside which the autonomous sciences arose. This is the situation, fraught with conflicts, in which theology finds itself up to now. This has become its undoing, for it contradicts its essential nature to be one science alongside other sciences. Consequently, theology is today approached either from a secular-rational or from a religious-heteronomous perspective. The secular-rational conception of theology makes of the latter the science of religion, of Christianity, of faith. This conception is based on the correct insight that God cannot be one object alongside other objects, and that therefore there can be no science of God alongside other sciences. What lies behind the liberal conception of theology is the protest against rational metaphysics, but it becomes evident that within a purely autonomous perspective theology necessarily disappears. The problem cannot be solved by putting some other object in the place of God as the subject of theology; for all other objects are apportioned among the autonomous sciences. Thus theology would have to constitute itself as a cooperative practical effort concerned with problems of religion in general and of Christianity in particular; but in doing so it would cease to exist as an independent science.

Over against this secular-rational type of theology stands its equally false counterpart, heteronomous theology.

The religious-heteronomous approach . . . seeks to retain theology's character as an independent science without having the courage, however, to make it into the theonomous cultural science as such. It attributes absolute significance to the confessional symbols (which originated in a theonomously charged intellectual situation) and thus comes into conflict with the autonomous dynamic in all areas. It clings to its metaphysical orientation and is conscious of itself as the science of God, but it forgets that the metaphysical symbols depend on the concepts and understandings produced by the autonomous cultural process. It thus makes of God one object alongside other objects and cannot arrest the transition to rational metaphysics.

Wherever it reigns it brings about a division of the consciousness between two kinds of truths, both of which lay claim to being valid in the same sense. This division would utterly disrupt the unity of the life of the mind if no permanent escapes could be found: the sacrifice of autonomy in the name of religious asceticism within Catholicism, the relegation of religion to the personal and practical sphere in the Anglo-American world, the concealment of the contradiction through the arts of theological apologetics within Lutheranism. But since all these means are inadequate, in the end, the dissolution of theology into a secular-rational discipline always ensues.

Theology is the theory of the theonomous norms of meaning. Only as such can it be justified. The truth of theology is dependent on the degree to which it ceases to be an independent discipline and, in union with autonomous systematics, constitutes the normative cultural science.[88]

To be sure, theology must take historical considerations into account. But it ought not to be viewed as simply an empirical science. Historical theology is not merely philology and history. It goes beyond these in a twofold direction: it is on the one hand theonomous intellectual history and on the other normative exegesis. As theonomous intellectual history it cannot limit itself to a particular religion or even to religion in general. It must take into account "the entire process of the actualization of spirit."

As normative exegesis, theology resembles the theory of law. It has a creatively individual character that is partially determined by its historical rootage, and on the basis of its inheritance it co-creates norms. Theology works out from a concrete intellectual process and is bound to the classical symbols (creeds) in which the theonomous conviction has found its expression. In this respect, theology has a twofold task: "to present the original spirit of the religious documents and to transmit this spirit to the present-day mentality." There are certain pitfalls to be encountered here: for example, the allegorizing of the substance of the documents and the absolutizing of the precise formulations of the documents. Normative exegesis in the proper sense is neither of these things. It aims to effect a living relationship with the religious intention of the document of revelation.

This connection of theology with historical symbols and documents is the basis for one of its distinguishing features: it is confessional.

Just as law is supported by the state as the community establishing justice, so religion is supported by the church as the symbol-creating

[88] *Das System der Wissenschaften,* pp. 150-51.

community. From this comes the concrete, confessional character of theology which would not be lacking even if the whole of humanity were bound together in one confession. Even then theology would be individually creative, that is, confessional. Just as little as the theory of law is permitted to seek a rational law of nature, just so little is theology permitted to seek a rational religion of reason. It can derive its normative system only from the concrete norms of the living confessions.[89]

The confessional character of theology does not, however, constitute an objection to its scientific character. The confessional element is essentially connected with theology as a normative cultural science, but the truth in the confessions is the thing that is of decisive importance. The confessions are not accepted properly if they are received in a heteronomous fashion. If the confessions were accepted merely on authority, the systematic theologian could aim only to present the symbols in an "orthodox" fashion.[90] In theonomous systematics the theologian not only exercises autonomy in the selection of symbols but also interprets the norms derived from the confessions, in a figurative, paradoxical sense. It is in this sense that theology is confessional.

Accordingly, systematic theology is directed always toward the universal. Even though it achieves its purpose in an individually creative way—especially because of its dependence upon the confessional symbols—it need not thereby become the less universal.

Nor does theology docilely accept the old symbols. It aims to be creative, maintaining the tension between autonomy and theonomy. When this tension is effective, theology co-operates in the formation and transformation of symbols. It can never stop doing this so long as there are theonomously imbued communities.

The unity and mutuality between theonomy and autonomy obtains in the relation between theology and the supporting and supported functions of the theoretical and the practical sciences. The dialectic of theonomy and autonomy is operative in all functions of meaning.

This dialectic manifests itself differently, however, in the supporting functions from the way it operates in the supported functions.

[89] *Ibid.*, p. 152.
[90] Hans von Soden, in asserting that the decisive character of the confession is "law" and not "truth," is only describing the heteronomous type of theology, which Tillich repudiates. ("Kirchentheologie und Kulturtheologie," *Zeitschrift für Theologie und Kirche*, II [1921], 473 ff.)

In the supporting functions the Unconditioned is supposed to be conceived and realized as the Unconditioned, in the supported functions the conditioned forms are supposed to achieve the fulfilment of meaning in their independence and validity. From this it follows that a direct theonomous intention is possible only in the supporting spheres of meaning, and a direct autonomous intention is possible only in the supported spheres of meaning. In the first case autonomy becomes operative only indirectly, in the way of symbol selection. In the second case theonomy becomes operative only indirectly, in the way of grasping the form. There is therefore an immediate expression of theonomy only in metaphysics and ethics.[91]

The important differences between theology's relation to the theoretical and to the practical disciplines should be noted here. In theology theonomous metaphysics is usually treated as dogmatics. The word "dogmatics" indicates that the symbols that find application in it are not subjectively selected. They are rather the normative expression of a community. Again the problem is to maintain the tension and unity between theonomy and autonomy. Having already touched upon this relationship between theology and metaphysics, we turn therefore to a consideration of the relation between theology and the supported theoretical functions—epistemology and aesthetics.

As suggested in the quotation above, theonomy can be operative only in an indirect fashion in the supported functions. And even then it can be concerned with them only in their character as expression and not in their character as validity. Hence there can be no theonomous epistemology or aesthetics; there can be only a theonomous and an autonomous attitude here. Theology can show which attitudes of epistemology and aesthetics correspond to theonomy and which concepts and outlooks come into consideration for a theonomous formation of symbols. But it cannot itself create material in the supported spheres. If theology attempts to do so, it will become heteronomous and will destroy the supported spheres of meaning.

The ideal demand would be that on the basis of a theonomous attitude in the supported functions entire creations in epistemology and aesthetics could serve immediately the formation of symbols in a theonomous metaphysics. But this ideal is unattainable in consequence of the infinity of the rational process.[92]

[91] *Das System der Wissenschaften*, p. 153. It should be recalled that metaphysics is the supporting function in the theoretical disciplines (epistemology and aesthetics) and that ethics (as ethos) is the supporting function in the practical disciplines (jurisprudence and political science).

[92] *Ibid.*, p. 155.

By constant reference to this ideal, theology should seek to avoid the absolutizing of the forms of the church community. This applies not only to doctrinal matters (as referred to above) but also to the practical disciplines, for example, liturgics, a descipline involving artistic considerations. Very frequently in Protestant circles liturgics is regarded as a theory of the specifically ecclesiastical forms of devotion. In consequence it becomes a heteronomous discipline and is then assigned to practical theology. Assignment of liturgics to practical theology, however, should hold only for its pedagogical, social-technical side, but in no way for its basic principles, which belong to systematic theology. "The theory of the forms of devotion is the radiation of theonomous metaphysics into the artistic and scientific conception of the world."[93]

Essentially the same relations should obtain between theology and ethics as between theology and metaphysics: if metaphysics is the supporting function in the theoretical cultural disciplines, ethics (or ethos) is the supporting function in the practical cultural disciplines. As pointed out in the previous chapter, theological ethics as a discipline alongside philosophical ethics presupposes a heteronomous ethics and results in a splitting of the consciousness and in a theory of double truth. This conflict can be overcome "only through uniting theonomous intention and autonomous forms of expression in a theonomous ethos."

The relation between myth and metaphysics finds its analogue in theonomous ethics. Just as myth precedes the rise of a rational science, so the cultus precedes the rise of a rational consciousness of law and community. On the other hand, just as metaphysics utilizes the rational forms of science for a theonomous symbolism, so ethics employs the rational forms of law and community for the theory of piety. Again we see the dialectic between autonomy and theonomy. Again, heteronomy and autonomy are to be avoided. Cultus and ethos should find their synthesis in a theonomous ethos. That is, piety finds its "meaningful fulfillment only in the unity of theonomous intention and autonomous forms of realization." Neither the heteronomy of ecclesiastical cultus nor the autonomy of community forms is to be left undisturbed. Moreover, even the forms adopted theonomously are interpreted as symbols and not as unconditioned forms. So much for Tillich's treatment of the relation between theology and the supporting practical function.

[93] *Ibid.* For further discussion of this point, see the treatment of the problems of religious art in the preceding chapter.

The same principles obtain in the discussion of the relation between theology and the supported practical functions (jurisprudence and political science) as we have observed in the relation between theology and the supported theoretical functions (epistemology and aesthetics). There can be, properly speaking, no theonomous jurisprudence and political science; there can be only a theonomous ethos informing jurisprudence and political science. In these supported functions the intention is necessarily autonomous—that is, it is directed to the autonomous forms. Theology can affect these disciplines only indirectly by influencing the attitude. Thus it cannot properly absolutize any particular forms, nor can it properly claim to draw its forms from any exclusive, holy sphere. Church law is either secular law for a spiritual community of conspicuous social significance or the symbol for ideal justice in all communities. Church law in the sense of a theonomous theory of law for a special religious community would lead to heteronomy.

The assertion that religion cannot properly draw its forms from an exclusive, holy sphere would seem to be contradicted by the existence of holy personalities and communities. Rightly understood, however, holy personalities and communities are by intention directed toward the Unconditioned, and they achieve realization in conditioned forms. But there can be no unconditioned community or personality.[94] Nor can there be a science of the Unconditioned.

Theology is concerned with a theonomous *attitude* prevailing in these areas; it selects from the forms of law and community those which are significant for the realization of a theonomous ethos. Hence it cannot properly limit itself to a consideration of the specifically ecclesiastical forms.

Rather, it seeks out, in all communal and legal relationships, those forms which are supported by the theonomous ethos. It thus shows the radiation of the theonomous ethos in the entire sphere of meaningful existential relations. Forms cannot, however, be created in these by theology itself. For theonomy can affect the law and the community only through the ethos.[95]

Any other course leads in the direction of heteronomy.

By definition theology enters and performs its function at the

---

[94] This view will have a marked influence upon Tillich's Christology and upon his conception of the kingdom of God. These matters, however, lie beyond the scope of our discussion.

[95] *Das System der Wissenschaften,* p. 158.

point where theonomy and autonomy stand in tension, always fending off heteronomy. The tension between theonomy and autonomy in the sphere of the practical functions, as elsewhere, can be resolved only by recognizing the symbolic, paradoxical character of the religious community, and not by the creation of a theonomous law but rather by bringing the theonomous ethos to bear upon autonomous law. But, as in the theoretical sphere, theology does not look for perfect realization.

Here also the ideal condition would be that all forms of community and personality would be imbued with theonomous import to such a degree that they could appear immediately as forms of realization for a theonomous ethos. But this ideal lies also in the infinite.[96]

From the foregoing description of the function of theology as theonomous ethos we see that theological ethics as often interpreted is repudiated. Any other course, Tillich believes, will lead to the theory of double truth and double morality. In conformity with the above exposition, Tillich assigns to systematic theology the task of presenting the general principles of a theonomous ethos on the border between the theory of the cultus-community and an autonomous theory of law and community. The really practical material of practical theology as traditionally understood is assigned to the disciplines of psychological and sociological technique.

Summarizing the whole discussion of theology we may now define its disciplines in this fashion: Systematic theology as a theonomous theory of the norms of meaning embraces theonomous metaphysics oriented to the living confessions (dogmatics), theonomous ethics or ethos (the theory of piety), the theory of the forms of devotion (liturgics), and the theory of the cultus-community; add to these disciplines the theonomous theory of the principles of meaning (philosophy or philosophy of religion) and the theonomous theory of the material of meaning (historical theology and theonomous cultural history); all together these disciplines constitute the theonomous cultural science of theology.

This brings to a conclusion the exposition of Tillich's conception of systematic theology as well as the exposition of his system of the sciences. We consider now the general significance of the system in its philosophical and theological aspects.

First it should be noted that we have here given only an outline of a book that is itself only an outline.[97] Moreover, a multi-

---

[96] *Ibid.*, p. 157.

[97] Philosophy of history, for example, which looms large in Tillich's other writings, is in this volume given only casual attention.

tude of considerations which have been presented in the book have not been mentioned. Every page contains penetrating observations on the methods and the objects of science, and many refinements of the general philosophical position are presented. It should be noted also that our principal interest in discussing Tillich's system of the sciences is of a philosophical and theological character. Hence we shall not be concerned here with the criticism of the details of the classification of the sciences. In confining our attention to the philosophical and theological considerations we assume that the volume under discussion has its primary significance in these areas. Indeed, so far as the present writer can discover, the same assumption is made by all the critiques of this work which have been published. No scholar primarily concerned with the comprehensive problem of the system of the sciences seems to have published a discussion of the volume.

No doubt one reason for the small amount of attention given to the book by students of the system of the sciences is the fact that Tillich himself devotes very little attention to other specific attempts at systematization. He contents himself primarily with general, brief comments on other types of system.

So far as the Anglo-American world of scholarship is concerned, Tillich's system, where known at all, is probably given scant attention because of what would be called its highly speculative character. The author explicitly renounces a psychological approach to the discovery of the principle of classification. "The pure science of knowing," he says, "is in question, regardless of how it comes into existence or where it exists." Hence he is concerned only with "the purely abstract meaning of that which is contained in the essence of the knowing process (*Wissen*)."[98] The same procedure is adopted for the understanding of the concept of being. "All ideas of a particular existing thing or of an existing substance are to be excluded."[99] Such ideas are, in Tillich's view, already contents of knowing. On these epistemological presuppositions Tillich rests his whole system, and, as we have already indicated, he therefore makes the principle of his system of the sciences "the idea of knowledge" as suggested by Fichte. In short, Tillich's approach is not in accord with the empirical traditions of Anglo-American philosophy of science. Instead, it reflects the idealistic tradition as supplemented by phenomenology and qualified by what he calls "belief-ful" realism. He

[98] *Das System der Wissenschaften*, p. 5.
[99] *Ibid.*

"intuits" the nature of thought and being and thus arrives at a speculative conception of the principle of classification. Thus he does not take into account the prevalent empirical methods of the sciences. It is true that much so-called empirical "investigation" of the nature of thought and being is itself speculative in its presuppositions. Insofar as Tillich's presentation makes one aware of the speculative character of any approach to the subject it serves a good purpose. But insofar as it does not concern itself with empirical investigation and confirmation it elicits inevitably the charge of being sheer assertion and speculation.

But even as a speculative effort Tillich's presentation leaves something to be desired, for he does not provide careful and extensive definitions of his central concepts—"the knowing act" and "being" or "reality." We have pointed out already the great variety of phrases and contexts in which he uses the term "act." A precise definition of "act" would alone indicate the common element that pervades these many varieties of "act." One wonders, for example, whether "the spiritual act" is involved when a thought-form is "found," when a law is "discovered," when a technical form is "invented," and when a cultural norm is "created." The basic "acts" in the cultural sciences would seem to be the apprehension of the unconditionally valid and the unconditionally real, and the creation or fulfillment of spiritual meaning. The use of the word, of course, immediately suggests the Husserlian terminology, but, although Tillich frequently criticizes Husserl, he does not indicate explicitly the connotation of his term "act" in comparison with, and in contrast to, the connotations of Husserl's term. Hence the reader does not discover the relation between a "spiritual act" and a perception, a conception, an intuition, and the like. Nor does he learn the relation between a Tillichian "spiritual act" and a Husserlian "intentional experience." Thus Tillich's concept of the "spiritual act" appears to be not only a speculative concept but also a somewhat vague one.[100]

[100] Cf. August Dell, "Der Charakter der Theologie in Tillichs *System der Wissenschaften,*" *Theologische Blätter,* II (1923), 242. Certainly, Robert Winkler is wrong when he speaks of Tillich as providing a fusion of phenomenological method with the theology of religious experience. Tillich's general method of examining and shaping concepts does show indebtedness to phenomenology, but his *Sachlichkeit* aims to look through the particularity of concrete reality to the Unconditioned and not to Husserlian essences; moreover, he generally exhibits a studied avoidance of the term "religious experience." For Winkler's discussion, see his article "Die Theologie des Philosophen Tillich in seinem Buch *Religiöse Verwirklichung,*" *Christentum und Wissenschaft,* VI (1930), 212-20.

The same ambiguity and lack of clarity attach to the correlative concept "being." As Kurt Leese points out, the "being" of the empirical sciences and the "being" of the cultural sciences "run into each other without mediation" and without one's learning the "how" of the transition.[101] Especially difficult is it to understand the relation between being as an ontological structure and the Unconditioned as the meaning or import of being. A clarification of this relationship would seem to be most desirable for the understanding of a philosophy that purports to be "existential" and yet finds its ultimate orientation "beyond being and freedom." Tillich only asserts that all existence is subject to the law of the unconditioned form (another concept not clearly defined) and that the Unconditioned is grasped as unconditioned only in the spiritual act. It is curious that a philosopher so apt at developing architectonic structures should leave the reader in a state of confusion as to the precise character and status of the various levels of reality and experience, and as to their relationship to the Unconditioned, the ultimate orientation.

In connection with the relation between the two things just discussed—between the spiritual act and that which is "intended" in it—another source of confusion in Tillich's exposition should be mentioned. On the one hand, he seems to accept the idealistic principle of the identity of thought and being. On the other hand, he insists that there is an infinite tension between thought and being. As we have indicated earlier, he goes even so far as to assert that the thought-forms are infinitely remote from being. Being, he says, is the abyss of cognition. True, he has repeatedly criticized idealism because of its static, sham dialectic and its tendency to insulate itself from the ground and abyss of being. Yet these criticisms do not explain the seeming contradiction referred to.

The greatest confusion attaches perhaps to the most characteristic of all Tillich's concepts—"the Unconditioned." As we have pointed out in the probably oversimplified synthetic definition of this concept set forth in Chapter II, the idea of the Unconditioned must be understood in relation to Tillich's conceptions of being, truth, and value, in connection with which it serves as a ground and "qualification" and also as a limiting concept. The concept is used also as a philosophical-religious synonym for the holy. But Tillich has not given a definitive statement concerning

[101] Leese, "Das System der Wissenschaften," p. 322.

these denotations and connotations of the concept. Without clarity in these matters the reader is uncertain not only with respect to the several ingredients of the concept but also with respect to the criteria by which its validity is to be judged.

The lack of clarity in definition respecting the relation between the Unconditioned and the conditioned order becomes especially confusing in Tillich's discussion of symbols. He asserts that there is something in every genuine symbol which is appropriate, but he says also that the genuine symbol carries a protest against itself by pointing to the Unconditioned. Thus the symbol is accepted paradoxically as affirming and still not adequately representing the Unconditioned. Yet the appropriateness of the symbol does not depend solely upon its pointing beyond itself. It depends in addition upon some intrinsic fitness of the form itself. The symbol is drawn from the conditioned order and therefore serves to enhance some aspect of that order. Now, an infinite number of autonomous forms present themselves for the "activity" of symbol-formation on the part of the theonomously imbued metaphysician or the theonomously imbued community. Conceivably, anything and everything could be a candidate for symbolization. Therefore the questions arise: What is the principle of selection? Among an infinite number of possibilities, which forms are the more appropriate? When opposite symbols are presented, how does one choose between them? Does the appropriateness of the symbol depend upon the soundness of the "spiritual act"? If so, how does one judge this soundness? Or is this also a matter of "phenomenological intuition"? For the answers to these questions the theologian would presumably find some light and leading in the "living" confessions. Yet, according to Tillich the theologian stands on a border between the confessions of a community and the newly emerging forms of the autonomous order. Moreover, there are many confessions and many interpretations of the spirit of the original documents to choose from. Even here, then, a question arises: What principle of selection determines the symbol-formations of the theologian?

This brings us to a consideration of Tillich's conception of the relation between theology and the "living confessions," and of his conception of the relation between theology and the other cultural sciences. Here we are not directly concerned with Tillich's own theological position. The discussion of his theological writings lies beyond the scope of our present study. The way in which he as a theologian would bring together motifs from what he calls kerygmatic theology and philosophical theology is treated at length in his later writings.[102]

We must now, however, raise analogous questions with respect to Tillich's conception of a theonomous ethos. Again we see the tension between theology and philosophy. Tillich has given theology the task of selecting forms that can become symbols of theonomous activity. It is the task of "radiating" theonomy into autonomous forms. Is this "radiation" of theonomy an explicitly Christian theological endeavor?[103] We may readily agree that theonomy is not only in conformity with but even derived from the spirit of the original documents. But we can scarcely agree that theonomy is equivalent to the Christian ethical principle. We must ask here, what is decisive in theology's relation to the practical cultural sciences? Is theonomy or *Agape* determinative? Approaching the issue from the side of autonomy, we may ask: Does the ingression of a theonomous attitude into any autonomous ethical form make it Christian? Does the theologian fulfill his ethical task by simply radiating theonomy? If so, does this mean that a theonomous ethos is equivalent to *Agape*?

These are questions that Tillich does not answer in this book.[104] Instead, he gives the impression that the process of making theonomous an autonomous ethical attitude or form is the theological-ethical task of the theologian. These questions lead on further to the question as to what the positive content of the Unconditioned is, as well as to the question of the relation between philosophy and theology. Insofar as the Unconditioned is interpreted as the unconditioned of value and of truth, it can, of course, be pregnant with content. The question is, however, whether this content is peculiarly Christian. Insofar as the Unconditioned is a symbol for the holy, it is a consuming fire as well as a limiting concept for all *our* moral values. But these

[102] Cf., for example, his article "Philosophy and Theology," *Religion in Life*, X (1941), 21-30. Reprinted in *The Protestant Era*, trans. James L. Adams (Chicago: University of Chicago Press, 1948), pp. 83-93.

[103] The question of the adequacy of Tillich's definition of theonomy we reserve for discussion in the next chapter, which deals with his philosophy of religion.

[104] In recent years Tillich has devoted attention to the concept of love. See his essay "Ethics in a Changing World," *The Protestant Era*, pp. 150-60. See also "Being and Love," in R. N. Anshen, ed., *Moral Principles of Action* (New York: Harper & Brothers, 1952), pp. 661-72. This essay was written in 1943. *Love, Power and Justice* was published in 1954 (New York, London: Oxford University Press) and *Morality and Beyond* in 1963 (New York: Harper & Row).

considerations do not answer the question posed as to the relations between theology and philosophy or between Christian ethics and autonomous ethics. Let it be noted, however, that such queries do not arise for the purely philosophical theologian. Only because Tillich defines theology as somehow bound to the living confessions and as commissioned to discriminate and transmit the spirit of the original documents of revelation do the questions referred to come under discussion. Many a contemporary theologian does not face these questions because he makes no claim to be anything other than a philosophical theologian.

Another comment should be made concerning the place of theology in the system of the sciences. Tillich views this discipline as different from all other disciplines. Though rooted in the living confessions and cognizant of autonomous cultural experience, it is immediately directed toward the Unconditioned. Hence the idea that it is a particular science dealing with a special object is rejected. Yet it is related explicitly only to the cultural sciences; indeed, it is classified as a cultural science, and as such it is defined as the theonomous systematic treatment of the norms of meaning. This formulation is, to be sure, somewhat confusing and it has elicited criticism again and again for its neglect of the being-element.[105] But this criticism is unjustified, for Tillich's concepts of meaning and of spirit presuppose the spheres of thought and being. Meaning has to do with the unconditionally real as well as with the unconditionally valid. More pertinent would be the criticism that theology, which is asserted as a science to be relevant to all other sciences, is not discussed in relation to the empirical sciences. Tillich holds that it may not be properly classified as an empirical science: it is concerned with the metaphysical problem of relatedness to the Unconditioned. Yet metaphysics and theology have to do with ontology. Indeed, Tillich insists that Kant is wrong in denying to metaphysics all scientific character. This ontological problem, nonetheless, is dealt with in his system by a cultural, normative science. On the other hand, the discrimination of the import of being is asserted to be the result of phenomenological intuition. Why then should the empirical order be ruled out when considering the nature of this import, espe-

---

105 Cf., for example, Friedrich Büchsel, "Die Stellung der Theologie im System der Wissenschaften. Eine Auseinandersetzung mit P. Tillichs *System der Wissenschaften*," *Zeitschrift für systematische Theologie*, I (1923-24), 399-411.

cially when the fulfillment of meaning is asserted also to be the fulfillment of being? Tillich would presumably answer that phenomenological intuition is a "spiritual act" and that as such it should be considered in the *Geisteswissenschaften*. This brings us back to the criticisms we have already made concerning Tillich's concept of the "spiritual act." They suggest, indeed, that perhaps the "spiritual act" should itself be brought under observation in the empirical sciences.

Some comments on the general character of Tillich's accomplishment in *The System of the Sciences* will bring this chapter to a close.

Regarding the speculative aspects of Tillich's system it must be conceded that the system presented does not simply fall because of the ambiguities and obscurities pointed out. Nor, for that matter, does the system need to rest solely upon a speculative basis. In fact, many features of the system could be defended by arguments and by the presentation of evidence acceptable to the empiricist. In any event, even if one does not accept Tillich's particular system, still the treatment of the cultural sciences requires nothing less than a speculative orientation, that is, if one is not to forfeit entirely a philosophical approach to the problem of values. Moreover, only a naïve empiricist would suppose that metaphysics can be made into a science, and only a naïve positivist would suppose that he possesses no metaphysics or that his alleged antimetaphysical position is anything more than a definitely metaphysical prejudice.

Something further must be said regarding the system as a whole. Tillich in his Fichtean structure for the system of the sciences has set forth a realistic rather than an idealist interpretation of the data treated by the empirical and cultural sciences, and he has at the same time retained an idealistic conception of logic and mathematics, the sciences of thought. He defends this idealistic conception by asserting that there must be a consonance between the structure of the mind and the structure of reality. One cannot deny this view so long as one recognizes any necessity in the realm of thought or of being. On the other hand, one must recognize that such categories as space and causation have received a variety of interpretations in the history of philosophy and of the sciences, and also that again and again they have been subjected to change at the hands of empirical method. This is true also for the conception of the "laws" of nature, however much previous conceptions of these laws may have appeared to be a necessity of thought or of being. In short, our categories are not "the actual preconditions of things but our modus of interpreting things, and as such, they are held subject to continuous modification."[106] The limitations and the fallibility of the a priori categories deserve to be recognized more than the Fichtean scheme and Tillich's interpretation of it demand.

With respect to Tillich's conceptual apparatus we venture to assert that his definitions and discussions of such concepts as "Gestalt," "space," "time," "spirit," "meaning," "creation," and "theonomy" are among the most original and suggestive in current theological writing. Further, these concepts represent only a part of the impressive corpus of seminal ideas that Tillich has set forth. It should be noted also that no small part of the value of his writings consists in the brilliant characterizations and criticisms of other similar and dissimilar positions. He possesses an uncanny sensitivity to the significant nuances of the great philosophical and theological systems and concepts.

Through his philosophy of the Unconditioned as the qualification of all existence Tillich has given to theology a metaphysical, ontological grounding (which was denied it by Kantianism) without resorting to the objectification and extrapolation of divine beings (which was made impossible by Kantian criticism). Through his doctrines of theonomy and creation he has restored a dynamic element from early Christian and Jewish as well as from *lebensphilosophische* sources and has thus shaken the complacency and "poise" of moralism, rationalism, and idealism. Through his philosophy of meaning he has given theology a comprehensive relevance that it seldom achieves, and he has broken the deadlock between absolutism and relativism. His construction of a system of the sciences is only one of the many ways in which he has made theology come to terms with the far-flung human adventure. And, although it should be observed that he fails to show what direct bearing theology has upon the empirical sciences—and vice versa—his definition of theology not only precludes its being simply one science alongside other sciences (with an "object" alongside other objects) but makes theology an indispensable discipline for any human being that recognizes an ultimate concern.

Hence, even though much that he considers essential will be

[106] F. E. England, *The Validity of Religious Experience* (New York: Harper & Brothers, 1938), p. 254. See also his volume, *Kant's Conception of God* (New York: L. MacVeagh, 1930), chap. V.

viewed by the Anglo-American reader as highly speculative, Tillich has given an original and comprehensive, a valuable and persuasive answer to those widely neglected questions which, as he says,[107] brought him to his task: How is theology possible as a science? How is it related to the other sciences? What is its outstanding method?

[107] *The Interpretation of History,* p. 38.

V

The Philosophy of Religion

The System of the Sciences proposes, as we have seen, an organization of the sciences depending upon a conception of meaning which Tillich had already employed in his treatment of art and in his theology of culture. This philosophy of meaning, as set forth in his theory of the system of the sciences, is related to a neo-Fichtean conception of the relations between thought, existence, and spirit. But, apart from its concern with a philosophy of meaning and apart from the idea that there is a certain identity between thought and existence, this philosophy of Tillich's is not idealistic. It aims rather in a special sense to be realistic. Despite the alleged identity of thought and existence, a gulf is asserted to exist between them. Through his conception of meaning Tillich interprets thought and spirit as manifestations of an infinite and inexhaustible reality which in its ultimate character is referred to as the unconditionally real and the unconditionally valid. This unconditional reality permeates and qualifies the whole of the conditioned order and is discriminated in terms of the correlative conceptions of form and import.

Tillich's conception of meaning is not merely axiological: meaning is the fulfillment of existence in the creativity of the spirit. The spirit-bearing Gestalt in monadological fashion gives expression through creative freedom to a cosmic Gestalt which is characterized by an inner infinity of being. In Tillich's mystical view, the principles of the macrocosm are given in the microcosm. Hence, Tillich's philosophy of meaning is the expression of a philosophy of being, characterized as "belief-ful realism" or "self-transcending realism." Belief-ful realism is the presupposition of Tillich's "Philosophy of Religion," even though the term and its definition were not presented until two years after the publication of this work. We shall, therefore, include some consideration of the philosophy of being in the present chapter on the "Philosophy of Religion." But first we must give our attention to certain formal aspects of Tillich's procedure.

He begins his study by a discussion of the object and the methods of the philosophy of religion. From this he proceeds to the question of the essence of religion: here he defines religion in its relation to the theory of meaning and to the elements of meaning. In discussing these elements of the essence of religion he considers the relations between religion and culture, between faith and "unfaith," between God and the world, between the sacred and the secular, and between the divine and the demonic. He then goes on to a discussion of the intellectual or cultural history of religion. On the basis of this cultural history he develops a "construction" of the history of religion which in turn serves as a preparation for a normative theory of religion. In the concluding section he delineates the religious categories in the theoretical sphere (myth and revelation) and in the practical sphere (the cultus and the religious community).

Inevitably many of the motifs previously referred to reappear here. Other motifs that appear in later writings will also be relevant for consideration. In the present chapter we shall therefore draw upon these other writings for the purpose of expanding some of the concepts treated in "The Philosophy of Religion."

The term *philosophy of religion,* according to Tillich, ordinarily implies a certain tension. On the one hand it suggests that as a *philosophy* it is an autonomous cultural science wholly sufficient unto itself. On the other hand it implies that *religion,* the subject of the philosophy of religion, is a special function alongside other functions and that this function is an independent one. If the former implication is correct, then religion will be dissolved by philosophy. If the latter is correct, then philosophy may have to accept something from religion as "given" and as exempt from radical questioning. In this case, religion would turn out to be a heteronomous function and not properly subject to philosophical discussion. But even when religion is not heteronomous, that is, even when it is theonomous, a tension may still obtain between philosophy and religion—the tension between autonomy and theonomy.

As we have seen, it is precisely the task of theonomous philosophy to establish the relation between theonomy and autonomy. For this reason, Tillich holds that philosophy of religion, understood in this context, is really theonomous philosophy deepening autonomy. It will be recalled, however, that he makes no independent place for philosophy of religion as such in his *System of the Sciences.* Since religion cannot be separated from other functions, philosophy of religion cannot be separated from the general theory of meaning. It is a part of philosophy, the theory of the principles of meaning. On this point we quote again the statement from *The System of the Sciences:*

> Philosophy of religion is legitimate only as a theonomous theory of the principles of meaning, which does not stand beside or above the autonomous sphere but rather furnishes it the *one* right theory of the principle of meaning. The ultimate goal of philosophy of religion is self-annihilation in favor of a theonomous philosophy that carries autonomy within it as an equally justified element.[1]

But in attempting to provide a theory of the principles of meaning, philosophy of religion must, as has been suggested, encounter resistance. The stronger, the purer, the more original a religion is, the more emphatically it claims to be exempt from all ordinary structures of ideas. Such tension poses the basic problem of religion, a problem analogous to that considered earlier in connection with the discussion of the metalogical method. This method is therefore applied also to the philosophy of religion.

The tension between the general and the individual, between philosophy and theology, becomes evident in Tillich's assertion that the concepts of revelation and redemption, for example, stand in clear opposition to the concept of "religion." "They express a singular once-for-all action, transcendent in origin and transforming in its effect on reality, while 'religion' subordinates under one general concept a whole series of spiritual acts and cultural phenomena. 'Revelation' speaks of a divine, 'religion' of a human act."

In so characterizing revelation and religion Tillich might seem at first to be accepting the definitions of these terms as they are employed by Barth. But the supposition would be erroneous. For Barth there is no valid place for the discipline, philosophy of religion. For Tillich, on the other hand, philosophy—or philosophy of religion—and theology must always stand in tension or in correlation with each other.

[1] *Das System der Wissenschaften* (Göttingen: Vandenhoeck und Ruprecht, 1923), p. 149.

Yet the contrast between philosophy of religion and theology is not merely dialectical. In one age theology occupies a dominant position; in another, philosophy—or philosophy of religion—rises to ascendancy.

The history of the relations of philosophy and religion includes movements that are almost pure actualizations of one or the other of these forms, such as the early Middle Ages and the Enlightenment, respectively. Other movements represent efforts at mediation and synthesis, initiated by champions of revelation in the high Middle Ages, and by partisans of philosophy in the period of Idealism and Romanticism. A third type maintains the coexistence of both forms; one thinks here of the late Middle Ages, of British empiricism, and of theological Kantianism. But no drawing of boundaries can bring about a solution here. Every attempt to force religion and philosophy to compete in the same field is bound to fail, for it constitutes as much of a violation of the philosophic sense of truth as of the unconditional character of revelation. The method of drawing boundaries is doomed by the question as to who shall determine the boundary; for both sides claim this right.[2]

It is futile to attempt to rule out the one or the other. Nor can a stark opposition be allowed to remain: it leads to the shattering of the unity of consciousness. A naïve faith may for a time hold exclusively to the one. But eventually the naïveté will be dissipated. Any calculated return to simple faith will not succeed. Even if it should do so momentarily, it would represent a false step. The only way left open is the inner overcoming of the antithesis. It may fail again and again, but it is required. This requirement does not involve the equation of philosophy with theology; ultimately, theology must provide a normative answer to questions raised by philosophy of religion. But there is a point in both revelation and philosophy in which the two are one. To find this point and from it to construct the synthetic solution is the critical task of the philosophy of religion. This demand leads immediately to the consideration of the place of philosophy of religion in the system of the sciences. More precisely, it leads to the consideration of the relations between philosophy, the empirical study of religion, and metaphysics.

The determination of the place of philosophy of religion—a branch of philosophy—in the system is important not only for philosophy of religion; it is equally important for the system. Each is affected by the other. The system of the sciences is conditioned

2 "Religionsphilosophie," in Max Dessoir (ed.), *Die Philosophie in ihren Einzelgebieten* (Berlin: Ullstein, 1925), p. 770.

by the conception of science, and since science in general is brought into question by the basic problem of philosophy of religion, it is conditioned decisively by philosophy of religion. A systematization of the sciences is in its totality dependent upon the solution of the problem of philosophy of religion. "This reciprocal action corresponds to the dynamic character of knowledge. It signifies that all aspects of knowing are conditioned by a fundamental, systematic, essential intuition (*Wesensschau*)".[3]

Three problems must be dealt with in order to determine the place of philosophy of religion in the system of the sciences: (1) the relationship of philosophy of religion to the phenomenological or empirical science of religion; (2) the place of philosophy of religion in the system of the normative sciences, particularly its relation to philosophy in general and to theology; and (3) the relation between philosophy of religion and metaphysics.

Philosophy of religion must presuppose a familiarity with the materials which the disciplines of the history of religions, the psychology of religion, the typology of religion, and the sociology of religion provide. But its own task is not empirical; it considers what ought to be and not what is. As a normative science it sets forth "what is deemed to be religion, in a creative, productive synthesis." The disciplines belonging to philosophy of religion proper are arranged in accord with the system set forth earlier for the normative sciences. That is, they are distributed in the tripartite classification: philosophy of meaning, intellectual history, and the normative system—theology. Every cultural science consciously or unconsciously flows in these three channels.

It moves out from the general function of the mind and the forms through which objects are constituted in this function of the mind. It points out in a critical way the realization of existence according to the lines of historical development. It gives a unified, systematic solution on the basis of the problems which the conception of existence and the development of intellectual history push to the fore.[4]

Accordingly, philosophy of religion is the theory of the religious function and its categories. The student of religion passes thence by way of transition through history of religions to theology, the normative and systematic presentation of the concrete realization of the concept of religion. Thus philosophy of religion and theology are two elements in a cultural science of religion. They may never properly be separated entirely. Every theology is dependent

[3] *Ibid.*, p. 771.
[4] *Ibid.*, p. 772.

upon the concept of the essence of religion already presupposed. Every philosophy of religion is in the end dependent upon the normative concept of religion. And both are dependent upon the comprehension of the socio-historical material.

By this systematization Tillich indicates not only that theology itself requires the work of a methodical philosophy of religion which deals with the problem of the essence of religion and with the theory of meaning. He indicates also that some particular normative system of religion—some theology—serves as a background for every philosophy of religion. In other words, the philosopher of religion is a theologian *malgré lui*. Tillich presents the evidence for this in many of his other writings.[5]

But not only philosophy of religion and theology stand in this reciprocal relation. As has been observed earlier, religion cannot be properly interpreted as one function alongside other functions. It is an attitude that is found in the other functions. The same thing holds for metaphysics, in the sense that its spiritual attitude affects the various sciences. The difference between philosophy of religion and metaphysics is that the former is the theory of the religious function and its categories and the latter is concerned with the demonstration that direction toward the Unconditioned is a necessary function constituting the fulfillment of meaningful reality.

We shall not present here Tillich's arguments against the use of certain methods in the philosophy of religion—methods which he calls heterogenous. Tillich dismisses what he calls the methods of the history of religions, the methods of the psychology of religion, the theological method, and the speculative method. Instead of examining these arguments, we may note that he claims to employ a "critico-dialectical" method. It aims to separate the principles of meaning from meaningful reality; in this respect it is critical. It aims also to envisage these principles in a "constructive" systematic fashion; in this respect it is dialectical. Where the philosopher of religion employs only the critical method, he will not be able to remain free from the use of empirically accidental concepts in the delineation of the functions and the categories—as, for example, is the case with Kant. Where the philosopher of religion employs only the dialectical element,

---

[5] We think especially of his recurrent argument that Christian elements such as the doctrine of creation, exclusive monotheism, and the presupposition of the omnipotence of God appear again and again by implication in philosophies set forth by thinkers who believe themselves to be emancipated from Christianity.

he develops an inadmissible metaphysic of being and of history —as, for example, is the case with Hegel.[6]

The critico-dialectical method presupposes the autonomy of the spiritual over against every immediately existing thing. But this does not mean that it advocates an idealistic epistemology. Here we find again that the decisive presupposition for Tillich is one that purports to transcend both idealism and realism. The implications of Tillich's philosophy of meaning (already presented) again become evident:

[The critico-dialectical method] need not assume that the mind gives its laws to nature. Nevertheless it cannot hold an epistemological realism to be true. It cannot assume that nature gives laws to the mind. It must assume that the principles of meaning to which consciousness submits itself in intellectual activity are at the same time the principles of meaning to which existence is subjected. It must assume that the meaning of existence is expressed in the meaning-oriented consciousness. If it hopes nevertheless to avoid the difficulties of an exclusive idealism as well as a doctrine of pre-established harmony, then it is best to speak of the meaning-fulfillment of existence through the activities of the spirit. On the basis of this premise, which is ultimately nothing other than a self-intuition of the spirit as spirit and not as existence, the critico-dialectical method develops the universal forms of meaning, which are at the same time functions of the mind and principles of meaningful reality.[7]

But the critico-dialectical method is not sufficient; it is not the only element of the normative, philosophical method. By this method alone, one may apprehend the forms of meaning. But if the method is employed in the manner of Neo-Kantianism, it will subordinate the principles of meaning to a logical, primary unity. In doing so it comes to terms with the forms of meaning but misses the real vitality of religion; it misses the import of meaning which is "the ground of reality presupposed in all forms of meaning"; it misses "the ultimate significance and the real quality of each act of meaning." Formal unity, like every individual form, is abstract and empty without the relation to the import of mean-

---

[6] This would apparently be Tillich's answer to E. Hirsch's objection to Tillich's philosophy of religion on the ground that it does not, like Hegel's system, depend upon a *Begriff* that contains "the principle of movement in itself." See Hirsch's review-article on Tillich's "Religionsphilosophie," *Theologische Literaturzeitung*, LI (1926), 97-103.

[7] "Religionsphilosophie," p. 779. Once more we see the adaptation of the tripartite distinctions drawn from Fichte (discussed in the previous chapter). But as has been indicated and as is made clear again in the next sentences, idealistic epistemology and metaphysics are transcended.

ing. Phenomenology has attempted to overcome this empty formalism by concentrating attention on essences representing a fullness and completeness in which existing things are supposed to participate. But here the element of content turns out again to be merely the rational-abstract aspect of things. The individual aspect of existence is missed. "The inner infinity and eternal significance of the individual is blotted out." Phenomenology has no organ for apprehending the singular character of the historical event. It must—as, for example, in the philosophy of religion—erect an "essence" of religion which either bears the features of one definite religion or represents in effect the construction of a new ideal religion. This attitude in some quarters has brought about a revolt in the direction of the pragmatic method. But, although the pragmatic method does recognize the dynamic, concrete character of existence, it becomes the victim of relativity and in the end degenerates into "the epistemologically formulated renunciation of knowledge." Both the phenomenological and the pragmatic methods are reflections of transitory cultural situations: phenomenology is for a static cultural situation; pragmatism, for a transitional phase. One must avoid a romantically conceived mysticism of essence on the one hand and an anti-intellectual, arbitrary dynamism on the other. Each offers a challenge, but each fails to meet the challenge.

What is needed is a method of phenomenological intuition and a dynamically developed critical method. This means that Tillich believes the demand is for the metalogical method (discussed in general terms in the previous chapter).

The metalogical method maintains the logical element of the critical method, but it goes beyond pure formalism in two ways: It aims to apprehend the import inhering in the forms, and it possesses an individual creative power to set up norms. In short, it aims to grasp both form and import. Yet it does not remain attached to particular forms but critically and intuitively reaches back to the principles of being and meaning.

It is evident that the metalogical method, with its attempt to reach back to the ultimate principle that gives meaning to existence, itself presupposes a general view of the nature of things. Indeed, in Tillich's words, already quoted, "All aspects of knowing are conditioned by the fundamental, systematic, essential intuition."[8] Tillich himself explicitly asserts that the method is not without relation to mysticism, particularly in its intuitive element," but the intuitive element in his system aims to grasp the integrat-

[8] "Religionsphilosophie," p. 771.

ing principle through the conditioned forms. To use the language of philosophical idealism, the metalogical method is devised in order to intuit the Absolute in its relation to the relative, to see the One in the Many.

We have previously observed that Tillich's general philosophy was presupposed in his classification of the sciences. We find here that his general philosophy is presupposed not only in his philosophy of religion but also even in his definition of religion. The description of the metalogical method reveals these general presuppositions. Hence it may be well to consider them before proceeding with an exposition of the philosophy of religion.

Speaking of the relation between the metalogical method and mysticism, Tillich (as we have noted) asserts that the basis of all mysticism is that the principles of the macrocosm are given in the microcosm.[9] This primary tenet, he says, finds its epistemological expression in the theory of the fulfillment of the meaning of existence through the spirit. Hence the elements of meaning, namely, form and import, are the absolutely essential elements of such a theory or of such a fulfillment. Tillich views his emphasis on the import of meaning, the "life-blood" of his whole system, as a break through idealism to a new realism and as an adaptation of a hitherto much-neglected tradition of European thought which has been overshadowed by rationalism and utilitarianism. The symbols that have been used to express the import of meaning, he says, have in the dominant rationalistic tradition been transcendentalized or rationalized; hence the real power that belongs to any concept of the import of meaning has been lost. Indeed, the feeling of emptiness in our present culture is partially the consequence of this fact. The following passage both expresses a lament for this situation and indicates the historical heritage that Tillich aims to appropriate:

The conception of the import of meaning has, in fact, in occidental mysticism used symbols derived from psychological language: the ground of the soul, the unconscious, the will, and the like. The last-named concept has gained its greatest significance through the voluntaristic metaphysics of Boehme, Baader, Schelling, Schopenhauer, Nietzsche, etc. In addition the symbolic character of the concept of the

[9] *Ibid.*, p. 786. Cf. *Rel. Verw.* (Berlin: Furche, 1929), p. 170: "Through confronting the macrocosm the microcosm becomes aware of its own character as itself a cosmos and conversely the apprehension of the world as a world would not be possible unless the subject had the character of being a microcosm." This view is to be compared to his statement about accepting the idealistic principle of the identity of subject and object in knowledge.

will has been misunderstood in many ways and the great epistemological conception of mysticism has been forced down to the level of a
rational metaphysics based on biology or psychology, and is therefore
impossible.[10]

If we continue, we find here also the correlation of this voluntaristic mysticism with the metalogical method:

It has not been recognized that there is a break-through to a new
method here, to a new fundamental attitude of mind, namely, the
metalogical-dynamic method. The implication for the implementa-
tion of metalogic is that while the dynamic of the elements of meaning can indeed be expressed in symbols derived from the affective side
of the consciousness, the goal of this symbolism is the intuition of the
forms of meaning filled with living import, not of any independent
metaphysical entities. For the elements of meaning belong together;
there is no import apart from a form, and no form without import.[11]

In these passages one may detect the basic features of Tillich's
philosophy of life as well as the presuppositions of his philosophy
of religion in the narrow, technical sense. In view of the fact
that the centrality of the concept of meaning has not generally
been emphasized in American expositions of Tillich's philosophy,
we must here not only stress its importance but also indicate
its connections with other ideas in the Tillichian philosophy.

In the exposition of these connections we now consider Tillich's "belief-ful realism." As the passage quoted above indicates,
the whole must be seen in terms of his interpretation of mysticism. After presenting these aspects of his thought we may turn
to the further exposition of the principal ideas set forth in his
"Philosophy of Religion."

Tillich's whole philosophical effort is motivated by the desire
to present a conception of the meaning of life as it may be
disclosed by a direct confrontation with concrete actuality. On
the one hand, he wishes to avoid the disruption of meaning that
is represented by supernaturalism or by an idealism that attempts to find unity and direction of meaning by resort to metaphysical entities or transcendental abstractions. These entities
and abstractions, besides being a disruption of meaning, are also
residues of types of metaphysics that are—on still other grounds
—not tenable. On the other hand, he has always exhibited a
desire to understand and appreciate secularism; indeed, he
believes that secularism sometimes carries within it not only

---

[10] "Religionsphilosophie," p. 786.
[11] *Ibid.*

valid criticisms of traditional religion but also a covert form of a religious approach to life.

Consequently, he wishes to make a fresh, direct approach to actuality. This is not to say that he approaches the world without presuppositions. Rather, he believes that men may become over-burdened with traditional, rationalized theological and philosophical concepts to such a degree that they cannot see reality in its freshness and vitality. "The world of the concept can become independent and envelop the factual in a fog. Concepts lead to concepts, and concepts are disposed of by concepts, without new or original perceptions."[12]

Exclusive preoccupation with concepts is usually called scholasticism. But this is the pejorative meaning of the word. The best thought of the Middle Ages cannot be characterized by such use of the word. A more favorable meaning must be intended if one wishes to describe the profound mystical-experiential view of reality which was the spirit of the Middle Ages.

The temptation of the intellect is to split up reality and create a new actuality out of itself, then to set it over the given actuality. But the true function of the intellect is to comprehend the truth of actuality. This does not properly end in formalism; it should rather lead to the awareness of the power and vitality of the real as it fulfills itself in meaningful creativity. In Tillich's view, "the true actuality is what is truly powerful, not powerful in a social sense, but powerful in being, filled with the power of being."[13]

This assertion must be interpreted in the light of the voluntaristic mysticism of Jacob Boehme (with his dynamic theogony) and of the later Schelling (with his theory of potencies and his attempted disruption of a static philosophy of identity by means of a theory of freedom).

The history of thought exhibits one attempt after the other to discriminate the truly powerful element in contrast to the impotent. The Greek, troubled by the changing and perishing of things, sought the truly powerful in eternal forms from whose power temporal realities derive their possibility of being. "Thus

---

[12] "Gläubiger Realismus," *Theologenrundbrief für den Bund Deutscher Jugendvereine* (1927), p. 1. (This is an earlier version of the longer essay published in *Theologische Blätter*, VII [1928], 109-18.) In Tillich's emphasis on *Sachlichkeit* Robert Winkler sees a motif to be found also in Reformation theology. Cf. his article "Die Theologie des Philosophen Tillich in seinem Buch *Religiöse Verwirklichung*," *Christentum und Wissenschaft*, VI (1930), p. 215.

[13] "Gläubiger Realismus," p. 2.

the Greek searched for the power of being in that which lies beyond time, to which he escaped from the changing and transitory, to contemplate it and to become one with it."[14] Mystical realism was his answer to the question as to the locus of the truly powerful. Combined with his reaching out for a world of essences, however, was a flight from an ambiguous, demonic power in the world of things.

For the Renaissance, the power of being is man. Demonic forces have been exorcised, largely under the influence of Christianity. Man is the summation of power and reason.

He is the bearer of intellect; in him the powers of all spheres are concentrated; he is mediator among them; he compels them to serve him, first through magic, then later through technology. He fixes the purposes, and all things are deprived of their powers in the service of these purposes.[15]

This attitude issues in utilitarian realism. Things are subordinated to human purpose, so much so that in the end man himself becomes a tool, a machine, working energy. Mystical realism and utilitarian realism have one thing in common: they both negate existence, the one in favor of essence, the other in favor of purpose.

There are, to be sure, aspects of these forms of realism which deserve great positive appreciation, but both have failed in the attempt to find enduring meaning. The one has given rise to irrationalism—in revolt against a static world-view—the other, to oppressive exploitation of natural and human resources.

Another approach to reality and to the power of being must be sought. The method called historical realism attempts to find the essence and the inner power of being in the concrete here-and-now. To be more exact, it attempts to find this essence and power in existence as well as beyond it. Such an attempt is peculiar to the Christian outlook, where the doctrine of creation implies a favorable or positive attitude toward matter and thus also toward existence in general. In this it is to be contrasted with ancient pagan thought, which interpreted the world as constituted of an eternal matter that resists "form." Historical realism does not require that one flee the world. "The true powers of being are manifest in the inner dynamic relationships of the historical process."[16] Here there is a sort of mutual inter-

---

[14] *Ibid.*, p. 4.

[15] *Ibid.*

[16] *Rel. Verw.*, p. 73. This quotation is from the revised and lengthened version of the previously quoted lecture on "Belief-ful Realism." This version

play between subject and object, through a simultaneous grasping of the object and being grasped by it. In this view Tillich finds a realism that lies beyond the simple alternative between utilitarian and mystical realism.

Its decisive characteristic is its vivid awareness of contemporaneity, its awareness of the meaning of the here-and-now. Utilitarian realism relates every moment to a purpose lying in the future, and in the name of progress it deprives nature and man of their intrinsic powers. Mystical realism, on the other hand, finds meaning and power only in the world of essences.[17]

Historical realism is not identical with bondage to the moment. It finds meaning and power in the here-and-now, but it does not become submerged in the immediate. It transcends the moment, the accidental, the merely changing. It finds the power of the here-and-now in its singularity, its unrepeatable character; yet it recognizes the demand for meaning that will fuse past and present in a meaningful drive towards the future. Hence historical realism does not negate utilitarian and mystical realism. It searches the element of permanence characteristic of power itself (mystical realism), and it recognizes the cleavage between subject and object and elevates the subject (utilitarian realism). But in face of historical potencies it leaves off the mystical-ascetic attitude, and it opposes the domineering "objective" attitude. Thus historical realism confronts the subject with something unconditionally powerful, an inner infinity of being, a power that is ever fresh and active and a power that makes a demand for the novel fulfillment of meaning.

This inner infinity of being, this inexhaustible power, which is to be discerned also in the inner infinity of ideas, is never to be identified with any actuality—in knowledge or in existence —yet it pulsates through all actuality, offering support and threat. Nor is it, in its aspect of demand, to be identified with any form or *nomos*. In its affirmation it grasps us, giving birth to the ecstasy that comes with breaking through given, fixed forms of our existence and of our thinking.

The "ecstatic" element can be seen in a preliminary way in primitive religions. It can be discerned also in the glowing passion of prophetic speech and action.

---

appears in revised form in *The Protestant Era,* trans. James L. Adams (Chicago: University of Chicago Press, 1948), pp. 66-82.

[17] *Ibid.*

It is likewise to be discerned in the profound sayings of Jesus in the Sermon on the Mount, in the mysterious Word of John and in the narrative of the Last Supper in the Synoptics, in the epistles where Paul speaks of the spirit and of love and particularly where he speaks of the triumph of the gospel over the law, in Luther's words of anger and defiance. . . . One might say that just as "power" is basic on the ontological level, so ecstasy is fundamental on the anthropological level.[18]

Here again we sense the numinous overtones of the Unconditioned.

In a previous chapter we have observed that Tillich sees something of this unconditioned power and ecstasy in the paintings of the expressionist school. He believes that expressionist painters were opening up and breaking through the outer forms of things to disclose an inner import. A new realistic intuition here turns its attention to the outer form in order to discern in and through it the inner power of things. Hence there is present in these paintings a wavering between the portrayal of an object and the expression of a meaning that transcends it.[19] Not that the productions offer pure examples of this tension. They exhibit rather a groping awareness of it.

What is apprehended is not a new metaphysical entity. It is an import that pulsates in and through and beyond the forms that reveal it, expressing the ecstasy of freedom through the creation of something new. The full apprehension of this import reveals the flatness of any two-dimensional realism exalting only the outer forms; it reveals also the pallid, stodgy character of a supernaturalism or an idealism that spatializes or transcendentalizes the infinite and inexhaustible ground and abyss of being and meaning.

It is difficult to find a rational symbol for the pulsating import in things which is the ground of meaning and a hallowed demand for creative newness. But one symbol devised by rational metaphysics must be avoided or at least used sparingly, namely, "the Absolute." This term suggests something separated from us by an infinite distance and something static. Moreover, under the influence of Hegelianism it suggests the synthesis of the absolute idea, an unfolding of something potential and immanent within nature and spirit. Meaningful creativity is no mere *Entfaltung.*

18 *Ibid.,* p. 83.
19 Compare what has been said (in the previous chapter) concerning the paradoxical character of the religious symbol.

It breaks through the closed circle of pure being; it produces the new, the unexpected which cannot be derived from natural motion. Therefore history also is more than the development of something enveloped. Every living being develops what is enveloped in its nature. This development, however, is not the production of an entirely new creation. It is the actualization of a definite potentiality; but it does not break through the circle of actuality and potentiality as history does. History transcends the natural limitations in creating the new which does not follow from the old by evolution. The new, which occurs wherever history occurs, is meaning. In creating meaning, existence rises above itself. For meaning—as we use the word here— is realized by freedom and only by freedom; in creating meaning, existence gains freedom from itself, from the necessity of its nature.[20]

Thus the Hegelian *Begriff* must be replaced by transcendent-immanent meaning which never arrives at a completed synthesis.

The rational symbol employed by Tillich for the inner infinity of existence and meaning is "the Unconditioned." One wonders why he did not adopt a word possessing greater *Symbolkräftig-keit.* The word "Unconditioned" communicates very little, "power-fully" little, to the average reader. Perhaps its principal merit is that it carries few familiar connotations for the average reader, and thus it requires definition. Moreover, it issues from a vener-able philosophical tradition reaching back through Kant and Spinoza to Plato.

The word connotes several meanings that are only hinted at in the previous discussion in Chapter II:

1. It is not a metaphysical entity. It is not a highest or supreme being. Such conceptions are ruled out as spatializations of the infinite. Since Kant all such entities and supranatural beings must be considered extrapolations. Accordingly, it cannot be said to "exist"; it is a qualification of all existence and meaning.

2. It is not unconditioned, however, in the sense that it is unrelated to us or to the conditioned order. Quite to the contrary, it is a symbol for that which pours upon us the blessings of signifi-cance, of enthusiasm, of creative courage. It is a symbol of the demand placed upon us in all meaningful thought and action, a symbol of that which unconditionally concerns us. It symbolizes the point at which subject and object meet, at which meaning is paradoxically fulfilled and confronts higher demand. (Hence it cannot be described or explained away in terms of a psychology that bases everything upon the infinity of desire.)

[20] *The Interpretation of History,* trans. Rasetzki and Talmey (New York: Charles Scribner's Sons, 1936), p. 273.

3. It is unconditioned in the sense that man has no control over it. Thus it aims to grasp an essential meaning of the doctrines of grace and of justification by faith.

4. It is a symbol of the ground and abyss of all existence and meaning. It is not to be equated with the totality of existence or with the totality of meanings. The inner infinity of existence, idea, and meaning is implied. Hence it is not to be fully grasped by any word or concept; it can only be pointed to in gratitude, in fear and trembling, as the unconditional aspect and qualification of existence, value, and meaning.

5. But none of these characterizations is adequate. The feeling-tone of the word (and concept) can be grasped only if one divines the utter sublimity, the *mysterium tremendum et fascinosum* of the numinous, the holy, expressed in the German words for the Unconditioned (*Das Unbedingte*) and the unconditionally real.

This concept constitutes the belief-ful and the realistic element in "belief-ful realism." Therefore the characterization of the attitude of "belief-ful realism" immediately reminds us of the characterization of the Unconditioned:

Belief-ful realism is a basic attitude toward reality. It is neither a theoretical view of the world, nor is it a practical discipline for life. It belongs to a level of life that lies underneath the cleavage between theory and practice. Nor is it a particular kind of religion or theology. Indeed, it is not any kind of separate, particular thing.[21]

This similarity of characterization indicates the relation of Tillich's conception of the Unconditioned to his philosophy of being. In his view, there is a structure of being which permeates, or which is an inner depth quality within, but "beyond," all existence. This structure cannot be disposed of by subjective idealism, for it supports and resists us at every turn. It is not something to be found on the surface of things, nor can it be said to exist as finite objects exist. Tillich does not accept the spatialized conception of a Superbeing, yet he insists that things

---

[21] *Rel. Verw.*, pp. 66-67. For the English translation of this essay in *The Protestant Era* (pp. 66-82) Tillich proposed the term "self-transcending realism" instead of "belief-ful realism." The passage here cited appears on p. 67 (*op. cit.*), in a revised translation proposed by Tillich. It should be observed here that in his later writings, Tillich does not use the substantive form, "the Unconditioned." He tends to use instead the existential formulation, "object of unconditional concern." If the substantive form appears, he speaks of "being itself," "ground of being," "power of being." For a succinct definition of the term "unconditional," see *The Protestant Era*, p. 32, n.1

cannot be taken as independent and ultimate in themselves and in their surface actuality. Taken as self-existent and independent, without a sense of their depth, things lose their powerfulness and their significance. Therefore, we must go beneath surfaces, we must go beyond the creatures to that in which they find their roots—and their "sap." This "going beyond" is a necessity of the human mind. The mind cannot, says Tillich, think of things existing in themselves, nor can it think of nonbeing even as a possibility. Even empty space as a nothingness is inconceivable; the empty space becomes a form of being. Hence something unconditional is presupposed when, with Schelling, one asks, "Why is there not nothing?"

The assertion that all existing things participate in some basic and ultimate being runs through the whole history of philosophy, and Tillich seems to accept the intent of the assertion. But he speaks of it as an inner structure, an ontological structure. Thus he wishes to avoid hypostatizing being. He views the unconditioned of being and meaning as an aspect or quality or qualification of existence, the aspect that gives meaning to existence. Anaximander speaks of the *Apeiron,* the infinite, from which all things come and to which they return (in payment for their guilt). Parmenides finds this ultimate structure in being itself, which is without genesis and decay—a static conception from Tillich's point of view, but one of the greatest insights of the Greek genius. Plato finds it in the Good. Spinoza speaks of substance as the necessary being: one cannot think that it could not be. Schelling and Hegel go beyond the cleavage of subject and object to an unconditioned identity. Schelling speaks of it as "immemorial being" (*das Unvordenkliche*), a reality presupposed by, anterior and inaccessible to, thought—in short, the unconditionally real and powerful. Schleiermacher speaks of that upon which man is absolutely or unconditionally dependent. Schopenhauer's Dark Will is something quiet within itself from which particular wills are derived and to which they return. The core of this conception of the primordial unity of existence Tillich accepts, and he applies it to thought and value as well as to being. It is for him implicit in monotheism and in the Christian doctrine of creation; and it is explicit, if inadequately expressed, in idealism.[22] But Tillich prefers the Old Testament and the theosophic

---

[22] *Ibid.,* pp. 282-83. Idealism is rejected insofar as it does not recognize the contradiction of essence in existence, that is, insofar as it does not recognize the "Fall." Schelling is highly esteemed by Tillich for having overcome this deficiency in idealism through his insistence upon the cleavage

versions of voluntaristic mysticism—versions that are more
dynamic than most of those listed in the foregoing references
to the history of philosophy (Anaximander and Schelling are
the principal exceptions). His use of the terms "Unconditioned,"
"inexhaustible," "power of being," "abyss of being," "depth" is
to be interpreted with this connotation of dynamism. In accord
with this conception of being, he designates the depth in things
as "the pure existentiality of things, their being supported by
the basis of existence, their sharing in the abundance of existence."

One aspect of Tillich's conception of the depth of things, of the
pure existentiality of things, is of sufficient importance to require
special emphasis. We have just referred to the disposition of
Schelling and Hegel to go beyond the cleavage of subject and
object to an unconditioned identity. One of the decisive features
of modern life and thought is the contrast seen betweeen "subject"
and "object," a contrast made explicit in Descartes' duality of
thought and extension. The sense of contrast has become per-
vasive in modern industrialism and technology. The dichotomy
between subject and object, in Tillich's view, superseded the subject-object unity of the high Middle Ages. But life originates
on a level that is deeper than the Cartesian duality. Kant, by
means of the transcendental dialectic, had ruled out the validity
of seeking this level of being: in his view, ontology could only
project an *object* behind the world to explain the world. So far
as Kant was concerned, man remains in a prison of finitude.
Fichte, going beyond Kant, asserted that God cannot be an object
among objects, but is rather beyond the cleavage between subject
and object. This view that one can penetrate deeper than the
dichotomy between subject and object became a persistent theme
in nineteenth- and twentieth-century thought. Rejecting the dichotomy, Tillich holds that man is immediately aware of something
unconditional, of a power of being, which is the *prius* of the
separation and interaction of subject and object.

This conception of the ground of being and meaning is so
fundamental in Tillich's outlook that it seems justifiable to quote
here a rather lengthy passage that deals with it:

This foundation and this suggestion by things of "another thing,"
which is yet no other thing, but a depth in things, is not rational, *i.e.*,

---

in human existence. Schelling qualifies the mystical assertion of the unified
structure of things by adding the concept of guilt. See Tillich's doctoral
dissertation, *Mystik und Schuldbewusstsein in Schellings philosophischer
Entwicklung* (Gütersloh: Bertelsmann, 1912).

demonstrable from the interrelation of things with the world; and the "other," to which the things point, is nothing discoverable by a rational process, but a quality of things which reveals—or conceals— a view into its depths. We say of this depth, that it is the basis of being of things, whereby "being" is taken absolutely, transcendently as the expression of the secret into which thinking cannot penetrate, because as something existing it itself is based thereon. In order to say this, however, we must also say something else: that the depth of things, their basis of existence, is at the same time their abyss; or in other words, that the depth of things is inexhaustible. If it were not inexhaustible, and if it could be exhausted in the form of things, then there would be a direct, rationally designable way from the depth of things to their form; then the world could be comprehended as the necessary and unequivocal unfolding of the basis of existence; then the supporting basis would pour out entirely into the cosmos of forms; then the depth would cease to be depth, cease to be transcendental and absolute. Every one of our relations in existence, however, suggests that it is directed to something that, despite its finiteness, shares the inexhaustibility of existence. . . . This inexhaustibility denoted here, however, is not to be interpreted as passive inexhaustibility, as a resting ocean, which any subject, form, or world fails to exhaust, but is to be understood as an active inexhaustibility, as a productive inner infinity of existence, *i.e.*, as the "consuming fire" that becomes a real abyss for every form.[23] Thus the inexhaustibility of being is simultaneously the expression of the fullness, the power of being and meaning of everything, and the expression for the inner insecurity, limitation, and fate of everything to succumb to the abyss.[24]

We have quoted so long a passage because Tillich's philosophy of religion presupposes this philosophy of being. The concept of meaning, which in his view is decisive for the understanding of either culture or religion, also presupposes this philosophy of being, this "belief-ful realism." If one is to grasp the deepest meaning of existence, Tillich holds that one must "by phenomenological intuition" penetrate reality in such a way as to find its inner infinity, its import rooted in the ground and the abyss of being. ("Phenomenological" here seems to mean a description of what one "sees." It is not to be taken in the sense of a Husserlian intuition of essences.) For him, then, there is "no approach to religion at all without what we call theological ontology, the understanding of the Unconditioned or the Tran-

[23] Again we detect the language of Jacob Boehme.
[24] *The Interpretation of History*, pp. 83-84. The last sentence should be connected with Tillich's conception of the boundary (already discussed) and also with his conception of Protestantism. Later on, for example in *Systematic Theology*, this ontology is elaborately presented.

scendent as that which gives meaning to existence, as the transcendent power of being." As we shall see, however, this approach of theological ontology is not one that belongs to some cloistered sphere of experience, nor is it one that requires some special way of knowing peculiar to "religious experience." Rather, it is that kind of "seeing" which discerns the infinite and inexhaustible ground and abyss of all experience, of all meaning, of all culture, of all being. By means of it realism—the looking at actuality—becomes belief-ful.

By what theory of knowledge does Tillich apprehend this transcendent meaning in things? His answer to this question is not easy to grasp. It is an elaborate answer involving a discussion of historical epistemologies. He is emphatic in insisting that no special way of knowing is involved. Rather, the way of knowing is appropriate and necessary for the apprehension of ultimate meaning in all spheres of the spirit, a way of knowing available to all men who look into the depths of being and meaning.

One way of knowing does, however, exclude penetration to the depth of things. It is the path of the "main methodical line" of Western thought, the path of rationalism. This main stream of thought has had boundlessly fruitful consequences, especially for gaining control of the world, but it misses the depths. It is that stream of thought which finds classical formulation in Descartes' *Discours de la méthode;* it reaches its mightiest expression in Kant's *Critiques.* A principal element in this tradition is to be discerned also in the mystical-mathematical-metaphysical type of thought, emanating from Neo-Platonism, reaching through Nicolas of Cusa to its climax in Spinoza. The stream also includes the line of English empiricism from Bacon and Hume to the later Positivists of the nineteenth century. It is characterized by an effort to grasp the form of the world, "the elements and the laws of their combination." It is the way of rationalism for which time "remains insignificant"; it is a "static type of thinking in terms of form, and for it even history presents only the unfolding of the possibilities and laws of the Gestalt, 'Man.' "[25]

To be contrasted with this main methodical line of thinking is a subsidiary—at times subterranean—line that goes back to the mysticism and nature-philosophy of the late Middle Ages

[25] The exposition in the ensuing paragraphs is based upon the essay entitled "Kairos und Logos," which appears in English translation in *The Interpretation of History,* pp. 123-75.

and the Renaissance. Its symbol is the name of Jacob Boehme; it appears also in the thought of Baader and the later Schelling. Influences from it are to be discerned markedly in Schopenhauer and Nietzsche, and in the *Lebensphilosophie* that revolted against "the methodical formalism of the Kantians." Whereas the eternal form of being is the goal of knowledge in the main methodical line, the world is understood as "creation, conflict, and fate" in the second, subsidiary line. Here the "form-creating process itself is to be perceived." The world is not viewed as a unified structure, or, to be more exact, it is interpreted as constituting an interplay between form-creating and form-destroying processes. As already indicated in the discussion of the essay "Philosophie und Schicksal," the world is seen to be moving towards unknown fates. Time and individuality are of fundamental significance. Hence it is presupposed that single, underivable happenings are of the essence rather than that the eternal essences realize themselves in universal laws. In short, this whole outlook is, in contrast to the main rationalistic line, a "historical philosophy" the main features of which have been delineated by Schelling and Troeltsch. Indeed, the terms "creation," "conflict," "fate" are frequently to be found in the writings of both of these men.

Tillich sums up the outlook in these succinct sentences:

> In this dynamic thinking in terms of creation, time is all-decisive, not empty time, pure expiration; not mere duration either, but rather qualitatively fulfilled time, the moment that is creation and fate. We call this fulfilled moment, the moment of time approaching us as fate and decision, *Kairos*.[26]

The historical development of the word "*Kairos*" illustrates the two conceptions of time characteristic of the two contrasting outlooks. In Greek linguistic usage the word meant time as pure duration; in its transformation under the influence of the historical consciousness of early Christianity it acquired the meaning of fullness of time. And thus in its two meanings it symbolizes the two types of thinking:

> The thinking in the *Kairos*, which is the determinant of the second line explained in our historical consideration, is opposed to the thinking in the timeless *Logos*, which belongs to the methodical main

[26] *The Interpretation of History*, p. 129. Similar formulations appear in the essay, "Philosophie und Schicksal," published in translation in *The Protestant Era*, trans. James L. Adams (Chicago: University of Chicago Press, 1948), pp. 3-15.

line. Thus the correctness of our original distinction becomes apparent, and at the same time the question of the essential relationship between *Kairos* and *Logos* becomes urgent.[27]

On the one hand, then, we have the world of the timeless *Logos*, which is "at best an immense abstraction," and on the other, "the passing fate and decision of immediate existence." The method peculiar to the former outlook is unable to come to terms adequately with fate, decision, and immediacy—that is, with the sense of historical individuality—stressed in the other outlook. Here we see, then, the carrying out of the distinction between the time-thinking and the space-thinking referred to in *The System of the Sciences*. Here, too, we see the basic distinction made by Tillich between Christian and pagan philosophies of history. In the Christian "*Kairos*-thinking," time is dominant over space, time is directed, the fulfillment of meaning is in time and history. In the pagan space-thinking, space is dominant over time, history moves in cycles; and meaning and knowledge come through escape from the temporal process into the world of eternal forms.[28]

But the two outlooks are to be contrasted not only in their attitude toward the eternal forms, toward individuality, and toward time. (These contrasts are an expansion of what has been earlier referred to as historical realism.) They are also to be contrasted with respect to the types of epistemology. In the main methodical line "the perceiving subject in its relation to reality" is an "empty" subject open to the eternal forms of *Logos*. This view is characterized by aloofness to historical fate, to *Kairos*. This is the attitude of pure theory, the attitude of distance. Hence the subject claims to occupy an absolute position. An element of universal validity is, to be sure, contained in this attitude of *Logos*. But the knowledge that accrues is insufficient. It is confined to "formal evidence and material probability." This two-dimensional knowledge apprehends only the surface level of existence. It misses the dynamic nature of reality and knowl-

[27] *Ibid.*

[28] These distinctions are worked out in detail in Tillich's two notable essays on philosophy of history, namely, "Kairos" and "Historical and Non-historical Interpretations of History," reprinted in *The Protestant Era*, trans. James L. Adams (Chicago: University of Chicago Press, 1948), pp. 16-31, 32-51. The same distinctions are also employed in Tillich's book *Sozialistische Entscheidung* (Potsdam: Protte, 1933), in order to contrast a religious-socialist program with a National-Socialist philosophy (bound to the "spaces" of blood and soil). Tillich points out that this contrast between space-thinking and time-thinking is adumbrated by the young Hegel.

edge; it destroys the community between the knower and the known, both of which stand in history, in fate, and in the context of creative freedom. As a consequence, it develops a sort of scientific asceticism in face of the immediate historical situation—symbolized by Max Weber's conception of "science as vocation." Thus the knowing subject and the objects of his knowledge become timeless.

To this sort of epistemology Tillich contrasts what he calls "the fundamental Protestant attitude," which "stands in nature, taking upon itself the inevitable reality." The Protestant attitude does not wish to flee from the sphere of the concrete, the historical, the sphere of decision, to the "world of ideal forms or into the related world of super-nature" (Catholicism). It turns rather to the concrete "here-and-now" and *through* it to the dynamic source of all being and meaning. This source or ground

should not be confused with the *Arché* of Greek metaphysics nor with the Absolute of German idealism. The means of access to the sort of basis here under discussion, is not through the objective world, nor through the dissolution of that world, nor through the idealistic absorption of it into the human self. Access to it comes rather through our being grasped or encountered by that in which our existence as our existence is grounded.[29]

But in confronting the "source" of existence and meaning we become aware of the fact that we are both dependent upon it and "separated" from it. The Protestant doctrine of justification by faith expresses this idea, for it "rends every human claim in the face of God and every identification of God and man";[30] thus it denies to the subject the possibility of an absolute position in knowledge as well as in the realm of works. "Fate and freedom reach into the act of knowledge and make it a historical deed: the Kairos determines the Logos."[31] This view is to be contrasted with the Catholic doctrine of supernatural grace, according to which, one is raised by grace into the world of unequivocal truth. "Catholicism knows only two possibilities of a historical fate: to belong to the church or not to belong to it. Radical Protestantism knows only the one historical fate: to stand under divine judgment."[32] The attitude of radical Protes-

[29] *Protestantisches Prinzip und proletarische Situation* (Bonn: Cohen, 1931), p. 8. This essay appears in translation in *The Protestant Era*, trans. James L. Adams (Chicago: University of Chicago Press, 1948), pp. 161-81.
[30] *The Interpretation of History*, p. 32.
[31] *Ibid.*, p. 135.
[32] *Ibid.*, p. 137.

tantism involves the consciousness of standing "in separation from the Unconditioned, and in the sphere of cleavage and decision, without being able to evade this situation even in knowledge."

Although Tillich speaks of this attitude as Protestant, it would be wrong to associate it only with explicitly Protestant tradition. Indeed, it is usually associated with the movement known as *Existenzphilosophie*. Existential philosophy has been set forth in opposition to rationalism in general, but its principal representatives have taken Hegel to be the symbol of the false philosophy.

The "pregnant" use of the term "existence" suggests the scholastic distinction between *essentia* and *existentia*. According to the schoolmen, there is in God no difference between essence and existence—in contrast to all finite beings. The term "existential philosophy" begins to play a decisive role with the revolt against Hegel. The German dialectician had interpreted the world as the self-unfolding of God. In effect, therefore, he denied the difference between essence and existence *for finite being*. Man is God coming to self-consciousness. To be sure, the identity between essence and existence was viewed as a dialectical one; nevertheless, man's creatureliness was in effect overcome in the completed philosophy of the absolute idea.

Tillich's characterization of the revolt against this identification of man's essence with his existence brings together so much in nineteenth-century thought which contributes to "existential thinking" and therefore to his own thinking that we quote it here at length. Referring to Hegel's philosophy he says:

Against this metaphysical arrogance—the profoundest expression of rational humanism—a whole generation of thinkers directed their powerful attacks, mainly in the years between 1840 and 1850. I only mention Schelling in his old age, Feuerbach, Marx, and Kierkegaard. These and many others emphasized the gap between man's essential nature and his actual situation. They disrupted the assumed unity between the infinite and the finite from all sides: Feuerbach from an anthropological, Marx from a sociological, and Kierkegaard from an ethical point of view. And they all did it in the name of existence as contradicting essence. Existential thinking is thus a thinking which is conscious of the finiteness and tragedy of all human existence—including human thought. For Kierkegaard this means that man's thought cannot be separated from his ethical existence, and this makes a detached attitude impossible because it demands passion and decisions with respect to truth. (Similarly Marx denies that theory can be separated from man's practical existence because this demands that the world be changed while it is being thought.) The word "existential" has, therefore, the connotation of a thinking in the realm of ethical decisions, of political radicalism, of ultimate concern and, consequently, of a thinking with passion and interest.[33]

This whole development took place in the context of a revolt against idealistic as well as naturalistic rationalism, against the modern mechanized world and its dehumanizing effects in an industrial society. Tillich's epistemology must be seen in the context of this conflict within modern Western society and philosophy.

The Protestant religious consciousness stands, then, in a state of cleavage. Confronting the Unconditioned it is conscious of alienation as well as of kinship. It hears not only the eternal Yes but also the eternal No. The No reminds it that it stands under divine judgment, that it is separated from the Unconditioned. The Yes affirms the presupposition of all our thinking, namely, "that truth is realized in a decision regarding the Unconditioned; stated in religions terms, that all knowledge of truth in a certain stratum is knowledge of God."[34] Here one is confronted with the ultimate seriousness of existence, its support and threat and promise: the support of (intimacy and community with) an infinite and inexhaustible reality, the threat of the blindness that comes from the *Hybris* or blasphemy of claiming absolute truth, and the promise of new, concrete, meaningful fulfillment.

Only by a decision for the unconditioned of being and truth, of meaning and value, can one come into community with being and truth, with meaning and value. Implicitly or explicitly everyone makes this sort of decision. "Decisions in the conditioned sphere mean nothing in themselves. As long as they do not have an unconditioned element in themselves they are, absolutely speaking, meaningless and do not contribute to the meaning of history."[35] Here we see again that Tillich is making religious decision the presupposition of all decision. As in *The System of the Sciences* and in "The Philosophy of Religion," concern with ultimate meaning is the concern that constitutes human striving.

But the decision for the Unconditioned can never properly

[33] "Kierkegaard as Existential Thinker," *Union Review*, IV, No. 1 (December, 1942), 6. For a more extensive discussion of these issues, see Tillich's article "Existential Philosophy," *Journal of the History of Ideas*, V (1944), 44-70.
[34] *The Interpretation of History*, p. 141.
[35] *Ibid.*, p. 138.

be unambiguous. To suppose it can be so is to suppose the absolute position of the knower, the identification of essence and existence. In face of the ultimate, no decision can be unequivocal. Nor, for that matter, can the decision for the Unconditioned be a single decision. "It cannot stand beside other decisions, for then the Unconditioned would stand beside something conditioned: the decision here discussed can be only a hidden, transcendental decision which is never apparent, but which may be the innermost meaning of each single decision."[36]

Since decision for the Unconditioned cannot be unequivocal, the subject can never overcome the separation from the Unconditioned. It can point to the Unconditioned as the ground of being and meaning: that is, it can intuit an ultimate meaning *in* the transitory moment, it can find eternity *in* time. But it cannot draw the Unconditioned into the finite sphere. It must stand "guard" against those who would attempt to domesticate it and gain the absolute position.

With this recognition of the ultimate seriousness and the ubiquitous insecurity of the subject, absolutism on the one side and relativism on the other are overcome. The creative depths issue forth in the subject, bringing the fateful knowledge of decision and demanding "timely" action. Again we see the scheme presented in *The System of the Sciences*. Thought and being are sublated in creative spirit, and the synthesis of the absolute idea is paradoxically and inchoately accomplished.

Both seriousness and insecurity offer themselves to a phenomenological intuition of things, supported by religious belief. No being fulfills its being but each participates in absolute being. That every being participates in absolute being shows the seriousness of things. That it is separated from the absolute shows the insecurity of things. No being has unconditioned power of being, but each points through positive and negative qualities to the absolute power of being which it shares. This absolute power is the transcendent meaning of things as they have being. To see things in this transcendent quality is the presupposition of religious ontology; or in dogmatic terminology, of the doctrine of creation.[37]

For an understanding of decision, certain of its prerequisites should be made evident. The first is not a possible subject of decision, namely, that personality is confronted with the necessity of decision—it stands in a fateful situation. "All those structures which constitute an Ego and make it capable of deciding belong

36 *Ibid.*, p. 137.
37 *Ibid.*, p. 271.

to it."[38] The Ego, considered in itself, confronts logical necessities and alternatives. It "rests" within the security of the Logos.

The second prerequisite of decision is "the material in which it is carried out." Decision cannot be merely abstract; it is possible "only in concrete material, in a formed, ambiguous world." Thought is confronted by a concrete existence. This world of concrete material is "given," stands opposite and, as it were, alien to the Ego and to Logos. Whereas the Logos can in pure thought remain in itself, here it is estranged from itself. Knowledge of the material in which meaning is fulfilled can "approach the ideal of evidence only in a slow progress." One does not look for certainty in this area. Self-evidence is possible only in the realm of pure thought. But in face of the concrete material through which decision expresses itself, "no evidence but probability is demanded." In this area, then, knowledge lies between "formal evidence" and "material probability." It lies between rationalism and empiricism. At this level one is still in the sphere of Logos. The full character of decision is not yet reached, for it is only with the creative fulfillment of meaning that knowledge becomes "spiritual." (Here we find again the Fichtean view which runs through *The System of the Sciences*.)

One can never achieve the level of the creative and the spiritual through the rational or empirical examination of the forms of the material, or through the technical application of form to material, or through the application of the evident to the probable. A third element in knowledge is indispensable. This is the third prerequisite for decision.

The third element of which we speak, is the meaningful interpretation of reality. We are not speaking of a religious-metaphysical interpretation of our world as a special task, but of an understanding of reality such as is inherent in all scientific work. All knowledge, even the most exact, the most subject to methodical technique, contains fundamental interpretations rooted neither in formal evidence nor in material probability, but in original views, in basic decisions. . . . This becomes immediately clear in the productive understanding of norms, the religious, the moral, the aesthetic, and so forth. The formal evidence here reaches only as far as the constitution of the field of meaning itself, no further, and no norms at all can be taken from the material. Where it comes to a concrete formation of norms, concrete decisions are effective, and only insofar as this is true are concrete sciences of norms meaningful.[39]

[38] *Ibid.*, p. 142.
[39] *Ibid.*, pp. 143-44.

This whole passage is reminiscent of the description of the creative, spiritual act, set forth in *The System of the Sciences*. What was there called "original positing" is now called "original views" and "basic decisions." The conception of the "third element" is analogous also to the metalogical discrimination of the import. It will be recalled that the metalogical method deals with the formal and material elements on the one side and with the import element on the other. The fulfillment of the meaning of being brings about a correspondence between the epistemological and the metaphysical spheres.

The fulfillment of meaning in face of the Unconditioned and in the dimension of fate and decision is "the fulness of time," Kairos. Time is interpreted as running, so to speak, through a funnel. The spirit-bearing Gestalt, both individual and social, bearing within it a sense of universal values, living in the context of the "concrete material," and oriented to the Unconditioned, creatively fulfills meaning for that particular, fated time. After this fashion fate and freedom are supported by the eternal. Knowledge born in the Kairos, then, is knowledge growing not out of accidental, arbitrary events but out of a sense of basic significance and possibility. "True knowledge is knowledge born of the Kairos, that is, of the fate of the time, of the point at which time is disturbed by eternity."[40]

But being disturbed by eternity is quite different from grasping it in an act of knowledge. The "third element" is not an object that presents itself in an act of perception. It can never become an object in the act of knowledge itself. This is the reason it must remain hidden from the formalistic and empirical epistemology.

It can become an object only for the metaphysics of knowledge. In the same way, style never lies in the intention of the creative artist, not even when he consciously follows a previous style. He can never consciously give himself *his* style. The style (the third element in artistic creation) is apparent only to the historian or observer of art (who under certain circumstances can be the same person as the artist).[41]

The "timely" moment (the Kairos) is one in which a living disinterested enthusiasm for creation is joined with the fatefulness of reality and the depth of life. But "as soon as attention is *directed to* the third element, freedom and fate are lost, and

[40] *Ibid.*, p. 174.
[41] *Ibid.*, p. 148.

subjective arbitrariness controlled by psychological necessity replaces them." Rigorous objectivity is demanded, but one cannot objectify the ultimate orientation, the Unconditioned. We cannot grasp it; it grasps us.

The third element is apprehended as unconditionally real and unconditionally valid, but "it transcends every conceivable and experienceable reality."[42] This formulation is, to say the least, confusing. One might wonder how one is to know anything about the Unconditioned if it is beyond conception and beyond experience. Indeed, Tillich's words remind one of Nietzsche's trenchant criticism of the concept of "the Unconditioned":

> An "absolute mode of existence" is nonsense, the concept "being," "thing," is always relative to us. . . . There are no things-in-themselves! But even supposing there *were* an "in-itself," an unconditioned thing, it could on that very account *not be known!* Something unconditioned cannot be known: otherwise, it would not be unconditioned! Knowing, however, is always a process of "coming into relation with something." . . . Knowing means: "to place one's self in relation with something: to feel one's self conditioning it." . . .[43]

When Tillich says that the Unconditioned "transcends every conceivable and experienceable reality," he of course does not mean that it can be of no concern to man. It is man's ultimate concern. He means rather that it is comparable to Schelling's "immemorial being" (*Das Unvordenkliche*), which is anterior to and inaccessible to thought. It is recognized as the *prius* of all thought and also as an abyss before all thinking. Nevertheless, the words quoted from Tillich can only be hyperbole, whether describing Tillich's or Schelling's point of view, for the ground and the abyss of meaning are asserted to characterize the ultimate. Evidently, the Unconditioned is not entirely inconceivable. If it were, how could Tillich know that it contains the dialectic of ground and abyss?[44]

With regard to Nietzsche's point about the conditioning of the Unconditioned through the mere knowledge of it, we shall not repeat here the considerations already set forth in the definition of the Unconditioned expounded earlier. Tillich would agree with

[42] *Rel. Verw.*, p. 67.

[43] Friedrich Nietzsche, *The Will to Power*, II, trans. Anthony M. Ludovici (New York: The Macmillan Company, 1924), *Works*, XV, 82.

[44] Siegfried Marck argues that by transporting the dialectic to the absolute Tillich is violating the demands of (Kantian) critical philosophy which he claims to observe. Cf. *Die Dialektik in der Philosophie der Gegenwart* (Tübingen: Mohr, 1929), I, pp. 116 ff.

Nietzsche if the Unconditioned were asserted to be a "thing." In Tillich's view, however, it is in every meaning; it is the meaning-reality that conditions all conditioned forms and meanings. (This answer to Nietzsche is scarcely adequate. We shall come back to it below.)

But no simple unequivocal formulation can grasp this meaning. A dynamic logic is necessary for a reality that is no mere imitation of eternal essences. According to Tillich, "there is no grasping of the essential nature of things except in decision, because the nature of things itself stands in fate and ambiguity."[45] Dialectics, then, is an observation of the essence in so far as it stands in fate, and not of the essence in so far as it remains fateless. If reality is dynamic, so also must the idea of it be dynamic. Here we confront the problem of the One and the Many. In order to be recognized at all the idea must have some element withdrawn from the fateful course of change. The Platonic conception of the idea stresses the immutable element in being, the unchanging element of reality. In later Occidental philosophy this element was minimized, but the concept of universal law maintained the view of the static character of the idea. This static space-thinking was challenged radically by the subdominant strain in modern philosophy. With Jacob Boehme, for example, something breaks through the confines of mystical striving for unification with the Superbeing. For him, "the world of ideas is the revelation of the divine abyss." Following Boehme and Schelling, Tillich holds that the idea carries within itself struggle, contrast, and harmony; this is the dynamic element that leads, or, as Tillich puts it, that leaps to history. "The world of ideas is not only the principle of completion, but in it there is an ambiguity, a threat, a power to enter into conflict with itself, to rush forward to the historical revelation of the contrasting elements unified in it."[46] The idea shares in the dynamic, dialectical character of reality, and therefore it does not promise a Platonic "eternal rest" but rather "a unity of rest and unrest, a movable, in itself questionable being, pregnant with infinite tensions."[47] Only through dynamic process in fate and freedom does the idea enter into history, the Logos into Kairos.

The idea has an inner infinity, not indeed for a supposed observer but for itself, and everyone who regards it is drawn into the inner infinity of the idea. There is indeed a rest, an eternal, static element in it; otherwise it would not be idea, and the unrest would have no

45 *The Interpretation of History*, p. 162.
46 *Ibid.*, p. 161.
47 *Ibid.*

resistance, no immutable point through which it could become evident as unrest but this static element is not to be severed from the dynamic.[48]

Accordingly, the participation of things in the idea corresponds to the participation of the idea in things. "The Logos becomes flesh; it enters into time and reveals its inner infinity."[49]

Now, this inner dynamic makes the idea ambiguous and in turn makes freedom and individuality possible. Man can turn towards the Unconditioned and thus follow the leap of the idea to a new meaningful creation. Or he can turn away from the Un-conditioned—that is, he can attempt to draw it entirely into the sphere of the conditioned; in this case he follows the leap of the idea into the ever present temptation to capsule the absolute in a demonic distortion.

But there is one point where ambiguity is overcome. The ap-prehension of the Unconditioned of meaning, being, and value does not share the decision character of other knowledge. What-ever stands in the context of knowledge is subject to ambiguity, but the knowledge of knowledge must arise from another sphere. The recognition of the third element in knowledge is an expres-sion of the relation of knowledge to the Unconditioned. Here we have to do with a basic metaphysical attitude. The recognition that our knowledge is relative is the one knowledge that is not relative; it is the knowledge that transcends formal and material elements, transcends the opposition between the absolute and the relative.

The absolute standpoint is therefore a position which can never be taken; rather it is the guard which protects the Unconditioned, avert-ing the encroachment of a conditioned point of view on the sphere of the Unconditioned. But the guardian is not the guarded, and if it claims to be such, it is the very one which abandons the watch and injures the holy. With these concepts the position of belief-ful relativism is grasped, i.e., of that relativism which overcomes relativism.[50]

This, then, is the outcome of the dynamic conception of truth: it is not relativistic.

It has nothing statically absolute, in reference to which it can be called relative, while the static thought of truth forces one to rela-tivism, as soon as the arrogance of the absolute position is broken down. The dynamic thought of truth overcomes the alternative

[48] *Ibid.*
[49] *Ibid.*, p. 164.
[50] Ibid., p. 171.

"absolute-relative." The Kairos, the fateful moment of knowledge, is absolute insofar as it places one at this moment before the absolute decision for or against the truth, and it is relative insofar as it knows that this decision is possible only as a concrete decision, as the fate of the time. Thus the Kairos serves to reveal rather than conceal the Logos.[51]

Now, if we ask by what standards man enters into the Kairos and moves towards the fulfillment of time and meaning, we do not readily find in Tillich's exposition a central integrating positive principle. We have already noted his early espousal of a mysticism of love for all living creatures. In his essay on "Kairos" he asserts the meaning of history to be the struggle for justice. In his sympathetic, if also critical, treatment of Marxism he asserts that the Marxist revolt against capitalist society represented a justifiable revolt against exploitation in the direction of a new meaning in life—a meaning that involves a wider participation of men in the satisfactions of security and creativity. In general, his material principles would seem to be drawn from Old Testament prophecy, from the New Testament idea of love, from Enlightenment conceptions of autonomy, and from modern socialist conceptions of a planned freedom and security. All of these conceptions are of course to be interpreted in terms of autonomy deepened by theonomy and also in a dynamic spirit oriented to the Kairos. But these norms do not represent Tillich's first concern. Whatever norms we employ or create, Tillich says, we must look beyond them to the Unconditioned of value and truth.

As noted in the previous chapter, however, this principle of theonomy represents more an attitude than a material principle. The point is not that Tillich's concept of the Unconditioned has no special relevance for ethical value and meaning, but rather that it seems to be relevant for any and all universal values. It seems to assert that the fulfillment of meaning will move in the direction of the harmony and fullness of value. But we are not

[51] *Ibid.*, p. 175. It is because of Emanuel Hirsch's repudiation of Logos that Tillich attacks his subordination of the demands of the Kairos to the goals of National Socialism. See Tillich's striking essay "Die Theologie des Kairos und die gegenwärtige geistige Lage. Offener Brief an Emanuel Hirsch," *Theologische Blätter*, XIII (1934), 305-28. It might appear that the absence of any explicit material principle (a point we have already discussed in Chapter IV and shall revert to presently) leaves Tillich's philosophy open to perversion in the hands of a Hirsch. But it should be noted that Hirsch completely violated the theonomous spiritual attitude desiderated by Tillich.

here concerned primarily with the ethical problem. His systematic treatment of this problem appears in his presentation of religious socialism and also in writings belonging to a later period not under discussion here.

Concerning the epistemological method Tillich proposes, we can only say of it that on the one hand it does not repudiate formal evidence and material probability and that on the other it is, like the ultimate aspect of any religious insight, based upon the intuition of the infinite splendor and promise of the dearest deep down freshness of things. The guarding against the absolutizing of the finite is a modern expression of the negative theology of Neo-Platonism and of the doctrine of justification by faith. All in all, the epistemological method presented is a way of faith whereby one through decision puts his trust in that effulgent and powerful mystery which vibrates through every part of creation, supporting and threatening, form-creating, form-bursting, form-transforming. One cannot prove or disprove its reality. One can only recognize that in it and through it we live and move and have our being. This is scarcely an epistemological method as ordinarily understood. It is rather an affirmation about the ultimate, a decision for that without which being and meaning and truth lose their life-blood. It is, in short, a method that presupposes the reality it is supposed to lead to. Tillich himself calls it an "original decision" in response to grace.

But Tillich is not merely the philosopher of grace. He is also the philosopher of sin; he is an existential philosopher. Belief-ful realism implies that existence is alienated from being, or, to use his more frequent formulation, man in his existential nature is separated from the Unconditioned. He uses also, as we have seen, the Platonic concepts of participation and separation to describe the existential situation. Sometimes he adapts the concept of tension implicit in Anaximander's view of existence poised precariously over the *Apeiron*. At other times he uses the medieval concepts of existence and essence, and thus he characterizes existence as an expression of essence and at the same time a contradiction of it.

Hence man's fate is that his existence is meaningful and also hostile to meaning. This is not a matter for explanation; it is rather a matter for description. In other words, Tillich accepts— as description and not as explanation of evil—a form of the doctrine of original sin, though he does not like to use the phrase because of mythological perversions that attach to it. Original sin is wrongly interpreted, in his view, if it cuts man off entirely from

meaningful reality, if it cuts man off entirely from the Unconditioned. It is also wrongly interpreted if it deprives man of
responsibility. Either of these views is a falsification of the existential situation; either of them calls for a nondialectical interpretation of existence.

On the one hand, then, Tillich aims to avoid the idealistic
conception of synthesis which makes man's existence an unfolding of essence. According to idealism, sin and guilt and separation
are actually not real. Thus man is described as God coming to
self-consciousness and self-realization through man's exercise of
freedom.[52] On the other hand, Tillich aims to avoid the undialectical (earlier) view of the Barthian, who deprives everything in the
natural order of its significance. In the (earlier) Barthian view
existence is merely the order of sin and guilt. Grace is the complete contradiction of the order of nature. For Tillich, man is both
fated and free; he is both related to the Unconditioned and separated from it. If he were not related to it, he could not even ask
the question concerning the ultimate meaning.

Since the elucidation of the concepts of sin and guilt really
belongs to Tillich's theology, we shall not here consider them in
detail. It must suffice to emphasize that his philosophy of religion
is shot through with the dialectical conceptions described above.
Thus the doctrine of creation and the doctrines of fate, guilt, and
sin are seen in relation to each other.[53]

As we proceed with the exposition of Tillich's philosophy of
meaning and of the philosophy of religion based upon it and as
we consider his conception of the Unconditioned, the conceptions
of participation and separation found in his philosophy of being
must be borne in mind. Otherwise, Tillich may be confused with
the idealists or with the Barthians.

Having indicated the main features of Tillich's belief-ful or
self-transcending realism, we are now ready for the exposition of
his philosophy of religion. Philosophy of meaning becomes central here, as in Tillich's philosophy of culture. Its general principles are presented under the following heads: (1) the definition
of the elements of meaning and their relations, (2) the general

---

[52] Schelling's essay *Of Human Freedom* represents for Tillich a decisive
denial and repudiation of idealistic monism. Schelling presents a more
dialectical view also in his treatment of mysticism and guilt (the subject
of Tillich's dissertation of 1914).

[53] Cf. "Estrangement and Reconciliation in Modern Thought," *Review of
Religion*, IX (1944), 5-19.

definition of the functions of meaning, (3) the structure of the functions of meaning, (4) religion in the various functions of meaning, and (5) the essence and truth of religion.

We have already had occasion to discuss Tillich's concept of meaning in connection with the theology of culture and in connection with the treatment of "belief-ful realism." In "The Philosophy of Religion" the elements of the consciousness of meaning are presented as follows:

1. An awareness of the context of meaning in which every separate meaning stands and without which it would be meaningless.
2. An awareness of the meaningfulness of the context of meaning and thus of every particular meaning, namely, the consciousness of an unconditioned meaning that is present in every particular meaning.
3. An awareness of the demand under which a particular meaning stands, to fulfill the unconditioned meaning.[54]

The first is an awareness of a totality, of a "world." But more than a totality is involved, for this alone could sink into the abyss of meaninglessness. In it there lives an unconditioned meaningfulness. The unconditionedness of meaning, however, is itself not a meaning but rather the ground of meaning. All particular meanings or contexts of meaning on up to the universal context may be designated as the *forms* of meaning. The unconditioned meaning is called the *import* of meaning. The latter is the meaningfulness that gives to every particular meaning its reality, its significance, its real existence. The unconditioned meaning is not only a ground of meaning but also a demand for fulfillment of meaning, a demand with which only the complete or perfect context of bringing together all meaning could comply—the unconditioned form. But such an unconditioned form would itself be a contradiction of the relation of form to import. If the ground of meaning could exhaust itself in an unconditioned form of meaning, the inner infinity of being and meaning would be abolished. Nevertheless, in every act of meaning there exists the demand for this perfect unity of form and import; only through the perfect unity of all meaning can meaning come to unconditioned realization, namely, to form.

The view of the elements of meaning just set forth provides the fundamental principles of the philosophy of religion and of culture. In other words, these elements of meaning may be

[54] "Religionsphilosophie," p. 789. We have cited this passage in our preliminary discussion on p. 59. For Tillich's treatment of meaning in the context of *The System of the Sciences*, see pp. 159 ff., *supra*.

exhibited in every sphere of meaning, in the theoretical as well as in the practical functions. With them in mind we turn now to the theoretical definition of religion and of culture.

Culture is interpreted as exhibiting an autonomous orientation, religion as exhibiting a theonomous orientation. In culture the consciousness is directed toward the particular, conditioned forms of meaning; in religion it is directed toward the unconditioned meaning, the import of meaning. "Religion is direction toward (or reference to) the Unconditioned; culture is relatedness to the conditioned forms and their unity."[55]

But religion and culture may not properly be placed in sharp juxtaposition, for form and import belong together. It is meaningless to posit the one without the other. Every cultural act depends upon the ground of meaning; insofar as it is an act of meaning, it is *substantially* religious. It aims at unity of form, and it implicitly recognizes the demand for unity of meaning.[56]

One may, it seems to the writer, question whether culture actually recognizes this demand. Autonomy and heteronomy would seem rather to be characterized by their ignoring of the demand. Indeed, Tillich in later writings characterizes secularism as self-sufficient finitude. It should be noted here that, so far from recognizing the demand for unity of meaning, autonomy is often to be seen as a fragmenting of meaning which may issue in what Dilthey calls the "anarchy of values."

In any event, Tillich holds that culture, though substantially religious, is not religious by intention. On the other hand, religion must assume a cultural form. The religious act cannot direct itself toward the unconditioned meaning except through the unity of the forms of meaning. Every religious act is therefore from the point of view of its form a cultural act; it is related to the totality of meaning. But it is not by intention cultural; it does not have in mind the totality of meaning, but rather the import of meaning, the unconditioned meaning.

Before continuing with our exposition it may be well to observe that Tillich in these formulations may appear to give a higher value to culture than the facts would seem to warrant, and also that he defines religion in the way he prefers to find it. Not all

---

[55] *Ibid.*, p. 791.

[56] Cf. Tillich's presentation of Schelling in his *Die religionsgeschichtliche Konstruktion in Schellings positiver Philosophie* (Breslau: Fleischmann, 1910), p. 50: "History is really history of religion. The cultural process has its roots everywhere in the religious, from which finally it reaches completion . . ."

types of religion are directed toward the unconditioned meaning, and certainly not toward what Tillich considers to be the unconditioned meaning. But Tillich takes these considerations into account. Indeed, precisely because many "religious" people identify the conditioned with the Unconditioned or dissolve the Unconditioned into the conditioned, Tillich has himself demanded the elimination or rather the transformation of the concept of "religion."[57] It would appear that in the above formulations about religion Tillich has given, not a definition of religion in accord with his conception of the task of philosophy of religion, but a norm concept. According to that conception, as pointed out earlier, the philosopher of religion should provide a theory of the religious function and its categories, or, in other words, a theory of the essence of religion and its categories. This theory of the essence of religion, to be sure, may imply a normative concept of religion (as Tillich says), but it should not itself represent that norm. It would seem, then, that Tillich's definition of religion should be formulated as follows: Religion is relatedness to that which is conceived to be of ultimate significance, to that which is *considered to be* the Unconditioned.

That Tillich has given a normative concept of religion and not a definition of the essence of religion becomes clear when we observe the argument cited to support his assertion that the distinction between religion and culture and the interrelatedness between religion and culture must always be maintained. Hegelianism, he says, overlooks the distinction and as a consequence identifies religion with a self-sufficient culture, "a synthesis of the world of spirit." In other words, Hegel is criticized because he uses the wrong norm-concept of religion. Again, Tillich says that supernaturalism overlooks the interrelatedness between religion and culture and as a consequence simply ranges religion above culture or against culture. In ranging the one above the other it forgets that religion signifies the ground and abyss of *all* meaning. In ranging the one against the other it destroys the unity of meaning. Frequently, Tillich goes on to say, this disruption of meaning takes place in the name of the irrational.[58] A similar disruption of meaning may occur, he says,

[57] "Die Ueberwindung des Religionsbegriffs in der Religionsphilosophie," *Kant-Studien*, XXVII (1922), 446-69. Barth has also demanded the *Ueberwindung* of the concept of religion, but in his case the concept of religion is entirely deprived of positive significance for Christian theology.

[58] In some quarters Tillich himself has been attacked as an irrationalist. His own intention is overlooked or misunderstood in these attacks. For him a fundamental, if undiscoverable, unity obtains between rationality and the

in idealism. Rudolf Otto, for example, distinguishes religion and culture in such a way as either to set the one above the other or to set the one against the other, the one being characterized as irrational and the other as rational.[59] In these comments on super-naturalism, on irrationalism, and on idealism, Tillich is again appealing to a normative concept of religion. It should be added that in some of his writings religion is referred to in accord with the alternative definition suggested by the writer. In other words, sometimes Tillich refers to religion in terms of a general theory of its essence, and sometimes he refers to it in accord with the norm-concept set forth in "The Philosophy of Religion." Indeed, when Tillich later on in "The Philosophy of Religion" discusses heteronomous and demonic forms of religion, he uses the definition and not the norm-concept.

From the definition of religion Tillich turns to a treatment of

---

unconditionally powerful. Irrationalism, he says, may be explained fre-quently as an attempt "to preserve the inner power of things" by setting up limits to the *ratio*. "But it fails to see that it is of the very essence of *ratio* to make evident the true, the ultimate power of existence. Conse-quently, it is the fate of irrationalism that, whereas it aims to go deeper than rationalism, in reality it becomes more shallow, that is, it remains fast within the bounds of less powerful levels of being" (*Rel. Verw.*, p. 70). On page 280 of this same book he sets forth a series of definitions of the rational and the irrational, then concludes by saying, "Altogether, it is better either to avoid the use of the concept of the irrational or to use it only in a strictly defined sense." Irrationalism as a protest against a limited form of rationality or as a demand for paradox or antinomy is not, strictly speaking, irrationalism. These matters should be dealt with in a "fully rational, i.e. in a self-consistent way; they can thus provide a basis for the necessity of antinomy."

[59] Otto's book *Das Heilige* is praised by Tillich for its acute description of the numinous experience and also for its overcoming of the rational rigidi-ties and burdens of the ecclesiastical and of the idealistic-philosophical mentality. Yet his conception of the holy is criticized not only because it provides an undialectical interpretation of the relation of the rational to "the irrational" ("the burning fire of the living thing") but also because his idea of the holy as the "Wholly Other" can be of little significance for man. In a lengthy review of Otto's *Das Heilige* the following typical sen-tences are to be found: "One cannot entirely avoid the impression that what Otto calls the rational is related to the irrational as something external. Otto himself feels this and considers it as an irrationality that is tied up with religion, but he does not indicate the essential relation that obtains between the *mysterium* and the rational form. . . . It must be shown in what essential relationship this 'Wholly Other' stands to the other forms of consciousness. For if it stands in no relation or even only in a supple-mentary relation, it splits the unity of the consciousness and it would not be *we* who experience the holy." "Die Kategorie des 'Heiligen' bei Rudolf Otto," *Theologische Blätter*, II (1923), 11-12.

the structure of the functions of meaning. This involves a discussion of the theoretical and the practical functions. Expanding what he had set forth already in *The System of the Sciences*, he asserts that there are two functions of meaning: In the one everything existent, including the spirit-bearing Gestalt itself, is viewed in terms of the fulfillment of meaning; in the other the spirit-bearing Gestalt tears itself away from its meaningful immediacy and establishes itself as a spiritual (or cultural) form. The first range of functions is the theoretical, the second is the practical. Now, although logical priority belongs to the practical range—for only insofar as the spirit-bearing Gestalt has subordinated itself to the valid form in its existence can it bring the existing thing to fulllment—the practical, of course, cannot exist without the theoretical and vice versa. The practical is a real, the theoretical an ideal fulfillment; the former is directed toward the connections of existence, the latter toward the form of things.

Thus there is tension between the real and the ideal. It is based upon the double relationship of the import of meaning to the form of meaning.

Insofar as the import of meaning comes to fulfillment in no form of meaning but yet is the ground of every form of meaning, it becomes the stuff or material of meaning. "Material" is the expression for the import of meaning considered as detached from its unconditionedness and making possible the particular contents of meaning. "Material" as absolute giveness (or datum) is a concept that is as impossible as *perfect* unity of form. For an exclusive, given material would be a form among other forms, but not the infinite possibility of forms, as is demanded by the unconditionedness of the import of meaning. The genuine concept of material has nothing to do with materiality in the sense of an objectification in the physical sphere of natural laws; it expresses the basic creative principle found in everything real, and reaches on into the sphere of the spirit-bearing *Gestalten*. A real fulfillment of meaning is one in which there is a bestowal of meaning in the sphere of the individual reality which is bound to nature; an ideal fulfillment is also one in which the giving of meaning signifies no transformation in the material sphere, but rather a fulfillment of the existent in its immediate formation. The first, however, is only possible *in* the spiritual personality, the second *through* the spiritual personality. That is the place of fulfillment of meaning, both real and ideal.[60]

We may recall here that the religious element in both the real and the ideal, in both the practical and the theoretical spheres, is the special concern with the import of unconditioned meaning; the cultural element is the concern with the forms which meanings take. To use the language of *The System of the Sciences,* the religious element has to do with the foundation of meaning (*fundierend*) and the cultural element has to do with the empirical forms of cultural creation (*fundiert*). By way of illustration Tillich applies these general principles to the various spheres, practical and theoretical, exhibiting again the dialectic between the form and the import, the conditioned and the Unconditioned. But always the theoretical and the practical are shown to belong together and to be necessary for the apprehension of the Unconditioned. When they are separated, the result will be abstractness and non-contemporaneity with respect to meaning, and this will lead to a loss of ultimate meaningfulness, with its consequent emptiness.

Following Tillich through example after example of the application of the theory of meaning one becomes aware of a marked advantage of the method. By means of it he avoids having to argue for religion. All men are seen to be religious, either implicitly or explicitly, for all men are concerned with meaning. Or, to put the matter in another way, all men recognize something as being of ultimate concern. Hence all men are religious in this broad sense. The differences between men are, so to speak, religious differences, that is, differences with respect to what concerns them unconditionally. This approach makes its unnecessary to discuss the usual problem posed by philosophy of religion, namely, the problem of the truth of religion. In the usual method, one first discusses the nature of religion and then raises the question of its truth. One examines the religious act for purposes of description, then turns the attention to the religious object for the purpose of scrutinizing the truth claim of the religious act.

The metalogical method of Tillich, however, repudiates this dual approach. For it, the question as to the nature and the question as to the truth of religion are identical.

In the proof that the religious function is the ground (*fundierend*) function of meaning, there is immediately given the evidence of the nature and the truth, an indication of the act and the object of the act. It is the superiority of the metalogical method that it apprehends the truth along with the nature of religion and it is not necessary for it to give the evidence of the truth, neither from outside religion, nor speculatively, nor ethically, nor through evaluation of religious evidences, nor pragmatically.[61]

Thus the question concerning the reality of an unconditional concern is meaningless. The very posing of the question presupposes that an ultimate meaning is discoverable.

It is meaningless to ask whether the Unconditioned "is," whether therefore the religious act is oriented to something real and is in that sense true or not. For the question as to whether the Unconditioned exists presupposes already the unconditioned meaningfulness of the sphere of knowledge, the unconditionally existing. The certainty of the unconditioned is the grounding certainty from which all doubt can proceed, which however itself can never be the object of doubt. Therefore the object of religion is not only real; it is the presupposition of all positing or recognizing (*Setzung*) of reality.[62]

The truth and meaning of this reality is known immediately. Here Tillich aligns himself with the Augustinian and medieval Franciscan view.

Tillich would no doubt admit that he may be challenged on whether he has correctly or adequately described the unconditional concern of human nature, but he denies that any meaningful interpretation of life can avoid the question: What is the unconditional concern? All men are thrown into this existential situation, which inevitably elicits the question and demands an answer in terms of the human situation in general and in terms of the particular historical situation. The question is both a practical and a theoretical one.

But Tillich does recognize that the Unconditioned is not something "given" as a datum. The Unconditioned is not real in the sense of being an entity. It is rather something that must be apprehended in and through and beyond the real and the ideal. To use a term drawn from speculative mysticism, the Unconditioned is "ungiven."

That the Unconditioned can never be anything objective or objectively given is an insight of which theology must be reminded again and again. The objectification of the divine is the fundamental danger of all religious cognition and corresponds exactly with the danger of nomism in the domain of the religious life. Here the mystics are better guides than the church theologians.[63]

Since the Unconditioned is not something objective, it must always be spoken of symbolically. A literal expression is in the nature of things impossible. The symbolic character of religious ideas in no way deprives them of their reality, but it lifts this

[61] "Religionsphilosophie," p. 798.
[62] *Ibid.*
[63] Tillich's review of Hermann Schwarz's *Das Ungegebene,* in *Theologische Blätter,* II (1923), 74.

reality out of the conditioned into the unconditioned sphere, that is, into the religious sphere.

The intention to speak nonsymbolically of religion is irreligious, impious; for it robs the Unconditioned of its unconditionality and leads in addition to the quite proper abandonment of the Unconditioned when transformed into an object, as a creature of fantasy.[64]

In line with his theory of meaning as the correlation, the transforming, and the transcending of the real and the ideal, Tillich gives extensive attention to the problem of the nature of religious symbols not only as references to the Unconditioned but also as the creations of spirit. Religious symbols have four major characteristics: figurative quality; perceptibility—"something intrinsically invisible, ideal, or transcendent, is made perceptible"; innate power; and social acceptability.[65] Any adequate symbolism must always be related to an apprehension of the Unconditioned, the abyss as well as the ground of meaning. Failure in this respect induces not only literalism but also relatedness to some conditioned object rather than to a truly unconditional concern. False and true symbolism may be distinguished on this basis.

There have been numerous and sundry attempts to negate the truth value of religious symbolism. When radical, they are attempts to separate the question of the essence of religion from the truth of religion. Subjective idealism, psychologism, and sociologism, try this separation in various ways. But the attempts must miscarry. Subjective idealism overlooks the fact that analyses of functions or of meanings are ultimately analyses of being. In this essay on "The Religious Symbol" Tillich gives considerable attention to the objections of psychologism and sociologism. Although he recognizes gratefully an element of truth in the charges of illusionism and ideology coming from depth psychology and from Marxism, he holds nevertheless that the psychologist and the sociologist must themselves presuppose something that is unconditionally real. Hence their criticisms are mainly relevant as a questioning of the particular *selection* of symbols, but not as denials of all symbols. And on their own part, they end by committing the *Hybris* of attachment to some particular autonomous forms. In reaction against the *Hybris* of autonomy—which appears in varying forms in different cultures and periods—"religion"

[64] "Religionsphilosophie," p. 798.

[65] *Rel. Verw.*, pp. 88-90. A translation by the present writer and Dr. Ernst Fraenkel of this essay on "The Religious Symbol" appears in the *Journal of Liberal Religion*, II (1940), 13-33. A slightly revised and abbreviated version appears in *Daedalus*, 87, No. 3 (1958), 3-21.

often commits the corresponding sin of the *Hybris* of heteronomy by setting up symbols that claim exemption from autonomous, rational criticism. This spurious form of religion does not recognize that in autonomy there is a response to demand for meaning; moreover, it gives unconditional loyalty to its own particular symbols, and all in the name of the Unconditioned. Both autonomy and heteronomy require at least an implicit theonomy, else they become empty, the one by identifying culture with religion, the other by separating culture from religion. Thus both lose the power of persuasion and become in the end demonic.

Autonomy and heteronomy are tensions within theonomy, which can lead to the tearing asunder and thus the catastrophe of the spirit, for the essential relationship of culture and religion is theonomy. Every philosophy of religion is to be reproached which proceeds from one of the two poles without coming to the synthesis and correcting the defect of the one-sided starting point.[66]

In short, relatedness to the Unconditioned must be seen to affect all spheres of meaning, yet it is not to be identified with any sphere of meaning or all of them (as such) together. Hence philosophy of religion and theology must ultimately be oriented to the Unconditioned.

If this relatedness to the Unconditioned is properly interpreted, as it affects both religion and culture, it may be called faith. It is the belief-ful aspect of self-transcending realism. It is effective in all functions of the spirit. It is not identical with any one or all of the functions, nor is it a special function apart. Nor is it belief in the truth of uncertain or doubtful objects; it has nothing to do with acceptance or probability. It is rather something that comes to expression in all meaningful activity—is, indeed, its root. Faith, then, has no special "object." The Unconditioned as such can never be an object; rather, the ground and abyss of meaning are intuited in the symbol. Faith transcends the immediacy of things and penetrates to the ground and abyss upon which all things rest.

Accordingly, the lack of faith is not the refusal or failure to recognize something or other that is objective. Its essence is rather that it stops with objects in their immediacy, in their conditioned forms, and does not penetrate to the supporting import. The unbelief-ful attitude is therefore the typically cultural-autonomous attitude. But it is unbelief-ful only by intention; it is not so in substance. For so long as it is creative it lives in faith.

[66] "Religionsphilosophie," p. 801.

Heteronomous faith, on the other hand, may be belief-ful in intention, but in substance it is the absolutization of some particular cultural form. Hence it, too, fails to penetrate to the ground and abyss of meaning and being.

At this point arises one of the most critical questions regarding Tillich's philosophy of religion. The Christian speaks of faith as faith in a personal God. But Tillich speaks of it as relatedness to the Unconditioned, which is beyond the personal. When we come to that section of his "Philosophy of Religion" where he discusses "God and the World," we naturally expect to learn something of the character of God and his relation to the world. Actually we find only statements concerning the nature of the Unconditioned. We are reminded that speaking about God must be symbolic speaking, that God cannot be one being alongside other beings. We are reminded that any symbol of God must be a self-immolating symbol, pointing beyond itself to the unconditioned abyss and ground of meaning. Here we find much that is reminiscent of the Neo-Platonic conception of transcendence. But we do not learn whether the Unconditioned *is* God.[67] Later on we shall discuss this question at length. First we shall consider the principal concepts which Tillich uses to refer to the ultimate, namely, the holy and the divine—with their accompanying concepts, the profane and the demonic.

In its fullest sense the word "holy" applies to the meaningful reality of an ideal theonomy. But a complete theonomy would be the perfected kingdom of God; hence when the word refers to the ideal theonomy it is a symbol and no reality. In any state less than that of the ideal theonomy, "a meaning-fulfilling act or a meaning-object is holy insofar as it is a bearer of the unconditioned meaning." In every such act or object there is implicit both an affirmation and a negation from the point of view of the Unconditioned. Thus the holy reality is related to the Unconditioned as the double symbol of the ground and the abyss of meaning and reality. The holy object is therefore never holy in itself, but rather only through a negation of itself; and in this negation of itself is included the negation of everything finite. What is involved here is the duality of absolute fulfillment of meaning and of the absolute abyss of meaning.

The holy breaks through the immediate forms of existence; it has ecstatic qualities. All holy existence is *ecstatic* existence; that is,

[67] In later writings Tillich speaks of the Unconditioned as a negative-rational term, whereas "God" is a positive-symbolic term. The distinction is not made in the "Religionsphilosophie."

existence that escapes from its immediate form. There is an inner transcending of its formal, cultural givenness. Subjectively this is true of every act of faith, whether it finds expression in personal prayer or in the consciousness-transcending intoxication of mystical ecstasy. Objectively it applies to every symbol of the divine, to the personal God resting upon his own depth as much as to the awesome figures of the gods of India.[68]

There are three typical ways of conceiving the ecstatic approach to the holy. From the point of view of heteronomy, the holy is the supernatural, for autonomy it is the ideal, and for theonomy it is the paradox. According to the Tillichian view of theonomy, then, the holy appears as the paradoxical immanence of the transcendent. The characterization of these three orientations is basic for Tillich's whole philosophy of culture and of religion. Hence his formulations should be quoted at length:

Supernaturalism asserts that the holy has so united with the holy object or event that the latter is raised as a whole into a higher sphere and stands over against everything else—the secular. In this view the insight is lost that the holiness of the holy reality is effected by the negation of its immediate existence, a negation that places the holy reality in the same situation with everything else secular.

Idealism, on the other hand, wishes to transcend the immediate givenness through the ideal demand. It makes ecstasy into enthusiasm for the ideal; it does not see that even the immediately existent is grounded in the Unconditioned, nor that the ideally existent is also negated by the Unconditioned.[69]

Here we see again Tillich's basic objection to idealism: with respect to the thing as it is, it forgets the ground; with respect to the thing as it should be, it forgets the abyss. Not so with theonomy:

Theonomy, which by definition sees the holy in all forms, must reject supernaturalism, because it sanctifies a definite form in and for itself, and thereby excludes all others. It must likewise reject idealism because it no longer places the theoretical and practical ideal forms under the No of the Unconditioned and thus wrongly profanes the real forms while falsely sanctifying the ideal forms. Theonomy itself discerns the *paradoxical* character of the holy and of ecstasy; it discerns the character of self-transcendence, of the break-through and of symbolism. As over against both supernaturalism and idealism, it comes to the insight that the holy reality is *grace* and not a stage above nature, nor the demand of a natural ideal. Grace is

[68] "Religionsphilosophie," p. 806.
[69] *Ibid.*, pp. 806-7.

always paradoxical; it breaks through the immediate form, but it has no form of its own.[70]

We have noted that for Tillich a Yes and a No inhere in every holy reality and also in every symbol of the holy. Indeed, the negation, he says, places the holy reality in the same situation as the secular. This could be taken to mean that nothing is in any special way holy, that all things, since they are conditioned, are profane. But such an interpretation would be erroneous. One must remember, to be sure, that the ground of the holiness of things is not in the things themselves. But certain things possess a peculiar and eminent symbolic power in their witnessing to the transcendent and the holy. Indeed, their destiny seems to be that they should become "holy things." Certain things and persons, forms and events, have a symbolic power due to associations that may not depend entirely upon their own character but depend rather upon a fateful juncture of meanings and associations. This symbolic power can be dissolved through an autonomy that secularizes the holy, or it may lose its effectiveness through a supernaturalistic sanctification and exaltation above the formal context of meaning. In both cases the ecstatic and paradoxical character of the symbol is destroyed.

One is reminded here of Otto's description of the numinous. Tillich seems to be saying that the holy involves a complex of that which is "other," of the ecstatic, the "fascinating," and the awesome. All of these elements are involved when the religious consciousness is aware of the ground and the abyss. The holy blesses man, for in it the consciousness finds an earnest of unconditioned fulfillment; but the holy is also inviolable and not to be approached by the secular consciousness. The first aspect is expressed in the hymns of blessedness of the mystics, the second in the taboo— the plastic symbol of the negative unconditionedness of the holy. These two aspects of the holy give rise to the two characteristic countertendencies in religion. The first aspect manifests itself in the attempt to achieve perfection through traffic with holy things and through ecstatic states of consciousness. The second aspect is to be seen in the ideas and practices of purification. Here there is an attempt to eliminate profane elements from the consciousness toward the end of preparing a receptacle for the reception of grace.

The upshot of this discussion is, then, that there are acts and objects that have a superior symbolic power for eliciting "ecstatic"

[70] *Ibid.*, p. 807.

relatedness to the Unconditioned and for eliciting movement towards new fulfillment of meaning. But this does not mean that secular or profane elements are viewed as the real antithesis to the holy. Culture is not the antithesis of religion. Of course the absolute antithesis to the sacred would have to be something totally incompatible with the structure of being; it would have to be something completely destructive—that is, nonexistent. If the term "Satanic" is taken to be symbolic of this absolute antithesis, "the Satanic has no actual existence. In order to have existence, it would have to be able to take on form, i.e., to contain an element of creation."[71]

In some sense, everything existing possesses significance. *Esse est bonum qua esse.* Indeed, Tillich suggests that this is the real meaning of the Christian doctrine of creation. The nature of the secular is not to be understood apart from this doctrine. As already observed, Tillich views the secular as substantially religious. Hence a new concept—the concept of the demonic— is required if the genuinely anti-religious or anti-holy is to be grasped.

Tillich's first discussions of the demonic appear in his "Outlines of Religious Socialism" (1923) and in his "Philosophy of Religion" (1925); his well-known essay on "The Demonic" did not appear until 1926. Shortly after the publication of the latter, Tillich wrote an article on "The Concept of the Demonic and Its Significance for Systematic Theology." In this article he tells how he arrived at the idea of the importance of the concept:

> The importance of the concept of the demonic occurred to me first in connection with the fundamental problem of philosophy of religion, the question of the relation between the sacred and the secular, between religion and culture. If the sacred is not to be one sphere among others, a sphere that may be put aside, if religion is not to be one sphere of culture among others, for or against which everybody may decide for himself according to his nature; if the sacred is rather that which absolutely claims me, which absolutely concerns me, then there can be no question of a coordination of these apparently contradictory concepts. Then the profane or the secular can be only an inchoate tendency within the sacred (which is all-embracing), and culture can be only a form that is substantially religious. . . . The categories profane, cultural, secular, autonomous, humanistic (by means of which Gogarten and Brunner attempt to deal with the problem) are obviously insufficient.[72]

[71] *The Interpretation of History,* p. 80.

[72] "Der Begriff des Dämonischen und seine Bedeutung für die systematische Theologie," *Theologische Blätter,* V (1926), 32.

In his view, then, the profoundest struggle of a religious movement can never properly direct itself absolutely against the profane, the secular, the unreligious. The secular lives in the
religious and has precisely as much of reality as it retains of
religious substance. The struggle of genuine religion is directed
much more against the anti-divine religion, against the demonic.[73]

Obviously, this conception of the demonic has nothing to do with
the mythical hypostatizing associated with the belief in demons,
though it does aim to grasp something suggested by the mythical
notion of demons. The demonic is not a tangible entity. Like the
terms "Unconditioned," "ground," "abyss," "divine," it is not
something that can be identified unambiguously. All of these
terms refer to aspects, to qualities of existence. Hence the demonic
is an aspect, a power, in the structure of existence.

The formulations which Tillich has given to the demonic vary
in emphasis and in implication. In the main, however, the concept is adapted from Boehme and Schelling. This fact is evident
in the terms used to describe the demonic. For example, he says:

> The possibility of the demonic is based on the fact, first, that the
> sacred is at the same time the absolute support and the absolute claim,
> the depth and the form, the ground and the abyss; and second, that
> in the creature these elements may separate. The creature desires to
> draw up into itself the inexhaustibility of the divine depth, to have
> it for its own. By this means the creative potency becomes destructive.
> For creation occurs where the abyss and the form are united in one
> entity, and destruction occurs where the abyss arises and dominates
> and breaks the form.[74]

Here the Boehme terms *Ground and Abyss* and the Schelling
term *Potency* appear. Equally reminiscent of Boehme are Tillich's
words characterizing the two polar forces that break apart (as

[73] "Grundlinien des religiösen Sozialismus." Reprint from *Blätter für
religiösen Sozialismus* (1923), p. 7. In his lecture "Nichtkirchliche
Religionen," *Volk und Reich der Deutschen*, ed. B. Harms (Berlin:
Hobbing, 1929), I, 456-75, Tillich asserts that the struggle between the
divine and the demonic replaces the struggle posited by supernaturalism
which interprets God as an "object" standing across an infinite gulf from
man. This problem posed by supernaturalism was "submerged long ago."

[74] "Der Begriff des Dämonischen. . . ," p. 33. These formulations remind us of Tillich's treatment of Schelling's idea of the bifurcation of
absolute being in the "Fall" and also of his treatment of Schelling's concept of the wrath of God. Tillich's description of the "separation of
ground and abyss" may be compared to Schelling's theory that the freedom of man consists in his capacity to put the potencies into imbalance.
Cf. *Die religionsgeschichtliche Konstruktion in Schellings positiver Philosophie*, pp. 46-49.

suggested in the quotation) and operate in a destructive fashion in the demonic: these polar forces Tillich calls "the impulse for power and the impulse for Eros."[75]

There is then a tension in existence between the ground and the abyss, between the form of being and the inexhaustibility of being. These elements belong together, and their unity in the depth of *essential nature* is the divine. "Their separation in *existence,* the relatively independent eruption of the 'abyss' in things, is the demonic."[76] But whereas an absolutely independent eruption of the "abyss," a mere destruction of every form, would be Satanic, the retention of the ground, of an element of the divine unity, is characteristic of the demonic. Therefore the demonic includes within it both creative and destructive force; it is the unity of form-creating and form-destroying strength, but the latter is predominant. Because the demonic contains this tension it can be a counterpositive to the divine and it can thus appear in the very sphere of the holy. Hence it exhibits an ecstatic, overpowering, creative quality.[77] Through it the personality is grasped by another power and is divided. All the power and the fascination to be associated with archaic art or to be found in the orgiastic practices of primitive religion are expressed in the concept of the demonic. Like the divine, the demonic does not belong to the level of the rational and the moralistic.

The concept of the demonic is not possible where only the rational Gestalt of things is yet visible, and where the creative depth of things is not visible. For this two-dimensional philosophy certain concepts such as chaos, the not-yet-formed matter, the notion of the infinite task, or the idea of criticism, may be logically necessary, but not active contradiction to form, a contradiction that arises precisely from what is at the same time the all-embracing ground.[78]

Since the Enlightenment—a justified revolt against "the possessed state of a whole era"—rationalism has lost the sense of depth, the sense of the depth of the demonic as well as of the divine. In the Enlightenment and in philosophical idealism God has be-

[75] *The Interpretation of History,* p. 89. Cf. Boehme's terms, *Liebe* and *der eigene Wille.*
[76] *Ibid.,* p. 84.
[77] *Ibid.,* p. 90.
[78] "Der Begriff des Dämonischen. . . ," p. 34. This passage is to be understood as a criticism of idealism. Cf. Tillich's comments on pantheism in this connection: "Pantheism is idealism. As idealism, however, it breaks down before the reality of the demonic." ("Religionsphilosophie," p. 818.)

come "the consecrating word for the closed world system, for the completed immanence and its rational structure." With this conception of a unified immanental structure, the nature and power of grace and of evil have been rationalized if not ignored.

Thinking is reduced to the two dimensions of form and matter, either in such a relationship that the matter is assumed as already formed, or in such a way that there exists the infinite task of impressing the form on the matter, or as a synthesis of both. The third dimension upward and downward, the divine-demonic, breaking through form, bestowing grace and destruction, is not seen. The negative element is finiteness, deficiency, laziness, but not active resistance, nothing contrapositive. In this manner it is possible to perceive the world and rule it. It offers no basic active resistance. It is capable of rationalization, even though in infinite labor. The mythical categories of creation, origin, miracle, of grace and frenzy, disappear or are sentimentally reinterpreted. . . . The individual is considered free. The possibility of forming much or little material, of pushing the limit of the rational far or not so far out, is not limited by anything.[79]

The demonic, like the divine, belongs to a third level: It is not something hostile to meaning which is to come to an idealistic synthesis. Nor is it mere inferiority of value or ethical deficiency. It is an actual contradiction to the divine and is to be fought without compromise. Hence it cannot be encompassed by any idealistic synthesis.

Accordingly, the demonic is something that cannot be fought with ordinary rational and moral means. It is not a matter of personal decision; it has the character of a suprapersonal power, operates as an obsession, a "possession." Hence it is a "principality and a power" of the character suggested in the Gospels and in the Pauline letters, and recognized today by psychopathology. This is its destructive side, as recognized also by Boehme and Schelling. But it has also a creative side, as is suggested by the usage made familiar by Socrates, Plato, and Goethe: for them it is a demonically ingenious, productive power. If the demonic combines destructive and creative aspects as fateful expressions of the eruption of the depths, then only something of greater and deeper creative power can oppose it, namely, grace.

The demonic comes, like grace, from "beyond," and it can be opposed only from "beyond." It cannot be the object of a merely reforming activity, for its character is to come out of a depth that breaks right through the formative law, and it is able to draw "the good will" into its service against its will. Demonries, whether

[79] *The Interpretation of History*, p. 109.

individual or social, always appear in the name of law, in the name of the unconditioned law, creating but also destroying. Indeed, the creative depth and power are so great that the enemy of the demonic may himself seem to be demonic. This is to be seen strikingly in the attitude of "the bourgeois man" toward the critics of capitalist society. Capitalism is a demonry just because it has combined great creative tendencies with great destructive tendencies. Analogously attractive forms of demonry are to be found throughout history. Religious history offers as many and as striking examples as secular history, powerfully expressed in the parable of the Grand Inquisitor.

The opposite of the demonic obsession is not freedom but rather being in a state of grace. The state of grace also emerges from the depths, not as destruction but as a new creation. It also comes from the third level. This does not mean that freedom plays no role: it is the formal element by which personality becomes personality, a responsible center to which the claim of the sacred is directed. Without freedom the absolute claim of the Unconditioned would not have any meaning. But freedom is not the material possibility to decide *ad libitum*. The freedom of the individual, his personal center, is no isolated point; it is embedded in greater contexts that are demonically or divinely controlled. (This reminds one of Luther's assertion that man is ridden by two cosmic powers; indeed, the whole conception of grace and of the demonic suggests the doctrines of the sovereignty of God and of justification by faith.) Only through grace may one pass from the anti-divine form-destroying to the divine form-creating tendency—that is, from sin to salvation.[80]

Illustrations of demonry are found in the psychic life of the individual, in the history of religion—and of Christianity—and in the history of culture in the broader sense. They include intellectualism, aestheticism, nationalism, capitalism. Illustrations of false means of overcoming demonry without benefit of grace include ascetic mysticism which in its negation and destruction of form may itself be semi-demonic, a monotheism that degenerates into an identification of God with the tribal deity, a sacramentalism depending upon an arbitrary mediator-god or ruled arbitrarily by a hierarchy, or dominated by "pure doc-

[80] Cf. "Redemption in Cosmic and Social History," *Journal of Religious Thought*, III (1946), 17-27. It should be noted that there are other forms of sin, e.g., uncreative weakness. But all forms of it represent lack of faith and "a separation from absolute being" (*The Interpretation of History*, p. 93).

trine." All of these can and have become demonries themselves: as Eduard von Hartmann would say, they are forms of "self-salvation." Secularism is one of the means of combating the demonic, and although in its initial struggle it contains something of the spirit and intent of prophetism, it ends by losing contact with the depth of the divine. Christ is the only adequate symbol of an antidemonic overcoming of the demonic.[81]

In his doctoral dissertation of 1910, on Schelling's "construction" of the history of religion, Tillich exhibited an interest not only in the theory of potencies, on the basis of which the theory of the demonic was developed, but also in a philosophical interpretation of the typology of religion. In the third section of his "Philosophy of Religion" he proposes a normative concept of religion founded on a philosophical interpretation of the typology of religion.

Continuing with his consideration of the divine and the demonic, Tillich turns to a treatment of the basic religious tendencies and then proceeds to a cultural-historical "construction" of the history of religion. First let us consider his "construction" or typology of the elemental forms of religion. An element of the essence of religion, he says, must be present in every religious phenomenon; hence the unity of form and import must be found in every form of religion. This unity of form and import is not only the ideal goal; it is also the essential presupposition of religious development. Between the point of departure in pure being and the movement towards the divine goal we find the struggle between the divine and the demonic. Of course, the starting point and the goal are not to be understood as temporal realities. They are constructs and not realities. The reality lies between them, but in such a way that through their inner dialectic it pushes always from one point to another, in progress or regress.

As a starting point for his typology Tillich posits an original sacramental "indifference" wherein all things possess equal significance with respect to form and import. The "indifference" disappears then in favor of one or the other of two basic tendencies, the sacramental and the theocratic. In the sacramental attitude, criticism of the forms of meaning makes it no longer possible indifferently to intuit the holy in everything real: particular realities and forms become the bearers of holy import. These things

[81] *The Interpretation of History,* p. 106. Here again philosophy is brought to the threshold of theology.

(or acts) receive a special sacramental quality. "Their significance depends upon the fact that in them as finite, conditioned realities, the presence of the unconditioned import of meaning is experienced."[82] If the criticism of the holy objects is pushed through radically, sacramentalism dissolves into mysticism.

The theocratic tendency stands at the opposite pole from the sacramental.[83] Its characteristic feature is that it aims to subject the forms of reality in action and knowledge to the unconditioned form, that is, to divine obedience. Hence it turns against the deification of certain sacramental realities. It demands obedience to the unconditioned form, which critically negates every particular form. In other words, it criticizes and struggles against all holy demonries connected with the sacramental type of religion. "It wishes to set up the rule of God."

These two types of religious emphasis are seldom to be found in pure form. Indeed, there is usually a sacramental element in theocracy and a theocratic element in sacramentalism.

In order to be concrete, the sacred demand must proceed from a sacred bearer, a mediator of revelation, which now on account of its theocratic power receives sacramental consecration. From this sacramental element of theocracy new demonries can develop which lead in turn to new theocratic reactions or to autonomous dissolution.[84]

This twofold classification of religion is employed by Tillich in such a way as to subsume a wide variety of phenomena. Some typologists would claim that it has left out of consideration a type of fundamentally different sort, namely, mysticism. Tillich disagrees with Friedrich Heiler, for example, who has attempted to make mysticism into a basic type, contrasting it with the prophetic. He holds that the opposition is inadequate. Indeed, he believes that the prophetic is also an inadequate characterization of a type. The theocratic type includes the prophetic element as a critical element but it also posseses a form-creating tendency. But what of mysticism?

Mysticism does not represent a separate basic attitude. Its

[82] "Religionsphilosophie," p. 810.

[83] The employment of the term "theocratic" represents a deviation from ordinary usage. "It has nothing to do with priestcraft, but it can be distorted into it."

[84] "Religionsphilosophie," p. 811. In the essay "Nichtkirchliche Religionen" Tillich characterizes these two types in accord with psychoanalysis: the sacramental is a mother-type, the theocratic a father-type. Autonomous culture, which wishes to break away from both, is characterized as the child-type. In the same essay these aspects of religion are related also to the sect type and church type of religious organization.

goal is union with the unconditioned import of meaning as the ground and abyss of everything conditioned. In this respect mysticism is essential to all religion. But as a special religious phenomenon mysticism appears where the desire to become one with the unconditioned import detaches itself from the other element of religion, the affirmation of the form. It arises where particular sacramental forms are radically questioned and where the theocratic will to create form is lacking. Mysticism is the radical ecstasy that seeks to grasp the import itself beyond all forms. Hence it is indifferent to the forms. It may agree with theocratic criticism but it aims mainly to seize the import that is contained in, though frustrated by, the sacramental. Consequently it does not criticize myth and ritual but rises above both. In its very indifference to forms it may become demonic. When it does not do so, it uses the sacramental forms, giving them often a new depth. But mysticism is not a tendency of its own; it is rather the radically critical form of the sacramental attitude. "Both sacramentalism and mysticism are directed toward the *present* Unconditioned, sacramentalism through given, concrete forms, and mysticism beyond every form."[85]

In contrast to sacramentalism, theocracy is directed towards the *demanding* Unconditioned. It is the "reformation" movement in the historical development of religion. It challenges the demonries and demands a just social order, an ethical form of personality, a true knowledge of God. Yet it presupposes sacramentalism as a point of departure and as an object of criticism; and in the religion of grace it achieves some synthesis with the sacramental and with the mystical element implicit in sacramentalism.[86]

From this typology Tillich turns to consider the history of religion, with a view to discovering a normative concept of religion. The goal of the whole movement towards fulfillment of meaning is "the union of the theocratic demand and mystical negativity with the sacramental sanctification of a concrete

---

[85] *Ibid.*, p. 812. In his early treatise on Schelling's conception of mysticism and the sense of guilt, Tillich stresses the fact that the danger of mysticism is its lack of the sense of distance from the divine, its lack of the sense of guilt. This aspect of mysticism makes it susceptible to demonic longings.

[86] It should be observed that the autonomous attitude of culture depends upon the theocratic attitude. Both are directed toward the demanded form. Theocracy seeks the form as the bearer of unconditioned import; autonomy seeks the form for its own sake.

[subject]."[87] Unity of the "present" and the "demanding" holy cannot be effected; it can be experienced or known only as something that breaks through both of these elements of the holy. Hence Tillich speaks of the religion of grace as the religion of paradox. The goal is reached by Christianity, which, Tillich says, combines in Christ the three desiderated elements of theocratic demand, mystical negativity, and concrete subject. We must now review the process whereby Tillich develops this construction.

Each of the types, the theocratic and the sacramental (with the mystical core), must play a role. The theocratic element is necessary in order to prevent relapse into "sacramental indifference" (where all things are of equal sacramental significance). The sacramental attitude must be retained: it is the concrete medium through which the theocratic element may express itself, and it serves as the point of resistance for theocratic protest. If the sacramental element is entirely destroyed, then radical mysticism will arise with its enervating negation of every concretely holy thing. Mysticism requires a theocratic element and a sacramental element—the first in order to avoid antinomianism (a sort of nomianism in reverse), the second in order to provide a starting point and also a supporting concrete discipline. Yet mysticism even in its radical form is not without significance for the religion of paradox: it is the great decisive criticism in religious history, the criticism of empty theocratic, autonomous, or heteronomous legalism. It is the most powerful symbol for relatedness to the holy import and as such it is the constant background even of the religious paradox.

In developing a "construction" one must avoid two interpretations of the goal or synthesis. In the one a theory of types places the orientations alongside one another. In the other the ideal is envisaged as a universal religion that would include all orientations in equal degree. This is no real synthesis: it is mechanical aggregation. Both interpretations overlook the inner dialectic.

The "construction" and the normative concept related to it are decisive for the concept of God and for the concept of faith. First, let us consider the relation to the concept of God. The formulations here are obscure:

The indifferent-sacramental attitude symbolizes the holy in manifold forms that have not found their synthesis in the unconditioned form, and therefore are bearers that possess at the same

[87] "Religionsphilosophie," p. 813.

time a divine and demonic character. The nearer a religion stands
to indifference, the less it achieves precise conceptions of gods;
things are regarded as vessels of the holy in their immediacy.
That is, the more completely conceptuality emerges from immediate perception, so much the more a genuine polytheism arises,
which reaches its highest form in monarchical polytheism, as
in Greek mythology.[88]

The intention of this passage is difficult to grasp, but the notion
seems to be that when a religion is one of general sacramental
indifference, divine and demonic elements are present indis-
criminately. As the religion moves towards differentiation, particular "spaces" are singled out as holy. Then these "spaces,"
which are representations of a divine power embracing and pulsating through them, come into conflict. The conflict is at first
overcome by means of a pantheon, but the head of the pantheon
in turn elicits new conflict. The whole situation is lucidly presented in the essay on "The Demonic":

> The less formed a religion is, the less is the demonic distinguished
> in it from the anti-demonic, the divine. The sacral quality, which is
> attributed to most things and events, even to the parts of many things,
> gives everything a simultaneously divine and demonic character.
> . . . The individual, accidental thing receives its holiness from this
> general, necessary thing and has no holiness outside it. The holy is
> embraced in divine figures that have symbolic force for this sphere,
> for this field of meaning. But the relation between these spheres of
> meaning remains doubtful and distorted in this instance also. To
> each other they remain single, accidental, and therefore demons. Even
> the raising of one divinity above the others as a monarch does not
> essentially change this situation. For this monarch among the gods
> himself rests on a limited, finite foundation. He cannot lose it with-
> out becoming the abstract absolute and therewith removing the
> multiplicity altogether. Therefore it is natural that the other divinities
> —of strange nations or of his own monarchy—should arise against
> him.[89]

With the destruction of polytheism there arises a mystical
monotheism "which elevates itself above all particular divinities
and symbolizes the pure import in paradoxical concepts like

[88] *Ibid.,* p. 814. Although Tillich does not say so explicitly, his presentation of the "construction" seems to imply that he rejects any idea of the
necessity of religion's developing in the precise stages here characterized.
That view would smack of Hegelian rationalism. Tillich's "construction" here is
in general patterned after Schelling's as set forth in Tillich's dissertation
on Schelling's "construction of the history of religion."

[89] *The Interpretation of History,* pp. 99-100.

Nirvana, the Beyond, the Abyss." But this mystical monotheism retains within it the polytheism from which it was abstracted. (As pointed out above, the mystical attitude remains bound to the sacramental.) Consequently, mystical monotheism is an unsteady attitude: it may allow the polytheism to stand (and allegorize it in the direction of mysticism) or it may fall back into the polytheism (worshiping a tribal deity).

An interesting example of the interplay between the sacramental and the theocratic tendencies is to be observed in ancient Persia. The sacramental tendency was there subjected to theocratic criticism in such a way as to lead to a mythical dualism between opposing powers, divine and demonic. Although this sort of dualism has strong antidemonic tendencies, it is itself subjected to the demonic, for it splits the absolute unity of form into two independent unities of form. This is a false solution, for the demonic is no unity of form: it is rather a form-bursting principle.[90] The consequence of this dualism is psychic and social schizophrenia. If the divine and the demonic are assigned *equal* power, then the demonic is in truth dominant. Unity in the ultimate is denied, and one finds only a more poignant example of the conflict of one sphere of being against another, the characteristic of polytheism. But just because of this, "religious dualism is the form in which the problem of the history of religion (of heathenism) is most clearly put.[91]

Moving beyond the national culture-religions and beyond religious dualism, one is driven by the theocratic tendency to exclusive montheism. Here the many divinities are negated in favor of one God who is the bearer of the unconditioned form: the jealous God tolerates no demonic cleavages. But the more the theocratic tendency cuts itself off from the sacramental tendency, the more it is removed from the polytheistic basis. Hence it becomes more and more abstract, transcendental, and formal.

At this point in the "construction" the religion of grace invades and passes beyond exclusive monotheism. It passes also beyond the religion of law characteristic of the theocratic tendency. The religion of grace "takes from sacramental polytheism a symbol that brings to full expression the religion of paradox, namely, the symbol of the divine mediator." A finite, conditioned reality becomes in a paradoxical way the bearer of the Unconditioned. For its sake it surrenders itself as a finite: the incarnate, humble,

[90] "Religionsphilosophie," p. 815. Cf. *The Interpretation of History*, p. 101.

[91] *The Interpretation of History*, pp. 101-2.

and dying God becomes the genuine religious *mysterium*. This becomes the center of the mystery religion, but in Christianity it is raised to decisive dignity for the history of religion.[92] It should be stressed, however, that "only where the radical theocratic criticism has overcome every demonic element in the divine mediator and made him into a bearer of the unconditioned form, is the synthesis of the tendencies of the history of religion achieved."

Only there can exclusive monotheism without danger of demonic splitting absorb a polytheistic element and thus change from the religion of law to the religion of grace. The presentation of this symbol in concrete form is the central task of the normative theory of religion or theology.[93]

In other words, the religion of paradox finds its normative expression in Christology. Hence, at this point a theological problem, in contrast to a problem in philosophy of religion, presents itself. So much for the application of the "construction" to the problem of God.

Tillich applies the "construction" also to the problem of faith. The same polarities and syntheses obtain here as in the sphere of the problem of God. Hence in the sphere of faith the indifferently sacramental situation, theocracy, and mysticism produce analogous effects. In the indifferently sacramental spiritual situation faith is not distinguished from autonomous lack of faith. All things are mediators of the Unconditioned. With the rise of criticism of form an element of unfaith which is at the same time autonomous obedience to form penetrates into the faith. As a consequence many of the forms of faith are attacked as superstition. On the other hand mysticism may break through all the forms for the sake of unification with the unconditioned import. Still, mysticism maintains some connection with the forms, absorbing and transforming them as they appear in the theocratic spiritual situation. In radical theocracy there arises the tension between lack of faith in face of all finite forms and faith

[92] "Religionsphilosophie," p. 815. From the point of view of "construction" this analogy between the mystery religions and the Christian doctrine of incarnation appears to be quite plausible. Tillich does not, however, examine the historical evidence which has in wide circles been interpreted as disproving actual historical connection between the two. This questionable procedure has been one of the main causes of the decline in prestige of the "constructive" approach. Cf. Joachim Wach, *Religionswissenschaft* (Leipzig: Hinrichs, 1924), pp. 73 ff.

[93] "Religionsphilosophie," p. 816.

in the unconditioned form. Here there will develop either a compromise between faith and lack of faith or, better, a recognition of faith in the paradox. In the latter instance faith will affirm the presence of the Unconditioned in a conditioned form. This brings us again to the resolution of the inner antinomy of faith. Again the answer to the problem presented by the "construction" is to be found in theology, a concrete norm that fulfills the goal of the construction and overcomes demonry.

It is not the task of philosophy of religion to decide what concrete symbol the religion of paradox can accept, or better, it is not the task of philosophy of religion to determine which concrete symbol is fundamental for the normative concept of religion. That is the task of theology, which is necessarily confessional, because it includes confession to a concrete symbol. Theology need not on that account be less universally valid than philosophy of religion. When it has conceived the paradoxical symbolic character of the content of faith, it must also place itself and its apprehension of the Unconditioned under the No of the Unconditioned. It will stand all the deeper in the religion of paradox, the more it succeeds in intuiting in its own symbol the No of the Unconditioned against every symbol.[94]

Up to this point the "construction" has been concerned with the history of religion and the positing of a normative concept of religion. In conformity with his idea that culture is substantially, if not by intention, religious, Tillich now asserts that the basic tendencies found in explicit religion are to be found also in analogous forms in the culture. The principal difference is only this: that culture, because it is directed to the particular forms and their law, does not carry in itself the negativity of the Unconditioned against every form. Accordingly, religious ecstasy and the ecstatic-symbolic character of the religious objects disappear. In their place we find the form-bursting, ecstatic element present as enthusiasm and subjective creative quality. If this ecstatic element pushes out against and beyond the form, the culture has in effect become religious. Where the form retains its autonomy in face of the abyss of the Unconditioned, the culture retains a cultural attitude, thus fending off the intentional religious attitude. Where the form is absolutized, we find a demonic tendency.

It would be highly instructive to follow Tillich through the exposition of the ways in which the basic tendencies of religion

[94] *Ibid.* When this conception is related to Christology we encounter a view similar to Schelling's idea of Christology as the "atonement of mythology." Cf. Otto Pfleiderer, *The Philosophy of Religion on the Basis of the History* (Eng. trans.; London: Williams, 1887), II, 25-27.

reappear on the cultural level. Here we would see the analogies within culture of the theocratic and the sacramental tendencies in religion. Tillich shows how the same antinomies occur within culture as within religion. Again, the antinomies can be resolved only through the religion of paradox. "Thus there are included in the religion of paradox all the essential elements of religion and culture. They create the theonomous spiritual situation which is the goal of all realization of meaning—a goal appropriate to the nature of meaning itself."

We turn now to the final section of "The Philosophy of Religion," dealing with the religious categories of the theoretical and the practical spheres. We shall confine attention to the theoretical sphere; the section on the practical sphere applies the categories of the theoretical sphere to the cultus and the religious community. The categories that have been dealt with in the first two sections of "The Philosophy of Religion" were concerned with the general principles of meaning and with their relation to the various areas of meaning. These principles were in turn related to the basic tendencies of religion and culture. Tillich speaks of all this as a *general* theory of categories. In the third and final section he deals with what he calls the *special* theory of categories, as applied to the theoretical and the practical spheres.

In the theoretical sphere Tillich distinguishes between the philosophy of myth and the philosophy of revelation. "Revelation is the form in which the religious object is given theoretically to religious faith. Myth is the form in which the content of the revelation is expressed."[95]

The treatment of myth and of revelation given in "The Philosophy of Religion" is brief and is related primarily to sacramentalism, theocracy, and mysticism. It will therefore be well to draw upon Tillich's later writings on myth and revelation for the exposition. (We shall, however, treat revelation only briefly in this chapter and then discuss it again in connection with Tillich's theology.)

In general, mythology is the history of the gods. It presupposes that there is a world of gods and that they act and are acted upon in time and space. At certain stages in the history of religion there are not yet very definite notions about the gods, and then much later comes a time when the gods are no longer pictured as acting or being acted upon in time and space. The first is

[95] "Religionsphilosophie," p. 820.

characterized as a premythical stage, the second as a post-mythical stage. Between them lies the mythical stage. A complete account of myth should include a treatment of the inchoate and unrefracted mythology and also of the growing and the refracted mythology. In all the stages, myth gives expression to a relatedness to the Unconditioned.

Philosophy and the empirical science of religion have long been concerned with the understanding of myth. In general, the theories of mythology may be classified as positive and negative. The latter deny to myth an independent spiritual or intellectual content. They attempt to explain mythology by tracing it back to something else and thus deprive it of its special significance.[96]

The positive theories of myth attribute to mythical creations an independent, intrinsic significance. Some theories stress the metaphysical significance and some the epistemological significance of mythology. In Tillich's opinion, the most fruitful metaphysical theory of myth was propounded by Schelling. He saw in mythology the expression of a theogonic process, that is, a process

[96] The negative theories are classified as psychological and sociological. Examples of the former are the theories of Wundt and Freud. An example of the latter is the Marxist theory of ideology. Recognizing the contributions of these theories to a critical estimate of the significance of myth, Tillich shows how neither the psychological nor the sociological theories have been carried out consistently, for if they were, the respective theories would themselves be hoist with their own petards. Moreover, the psychological negative theories shed more light on the *selection* of symbols than on the general problem of the nature and validity of symbols. The way these theories break down when they attempt to devise a general theory of the religious symbol may be illustrated by Tillich's comments on Jung's theory: "Jung in his analysis of Meister Eckhart has explained the latter's idea of God on the basis of the infinity of the repressed desires of the libido. But the use of the category of the infinite cannot be derived from the immediacy of the vital urges. All such discussions have to do with a finite datum that is immediately given, and however strong the libido may be, it remains a finite datum. The category of the infinite requires on principle something that is beyond everything given. Even if one concedes that psychoanalysis is able to explain the actual psychological processes that control the personality (for example, the 'demand' that arises from the authority of the father), yet the quality of unconditionedness, which under certain circumstances even the demand of a real father can acquire, can never be posited on the basis of psychoanalysis. The leap into the Unconditioned is at the same time a leap out of the 'analytical' sphere, and there is no analyst who has not made this leap at some point or other, for example, when he becomes convinced of the validity of the findings of his own researches" *Rel. Verw.*, p. 285; cf. "The Religious Symbol," *Journal of Liberal Religion,* II (1940), 18, n. 8.

in which "the principles that are united in God establish themselves in a thoroughly contradictory way in the human consciousness."[97]

An important form of the epistemological theory is set forth by Ernst Cassirer. He attributes to the myth its own inner reality, manifesting itself in a meaningful structure that exhibits regularity according to a sort of law of mythology. According to this theory, myth, like science, art, and language, is a necessary element of cultural and intellectual life. But its significance is not to be understood in terms of the correctness of its representation of reality; it is rather to be viewed as an aspect of cultural creations meaningful in themselves.[98]

Tillich characterizes his own theory as realistic, and through it he attempts to overcome the opposition between the two previously mentioned theories. According to his view, the myth is the symbol for the Unconditioned which is grasped in the religious "act," that is, it is a symbol of the transcendent. (It should be noted that frequently the terms "religious symbol" and "myth" are used interchangeably, though the latter is defined originally as meaning stories of the gods.) The myth is no mere extrapolation of the creative spirit. It has reality or intrinsic significance, for it is an expression of relatedness to the Unconditioned, to the unconditionally real. This is the truth of the metaphysical theory. But the myth does not have the reality of a copy; it lives in symbols that are conditioned by a particular view of the Unconditioned, and it does so in accordance with discoverable laws. This is the truth of the epistemological theory.

In myth the logical and the aesthetic apprehension of the Unconditioned come together. But the myth is not only aesthetic: it aims to give expression to the true and the real. Nor is it merely logical: it wishes to apprehend the import of the Unconditioned in a perceptible, tangible fashion. These two elements are united in the original myth.[99]

The myth takes on concrete form only after theocratic criticism has centered attention on the forms accepted and has emancipated men from a primitive bondage to nature. A poly-

[97] "Mythos," *Die Religion in Geschichte und Gegenwart,* (2nd ed. Tübingen: Mohr, 1930), IV, 363.

[98] Tillich has vigorously criticized Cassirer's pansymbolism and his critical-idealistic conception of religious symbols as merely cultural creations. See "Das Problem des Mythos," *Theologische Literaturzeitung,* XLIX (1924), 115-17; *Rel. Verw.,* pp. 95 ff.; "Symbol and Knowledge," *Journal of Liberal Religion,* II (1941), 203-4.

[99] "Religionsphilosophie," pp. 820-21.

theistic mythology develops which later on takes the form of a monarchic mythology, meanwhile perhaps retaining belief in a lower sphere of sprites and demons. Mysticism may appear and "empty" the myth of its particular content: and theocratic criticism may even wish to abolish the myth altogether. But both the mystical and the theocratic tendency can restore the myth. Mysticism, for example, did just this by absorbing the hierarchical form of mythology into a Neo-Platonic hierarchy.

In autonomous culture the myth passes over into metaphysics. The rational dynamic forms take possession of the holy symbols, now more in an aesthetic form, now more in a logical form. In this way the symbols are transformed into cultural creations. The transformation may of course move also in the direction of annihilation.

Metaphysics is alive so long as the holy import of its creations is retained, so long as the sacramental element is preserved. Great metaphysics is full of mythical power, even though it is by intention directed no longer to the import but rather to the form. But through this formal intention its import is more and more lost until rational science and art take its place.[100]

One is reminded here of the Hegelian dictum that the owl of Minerva takes her flight with the coming of the shadows of evening. Thus theonomous metaphysics begins by attempting to give new form to religious dogmas. This process may be accompanied by an attack on heteronomously accepted dogma. Eventually, however, there is a striving for dogmatic form, but now dogmatics becomes a theory of theonomous metaphysics. This outcome is a central synthetic task for every period.

In general, mythology is concerned with three things: the myth of existence, the myth of history, and the myth of the absolute idea; or, to use mythical language, the myth of creation, the myth of redemption, and the myth of consummation.[101] This formulation is clearly related to the view set forth in *The System of the Sciences:* the apprehension of the Unconditioned is directed to the real and the ideal elements, and thence to concern with the immediately existing, with the meaning-fulfilling spirit, and with the completed unity of being and spirit. The absence of any one of these aspects is a sign of declining mythology. Only

[100] *Ibid.,* p. 822.

[101] In the article on "Mythos" the myths are given a more extensive classification into theogonic, cosmogonic, anthropological, soteriological, eschatological myths. These forms of myth express different basic concerns of the religious consciousness with reference to the transcendent.

in their unity does the relation of the Unconditioned to the conditioned find complete expression. In this way only is a true symbolism achieved.

We have observed how the mythical element may be weakened through rational metaphysics. A similar tendency is brought about by science, for the goal of science is an unmythical world-view. To this end science can deprive things not only of their divinity but also of their vitality, their individuality, their singularity. It can dissolve them into quantitatively determinable functions. But an absolute limit exists for this attempt of science. In everything there is an element of "being," an indissoluble, original datum, a power that still shines forth despite the most rational penetration. It makes possible—and even inevitable— a connection with the mythical element in religion. When science communicates a sense of the living power and inwardness of everything real, it begins to create myths—for example, evolution, Life, will to power. Thus myths are broken and then newly created.

The "breaking" of the myth in its immediacy, however, is a necessity not only for science but also for genuine religion. Scientific awareness of immanent realities breaks the myth scientifically; religious awareness of transcendence breaks it religiously. Accordingly, the mythical consciousness may be said to be either broken *or* unbroken. In any case, it does not disappear. In accord with his theory of culture and religion, Tillich does not view the conflicts of thought as conflicts between a mythical and an anti-mythical consciousness. The conflicts are between different unbroken myths, and between broken and unbroken myths. Hence, as suggested above, science itself may be said to exhibit a mythical consciousness, at least insofar as it uses symbols that pulsate with the depths of reality. This situation is analogous to that already observed in metaphysics: in both science and metaphysics rational and mythical power go together.

Despite the great influence of science, the most profound source of the "breaking" of myths is genuine religion itself. In genuine religion the myths are recognized as representations of an unconditioned transcendent that surpasses every possible conception of a being, including even the conception of a Supreme Being. This aspect of the religious consciousness is characterized as the atheism immanent in the religious act.

Wherever this aspect is lost sight of, there results an objectification of the Unconditioned (which is in essence opposed to objectification), a result that is destructive of the religious as well as of the cultural life. . . . It is the religious function of atheism ever to remind us that the religious act has to do with the unconditioned transcendent, and that the representations of the Unconditioned are not objects concerning whose "existence" or "non-existence" a discussion would be possible.[102]

This estimate of the role of atheism, taken at face value, would seem to represent a definitely strained, if not eccentric, interpretation. But Tillich qualifies his statement when he says, "Not the unbeliever, but rather the believer is the real atheist; and in every genuine *theism*, in every affirming of God as the Unconditioned an abyss (*Abgrund*) of *atheism* is contained and the affirmation is again dissolved."[103]

Wilbur M. Urban, like some of Tillich's German critics, has questioned Tillich's formulations here.[104] He infers that Tillich gives a purely symbolic significance to religious language. Hence, he concludes, Tillich denies that there is a knowledge-content in religious symbols. It is precisely this interpretation which Tillich repudiates in Ernst Cassirer's theory of pansymbolism. Commenting on Cassirer and on Urban's criticism, Tillich asserts:

> The non-symbolic element in all religious knowledge is the experience of the Unconditioned as the boundary, ground, and abyss of everything conditioned. This experience is the boundary-experience of human reason and therefore [it is] expressible in negative-rational terms. But the Unconditioned is not God. God is the affirmative concept pointing beyond the boundary of the negative-rational terms and therefore is itself a positive-symbolic term.[105]

Accordingly, Tillich accepts the principle of "analogia entis," for the immediate reality which is referred to in the symbol "has something to do with the transcendent reality which is symbolized in it."[106] But he does not accept the principle of "analogia entis" if it is used as a basis for rational construction. The truth in the symbol is not a theoretical truth—in Tillich's view, Kant has refuted this theoretical conception of truth for religious objects. For Tillich, the symbol represents "existential truth," that is, a truth toward which one cannot have the spectator-attitude, and to which one must surrender in order to experience it. "In this

[102] *Rel. Verw.*, p. 102.
[103] "Religionsphilosophie," p. 804.
[104] "Tillich's Theory of the Religious Symbol," *Journal of Liberal Religion*, II (1940), 34-36.
[105] "Symbol and Knowledge," p. 203.
[106] *Ibid.*, p. 204.

sense the 'symbols provide no objective knowledge but yet a true awareness,' namely, of the mystery of the ground, which never can become an object for a subject, but that draws the subject into the object thus overcoming the cleavage between them."[107] Here we see again Tillich's mystical, existentialist view that true community between the knower and the known overcomes the cleavage between subject and object.

The appropriateness of a symbol is dependent upon a certain inherent power that gives expression to, and possesses an original affinity to, the symbolic content represented in the symbol. As we have pointed out earlier, Tillich does not indicate how one chooses from among autonomous forms for the purpose of expressing the immanent aspect of the divine. But through the formulation just given, he attempts to avoid subjectivism on the one hand and simple objectivism on the other. He aims also to escape the charge of allegorizing. The symbol expresses a relation between the religious man and that which is of ultimate concern, and the symbol that he uses is the result of the work of creative spirit. But it expresses more than the autonomy of the subject; or rather, it expresses it properly only when the referend is not viewed as one object among others. The ignoring of this principle is, in Tillich's opinion, the justified cause of much atheism. The "atheism" immanent in the religious act is not necessarily a denial of that which is intuited in the symbol. It is rather a denial of the theoretical conception that uses the principle of analogy as a basis for rational construction whereby God or the Unconditioned is made into an object. A god who is a being behind the world or who is a probable hypothesis cannot be of ultimate concern. Such a view of deity is not so much false as it is a distortion. "Atheism" is a protest against this distortion. It is an implicit affirmation of the Unconditioned as a qualification of existence and a denial that the Unconditioned is one element among others. It is an implicit affirmation of the paradoxical character of the immanence of the transcendent.

We shall reserve for later discussion the treatment of the types of symbols, for it belongs with our discussion of theology. We turn now to consider briefly the concept of revelation. Like the subject of types of religious symbols, the concept of revelation brings us to the threshold of a normative theology. Yet it is a special category of the philosophy of religion. In his treatment of the concept of revelation Tillich again attempts to show

[107] *Ibid.*

that any fundamental conflict between philosophy of religion and theology must be overcome. Since, in his view, all the spiritual (or cultural) life of humanity represents an inner unity, this spiritual life both as a whole and in its parts is to be understood only in its religious roots. Revelation is therefore made the basis of the synthesis. It is defined as "the eruption of the unconditioned meaning-import through the meaning-form."[108] Wherever the unconditioned meaning-import is mediated through a meaning-form, revelation is present. Even when the autonomous attitude is dominant—that is, even when the demands of theonomy are not recognized—revelation is in effect present. Behind "every real creation there stands revelation: every creation lives on the import which it forms."[109] Heteronomous faith is judged more severely, for it gives to the mediator of revelation an absoluteness that destroys autonomy and, with it, the autonomous creation of forms. This tension between autonomy and heteronomy, the tension between the avowed denial of revelation and the affirmation of absolutized revelation is to be resolved only through insight into the paradoxical-symbolic character of revelation.

In this section of his "Philosophy of Religion" Tillich illustrates the different types of revelation as they are represented in the indifferent-sacramental situation, in the theocratic attitude, in sacramentalism, and in mysticism. These different emphases, with their characteristic defects, are illustrated also through a discussion of the uses of a sacred literature. Here heteronomy and literalism are seen as the demonic distortions of revelation. The distorters of revelation overlook the two elements of genuine revelation, namely, that it brings a relatedness to the unconditioned import and that the form through which the Unconditioned is revealed is symbolic. Hence genuine revelation elicits awareness of the Unconditioned, but it places the symbols of revelation under the eternal No that guards against "attributing the dignity of the Unconditioned to any conditioned thing." Again we confront the demand for a religion of paradox.

At the conclusion of the discussion of revelation Tillich turns to the study of the religious categories of the practical sphere, worship (the cultus) and the religious fellowship. Here the concepts of autonomy, heteronomy, and theonomy are related to different types of worship and to different types of re-

[108] "Religionsphilosophie," p. 823.
[109] *Ibid.*

ligious community. In view of the fact that no new principles are
introduced in this discussion of the practical sphere, we shall not
present an exposition of this brief section.

Tillich's philosophy of religion has been called one of the most
mature accomplishments of recent German systematic philosophy.[110] Certainly, it is also one of the most subtle and abstract.
Indeed, Wilhelm Bruhn says it scarcely belongs in the so-called
textbook in which it appears; it is "caviar for the epicure."[111] In
view of its great complexity we give now a brief resumé or synoptic outline of it, indicating also its connection with modern
German philosophy of religion.

In summary, its main positions may be stated as follows:
Taking as his starting point the idealistic presupposition that the
spiritual life of humanity represents an inner unity and can be
understood only in terms of its religious roots, Tillich insists on
three things, and these characteristics distinguish him from the
Hegelian idealist: (1) He holds that there is a tension between
every synthesis and the Unconditioned which constitutes its
meaning or import. There is no complete synthesis. The religion
of paradox with its view of the immanence of the transcendent
asserts that the unconditioned import erupts through every synthesis, through every form, whether it be cultural or "religious."
This tension between every synthesis and the inexhaustible Unconditioned applies to both the practical and the theoretical order,
to conduct and knowledge. Tillich goes beyond epistemological
idealism to a metaphysical realism, to a belief-ful realism and
relativism. The ultimate orientation of this belief-ful realism is
not an object of the temporal order or of a supranatural order; it
is the meaning-reality which is discriminated by the spiritual
act in and beyond the existential order—a reality that transcends subject and object. (2) But within each synthesis there is
also another tension—actual or potential—which comes from the
depths. Tillich insists that a creative-destructive, a demonic element, coming from the ground and abyss and expressed in fate
and freedom, operates in a dialectical fashion with the meaning-
fulfilling, creative, divine element. The demonic element can
never be sublated. It is a fateful, guilty aspect of the human
condition, and its presence vitiates all moralism. It is anti-holy and

110 Emanuel Hirsch, review of "Religionsphilosophie," *Theologische Literaturzeitung*, LI (1926), 96.

111 Wilhelm Bruhn, "Zur Religionsphilosophie," *Zeitschrift für Theologie
und Kirche*, VIII (1927), 77.

can never be dissolved by rationalism or by mysticism, but only by the creative, "blessing" gift of grace. (3) Combining these motifs with a "historical realism," Tillich says every synthesis represents a tension between the conditioned and the Unconditioned and between the creative and the destructive, which in the fullness of time and in a suspended fashion manifests itself in the concrete *here-and-now*. It stands over, and is made precarious by, the abyss, the inner infinity of being and idea, which through freedom and fate may receive divine fulfillment or demonic distortion. Hence the possibility of a demonic perversion is always present, as is also the possibility of a new eruption of the unconditioned import demanding a new form in the here-and-now. In both of these tendencies there is always something creative, though the creative predominates in the latter. With the complete loss of import "the spiritual exhaustion of substance" ensues. Creativity degenerates into lassitude and emptiness of meaning.

By definition, then, Tillich's "existential philosophy" stresses both creative participation in, and fated, guilty separation from, "essential being," with the ultimate ground of meaning ("beyond" fate and freedom and existence) qualifying them by relating them to the inner transcendence of things and spiritualizing them by demanding decision. The influence of Fichte and Kierkegaard are to be seen in this view of *Existenz,* but other similar influences are also evident. Tillich's awareness of the tension between every synthesis, even of the highest, and the absolute referred to in it is reminiscent of the early Fichte, though the latter finds the tension only in the field of practical conduct whereas Tillich finds it also in that of theoretical knowledge.[112] Tillich also bears resemblance to Schleiermacher with his "higher realism," which gives religious expression to a dual relation of the finite to the infinite, the envisaging of "the infinite in the finite and at the same time the negation of the finite for the sake of the infinite."[113] With respect to both participation and separation, both mystical unity and the sense of guilt, Tillich exhibits affinity to Boehme and the later Schelling.[114] With some similarity to Schelling's later outlook, the philosophy of belief-ful realism is presented in the dimension of

[112] Cf. Hirsch, *loc. cit.,* p. 96.

[113] G. Wehrung's review of *Religiöse Verwirklichung, Kant-Studien,* XXXVIII (1933), 487. We have pointed out earlier the similarity of this idea to Schelling's theory of the atonement of mythology.

[114] In Boehme these ideas are related to the theory of the theogonic process through the *Quellengeister;* in Schelling they are related to the theory of potencies.

the philosophy of history. In "The Philosophy of Religion" this philosophy of history takes the form of a "construction" of the history of religion and culture. In the writings on social ethics and religious socialism, it should be added, this philosophy of history takes the form of a criticism of "the present religious situation" and issues in the positing of a spiritual and social, theonomous "reconstruction" of society.

Although Tillich has transcended philosophical idealism in these ways, he nevertheless retains the idealistic presupposition that there is a certain identity between knower and known. Hence he asserts that in the religious act the cleavage between subject and object is in principle overcome and a new community (of meaning-fulfillment) between knower and known is established. Thus the questions concerning the nature and the truth of religion become the same question. As Hirsch points out, Tillich here approaches the Hegelian view of the unity of the consciousness of God and the reality of God, for the religious function and the fundamental meaning-function are one.[115] On the other hand, the unconditioned transcendent (as Tillich presents it) breaks through the idealist's bondage to a closed system of forms. In breaking through these forms it confronts both religion and culture with the judgment of the eternal and the demand for theonomy and "timely" new creation. In other words, in the apprehension and re-alization of meaning the community between knower and known yields a No as well as a Yes.

In *The System of the Sciences* Tillich distinguished between the supporting functions and the supported functions. The former are represented in theonomous metaphysics and ethos. The latter unfold in epistemology and aesthetics, in juridical and political science. In "The Philosophy of Religion" the supporting function is referred to as religion and the supported functions as culture. This distinction posits a double directedness of the consciousness, that toward the conditioned forms of meaning and their unity, and that toward the unconditioned meaning. Both are related to the same spiritual and cultural life. But whereas culture is sub-stantially religious, religion is intentionally so. On the other hand, in its form every religious act is a cultural act. Thus religion and culture are not to be divorced, nor are they to be identified. "Cul-ture is the expression-form of religion, and religion is the content of culture."

Since religion must assume cultural form, what is the difference

[115] Hirsch *loc. cit.*, p. 99.

between religious and cultural forms? Tillich answers that the former are viewed as symbols of the unconditioned transcendent which are cherished for the sake of the ultimate import, and the latter are viewed as autonomous forms of self-expression which are cherished for their own sake. If the symbols of religion are not viewed heteronomously, the faith they express must carry within it a certain protest or "atheism" that denies the adequacy of the symbols and renounces the objectification of the religious "object." These symbols may take theoretical or practical form. In the theoretical sphere myth and revelation are the characteristic categories; in the practical sphere they are the cultus and the religious community.

The propelling force in the history of religion is the tension between culture and religion, between autonomy and theonomy. The greatest struggle in the history of religion, however, is not the struggle between culture and religion but the struggle between the holy and the anti-holy, the divine and the demonic. The beginning of the struggle appears in principle with the transition from sacramental indifference—where everything is holy—to the situation where certain objects are sacramentally enhanced. Sacramentalism in turn is attacked or qualified by theocratic elements—which point to the demand of the Unconditioned—or by mysticism, which devaluates all form. The end-goal of this "construction" of the history of religion is the synthesis or reconciliation of these opposites in a new unity: the holy that is present and the holy that is demanded become one in the paradoxical experience of the Unconditioned as grace. If we consider competing sacramentalisms to be polytheism and theocracy to be monotheism, then the ideal synthesis is one in which the concrete symbol is a divine mediator who is at the same time the bearer of a sacramental presence and the bearer of the holy demand. He is a concrete symbol pointing beyond himself to the Unconditioned. With the characterization of this ideal synthesis philosophy of religion reaches the threshold of theology, whose task it is to determine the concrete symbol of the normative concept of religion.

We conclude this chapter with some brief comments and criticisms on certain of these concepts. We shall not summarize the critical comments already made on the central idea of Tillich's philosophy—the concept of "the Unconditioned"—but shall offer some further remarks and queries.

It will be recalled that Tillich says one must not play with concepts and essences but rather go directly to the things themselves. Yet, as we have observed, his existential philosophy with its method of "phenomenological intuition" is not empirical in the usual sense. "Phenomenological intuition" looks into the depths and discriminates the inner transcendence of things. It discriminates an import that is manifest in existence but is related to a qualification that lies "beyond" the existential order. Hence the word "existential" as a description of this philosophy can give a wrong impression, if, that is, it is interpreted only at face value and in a popular sense. The realization of meaning involves an inexhaustible form with which empiricist and positivist methods cannot adequately cope. The ultimate concern of man is not an "objective," existing thing in the temporo-spatial order; it has to do with something that is unconditionally valid and unconditionally real. How, then, we may ask, can this ultimate orientation be said to relate not to concepts and essences but rather to a direct apprehension of things themselves? Tillich answers that ideas are not born out of logic but "leap" out of real living. To find the depth of real living one must go beneath the surfaces. And if one goes beneath the surfaces one will find that which in paradoxical fashion contradicts the surfaces. One will confront that which is at the same time an unconditional, inexhaustible meaning-reality and our unconditional concern. Thus his existential philosophy finds its ultimate orientation in essential being. This is a reality that is the ground of all meaning and of all concepts and is at the same time unamenable to adequate conceptual description, Hence the concepts we use to describe this unconditionally valid and unconditionally real "object" must be viewed as symbols of an inexhaustible form, the unconditioned transcendent.

The question now arises as to what the unchanging element in the inexhaustible form is. It is the ontological structure of being. Yet the ontological structure is itself characterized as ground *and* abyss. Ground and abyss must be interpreted dialectically, so that each may be understood in relation to the other. The ground is in one sense an abyss, and the abyss is in one sense a ground. This dialectical conception is partially expressed in the German words for ground and abyss: *Grund* and *Abgrund*. Thus the unchanging element would seem to be the ontological structure of an inexhaustible, flowing reality. The balance between form and eruption of form is very delicate here, so delicate indeed that one may easily lose it. Emanuel Hirsch is, in the writer's opinion, wrong when he says that Tillich's ultimate orientation is the abyss, *das Bodenlose*.[116] In asserting this, Hirsch seems to have interpreted the ground and abyss undialectically; he has made the abyss into a separate, fundamental cosmological principle.

Tillich attempts to retain the delicate balance by his dynamic conception of essential being and of truth. But if we read his formulation of this dynamic conception of truth, for example, we find ourselves brought almost into a vertigo over the abyss:

> The dynamic conception of truth is not relativistic. It has nothing statically absolute in reference to which it can be called relative, while the static conception of truth forces one to relativism, as soon as the arrogance of the absolute position is broken down. The dynamic thought of truth overcomes the alternative "absolute-relative." The Kairos, the fateful moment of knowledge, is absolute insofar as it places one at this moment before the absolute decision for or against truth, and it is relative insofar as it knows that this decision is possible only as a concrete decision, as the fate of the time. Thus the Kairos serves to reveal rather than to conceal the Logos.[117]

But that is the question: Does the Tillichian conception of Kairos reveal the Logos? And even if it does, is the Logos revealed in anything more than a formal way? We can pose the same problem in another fashion. According to Tillich, man's action acquires meaning in the theonomous spiritual act. But then we must ask, What meaning? Tillich replies that it is the meaning involved in bringing together thought and existence, and interpreting both in the light of the inexhaustible import of being. This answer in turn suggests the question: How does one test this meaning; what is its criterion? On Tillich's principles it cannot for the religious consciousness be tested by anything in the existential order; it must be tested by reference to the unconditioned transcendent. In religious terminology, this is tantamount to saying that one tests it by reference to the will of God, and in any traditional frame of reference the answer would generally be considered satisfactory. The will of God is there understood to possess a definite content. But in Tillich's frame of reference a difficulty presents itself. The question arises as to what the *character* of the transcendent is. In Tillich's exposition we have found that the transcendent is the unconditioned of meaning and value and being. But, reduced to its essence, the transcendent as a standard only pronounces an eternal Yes and an eternal No upon human endeavor and demands a theonomous attitude. This

[116] *Ibid.*, p. 102.
[117] *The Interpretation of History*, p. 175.

ultimate reference is therefore of a purely formal character. To be sure, the theonomous attitude, in Tillich's view, issues in decision according to the Kairos. But when one asks on what principle timely action is to be determined, one searches in vain for anything other than formal principles. The Kairos is a matter of creation and fate. Beyond these indications any number of plausible principles can present themselves. Hence with respect to both the Unconditioned and the Kairos one fails to find in Tillich's exposition a decisive material principle that may serve as a criterion for the testing of meaning.

In this connection, it should be emphatically pointed out that Tillich's more recent writings reveal his concern with finding this principle in a dynamic conception of *Agape*.[118] It is a principle that can be tested in experience even if it is posited as transcendently demanded. Without it, however, one is left primarily dependent upon the merely formal principle of theonomy. Tillich's writings just referred to may be interpreted as a recognition of the validity of the criticism we have made of "The Philosophy of Religion."

Another question with respect to the changing and unchanging elements in the Unconditioned and in essential being must be raised. Ordinarily we ask: Is God perfect? If so, how can he change? If he cannot change, then what significance does the activity of the creature possess for him? If he does change, in what respects does he change and in what respects does he abide unchanging? One would suppose from Tillich's characterization of the dynamic nature of essential being that it must change in some respects. On the other hand, one might logically infer that *essential* being could not change, else it would lose its essentiality. The question concerning the changing and the unchanging elements in essential being becomes acute when we take into account the consideration that essential being is related to existence. If the latter has no effect on the former, or, in religious parlance, if the creature's activity in no way affects the Creator, then of what significance is the creature's activity? Harold Buschman has posed the issue in a pertinent fashion:

[118] Cf. "Ethics in a Changing World," in *Religion in the Modern World* (Philadelphia: University of Pennsylvania, 1940), pp. 51-61; "Fragments of an Ontology of Love," mimeographed MS of an address given on May 19, 1943, under the auspices of the National Council on Religion in Higher Education; "The Idea of a Transmoral Conscience," promised for early publication. In the second item here listed, Tillich says, "Love belongs to the structure of Being itself."

Obviously the idea [of the Unconditioned] is not meant to convey complete transcendence, for Tillich is opposed to Karl Barth and holds that the Idea becomes manifest in actual human living. It is not the not-yet-conditioned. It is not the to-be-conditioned. Is it the unconditionable aspect of existence? That is to be doubted, for Tillich insists that though it is manifested it remains inviolably transcendent. It is not objectively existent and yet is related to the world. How? By projection? Certainly not, for then it is subject to recall and change, i.e., human conditioning.[119]

Tillich has not addressed himself to these questions. Hence, we do not know whether in his conception of God there is a passive as well as an active element. Insofar as the Kairos is a fulfillment of unconditioned meaning, it might be expected to add richness to Being. Likewise, if meaning is frustrated or distorted, one might expect that essential being would somehow be affected. But if essential being can be affected, then we ask in what sense it can be conditioned. In short, we ask whether the Unconditioned can be unconditioned. Perhaps Tillich would reply that these questions wrongly presuppose an objectification of the divine. But if the questions are to be disposed of in this fashion, we are still left with the relevant question: Is the Unconditioned conditionable?

The question of the relation of the Unconditioned to the conditioned has a bearing upon another problem, namely, that of the relation between religion and culture, between theonomy and autonomy. Religion, it will be recalled, is defined as direction toward the Unconditioned, and culture is defined as direction toward the autonomous forms and their unity. The former is substantially and intentionally religious; the latter is substantially but not intentionally so. One may question here whether these formulations bring into sufficiently bold relief the difference between religion and culture. At the most, the formulation would seem adequate for only one type of spiritual attitude in culture, that type bordering so closely upon the religious attitude as to make the difference between the presence and the absence of intentionality insignificant. But the sort of spiritual attitude which Tillich characterizes and criticizes as "self-sufficient finitude" seems to be lacking substantial religious quality in any significant degree. The intention of "self-sufficient finitude" seems in principle to be an intention that deprives culture of the substantial religious element. Indeed, "self-sufficient finitude" characterizes a religious or rather a nonreligious attitude that is mov-

[119] Harold Buschman's review of *The Interpretation of History, Review of Religion*, I (1937), 430.

ing either towards lassitude and emptiness of meaning or towards demonic distortion.

This ambiguity of definition is probably partially due to Tillich's antipathy for piety on the coat sleeve and to his high regard (in the spirit of Nietzsche) for the unconventionality and vitality of certain types of secularism. It is due also to the fact that both religion and culture (secularism) are themselves ambiguous. Yet it is difficult to see how secularism with its matter-of-fact attitude and its fragmentation of meaning is substantially religious. Therefore we must ask whether culture is substantially religious in the same sense as religion is.

Despite these criticisms, it should be clear that Tillich's "Philosophy of Religion" draws upon the major themes of European philosophy as well as upon the ample resources of the history of religion and gives them a new, impressive conceptual expression and structure. When taken in connection with his writings on the philosophy of culture, on religious socialism, and on "historical belief-ful realism," it represents the most comprehensive and original production of its kind in our time. Even if the reader is not disposed to accept the "system" as a whole or some of its fundamental supporting structures, he must gratefully concede that the discrimination of the aspects of religion—and of its relation to culture—as set forth in the characteristic Tillichian concepts provides a basis for a new understanding of both religion and culture, as well as offering a new language that discloses treasures both new and old.

VI

Philosophy and Theology

According to Tillich, philosophy is a theory of the principles of meaning; philosophy of religion deals with these principles of meaning, relating them to a theory of the essence of religion; and theology provides a normative system of religion based on the classical symbols of a particular confession.[1] These disciplines must never be separated if one is to avoid the disruption of meaning, that is, if one is to avoid demonic heteronomy on the one side and self-sufficient autonomy on the other. Accordingly, theology is defined as a theonomous theory of meaning-norms, bound to "the classical symbols in which the theonomous conviction has found its expression."

The definitions are clear enough, but the very fact that the disciplines are interdependent presents a difficulty for the reader who would discriminate the lines of demarcation in Tillich's writings. Precisely because of Tillich's effort to avoid a disruption of meaning it is often hard to determine where, for example, philosophy of religion leaves off and theology begins. Up to the time of his coming to the States most of Tillich's writings were of a philosophical character rather than systematically theological. Only in his *Systematic Theology* does one find a comprehensive conception of his normative system.

There are two main reasons for the difficulty involved in identifying Tillich's *theology*—of discovering, that is, a norma-

[1] *Das System der Wissenschaften* (Göttingen: Vandenhoeck und Ruprecht, 1923), p. 151.

tive system derived from the Bible and "from the concrete norms
of the living confessions." The first reason is that his philosophy
of religion frequently presents ideas that are obviously drawn
from Christian theology or that presuppose some Christian idea.
Indeed, at times the reader supposes that he is reading general
philosophical discourse; then he is told that the idea just expounded is the essential meaning of the doctrine of justification
by faith or of the *Logos*. As a pedagogical method and as a
method of persuasion this procedure has been markedly successful, particularly in his philosophy of culture and his philosophy
of religion. It represents the fulfillment of the task Tillich set
for himself: to express in an effective way the enduring but
language-frustrated doctrines of Christianity. Yet one is frequently
left wondering, Is this supposed to be Christian doctrine, or is
this Tillichian philosophy, or has Tillich read his philosophy
into the Christian terms?[2] One might of course dismiss such
questions as irrelevant, on the ground that one should be primarily concerned with the truth of the ideas presented. This is a
pertinent consideration, but it does not come to terms with the
problem here under consideration.

The second reason for difficulty in determining the lines of
demarcation is that in the course of his development Tillich has
apparently changed his conception of the relations between
philosophy and theology. This change may be taken as evidence
of his desire to make the lines of demarcation clearer and thus
to indicate more explicitly the Christian character of his theology.
In any event, a change in the definitions of the two disciplines
may be discovered in his later writings. In his "Philosophy of
Religion" (1925) and in other writings of that period he viewed
philosophy as dealing with the theory of the principles of meaning. But later he began to assert that philosophy examines the
categories of thought and being, and raises the ultimate *questions*, and that systematic theology gives the *answers*. He has
characterized this relationship as "the method of correlation."[3]
Another formulation of the changed conception of the relation
between philosophy and theology should be mentioned. In his
inaugural lecture on "Philosophy and Theology," given at Union
Theological Seminary in 1933, Tillich speaks of philosophy as

[2] This question is the more pressing when we consider that Tillich says
that philosophical theology is based on the Christian "kerygma." Cf. "Philosophy and Theology," *Religion in Life*, X (1941), 21. Reprinted in *The Protestant Era* (Chicago: University of Chicago Press, 1948), pp. 83-93.

[3] *Systematic Theology* (Chicago: University of Chicago Press, 1951), I,
59-66.

dealing with the meaning of being, and of theology as dealing with the meaning of being, not as it is in itself, but as it is *for us*.[4] In the same lecture he distinguishes between philosophical and "kerygmatic" theology. The latter aims to reproduce "in a systematic way the content of the Christian message without referring to philosophy"; the former tries to explain the content of the *kerygma* in "keen interrelation with philosophy."

To add to the complexity, Tillich has changed the formulations defining certain of his concepts. New nuances of meaning are given to terms like "the Unconditioned" and "God." We shall presently discuss some of these changes. But before doing so, we must consider the concepts as they are presented in "The Philosophy of Religion" and in other similar writings of the period of the 1920's.

The concept of the Unconditioned is a decisive concept of Tillich's thought. Yet, curiously enough, his writings lack any systematic presentation of the principal meanings he attaches to the term. Nor do we find any systematic survey of the historical lineage of the concept. Moreover, we encounter a bewildering variety of usage.[5] In one passage, for example, the discussion will be on an ethical point; in another it will deal with a metaphysical question; in another it will have to do with the definition of religion; and in still another it will be concerned with public worship. In each context the word is of course introduced as a symbol of the Ultimate, but the distinctive meanings vary in the different contexts.

The term therefore acquires considerable ambiguity. Indeed, it is related to so great a variety of phenomena and attitudes that it becomes well-nigh a universal solvent. This fact will be readily evident if we list here a number of typical statements. In "The Philosophy of Religion" the ground of meaning is spoken of as the unconditionedness of meaning. Religion is defined as direction toward the Unconditioned. "God" is said to be "the symbol for the Unconditioned." Or again, "metaphysics is a theoretical and ethos a practical relatedness to the Unconditioned." "Myth apprehends in a perceptible way the import of the Uncon-

[4] "Philosophy and Theology," pp. 21-22.
[5] The definition of "the Unconditioned," presented in Chapter II is a synthetic definition drawn from the scattered references in his writings and from lecture notes. According to this synthetic definition, it will be recalled, the Unconditioned refers to the unconditioned of being, of truth, and of meaning. It is also at times presented as a synonym for "the Holy." The ensuing discussion will show, however, that these meanings are assimilated to a good many others.

ditioned."[6] "Revelation is the eruption of the unconditioned meaning-import through the meaning-form."[7] "Relatedness to the Unconditioned we call faith. Faith is a turning towards the Unconditioned, effective in all functions of the spirit."[8] An "ecstatic" painting is said to point to the Unconditioned.[9] In the 1922 book *Masse und Geist*—a religious interpretation of different types of mass man—certain mass movements for the achievement of justice are spoken of as "holy" masses; they too pulsate with the unconditioned meaning-import. In the 1922 essay entitled "Kairos" (which appears in *The Protestant Era*) we read that it is "that element in every religious experience which makes it religious. In every symbol of the divine an unconditional claim is expressed, most powerfully in the command: 'Thou shalt love the Lord thy God with all thy heart and with all thy soul and with all thy mind.' No partial, restricted, conditioned love of God is admitted." In the essay on "The Religious Symbol" (1928) we learn that "devotion to the crucifix is really directed to the crucifixion on Golgotha and devotion to the latter is in reality intended for the redemptive action of God, which is itself a symbolic expression for an experience of the unconditioned transcendent."[10] And so one could go on adding example to example of Tillich's all-embracing divination.

Ferdinand Kattenbusch says in this connection, "All concepts, doctrines, ideograms, sacraments, orders [of cultural creation] are bearers and hindrances of the Unconditioned, of God."[11] The above quotations, selected almost at random, would seem to justify Kattenbusch's complaint. Kattenbusch, it should be added, delivers an extravagant and unjustifiable criticism of Tillich's conception of the Unconditioned when, like Hirsch, he speaks of it as a *"Nichts,"* as a reflection of indifference to good and evil. It is of course nonsense to imply that Tillich's conception of man's ultimate concern involves an indifference to good and evil. Yet there is a sense in which Tillich's Unconditioned is "indifferent." It does not provide a basis for distinguishing between different conceptions and aspects of religion. So long as a mean-

---

[6] "Religionsphilosophie," in Max Dessoir (ed.), *Die Philosophie in ihren Einzelgebieten* (Berlin: Ullstein, 1925), pp. 804, 821.

[7] *Ibid.,* p. 823.

[8] *Ibid.,* p. 802.

[9] "Religiöser Stil und religiöser Stoff in der bildenden Kunst," *Das neue Deutschland,* IX (1921), 156.

[10] *Rel. Verw.* (Berlin: Furche, 1929), p. 88.

[11] "Das Unbedingte und der Unbegreifbare," *Theologische Studien und Kritken,* XCIX (1926), 349.

ing-import is discernible in a religion, in a conception of God, in a ritual, in a sacrament, in a cultural act, relatedness to the Unconditioned is asserted to be operative. Accepting Tillich's basic definition of the concept, one cannot deny that his assertion is correct. The point is that the concept of "the Unconditioned" does not provide a criterion for discriminating between qualitatively different types of religious mentality. In this respect Tillich's "Unconditioned" may be compared to Rudolf Otto's conception of "the Holy." The concept has such wide applicability that it may be used only as a description of a generic religious attitude. Accordingly, "the Holy" may be intuited in the worship of Shiva, in a powerful scientific symbol, in Christian "grace," and so on. Christ and the Buddha are religious symbols in so far as the unconditioned transcendent is envisaged in them. Likewise with Tillich, the Unconditioned would seem to be intuited in an impersonal as well as in a personal conception of God. As a consequence of this possible variety of application, the concept has the effect of dissolving individually creative elements at the same time that it discriminates the universal element. We have pointed out earlier that form is thus deprived of significance in favor of import. One begins to wonder, however, whether the concept of unconditioned import, as defined by Tillich, is itself adequate to discriminate the nuances of "substance."

In defense of this seemingly bewildering variety of examples one might respond that they all illustrate Tillich's statement that the Unconditioned refers to "that element in every religious experience which makes it religious." Certainly, one must recognize that the attempt to discriminate and to name this "element" is a necessary task for any critical view of religion. But, as Tillich himself points out, one must distinguish between a definition of the nature of the religious and a normative conception of the authentic religion. The examples cited above indicate that Tillich has used the concept of the Unconditioned in both ways. This ambiguity, we may observe, illustrates the confusion we have mentioned earlier which causes one to question whether at a given moment Tillich is speaking as a philosopher or as a philosophical theologian.

We should observe, however, that Tillich has provided an elaborate apparatus for discerning different types of piety within a given religion—for example, the distinction between the theocratic, the sacramental, and the mystical elements or emphases, and also the distinction between emphasis on the form and emphasis on the import. These distinctions are pertinent also for analyzing analogous features in the culture, whether the culture is religiously oriented or is secularized. At the same time the assumption is made that the different types of piety are directed toward the Unconditioned. Of what significance is it to know, that both a world-renouncing mysticism and a world-transforming historical realism represent "the intuition of the unconditioned import in the conditioned forms"?[12]

The concept of the Unconditioned appears, then, to be a universal solvent. All culture, all religion, every intuition of the divine expresses, substantially if not intentionally, a relatedness to the Unconditioned. This view may be accepted as a sound observation insofar as one may say that all culture and all religion are oriented to meaning. But orientation to meaning is not necessarily orientation to the Unconditioned, and ultimate meanings possess considerable variety in different religions, cultures, and epochs. The meaning is assuredly not always the same even if the paradoxical immanence of the transcendent is intended. The Buddhist concept of "Nirvana"—which "reflects a relatedness to the Unconditioned"—is certainly not adequately characterized if its difference from, say, the Christian conception of salvation is not brought into relief. And the converse is also true.

The point here being stressed can be confirmed if we consider Tillich's theory of the types of religious symbol. Taking up the discriminations set forth in *Das System der Wissenschaften*, Tillich distinguishes two levels of symbols: the level of the supporting (*fundierend*) symbol and the level of the supported (*fundiert*) symbol. The symbols of the first level he calls "objective religious symbols" or "positive-symbolic" terms. In this type of symbol "religious objectivity is established," something "based in itself." The symbols of the second level he calls the "pointing religious symbols." The "pointing" symbols are certain religious acts themselves and certain objects that symbolize the religious attitude. The "pointing" symbols presuppose those of the first level and are exemplified by cultic gestures and by illustrative symbols such as the cross, arrows, and the like.

The "objective" or "supporting" symbols are divided into three groups. The first and basic group varies in form according to the stage of development in a particular religion. If it appears

---

[12] In *Das System der Wissenschaften* (pp. 132-33) Tillich says, "Concepts like 'intellectual insight,' 'pure intuition,' 'grasping of the absolute identity,' of the 'paradox' and the like, are expressions for the method of coincidence."

in the stage before the "breaking of the myth," the symbol refers to the whole sphere of divine beings. If it appears after the "breaking of the myth," it refers to the one God. But, as already indicated in our earlier exposition of Tillich's philosophy of being, the symbol does not refer to an "object" or *a* "being." The symbol must not be reified, else it is not a symbol of the unconditioned transcendent.

The word "God" produces a contradiction in the consciousness, it involves on the one hand something figurative that is a concrete object of the consciousness and on the other something not figurative, something that is merely represented by this concrete object. The latter is what we really have in mind when we use the word "God." . . . The religious act has to do with the unconditioned transcendent.[13]

To return now to our argument, we may say that this first group of the "objective" symbols represents a type of symbol which may be found wherever the unconditioned import of meaning is intuited. Again there is nothing to distinguish the symbols of one religion from those of another religion.

When we turn to Tillich's description of the second group of "supporting" symbols there can be little doubt that his concept of the Unconditioned is a devouring abyss for all symbols. The second group presents the characterizations of the nature and actions of God. Here the first group is presupposed. Again, the symbols used are, when properly understood, recognized as figurative. "But," he says, "this by no means signifies that statements about the nature of God are lacking in truth or that these symbols are interchangeable at will. Genuine symbols are not interchangeable at all, and authentic symbols provide no objective knowledge, but yet a true awareness."[14] But now we come to the crucial point. What is the criterion for a true symbol in this group? In reply to this question Tillich says, "The criterion of the truth of a symbol naturally cannot be the comparison of it with the reality to which it refers, if this reality is absolutely beyond comprehension."[15] If this sentence were accepted to the foot of the letter, one would simply have to stop speaking altogether about God or the Unconditioned. Neither of them could be of any concern to us. Tillich does not stop speaking: he continues

[13] *Rel. Verw.*, p. 102.
[14] *Ibid.*
[15] *Ibid.*, p. 103. As we have indicated in the previous chapter, this sort of hyperbole is not consistent with Tillich's expositions in other passages. We have already quoted a passage in which he subscribes in a special way to the principle of "analogia entis."

to speak of the Unconditioned as that which ultimately concerns us. To return to the particular point now under discussion: Tillich gives two criteria for the truth of symbols concerning the character and actions of God. First, he says, "the truth of a symbol depends on its inner necessity for the symbol-creating consciousness. Doubts concerning its truth indicate a change of mentality, a new attitude toward the unconditioned transcendent." But this is only a psychological criterion: the symbol must be accepted in earnestness. It is not a criterion for the truth of a symbol. One has difficulty in understanding why it should be mentioned as a criterion for truth. At all events, Tillich continues by saying, "The only criterion that is at all relevant is this: that the Unconditioned is clearly grasped in its unconditionedness. A symbol that does not meet this requirement and that elevates a conditioned thing to the dignity of the Unconditioned is not false but it is demonic."[16]

This criterion for the truth of a symbol of the character and actions of God really provides no basis for selecting a Christian symbol as over against any other which "clearly grasps the Unconditioned in its unconditionedness." Again, the Unconditioned serves as a solvent and provides no basis for discrimination among symbols except unconditionedness.

We must come to a similar conclusion when we consider the third group of "supporting" symbols. In it are "the natural and historical objects that are drawn as holy objects into the sphere of religious objects and thus become religious symbols." In the discussion of the third group of symbols we find certain formulations that are utterly confusing. We shall not dwell upon them, but they should be quoted nevertheless in order to show that Tillich is himself at least partially to blame if even friendly critics like Kurt Leese fail to understand him.[17]

In the foreground stand the historical personalities that have become the object of a religious act. It would of course be entirely contradictory to the religious consciousness if one characterized these personalities, or what they did and what happened to them, as symbols. For the perculiarity of this kind of object of the religious consciousness depends precisely upon its historical reality, its reality in the objective sense. The use of symbolism with regard to this sphere in which the

[16] *Ibid.* Since coming to America Tillich has characterized the first group mentioned above as "ontological symbols" and the second group as "ontic symbols." Cf. Georgia Harkness, "The Abyss and the Given," *Christendom,* III (1938), 508-20.

[17] Cf. *Rel. Verw.,* p. 286, note 15.

holy is supposed to be really present would involve a denial of its presence and hence the destruction of its existence. And yet this denial is inevitable as soon as these holy realities are looked upon as being rationally objective. For in the context of the rationally apprehended world of concrete objects they have no place. . . . These historical personalities, insofar as they are considered as symbols, therefore, have no place in the objective world. More than this, they cannot have such a place if their quality of holiness is to be preserved.[18]

We find some sentences in this passage astonishing. They would mean that nothing in the actual life of Jesus may properly be taken as religiously symbolic. The discussion immediately following, however, is inconsistent with these formulations. Tillich goes on to say that all this signifies that

these objects that possess a holy character are not empirical even if they can only be perceived in connection with the empirical order. This means that they are symbols, they represent the presence of the unconditioned transcendent in the empirical order. The very fact that this presence is viewed as an empirical event (for example, the resurrection), indicates the figurative character that attaches to every objectification of the transcendent. It is therefore correct to say that Christ and the Buddha, for example, are symbols insofar as the unconditioned transcendent is envisaged in them.[19]

We shall have something further to say on this problem later, as it relates to Tillich's Christology.

With respect to Tillich's treatment of the second group of "supporting" symbols a further comment is to be made. We have reserved it until now because it has to do with another aspect of the question concerning the nature of the Unconditioned and its relation to the concept of God. As several critics of Tillich (for example, Kattenbusch and Brunner) have observed, the concept of the Unconditioned as presented by Tillich denies the personality of God—if God is the Unconditioned. Perhaps for this reason Brunner has spoken of Tillich's theology as Gnostic,[20] and Kattenbusch has asserted that Tillich's concept of God is unchristian: it is neither a personal nor a loving God.[21] As we

[18] *Ibid.,* p. 104. It would seem likely that this depreciation of the empirical reality of the historical personality as a basis for religious symbolism was the result of the wave of extreme skepticism concerning the authenticity of the Gospel records, a heavy wave at the time of the writing of the essay on "The Religious Symbol" (1928).

[19] *Ibid.*

[20] Emil Brunner, *Philosophy of Religion,* trans. A. J. D. Farrer and Bertram Lee Woolf (London: Ivor Nicholson and Watson, 1937), p. 42.

[21] *Op cit.,* pp. 394ff.

have seen in Tillich's description of the second group of "supporting" symbols, the attributes of God are to be tested only to determine their unconditionality. Evidently the attributes of love and personality, like countless others, would be acceptable to Tillich as ontic symbols providing they grasp the unconditionedness of the Unconditioned. But this means that the ontic symbols are significant only in terms of the first "supporting" group. Again we see, as in the preceding chapter, that the form is deprived of its significance in favor of the import. As Hirsch has suggested, there is too much emphasis on the *meta* in Tillich's metalogic. Because of this, Hirsch, we have already seen, wrongly asserts that Tillich's Unconditioned is *das Bodenlose*.

One further comment should be made concerning the ontic symbols of the second group. In 1940 Albert Einstein delivered an address at the Conference on Science, Philosophy, and Religion challenging the ideas of the omnipotence and personality of God. In reply to the denial of the omnipotence of God, Tillich, after agreeing that the symbol cannot be accepted in the sense of "omni-activity in terms of physical causality," says that the symbol means something else:

> The symbol of omnipotence expresses the religious experience that no structure of reality and no event in nature and history has the power of preventing us from community with the infinite and unexhaustible ground of meaning and being. What "omnipotence" means should be found in the words Deutro-Isaiah (Isa. 40) speaks to the exiled in Babylon when he describes the nothingness of the world-empires in comparison with the divine power to fulfil its historical aim through an infinitely small group of exiled people.[22]

This statement seems to say nothing other than what we have already attributed to Tillich, namely, that God is the unconditioned transcendent which is paradoxically present in all creation, either destroying or creating form. What particular character in God it is that impels him to fulfill a purpose in history is not made evident by the assertion that nothing can "prevent us from community with the infinite and unexhaustible ground of meaning and being." Nor is it implicit in the concept of the Unconditioned.

This same question as to the character of God is brought to the fore by Tillich's response to Einstein's denial of the personality of God.

[22] "The Idea of the Personal God," *Union Review*, II (1940), 8-9.

Philosophy and Theology 269

The depth of being cannot be symbolized by objects taken from a realm which is lower than the personal, from the realm of things or subpersonal living beings. The suprapersonal is not an "It," or more exactly, it is a "He" as much as it is an "It," and it is above both of them. But if the "He" element is left out, the "It" element transforms the alleged suprapersonal into a subpersonal, as it usually happens in monism and pantheism. And such a neutral subpersonal, cannot grasp the center of our personality; it can satisfy our aesthetic feeling or our intellectual needs, but it cannot convert our will, it cannot overcome our loneliness, anxiety, and despair. For as the philosopher Schelling says: "Only a person can heal a person." This is the reason that the symbol of the Personal God is indispensable for living religion. It is a symbol, not an object, and it never should be interpreted as an object. And it is one symbol beside others indicating that our personal center is grasped by the manifestation of the unaccessible ground and abyss of being.[23]

Here we have hyperbole again. In the preceding paragraph quoted above, Tillich says that "omnipotence" means that nothing has "the power of preventing us from community with the infinite and unexhaustible ground"; here we are told that the ground and abyss of being is "unaccessible." But to return to the main point with which we are now concerned: Even if we grant that God is not an object and that the term "personal" is a symbol, still we are left in doubt as to whether God has a character somehow suggested by the symbol or is merely said to have it in order that our loneliness, anxiety, and despair may be overcome.

The same anthropological rather than theological approach is evident in another statement of Tillich's on the same point: "Only

[23] Ibid., p. 10. In his essay on "The Transformation of the Ideal of Personality," Rel. Verw., p. 171, he says, "The power of self-determination (in personality) is the very essence and the highest form of the power of being, and it is in personality that this power of being finds its fulfilment in the existential order." But to attribute personality to the Ultimate is to be guilty of idolatry, for then "the supporting and yet transcendent ground of all existence becomes merely one part of the world." The concept of God as a personality—a being having consciousness and will—is "a degenerate product of the nineteenth century. Earlier theology, nourished as it was by a great ontological tradition, did not use such a concept" (ibid., pp. 172, 297).

In connection with Tillich's assertion that "the symbol of the Personal God is indispensable for living religion" we may mention a fundamental religious and theological problem, namely the question as to whether Tillich's conception of God permits any genuine response in God to the believer or the repentant sinner. Tillich's negative and positive conception of the Unconditioned—the inaccessibility of the Unconditioned and God viewed as the power of being—appears to make no place for God as a passive power, able to respond to men and to history. On this question, see pp. 256-57 supra.

personality can be confronted by the Unconditioned, can strive toward the Unconditioned."[24] But the human possibility cannot be decisive for determining the character of God.

The present writer is inclined to conclude that it is because Tillich has been so prone to show that God is not an Object or a Supreme Being that he has inadequately dealt with the question of the character of God—at least, when considered under the rubric of the Unconditioned. This evaluation obtains even if we take into account Tillich's statement that, in place of the term "the Unconditioned" one may use such terms as "Being as such" or "the power of being."

Hence his critics will not allow him to rest. Wilbur M. Urban, for example, has asked whether God is only a symbol and also whether God is the Unconditioned. In this connection Urban has pointed out that if all knowledge of God is symbolic, then there can be no nonsymbolic knowledge of God. Tillich, as we have seen, asserts that knowledge of the unconditioned transcendent is not figurative or symbolic. In response to Urban he states that "any symbolic knowledge presupposes some basis of nonsymbolic knowledge. The nonsymbolic element in all religious knowledge is the experience of the Unconditioned as the boundary, ground, and abyss of everything conditioned. This experience is the boundary-experience of human reason and therefore expressible in negative-rational terms."[25] Obviously, such a conception comes short of what religious people (including Christians) have called God.

At this point we should note a change in Tillich's formulations. In his "Philosophy of Religion" (1925) he speaks of God as the symbol for the Unconditioned.[26] It may well be that in making this assertion he had in mind the more positive implications of the concept (explained in Chapter II). At all events he now says, "The Unconditioned is not God. God is the affirmative concept pointing beyond the boundary of the negative-rational terms and therefore is itself a positive-symbolic term."[27] But then he goes on to say that Kant has refuted every attempt to establish the idea of God in "positive-rational terms." What then is possible? The answer is: "Positive-symbolic terms presuppose—in this I agree fully with Urban—that the immediate reality which is used in

24 *The Interpretation of History*, trans. Rasetzki and Talmey (New York: Charles Scribner's Sons, 1936), p. 142.

25 "Symbol and Knowledge," *Journal of Liberal Religion*, II (1941), pp. 202-6.

26 "Religionsphilosophie," p. 804.

27 "Symbol and Knowledge," p. 203.

the symbol has something to do with the transcendent reality which is symbolized in it."[28] Tillich goes on to say that he accepts the classical doctrine of "analogia entis," pointing out that he stands resolutely against Barth on this matter. Then he seems to repudiate the principle immediately:

> But while accepting the method of "anologia entis," I cannot accept any attempt to use it in the way of rational construction. The symbolic, affirmative concepts about God, his qualities and his actions, express the concrete form in which the mysterious ground and abyss of being has become manifest to a being as his ultimate concern in an act which we call "revelation." The special symbols are dependent upon the concrete situation and configuration in which the mystery of the ground appears to us. The knowledge about God arising from such a concrete manifestation of the unconditioned is true, although it may be a relative, preliminary or distorted truth. But it is not a theoretical, it is an existential truth, that is a truth to which I cannot have the spectator-attitude, to which I must surrender in order to experience it. In this sense the "symbols provide no objective knowledge but yet a true awareness," namely, the mystery of the ground, which never can become an object for a subject, but which draws the subject into the object thus overcoming the cleavage between them.[29]

Tillich has made a great change by stating that God is not the Unconditioned. That must be admitted: the Unconditioned is now presented as only a negative-rational symbol. But the reader is still left groping in search of a positive Unconditioned. And even if he finds it, or even if he finds a positive-symbolic knowledge of God—"with true awareness"—still he has no criterion for judging its truth value. We are told only that "the symbols are dependent on the concrete situation and configuration" and hence are still unable to state what the character of God is. And we get no nearer the answer by being told that we must not adopt a spectator-attitude, and that we must surrender to existential truth in order to experience it.

From this whole discussion we conclude that when Tillich moves from philosophy of religion to theology (the normative system) he carries over with him the concept of the Unconditioned, inserting it into and identifying it with the Christian categories. It is not our purpose to make an extended examination of his statements on theology. Yet, a few further observations may be made in order to confirm the general tenor of our criticism.

28 *Ibid.*
29 *Ibid.*, p. 204.

Consider, for example, his treatment of the concept of revelation. Tillich points out that the idea of revelation is as old as religion, but that the concept has two sources: Semitic apocalypticism and Hellenistic philosophy. In the Semitic literature the concept refers to a disclosure of the divine world-plan, particularly with reference to a coming catastrophic end.[30] The bearer of the revelation is a seer who has been privileged to behold transcendent mysteries. The second source, Hellenistic philosophy, is the result of the need of late Greek philosophy for a truth exempt from the uncertainties of philosophical discussion and skepticism. Revelation, then, has two constituent elements: the unveiling of a hidden, hitherto unknown event and the disclosure of a faith which reason is unable to develop. Tillich says in passing that these two concepts were joined on Christian soil and were enriched by a third element: "The revelation has taken place in a personal life. The unveiling of a divine plan for the world in Jesus Christ is at the same time its fulfilment; and in this fulfilment the truth has appeared for which the Greeks sought in vain."[31] He goes on to indicate some of the complex problems that arose because of the double source of the theory and because of intellectualistic and ecclesiastical perversions. But in the end he reduces the concept of "revelation" into meaning the disclosure of the Unconditionally Hidden. In short, it is the shattering and transformation of the conditioned by the grace of the Unconditioned Transcendent. A revelation is said to be perfect insofar as it places itself at every moment of its concrete realization under the shattering and transformation that are bound up with the genuine revelation. "That revelation is complete in which there is nothing unconditioned except the Unconditioned-Hidden itself which is revealed in it."[32] So he goes on to speak of the concrete norm as being derived from the Christian proclamation of "the cross of Christ" as an event of revelation. The concrete norm provided by the cross of Christ is this: Every revelation in which the revelation-bearer lays claim through itself to unconditionality is a demonized revelation, for the principle of the demonic is the elevation of a limited finite to unconditionality, to the dignity of the Unconditioned-Hidden. Here again we have the positive and the negative Unconditioned

[30] Here again is a characterization of God's purpose for which the concept of "the Unconditioned" is inadequate.

[31] "Offenbarung," *Die Religion in Geschichte und Gegenwart*, 2nd ed. (Tübingen: Mohr, 1930), IV, 664.

[32] *Ibid.*

imported into theology and made the concrete norm. The negative Unconditioned adopts Christ as the symbol of self-immolation. The positive Unconditioned adopts Christ as the symbol of the new being that shatters, transforms, and fulfills every finite. Christ, the center of history, is adopted as the symbol for the Tillichian synthesis of being, thought, and spirit. "Christianity, in calling Christ the center of history, considers a personal life which is completely determined by its relation to God, the principle of meaning in history." Tillich makes it clear that the meaning of meaning set forth in his "Philosophy of Religion" is the one he has in mind, for he goes on to say,

That implies first, that salvation occurs in that sphere which we call religion and which can be defined as the human answer to the manifestation of a transcendent, unconditioned meaning. . . . Only in the appearance of an unconditioned meaning is the ambiguity of time overcome, only by it can the threat of meaninglessness be conquered. Therefore being grasped by the center of history means being grasped without limitations and conditions, by an absolute power.[33]

If we recall now the "construction" of the history of religion set forth in the preceding chapter, we must ask how the "polytheistic" element has been taken up into this Christology. According to the "construction," a concrete symbol should form the capstone of the arch provided by ethical monotheism, but when we examine the capstone we find that it is the Christ symbol and that it is an expression of Tillich's philosophy of meaning. To be sure, Tillich says that the Christ symbol cannot be separated from the historical figure. But nothing concrete is taken up by the Christ symbol from the historical reality except the symbol of the cross, which, as he himself says, is a symbol of self-immolation before the unconditioned transcendent—surely, a reductionist interpretation.

Not through itself, not through its finite merits, nor through its highest ethical discipline does a creature acquire holiness but alone through its character of being a bearer of revelation, pointing to the Unconditioned-Hidden. But this is not its empirical character; the latter is that which is in revelation grasped, broken through, made into a pointer; but this empirical character is not itself revelation. Revelation is bound to nothing conditioned, i.e., to nothing humanly great or sublime, and it is excluded from nothing conditioned, i.e., from nothing humanly lowly. Hence the "witness" (pointer) of the revelation appearing in Jesus Christ does not signify a witness to his

[33] *The Interpretation of History*, p. 260.

empirical character with all its historical relativity and problematic character, it does not involve a witness to his ethics, his prophecy, his inner life, his numinous power—rather it signifies a witness to the transcendent being appearing in all these contingencies, to the revelation appearing through and in contrast to his empirical character. Only thus can it be a revelation to us and penetrate to our contemporaneity, because it is not a coercion, a destruction of our contingency through an alien contingency, but rather a breaking-in of the Unconditioned-Hidden through every contingency into our contingency. If revelation were identical with the object in which it appears, the cross would not stand over every bearer of revelation . . . and revelation would be a coercion.[34]

These are curious words indeed from a writer who only a few paragraphs earlier has said that revelation is something particular and once-happened. They are curious words also from a philosopher of religion who asserts that the normative system must be concrete and must be based upon the living confessions of a religious community.

No new light on our dilemma is shed by Tillich's later discussion of the doctrine of the Incarnation, for here we find that the Incarnation was a new being, a manifestation of original and essential God-manhood within and under the conditions of existence, in the *picture* of Jesus as the Christ. Yet although it is a picture of something once-happened in character, a picture behind which we cannot go, it presents Jesus in the totality of his being as the Christ.[35] Some of the formulations in this article are new for Tillich, but on the whole the doctrine of Incarnation set forth is again a reading into it of essence-existence philosophy—transformed by a superseding "New Being."

We could follow through with other doctrines showing the same tendency to carry over the conclusions of philosophy and philosophy of religion into the normative system.

Now, there is no compelling argument against a philosopher's reading his system into the categories of Christian theology. It has been done again and again with varying benefits and injuries. The reason we have stressed the fact in Tillich's case is twofold: First, we have wished to show the gulf between his theory and his practice. His *Das System der Wissenschaften* and his "Philosophy of Religion" assert that philosophy of religion should study only the principles of meaning and the intellectual history of religion,

[34] "Die Idee der Offenbarung," *Zeitschrift für Theologie und Kirche*, VIII (1927), 409-10.
[35] "A Misinterpretation of the Doctrine of Incarnation," *Church Quarterly Review*, CXLVII (1949), 113-48. This essay was written around 1941.

and that systematic theology on the basis of the confessions of the supporting religious community should present the normative system. His own practice all too often fails to follow these principles. Second, we have wished to show how his conception of the Unconditioned serves as an abyss into which sink the differences between one religion and another, and between different aspects of the same religion. Consequently, often when the reader turns, to read about the Buddha, the Christ, faith, revelation, God, prophetism, sacramentalism, mysticism, prayer, or the kingdom of God, he will find these realities penetrated and then replaced by the ground and abyss of the Unconditioned, which is inaccessible and which yet places a radical question mark over every kind of religious knowledge.

The criticisms presented here are directed toward Tillich's writings of the earlier period. Many of these criticisms are familiar to anyone who has followed the dialogues which his writings have engendered. Some of the criticisms no doubt bespeak the present writer's lack of understanding. Obviously, they cannot properly be taken as final. Since 1945, the terminus of the present study, Tillich has dealt with many of the criticisms. Moreover, since 1945 he has written more extensively and systematically on theological questions than in the earlier period. The reader must therefore view much that has been said here as serving at best to provide a background for dealing with his later writings. Certainly, the questions posed here should not give reason for anyone's overlooking the remarkable capacity of Tillich to interpret dialectically religion and culture, and the relations between them.

In 1928 Tillich expressed the view that the present task of the churches is to "discover anew the reality which was apprehended in earlier times and which is in essence the same today, and then present it in quite new terms."[36] If we should add nothing to the above discussion and estimate of Tillich's philosophy of religion, we would give the impression that he has failed in the accomplishment of the purpose just mentioned. The foregoing criticisms of Tillich imply that his philosophy of religion is only a form of Gnosticism, that it is something read into Christianity and nothing else.

It would, however, be just as accurate to say that this philosophy of religion is a powerful restatement of highly significant elements of the doctrines of Christianity—especially of the doc-

[36] *Rel. Verw.*, p. 31.

trines of creation, of justification by faith, of sin, and of grace. By his presentation of the first, the dimension of depth and the sense of dependence upon God is accented; by means of the second, every sphere including the "religious" sphere is brought into question and all false security is shattered; by means of the third the powerfulness and temptation of the threatening, form-destroying forces is discerned; and by means of the last the promise of newness of life is made plausible and is presented in existential terms as "at hand." All of these concepts destroy the self-enclosure of moralism and the false hopes of utopianism, turning us to the order of grace.

With respect to the doctrine of God, his formulations concerning the infinite and inexhaustible ground and abyss of meaning and being, concerning the impossibility of conceiving of God as an Object or as one Being among other beings, concerning the divine as a qualification of existence, concerning the "ecstatic" relationship to the divine, concerning the relation between the divine and the demonic, and concerning the theonomous attitude as a deepening of autonomy—all of these formulations have assisted many people to regain a sense of the decisive importance of religion in general and of the Christian religion in particular. Thus he has healed or prevented casualties among those who have been repulsed by the irrational and the rationalistic constructions of orthodoxy and of theism.

In more general terms, we may say that by centering attention on the principles of meaning he provides a way to bring the reader into the moment of decision where he will confront the question: What is of ultimate concern for *me*? By means of his interpretation of the nature of religion and culture and of the relations between them, he offers a religious interpretation of life whereby the positive significance of both religion and culture can be appreciated and whereby a basis for the prophetic criticism of both may be found.

It is true that at times Tillich insists so strongly upon the substantial, if not the intentional, religiousness of culture that sin and perversion seem to be exorcised. Indeed, one wonders whether the high valuation placed on culture is not due to the fact that he sees more religiousness there than it possesses by nature.[37] At other times he so much emphasizes the ambiguousness of

---

[37] His essay "Kirche und humanistische Gesellschaft," *Neuwerk*, XIII (1931), 4-18, gives a brilliant exposition of the dependence of secularism upon Christianity. Is this type of secularism the basis for the high estimate? If so, the estimate is really an evaluation of Christianity and not of secularism.

religion and culture, of knowledge and decision, that the order of time seems to be mainly the order of guilt. On the other hand this emphasis gives all the more relevance to the doctrine of forgiveness which is stressed in his writings on psychotherapy (writings that lie beyond our concern here).

Here we must say with emphasis that Tillich by no means contents himself with reading his philosophy of being and of the Unconditioned into everything Christian and religious which he treats. In his theological writings he exhibits an extraordinary ability to give a penetrating and intrinsic rendering of the major themes of the Judeo-Christian heritage. The reader should be reminded that this aspect of his work has not been the *center* of attention in the present study. We have been concerned to show how he has employed a particular method and terminology in presenting a philosophy of culture, science, and religion.

The greatest achievement of Paul Tillich has been manifest in his genius for devising new categories or for giving old or forgotten categories new meaning. Few theologians in our time have given currency to so many novel or virtually novel concepts. Belief-ful realism, the dimension of depth, the boundary-situation, form of grace, theonomy, the demonic, and *Kairos* are concepts to which he has given vivid and powerful meaning. These are words "in which the powerfulness of the word pulsates." In Tillich's hands they also readily lend themselves to the illuminating of specific elements in the Biblical and in church traditions. He has discovered anew a reality that was "apprehended in earlier times" and has presented it in new ways. By this means he has given new vitality and significance to figures and movements and ideas of the major traditions of the West—an impressive accomplishment indeed. This accomplishment, in fact, involves much more than his explication of themes from German classical philosophy, important as this may be. Moreover, he has had measurable success in accomplishing what he originally envisaged as a worthy task for the Protestant theologian of our day.

That task he has so well formulated in his autobiographical sketch that it is fitting and instructive to quote the passage at length. Thus we end our study with a reminder of what Tillich's major intention has been with respect to his speaking about the great themes of time and eternity.

Wherever the question of the language of the Christian gospel is taken seriously . . . , great difficulties arise. It is certain that the original religious terminology, as it is used in the Bible and in the liturgies of the Ancient Church, cannot be supplanted. There are religious original or archetypal words (*Urworte*) of mankind, as Martin Buber remarked to me some time ago. But these original or archetypal words have been robbed of their original power by our objective thinking, and the scientific conception of the world, and thus, have become subject to dissolution. In face of what the archetypal word "God" means, rational criticism is powerless. In face of an objectively existing God, atheism is right. A situation is hopeless and meaningless in which the speaker means the original word, and the listener hears the objective word. Thus, we may understand the proposal which is meant symbolically rather than literally, that the Church impose a thirty-year silence upon all of its archetypal words. But if it should do this, as it did in a few instances, it would be necessary to develop a new terminology. But all such attempts to translate the archaic language of liturgy and the Bible into a modern one have been deplorably futile. They represented disintegration and not a new creation. Even the use of the terminology of the mystics, especially in sermons (an attempt which I have made myself), is dangerous, since it conveys a different content with the different word; a content which hardly comprises all facts of the Christian gospel. Thus, the only solution is to use the religious "original words," and at the same time to make clear their original meaning, by disavowing their secular and distorted usage, i.e., to stand between the two terminologies and recapture anew the original religious terminology from the border. The present peril of society has driven many to this border where the religious terminology can be heard in its original meaning. It would be regrettable if a blind and arrogant orthodoxy should monopolize these words and thus confuse many who have a feeling for religious reality, either driving them into paganism or thrusting them finally out from the Church.[38]

In this passage Tillich reveals his acute sensitivity in face of the present religious and cultural situation. Because of this interpretation of the situation he has felt bound to live on the border, whence he has exercised a marked and salutary influence, on both sides of the border.

Those within the churches who have been instructed by Tillich have received a new and vivid understanding of the enduring meaning of certain Christian doctrines and of the Protestant, prophetic spirit. With this new understanding they have come to a recognition of the irrelevance of much present-day Christianity in face of the significant spiritual and cultural forces of our time. Hence they have acquired a new appreciation of the need for the criticism of "religion"; they have received a new understanding of the demands placed upon them as Protestants and Christians to achieve a religious interpretation of the arts and the sciences.

[38] *The Interpretation of History*, pp. 46-47.

Those outside the churches have gained a new understanding of the religious roots of culture and an appreciation of the decisive need for a religious criticism of culture as well as of "religion." Certainly, no small degree of Tillich's success as an apostle to the Gentiles is due to the fact that in many of his writings he largely avoids using traditional Christian language. This abjuring of traditional, smeared, bleared words prevents his writings from eliciting the misinterpretations of religion which obstruct the typical "modern" man's taking seriously either religion or Christianity, misinterpretations that in fact make this "modern" man boast that he would not so much "abandon" his mind as to read theology.

For both groups, the insiders and the outsiders, the disruption of meaning implied in the dualism of the old conflict between the natural and the supernatural, or between culture and religion, is partially overcome in the theonomous criticisms of all religion and culture and in the recognition of the demand for timely, new creation. They are both brought to the border where new promise as well as new tensions and distortions are to be found.

Bibliography

(1910–1945)

ABBREVIATIONS

GW Paul Tillich, *Gesammelte Werke*. Edited by Renate Albrecht. Stuttgart: Evangelisches Verlagswerk. Volumes published thus far: I (1959), II (1962), IV (1961), V (1964), VI (1963), VII (1962).

IH Paul Tillich, *The Interpretation of History*. Translated by N. A. Rasetzki (Part I) and Elsa L. Talmey (Parts II, III, IV). New York: Charles Scribner's Sons, 1936.

PE Paul Tillich, *The Protestant Era*. Translated and with a Concluding Essay by James Luther Adams. Chicago: University of Chicago Press, 1948.

RGG Hermann Gunkel and Leopold Zscharnack and others (eds.). *Die Religion in Geschichte und Gegenwart; Handwörterbuch für Theologie und Religionswissenchaft*. Second edition, completely revised. 6 vols. Tübingen: Mohr, 1927-1932.

SF Paul Tillich, *The Shaking of the Foundations*. New York: Charles Scribner's Sons, 1948.

A. *Books by Tillich*

1910 *Die religionsgeschichtliche Konstruktion in Schellings positiver Philosophie, ihre Voraussetzungen und Prinzipien*. Inaugural Dissertation. Breslau: Fleischmann, 1910. Pp. vi, 143.

1912 *Mystik und Schuldbewusstsein in Schellings philosophischer Entwicklung*. (*Beiträge zur Förderung christlicher Theologie*, XVI, No. 1.) Gütersloh: Bertelsmann, 1912. Pp. 135. (*GW, I*, 11–108.)

1915 *Der Begriff des Uebernatürlichen, sein dialektischer Charakter und das Prinzip der Identität, dargestellt an der supranaturalistischen Theologie vor Schleiermacher*. (Habilitationsschrift, Halle.) Königsberg: Madrasch, 1915. pp. 58.

1919 *Der Sozialismus als Kirchenfrage*. In collaboration with Dr. Carl Richard Wegener. Berlin: Grachverlag, 1919. pp. 18. (*GW, II*, 13–20.)

  Religionsphilosophie der Kultur; Zwei Entwürfe von Gustav Radbruch und Paul Tillich. ("Ueber die Idee einer Theologie der Kultur," by Tillich, pp. 27–52.) Berlin: Reuther und Reichard, 1919. Pp. 52. (2nd ed., 1921.)

1922   *Masse und Geist; Studien zur Philosophie der Masse.* Berlin and Frankfurt a.M.: Verlag der Arbeitsgemeinschaft, 1922. Pp. 55. (*GW*, II, 35–90.)

1923   *Das System der Wissenschaften nach Gegenständen und Methoden. Ein Entwurf.* Göttingen: Vandenhoeck und Ruprecht, 1923. Pp. 167. (*GW*, I, 109–293.)

1924   *Kirche und Kultur.* (*Sammlung gemeinverständlicher Vorträge und Schriften aus dem Gebiet der Theologie und Religionsgeschichte,* No. 111.) Tübingen: Mohr, 1924. Pp. 22. (English translation in *IH*, pp. 219–41.)

1925   "Religionsphilosophie," in Max Dessoir (ed.), *Die Philosophie in ihren Einzelgebieten,* II, 769–835. Berlin: Ullstein, 1925. (Separate reprint, Stuttgart: Kohlhammer, 1962. Pp. 119. Also *GW*, I, 295–364.)

1926   *Das Dämonische; Ein Beitrag zur Sinndeutung der Geschichte.* (*Sammlung gemeinverständlicher Vorträge und Schriften aus dem Gebiet der Theologie und Religionsgeschichte,* No. 119.) Tübingen: Mohr, 1926. Pp. 44. (English translation in *IH*, pp. 77–122. *GW*, VI, 42–71.)

    Kairos: I: Zur Geisteslage und Geisteswendung. Edited by Tillich. Darmstadt: Reichl, 1926. Pp. 481.

    Die religiöse Lage der Gegenwart. Berlin: Ullstein, 1926. Pp. 153. (English translation [with Introduction] by H. Richard Niebuhr: *The Religious Situation.* New York: Henry Holt and Co., 1932. Pp. XXV, 182. Other English editions: New York: Meridian Books, 1956; London: Thames & Hudson, 1956.)

    Das Berneuchener Buch. Hamburg: Hanseatische Verlagsanstalt, 1926. Pp. 181. Tillich is listed as a collaborator.

1929   *Kairos: II: Protestantismus als Kritik und Gestaltung.* Edited by Tillich. Darmstadt: Reichl, 1929. Pp. 407.

    Religiöse Verwirklichung. Berlin: Furche, 1929. Pp. 312. (2nd ed., 1930.)

1931   *Protestantisches Prinzip und proletarische Situation.* Bonn: Friedrich Cohen, 1931. Pp. 33. (English translation in *PE*, pp. 161–81. *GW*, VII, 84–104.)

1932   *Hegel und Goethe. Zwei Gedenkreden.* (*Sammlung gemeinverständlicher Vorträge und Schriften aus dem Gebiet der Theologie und Religionsgeschichte,* No. 158.) Tübingen: Mohr, 1932. Pp. 48.

1933   *Die sozialistische Entscheidung.* Potsdam: Alfred Protte, 1933. Pp. 201. (Suppressed in 1933. Reissued in 1948. *GW*, II, 219–65. Partial English translation in *IH*, pp. 203–15.)

1936   *The Interpretation of History.* Translated by Rasetzki and Talmey. New York: Charles Scribner's Sons, 1936. Pp. xi, 284.

1941   *War Aims.* (Pamphlet reprinting three articles appearing in *The Protestant.*) New York: The Protestant, 1941. Pp. 22.

B.   *Articles by Tillich*

1912   "Selbstanzeige," *Kant-Studien,* XVII (1912), 306–7. Author's note on *Mystik und Schuldbewusstsein in Schellings philosophischer Entwicklung.*

1915 "Predigt gehalten nach den Kämpfen bei Tahure am 30. und 31. Oktober 1915." Privately printed.

1919 "Revolution und Kirche," *Das neue Deutschland*, VII (July 1919), 394–97.
"Christentum und Sozialismus," *Das neue Deutschland*, VIII (December 1919), 106–10. (*GW*, II, 21–28.)

1920 "Die Jugend und die Religion," in A. Grabowski and W. Koch (eds.), *Die freideutsche Jugendbewegung; Ursprung und Zukunft*. Third supplementary issue of the semimonthly *Das neue Deutschland*. Gotha: F. A. Perthes, 1920, pp. 8–13. (2nd ed., 1921.)
"Christentum and Sozialismus," *Freideutsche Jugend*, VI (1920), 167–70. (*GW*, II, 29–33.)
"Masse und Persönlichkeit," *Die Verhandlungen des 27. und 28. Evangelisch-Sozialen Kongresses*. Göttingen: Vandenhoeck und Ruprecht, 1920, pp. 76–96. (Reprinted in *Masse und Geist*, pp. 5–23. *GW*, II, 36–56.)

1921 "Religiöser Stil und religiöser Stoff in der bildenden Kunst," *Das neue Deutschland*, IX (1921), 151–58.
"Masse und Religion," *Blätter für religiösen Sozialismus*, II (1921), 1–3, 5–7, 9–12. (Reprinted in *Masse und Geist*, pp. 37–55. *GW*, II, 70–90.)
"Die Theologie als Wissenschaft," *Vossische Zeitung*, No. 512 (October 30, 1921), pp. 2–3.

1922 "Die Ueberwindung des Religionsbegriffs in der Religionsphilosophie," *Kant-Studien*, XXVII (1922), 446–69. (*GW*, I, 367–88.)
"Albrecht Ritschl; Zu seinem hundertsten Geburtstag," *Theologische Blätter*, I, No. 3 (March 1922), 49–54.
"Anthroposophie und Theologie," *Theologische Blätter*, I, No. 4 (April 1922), 86–88.
"Religiöse Krisis," *Vivos voco*, No. 11 (April–May 1922), pp. 616–21.
"Kairos," *Die Tat*, XIV, No. 5 (August 1922), 330–50. (English translation in *PE*, pp. 32–51. *GW*, VI, 9–28.)
"Gotteslästerung," *Vossische Zeitung*, No. 485 (October 13, 1922), pp. 1–2.
"Zur Klärung der religiösen Grundhaltung," *Blätter für religiösen Sozialismus*, III, No. 12 (December 1922), 46–48.
"Renaissance und Reformation; Zur Einführung in die Bibliothek Warburg," *Theologische Blätter*, I, No. 12 (December 1922), 265–67.

1923 "Die Kategorie des 'Heiligen' bei Rudolf Otto," *Theologische Blätter*, II, No. 1 (January 1923), 11–12.
"Ernst Troeltsch," *Vossische Zeitung*, No. 58 (February 3, 1923), pp. 2–3.
"Grundlinien des religiösen Sozialismus; Ein systematischer Entwurf." Reprint from *Blätter für religiösen Sozialismus*, IV, Nos. 8–10 (1923). Pp. 24. (*GW*, II, 91–119.)
"Kritisches und positives Paradox; Eine Auseinandersetzung mit Karl Barth und Friedrich Gogarten." *Theologische Blätter*, II, No. 11 (November 1923), 263–69. (*GW*, VII, 216–25.)
"Antwort," *Theologische Blätter*, II, No. 12 (December 1923), 296–99. (*GW*, VII, 240–43.) (Replies to Karl Barth, "Von der Paradoxie des 'positiven Paradoxes,'" *GW*, VII, 226–39.)

1924 "Rechtfertigung und Zweifel," *Vorträge der Theologischen Konferenz zu Giessen*, No. 39 (1924), pp. 19–32. Giessen: Alfred Töpelmann, 1924.

"Antwort [auf Mennicke: 'Zu Tillichs Systematik']," *Blätter für religiösen Sozialismus*, V (1924), 18–22.

"Die religiöse und philosophische Weiterbildung des Sozialismus," *Blätter für religiösen Sozialismus*, V (1924), 26–30. (*GW*, II, 121–31.)

"Ernst Troeltsch; Versuch einer geistesgeschichtlichen Würdigung," *Kant-Studien*, XXIX (1924), 351–58.

"Erwiderung [auf Heppe, 'Nationale Erneuerung,']," *Wingolf-Blätter*, LIII (1924), 27.

"Christentum, Sozialismus und Nationalismus," *Wingolf-Blätter*, LIII (1924), 78–80.

"Jugendbewegung und Religion," *Werkland*, IV (1924), 61–64.

1925 "Die Staatslehre Augustins nach *De civitate Dei*," *Theologische Blätter*, IV, No. 4 (April 1925), 77–86.

"Denker der Zeit: Der Religionsphilosoph Rudolf Otto," *Vossische Zeitung*, No. 308 (July 2, 1925).

1926 "Denker der Zeit: Karl Barth," *Vossische Zeitung*, No. 32; *Das Unterhaltungsblatt*, No. 16 (January 20, 1926).

"Der Begriff des Dämonischen und seine Bedeutung für die systematische Theologie," *Theologische Blätter*, V, No. 2 (February 1926), 32–35.

"Zum Problem der evangelischen Sozialethik," *Blätter für religiösen Sozialismus*, VII (July–August 1926), 73–79. (Reprinted in *Religiöse Verwirklichung*, pp. 307–12.)

"Die religiöse Lage der bürgerlichen Gesellschaft im 19. Jahrhundert," *Neuwerk*, VIII (1926), 407–12.

"Die geistige Welt im Jahre 1926," in *Reichls Bücherbuch*, 17th year. Darmstadt: Reichl, 1926, pp. 6–14.

"Kairos: Ideen zur Geisteslage der Gegenwart," in *Kairos: I*, Darmstadt: Reichl, 1926, pp. 1–21. (*GW*, VI, 29–41.)

"Kairos und Logos; Eine Untersuchung zur Metaphysik des Erkennens," in *Kairos: I*. Darmstadt: Reichl, 1926, pp. 23–75. (*GW*, IV, 43–76. English translation in *IH*, pp. 123–75.)

1927 "Predigt zum Semesterschluss vor der Theologenschaft der Universität Marburg," *Neuwerk*, VIII, No. 11 (February 1927), 469–72. (Reprinted in *Von der Heiligung des Lebens*, edited by H. Hartmann. Leipzig: Hinrichs, 1928, pp. 13–16.)

"Die Ueberwindung des Persönlichkeitsideals," *Logos*, XVI, No. 1 (March 1927), 68–85. (Reprinted in *Religiöse Verwirklichung*, pp. 168–89. English translation in *PE*, pp. 115–35.)

"Ostern," *Hannoverscher Kurier*, LXXIX, No. 179 (April 17, 1927), 1.

"Eschatologie und Geschichte," *Christliche Welt*, XLI, No. 22 (November 1927), 1034–42. (Reprinted in *Religiöse Verwirklichung*, pp. 128–41; additional notes, pp. 290–93. English translation in *IH*, pp. 266–84. *GW*, VI, 72–82.)

"Gläubiger Realismus." Reprint from *Theologenrundbrief für den Bund Deutscher Jugendvereine*, II (July–August 1927), 3–13. (*GW*, IV, 77–87.)

"Paul Tillich über das Dämonische," *Philosophie und Leben,* III, No. 9 (September 1927), 260–64. A résumé.

"Logos und Mythos der Technik," *Logos,* XVI, No. 3 (November 1927), 356–65.

"Die Idee der Offenbarung," *Zeitschrift für Theologie und Kirche,* VIII, No. 6 (December 1927), 403–12.

1928 "Das religiöse Symbol," *Blätter für deutsche Philosophie,* I, No. 4 (January 1928), 277–91. (Reprinted in *Religiöse Verwirklichung,* pp. 88–109; additional notes, pp. 284–86. *GW,* V, 196–212. English translation by J. L. Adams in *Journal of Liberal Religion,* II, No. 1 [Summer 1940], 13–33. Slightly revised and abbreviated by the author in *Daedalus,* LXXXVII, No. 3 [Summer 1958], 3–21.)

Diskussionsrede. *Sozialismus aus dem Glauben: Verhandlungen der sozialistischen Tagung in Heppenheim.* Zürich und Leipzig: Rotapfel, 1928, pp. 101–4.

"Die technische Stadt als Symbol," *Dresdner Neueste Nachrichten,* No. 115 (May 17, 1928), p. 5.

"Ueber gläubigen Realismus," *Theologische Blätter,* VII, No. 5 (May 1928), 109–18. (Reprinted in *Religiöse Verwirklichung,* pp. 65–87. *GW,* IV, 88–106. English translation, "Realism and Faith," in *PE,* pp. 66–82.)

"Die Bedeutung der Gesellschaftslage für das Geistesleben," *Philosophie und Leben,* IV, No. 6 (June 1928), 153–58. *GW,* II, 133–38.)

"Zum 'theologischen Nachwort zu den Davoser internationalen Hochschulkursen,'" *Theologische Blätter,* VII, No. 7 (July 1928), 176–77.

"Das Christentum und die Moderne," *Schule und Wissenschaft,* II (1928), 121–31, 170–77.

"Das Christentum und die moderne Gesellschaft," *Student World,* XXI (1928), 282–90. (English summary, pp. 290–92.)

"Der soziale Pfarrer" (Diskussionsrede), *Die Verhandlungen des 35. Evangelisch-Sozialen Kongresses in Dresden.* Göttingen: Vandenhoeck und Ruprecht, 1928, pp. 74–77.

"Der Geistige und der Sport," Second Supplement to *Vossische Zeitung,* No. 608 (December 1928), p. 2.

1929 "Religiöse Verantwortung," *Berliner Tageblatt,* No. I, Supplement No. 5 (January 1, 1929), p. 2.

"Gegenwart und Religion," *Neuwerk,* XI, No. 1 (April 1929), 2–11.

"Philosophie und Schicksal," *Kant-Studien,* XXXIV (1929), 300–311. (*GW,* IV, 23–35. English translation, revised by the author, in *PE,* pp. 3–15.)

"Der Protestantismus als kritisches und gestaltendes Prinzip," in *Kairos: II.* Darmstadt: Reichl, 1929, pp. 3–37. (*GW,* VII, 29–53.)

"Nichtkirchliche Religionen," in *Volk und Reich der Deutschen,* edited by B. Harms. Berlin: Reimar Hobbing, I, 456–75. (*GW,* V, 13–31.)

1930 "Kult und Form," *Die Form,* V, No. 23/24 (December 1930), 578–83. (Reprinted in *Kunst und Kirche,* VIII [1931], 3–6.)

"Sozialismus," *Neue Blätter für den Sozialismus,* I, No. 1 (January 1930), 1–12. (*GW,* II, 139–50.)

"Religiöser Sozialismus," *Neue Blätter für den Sozialismus,* I, No. 9 (September 1930), 396–403. (*GW,* II, 151–58.)

"Mythus und Mythologie: I. Mythus, begrifflich und religions-psychologisch," *RGG*, IV, 363–70. (*GW*, V, 187–95.)

"Offenbarung: V A. Religionsphilosophisch," *RGG*, IV, 664–69.

"Philosophie: I. Begriff und Wesen," *RGG*, IV, 1198–1204. (*GW*, IV, 15–22.)

"Philosophie: III. Philosophie und Religion," *RGG*, IV, 1227–33. (*GW*, V, 101–9.)

"Neue Formen christlicher Verwirklichung; Eine Betrachtung über Sinn und Grenzen evangelischer Katholizität," *Reclams Universum*, XLVII (1930), 194–95.

1931 "Das Problem der Macht; Versuch einer philosophischen Grundlegung," *Neue Blätter für den Sozialismus*, II, No. 4 (April 1931), 157–70. (*GW*, II, 193–208. English translation in *IH*, 179–202.)

"Kirche und humanistische Gesellschaft," *Neuwerk*, XIII, No. 1 (April–May 1931), 4–18.

"Mensch und Staat," "Blut gegen Geist," "Kunstpolitik," "Einheit des Widerspruches," "Dämonen," "Neue Schöpfung," "Utopie," "Drei Stadien," "Menschliche Möglichkeiten," "Das Fragen," "Menschheit," *Der Staat seid Ihr*, Vol. I, Nos. 1–4, 6–10 (March 2–23, April 6–May 4, 1931).

"Zum Fall Eckert!" *Neue Blätter für den Sozialismus*, II, No. 8 (August 1931), 408–9.

"Die Doppelgestalt der Kirche," *Neuwerk*, XIII (1931), 239–43.

"Zum Problem des evangelischen Religionsunterrichts." Special issue of *Zeitschrift für den evangelischen Religionsunterricht*, XLII (1931), 289–91.

"Sozialismus: II. Religiöser Sozialismus," *RGG*, V, 637–48. (*GW*, II, 159–74.)

"Theonomie," *RGG*, V, 1128–29.

"Wissenschaft," *RGG*, V, 1985–87. (*GW*, IV, 36–39.)

"Gibt es noch eine Universität? Fachhochschulen und Universität," *Frankfurter Zeitung*, LXXVI, Nos. 869–71 (November 1931), 11.

"Das Wasser," in W. Stählin (ed.), *Das Gottesjahr 1932*. Kassel: Bärenreiter, 1931, pp. 65–68. (English translation by J. L. Adams and Mrs. George W. W. Brewster in *Paul Tillich's Philosophy of Culture, Science, and Religion* [New York: Harper & Row, 1965], pp. 62–64.)

"Goethe und die Idee der Klassik," *Bühnenblätter*, No. 17 (1931–1932), pp. 193–207. (Reprinted in *Hegel und Goethe*, pp. 33–48.)

1932 "Der Sozialismus und die geistige Lage der Gegenwart," *Neue Blätter für den Sozialismus*, III, No. 1 (January 1932), 14–16.

"Protestantismus und politische Romantik," *Neue Blätter für den Sozialismus*, III, No. 8 (August 1932), 413–22. (*GW*, II, 209–18.)

"Zehn Thesen," in Leopold Klotz (ed.), *Die Kirche und das Dritte Reich; Fragen und Forderungen deutscher Theologen*. Gotha: Klotz, 1932, No. 1, pp. 126–28.

"Selbstanzeige," *Neue Blätter für den Sozialismus*, III (1932), 667–68. Author's note on *Die sozialistische Entscheidung*.

1933 "Das Wohnen, der Raum, und die Zeit," *Die Form*, VIII, No. 1 (January 1933), 11–12. (Reprinted in *Das ideale Heim*, VII, No. 5 [May], 176–80.)

1934 "The Religious Situation in Germany Today," *Religion in Life*, III, No. 2 (Spring 1934), 163–73.

"The Totalitarian State and the Claims of the Church," *Social Research*, I, No. 4 (November 1934), 405–33.

"Die Theologie des Kairos und die gegenwärtige geistige Lage; Offener Brief an Emanuel Hirsch," *Theologische Blätter*, XIII, No. 11 (November 1934), 305–28.

1935 "What Is Wrong with the 'Dialectic' Theology?" *Journal of Religion*, XV, No. 2 (April 1935), 127–45. (German translation in *Christliche Welt*, L, No. 8 [April 25, 1936], 353–64. *GW*, VII, 247–62.)

"Um was es geht; Antwort an Emanuel Hirsch," *Theologische Blätter*, XIV, No. 5 (May 1935), 117–19.

"Natural and Revealed Religion," *Christendom*, I, No. 1 (Autumn 1935), 159–70. (Reprinted in part in *Contemporary Religious Thought*, edited by Thomas S. Kepler. New York: Abingdon-Cokesbury Press, 1941, pp. 64–69.)

"Marx and the Prophetic Tradition," *Radical Religion*, I, No. 4 (Autumn 1935), 21–29.

1936 "An Historical Diagnosis: Impression of a European Trip," *Radical Religion*, II, No. 1 (Winter 1936), 11–17.

"The Social Functions of the Churches in Europe and America," *Social Research*, III, No. 1 (February 1936), 90–104.

"Christianity and Emigration," *Presbyterian Tribune*, LII, No. 3 (October 29, 1936), 13–16.

"Prophetische und marxistische Geschichtsdeutung," ca. 1934–1936. (First published in *GW*, VI, 97–108.)

1937 "The End of the Protestant Era," *Student World*, XXX, No. 1 (First Quarter 1937), 49–57. (*GW*, VII, 151–58.)

"The Church and Communism," *Religion in Life*, VI, No. 3 (Summer 1937), 347–57.

"Brief an die Redaktion," *Aufbau/Reconstruction*, III, No. 3 (1937), 6.

"Mind and Migration," *Social Research*, IV, No. 3 (September 1937), 295–305. (Reprinted under the title "Migrations Breed New Cultures," *Protestant Digest*, III, No. 2 [February 1940], 10–19.)

"Protestantism in the Present World-Situation," *American Journal of Sociology*, XLIII, No. 2 (September 1937), 236–49. (Reprinted under the title "The End of the Protestant Era?" in *PE*, pp. 222–33. *GW*, VII, 159–70.)

1938 "Nicholas Berdyaev," *Religion in Life*, VII, No. 3 (Summer 1938), 407–15.

"The Gospel and the State," *Crozer Quarterly*, XV, No. 4 (October 1938), 251–61.

"The Attack of Dialectical Materialism on Christianity," *Student World*, XXXI, No. 2 (1938), 115–25. (Also in *World's Youth*, XIV, No. 2 (1938), 147–57.)

"The Significance of the Historical Jesus for the Christian Faith, *Monday Forum Talks* (Union Theological Seminary, New York), No. 5 (1938), p. 6.

"The Kingdom of God and History," in *The Kingdom of God and History*. Church, Community and State Series. London: George Allen and Unwin, Ltd., 1938, pp. 105–42. (American edition: Chicago and New York: Willett, Clark and Co., 1938, pp. 107–41. [Oxford Conference Books.] Partially [119–27] reprinted in Thomas

S. Kepler [ed.], *Contemporary Thinking about Jesus*, New York: Abingdon-Cokesbury Press, 1944, pp. 217–22.)

"The Meaning of Our Present Historical Existence." The Hazen Conferences on Student Guidance and Counseling. Haddam, Conn.: Edward W. Hazen Foundation, 1938, pp. 19–20.

"German-Americans Take Stand For Democracy Against Nazis," *Deutsches Volksecho/German People's Echo*, II, No. 48 (November 26, 1938), 1–2. (Reprinted under the title "Germany Is Still Alive," *Protestant Digest*, I, No. 3 [February 1939], 45–46.)

"The Meaning of Anti-Semitism," *Radical Religion*, IV, No. 1 (Winter 1938), 34–36.

1939   "History as the Problem of Our Period," *Review of Religion*, III, No. 3 (March 1939), 255–64.

"The Conception of Man in Existential Philosophy," *Journal of Religion*, XIX, No. 3 (July 1939), 201–15. (Reprinted in *The Examined Life; An Introduction to Philosophy*, edited by T. W. Organ. Boston: Houghton Mifflin, 1956, pp. 339–46.)

"De Situatie van Europa: religie en christendom," *Het Kouter*, IV, Nos. 9–10 (September–October 1939), 325–37.

"Und die Kirche?" *Press Service of the German-American Writers' Association* (New York), No. 5 (1939), pp. 1–2.

"The European War and the Christian Churches," *Direction*, II, No. 8 (December 1939), 10–11. (Reprinted in *Protestant Digest*, III, No. 1 [January 1940], 15–20.)

1940   "Freedom in the Period of Transformation," in *Freedom: Its Meaning*, edited by Ruth Nanda Anshen. Science of Culture Series, Vol. I. New York: Harcourt, Brace and Co., 1940, pp. 123–44.

"Has Higher Education an Obligation to Work for Democracy?" *Radical Religion*, V, No. 1 (Winter 1940), 12–15.

"The Meaning of the Triumph of Nazism," *Christianity and Society*, V, No. 4 (1940), 45–56. Résumé by Charles Stinnette, Jr.

"The Idea of the Personal God," *Union Review*, II, No. 1 (November 1940), 8–10. (Reprinted in *Theology of Culture*, edited by Robert C. Kimball. [New York: Oxford University Press, 1959], pp. 127–32. Reply to Albert Einstein, "Science and Religion," in *Science, Philosophy and Religion*. New York: Harper & Brothers, 1951, pp. 209–14.)

1941   "Ethics in a Changing World," in *Religion and the Modern World*. University of Pennsylvania Bicentennial Conference. Philadelphia: University of Pennsylvania, 1941, pp. 51–61. (Reprinted in *PE*, pp. 150–60.)

"The Permanent Significance of the Catholic Church for Protestantism," *Protestant Digest*, III, No. 10 (February–March 1941), 23–31. (*GW*, VII, 124–32.)

"Philosophy and Theology," *Religion in Life*, X, No. 1 (Winter 1941), 21–30. (Reprinted in *Theology*, XLIV, No. 261 [March 1942], 133–43. *PE*, pp. 83–93. *GW*, V, 110–21.)

"Symbol and Knowledge," *Journal of Liberal Religion*, II, No. 4 (Spring 1941), 202–6.

"Our Disintegrating World," *Anglican Theological Review*, XXIII, No. 2 (April 1941), 134–46.

"Religion and Education," *Protestant Digest*, III, No. 11 (April–May 1941), 58–61.

"I Am an American," *Protestant Digest*, III, No. 12 (June–July 1941), 24–26.

"War Aims. I. Why War Aims?" *Protestant Digest*, III, No. 12 (June–July 1941), 33–38.

"War Aims. II. What War Aims?" *Protestant Digest*, IV, No. 1 (August–September, 1941), 13–18.

"War Aims. III. Whose War Aims?" *The Protestant*, IV, No. 2 (October–November 1941), 24–29.

"Dr. Richard Kroner," *Alumni Bulletin*, Union Theological Seminary (New York), XVII, No. 1 (November 1941), 3–4.

"Love's 'Strange Work,'" *The Protestant*, IV, No. 3 (December 1941–January 1942), 70–75.

1942   "Challenge to Protestantism," *The Protestant*, IV, No. 4 (February–March 1942), 1–4.

"The Word of Religion to the People of This Time," *The Protestant*, IV, No. 5 (April–May 1942), 42–48. (Reprinted in *PE*, pp. 185–91.)

"Marxism and Christian Socialism," *Christianity and Society*, VII, No. 2 (Spring 1942), 13–18. (Included in *PE*, pp. 253–60.)

"Protestant Principles," *The Protestant*, IV, No. 5 (April–May 1942), 16–19.

"Was soll mit Deutschland geschehen? Gegen Emil Ludwigs neueste Rede," *Aufbau/Reconstruction*, VIII, No. 29 (July 17, 1942), 7.

"Spiritual Problems of Post-War Reconstruction," *Christianity and Crisis*, II, No. 14 (August 10, 1942), 2–6. (Reprinted in *PE*, pp. 261–69.)

"Läuterndes Feuer," *Aufbau/Reconstruction*, VIII, No. 22 (1942), p. 10.

"Es geht um die Methode," *Aufbau/Reconstruction*, VIII, No. 32 (1942), pp. 7–8.

"Our Protestant Principles," *The Protestant*, IV, No. 7 (August–September 1942), 8–14. (*GW*, VII, 133–40.)

"Kierkegaard in English," *American-Scandinavian Review*, XXX, No. 3 (September 1942), 254–57.

"'Faith' in the Jewish-Christian Tradition," *Christendom*, VII, No. 4 (Autumn 1942), 518–26.

"Kierkegaard as Existential Thinker," *Union Review*, IV, No. 1 (December 1942), 5–7.

1943   "Storms of Our Times," *Anglican Theological Review*, XXV, No. 1–2 (January–April 1943), 15–53. (Includes comments by F. C. Grant, Angus Dun, J. F. Fletcher, George F. Thomas. Reprinted, without the comments, in *PE*, pp. 237–52.)

"Flight to Atheism," *The Protestant*, IV, No. 10 (February–March 1943), 43–48. (Reprinted under the title "The Escape from God" in *SF*, pp. 38–51. Also in *Best Sermons 1949–1950*, edited by G. Paul Butler. New York: Harper & Brothers, 1949, pp. 138–46.)

"What Is Divine Revelation?" *The Witness*, XXVI, No. 46 (April 15, 1943), 8–9.

"Man and Society in Religious Socialism," *Christianity and Society*, VIII, No. 4 (Fall 1943), 10–21.

"Comment [on the report of the Commission on a Just and Durable Peace]," *The Witness*, XXVI, No. 45 (1943), 4.

"Immigrants' Conference: Why Immigrants' Victory Council?" *Aufbau/Reconstruction*, IX, No. 27 (1943), 3.

1944   "A Statement," *Bulletin of the Council for a Democratic Germany*, I, No. 1 (1944), 1–4.

"Existential Philosophy," *Journal of the History of Ideas*, V, No. 1 (January 1944), 44–70. (Reprinted in *Theology of Culture*, edited by R. C. Kimball, pp. 76–111.)

"Russia's Church and the Soviet Order," *Think*, X, No. 1 (January 1944), 22–23. (Reprinted in *The Cathedral Age*, XIX, No. 1 [Easter, 1944], 14–15, 31–32.)

"Critiques," in *Approaches to World Peace*, edited by L. Bryson and others, New York: Harper & Brothers, 1944, pp. 684–85, 816–17. Critiques of F. S. C. Northrop, "Philosophy and World Peace," and John A. Ryan, "Religious Foundations for an Enduring Peace."

"The God of History," *Christianity and Crisis*, IV, No. 7 (May 1944), 5–6. (Reprinted under the title "The Two Servants of Jahweh" in *SF*, pp. 29–33.)

"Trends in Religious Thought That Affect Social Outlook," in *Religion and the World Order*, edited by F. Ernest Johnson. New York: Harper & Brothers, 1944, pp. 17–28. (Reprinted in *Outside Readings in Sociology*, edited by F. A. Schuler and others. New York: Thomas Y. Crowell Co., 1952, pp. 420–30.

"A Program for a Democratic Germany," *Christianity and Crisis*, IV, No. 8 (1944), 3–5. A declaration by members of the Council for a Democratic Germany, Paul Tillich, chairman. (Reprinted in the *St. Louis Star-Times*, May 18, 1944, p. 15.)

"Depth," *Christendom*, IX, No. 3 (Summer 1944), 317–25. (Reprinted under the title "The Depth of Existence" in *SF*, pp. 52–63.)

"Estrangement and Reconciliation in Modern Thought," *Review of Religion*, IX, No. 1 (November 1944), 5–19. (German translation: "Entfremdung und Versöhnung im modernen Denken," *Eckart*, XXVI [1957], 99–109.)

"Now Concerning Spiritual Gifts . . . ," *Union Review*, VI, No. 1 (December 1944), 15–17. (Reprinted under the title "The Theologian. Part 1" in *SF*, pp. 118–21.)

1945   "Outlook for 1945," *Bulletin of the Council for a Democratic Germany*, I, No. 3 (January 1945), 1.

"The Crimea Concept and the Council," *Bulletin of the Council for a Democratic Germany*, I, No. 4 (February 1945), 1.

"All Things to All Men," *Union Review*, VI, No. 3 (May 1945), 3–4.

"Nietzsche and the Bourgeois Spirit," *Journal of the History of Ideas*, VI, No. 3 (June 1945), 307–9.

"The Redemption of Nature," *Christendom*, X, No. 3 (Summer 1945), 299–306. (Reprinted under the title "Nature Also Mourns for a Lost Good" in *SF*, pp. 76–86.

"The Christian Churches and the Emerging Social Order in Europe," *Religion in Life*, XIV, No. 3 (Summer 1945), 329–39.

"The World Situation," in *The Christian Answer*, edited (with Introduction) by Henry P. Van Dusen. New York: Charles Scribner's Sons, 1945, pp. 1–44. (English edition: London: Nisbet, 1946, pp. 19–71.)

"Comments," in *Approaches to National Unity*, edited by L. Bryson and others. New York: Harper & Brothers, 1945, pp. 407–8, 522–23, 537, 923. On Robert J. Havighurst, "Education for Intergroup Cooperation," Rudolf Allers, "Some Remarks on the Problems of Group Tensions," A. Campbell Garnett, "Group Tensions in the Modern World," and Amos N. Wilder, "Theology and Cultural Incoherence."

c. Books Reviewed by Tillich

1919 F. Thimme and E. Rolff (eds.), *Revolution und Kirche*. (Das neue *Deutschland*, VIII [1918–19], 394–97.)

1922 L. Bendix, *Die Neuordnung des Strafverfahrens*. (*Kant-Studien* XXVII [1922], 203–5.)

Theodor Birt, *Von Homer bis Sokrates*. (*Theologische Literaturzeitung* XLVII [1922], 349.)

Paul Feldkeller, *Graf Keyserlings Bekenntnisweg zum Uebersinnlichen*. (*Theologische Blätter*, I [1922], 210.)

Joseph Geyser, *Neue und alte Wege der Philosophie*. (*Theologische Literaturzeitung*, XLVII [1922], 380–81.)

A. V. Gleichen-Russwurm, *Philosophische Profile*. (*Theologische Literaturzeitung*, XLVII [1922], 478.)

Helmut Hatzfeld, *Dante: Seine Weltenschauung*. (*Theologische Literaturzeitung*, XLVII [1922], 350.)

Emanuel Hirsch, *Die Reich-Gottes-Begriffe des neuren europäischen Denkens*. (*Theoelogische Blätter*, I [1922], 42–43.)

Emanuel Hirsch, *Der Sinn des Gebets*. (*Theologische Blätter*, I [1922], 137–38.)

Werner Leopold, *Die religiöse Wurzel von Carlyles literarischer Wirksamkeit*. (*Theologische Literaturzeitung*, XLVII [1922], 433.)

Joseph Mansbach, *Der Geist Dantes und seine Kulturaufgaben*. (*Theologische Literaturzeitung*, XLVII [1922], 350.)

Eduard Spranger, *Der gegenwärtige Stand der Geisteswissenschaften und die Schule*. (*Theologische Blätter*, I [1922], 235.)

R. Stammler, *Lehrbuch der Rechtsphilosophie*. (*Theologische Literaturzeitung*, XLVII [1922], 417–20.)

Ernst Troeltsch, *Der Berg der Läuterung; Rede zur Erinnerung an den 600–jaehrigen Todestag Dantes*. (*Theologische Literaturzeitung*, XLVII [1922], 350.)

1923 Heinrich Eilderman, *Urkommunismus und Urreligion*. (*Archiv für Sozialpolitik*, L [1923], 247–48.)

Ernst Horneffer, *Der junge Platon. Erster Teil: Sokrates und die Apologie*. (*Kant-Studien*, XXVIII [1923], 437.)

Kurt Leese, *Die Geschichtsphilosophie Hegels*. (*Theologische Blätter*, II [1923], 72.)

Ernst Lohmeyer, *Soziale Fragen im Urchristentum*. (*Archiv für Sozialwissenschaft und Sozialpolitik*, L [1923], 250.)

Emil Walter Mayer, *Ethik*. (*Theologische Blätter*, II [1923], 16–17.)

Hermann Schwarz, *Das Ungegebene*. (*Theologische Blätter*, II [1923], 74.)

1924 E. Cassirer, *Die Begriffsform im mythischen Denken*, and Artur Liebert, "Mythos und Kultur," *Kant-Studien*, XXVII (1922). (*Theologische Literaturzeitung*, XLIX [1924], 115–17.)

Ernst Troeltsch, *Der Historismus und seine Probleme.* (*The-ologische Literaturzeitung*, XLIX [1924], 25–30.) English translation in *Journal for the Scientific Study of Religion*, I, No. 1 (October, 1961), 109–14.

Ernst Troeltsch, *Der Historismus und seine Ueberwindung.* (*The-ologische Literaturzeitung*, XLIX [1924], 234–35.)

1926 Paul Hoffmann, *Das religiöse Erlebnis;* J. P. Steffes, *Religionsphilos-ophie;* Emil Mattieson, *Der jenseitige Mensch; Zeitschrift für kritischen Okkultismus und Grenzfragen des Seelenlebens.* (*Vossische Zeitung*, No. 324; *Literarische Umschau*, No. 27 [July 11, 1926], 1–2.)

A. Faut, *Romantik oder Reformation;* W. Lüttge, *Das Christentum in unserer Kultur;* A. F. Stolzenburg, *Anthroposophie und Christen-tum;* H. Hermelink, *Katholizismus und Protestantismus in der Gegenwart;* G. Bäumer, *Die seelische Krisis;* N. Arseniew, *Ostkirche und Mystik;* W. Heinsius, *Krisen katholischer Frömmigkeit und Konversionen zum Protestantismus;* C. S. Macfarland, *Die interna-tionalen christlichen Bewegungen.* (*Vossische Zeitung*, No. 480 [October 10, 1926], 2.)

Wilhelm Dilthey, *Gesammelte Schriften*, Vols. V and VI. (*The-ologische Literaturzeitung*, LI [1926], 148–50.)

G. Ritter, *Martin Luther: Gestalt und Symbol;* Lamm, *Emmanuel Swedenborg;* E. Swedenborg, *Himmel und Hölle;* K. Müller (ed.), *Der Weg des Matthäus Stach;* E. Jäckh, *Blumhardt Vater und Sohn;* Christof Blumhardt, *Predigten und Andachten;* C. Blumhardt, *Hausandachten;* Anna Kähler, *Theologe und Christ: Erinnerungen und Bekenntnisse von Martin Kähler;* Erich Stange (ed.), *Die Re-ligionswissenschaft der Gegenwart;* H. Prager, *Die Weltanschauung Dostojevskis.* (*Vossische Zeitung*, No. 52 [January 31, 1926].)

1927 F. Brunstäd, *Die Idee der Religion;* E. Brunner, *Philosophie und Offenbarung;* W. Lütgert, *Die Religion des deutschen Idealismus und ihr Ende;* E. Hirsch, *Die idealistische Philosophie und das Christen-tum.* (*Theologische Blätter*, VI [1927], 29–40.)

Gerhard Heinzelmann, *Glaube und Mystik.* (*Theologische Litera-turzeitung*, LII [1927], 597–98.)

Paul Wernle, *Der schweizerische Protestantismus im 18. Jahr-hundert;* F. X. Kiefl, *Leibniz und die religiöse Wiedervereinigung Deutschlands;* E. Buchner, *Religion und Kirche;* J. Schlosser, *Vom inneren Licht: Die Quäker;* O. Holtzmann (trans.), *Das Neue Testa-ment;* G. Brandes, *Die Jesussage;* Bauer, Bertholet, Ködderitz, und Krohn, *Der Christus.* (*Vossische Zeitung*, No. 274; *Literarische Umschau*, No. 24 [June 12, 1927].)

Hendrik de Man, *Psychologie des Sozialismus.* (*Blätter für religiösen Sozialismus* [October, 1927], pp. 21–25.)

H. Groos, *Der deutsche Idealismus und das Christentum.* (*The-ologische Blätter*, VI [1927], 196–98.)

Hans Wilhelm Schmidt, *Zeit und Ewigkeit.* (*Theologische Blätter*, VI [1927], 234–35.)

1928 Eugen Rosenstock und Josef Wittig, *Das Alter der Kirche.* (*Vossische Zeitung*, No. 259; *Literarische Umschau*, No. 23 [June 3, 1928].)

Georg Brandes, *Urchristentum;* Ernst Barnikol, *Das entdeckte Christentum im Vormärz; Bruno Bauers Kampf gegen Religion und Christentum und Erstausgabe seiner Kampfschrift.* (*Vossische*

Zeitung, No. 97; *Literarische Umschau,* No. 9 [February 26, 1928], 1–2.)

Kaevels, *Expressionismus und Religion;* H. Frick, *Wissenschaftliches und pneumatisches Verständnis der Bibel;* K. Müller, *Die Forderung der Ehelosigkeit für alle Getauften in der alten Kirche;* L. Köhler, *Das formgeschichtliche Problem des Neuen Testaments.* (*Vossische Zeitung,* No. 343; *Literarische Umschau,* No. 30 [July 22, 1928].)

Emil Ludwig, *Der Menschensohn; Geschichte eines Propheten.* (*Vossische Zeitung,* No. 219; *Das Unterhaltungsblatt,* No. 109 [May 10, 1928], 1–2.)

Walter von Molo, *Der Mensch Luther.* (*Vossische Zeitung,* No. 535; *Literarische Umschau,* No. 46 [November 11, 1928], 2.)

Richard Kroner, *Die Selbstverwirklichung des Geistes.* (*Dresdner Neueste Nachrichten,* No. 171 [July 24, 1928], 2.)

F. Blanke, *J. G. Hamann als Theologe;* H. R. G. Günther, *Jung-Stilling;* A. Gilg, *Sören Kierkegaard;* G. Schenkel, *Die Freimaurerei im Lichte der Religions- und Kirchengeschichte;* E. Peuckert, *Die Rosenkreuzer.* (*Vossische Zeitung,* No. 499; *Literarische Umschau,* No. 43 [October 21, 1928], 3.)

Robert Jelke, *Das Erbe Martin Luthers und die gegenwärtige Forschung;* Joseph Schnitzer, *Hieronymus Savonarola: Auswahl aus seinen Schriften und Predigten;* Franz Strunz, *Johannes Huss;* F. Gogarten, *Martin Luthers Predigten; Theologische Studien und Kritiken: Lutherana;* Hartmann Grisar, *Martin Luthers Leben und sein Werk.* (*Vossische Zeitung,* No. 427; *Literarische Umschau,* No. 37 [September 9, 1928], 2–3.)

Feiler, *Die Entstehung des Christentums aus dem Geiste des magischen Denkens;* W. Michaelis, *Täufer, Jesus, Urgemeinde;* K. Völker, *Mysterium und Agape;* K. Holl, *Gesammelte Aufsätze zur Kirchengeschichte,* II. (*Vossische Zeitung,* No. 376 [August 5, 1928].)

1929 Richard Kroner, *Die Selbstverwirklichung des Geistes.* (*Vossische Zeitung,* No. 46; *Literarische Umschau,* No. 5 [January 27, 1929], 2.)

Karl Mannheim, *Ideologie und Utopie.* (*Gesellschaft,* VI, No. 10 [1929], 348–55.)

1934 H. Emil Brunner, *The Mediator.* (*Christian Century,* LI [1934], 1554–56.)

Theodor Wiesengrund-Adorno, *Kierkegaard.* (*Journal of Philosophy,* XXXI, [1934], 640.)

1935 Fedor Stepun, *The Russian Soul and Revolution.* (*Christendom,* I [1935], 366–67.)

1940 H. N. Wieman and W. M. Horton, *The Growth of Religion.* (*Journal of Religion,* XX [1940], 69–72.)

1941 H. R. Niebuhr, *The Meaning of Revelation.* (*Religion in Life,* X [1941], 452–5.)

Reinhold Niebuhr, *The Nature and Destiny of Man,* Vol. I, *Human Nature.* (*Christianity and Society,* VI, No. 2 [1941], 34–37.)

1942 Herbert Marcuse, *Reason and Revolution.* (*Studies in Philosophy and Social Science,* IX [1942], 476–78.)

Raymond B. Blakney, *Meister Eckhart; A Modern Translation.* (*Religion in Life* XI [1942], 625–26.)

1945 Nicholas Berdyaev, *Slavery and Freedom.* (*Theology Today,* II [April, 1945], 130–32.)

D. *Unpublished Materials by Tillich**

1935   Informal Report of a Seminar on Religion. Fletcher Farm, Proctors-
        ville, Vermont, May 22–31, 1935, pp. 28–32, 46–53, 56–58, 67–72.
        (Mimeographed. Confidential, not to be printed.)
        "The Christian and Marxist View of Man." Universal Christian
        Council for Life and Work. December, 1935. Pp. 19. (Mimeographed.)

1936   "The Kingdom of God and History." Universal Christian Council for
        Life and Work. October, 1936. Pp. 19. (Mimeographed.)

1938   "The Significance of the Historical Jesus for the Christian Faith."
        A Monday Forum Talk at Union Theological Seminary, February
        28, 1938. Pp. 9.

1942   "Man and Society in Religious Socialism." 1942. Pp. 10. (Mimeo-
        graphed.)

1943   "Depth." A sermon. February, 1943. Pp. 3.
        "Fragments of an Ontology of Love." Paper read at a meeting of
        the National Council on Religion in Higher Education, May 19,
        1943. Pp. 9. (Mimeographed.) Notes on the discussion are appended.
        "The Mystery of Time." A sermon. June, 1943. Pp. 4.

1944   "Estrangement and Reconciliation in Modern Thought." Presidential
        Address for the American Theological Society, April 14, 1944. Pp.
        13. (Mimeographed.)

1945   "Redemption in Cosmic and Social History." 1945. Pp. 17. (Mimeo-
        graphed.)

No   "Christian and Other Philosophies of History." Address given at the
date   Annual Meeting of the American Theological Society. Pp. 14.
        "Comments on Edwyn Bevan's, E. W. Lyman's, and H. G. Wood's
        Manuscripts on 'The Kingdom of God and the Meaning of History.'"
        Universal Christian Council for Life and Work. Pp. 3. (Mimeo-
        graphed.)
        "I Cor. 2:10; Ps. 130:1." A sermon. Pp. 10. (Mimeographed.)
        "II Cor. 6:3–10." An ordination sermon. Pp. 7.
        "Eschatology and Personal Destiny." (Immortality, Resurrection,
        and Judgement.) Pp. 10.
        "Hebrews 2:10-18." A sermon. Pp. 2.
        "Luke 6:27 and Luke 23:24." A sermon. Pp. 2.
        "Marxism and Christian Socialism." Pp. 10.
        "Marxism and Christian Socialism." Pp. 2. (Mimeographed.)
        "The Ontological Foundation of Values." An address as part of a
        symposium, with Sidney Hook. Pp. 11.
        "Psalm 19:2–5, Romans 8:19–22, Revelation 21:1, 2." Sermon
        given at Union Theological Seminary, March 25, 1945. Pp. 6. (Mimeo-
        graphed.)
        "Psalm 90." A sermon. Pp. 7. (Mimeographed.)
        "Psalm 139." A sermon. Pp. 6. (Mimeographed.)
        "A Reinterpretation of the Doctrine of the Incarnation." Pp. 19.
        "The Rise of Protestantism." Pp. 15.
        "Systematic Theology. Preliminary draft for the use of students
        only." Parts I, III, V. (Mimeographed.)
        "Die weltgeschichtliche Zukunft Europas." Pp. 15. (Mimeographed
        —about 1943.)

    * Many of these items have been published subsequently.

E. *Books Discussing Tillich*

Allwohn, Adolf. *Der Mythos bei Schelling.* Charlottenburg: Rolf Heise, 1927.

Barth, Karl. *The Doctrine of the Word of God.* Translated by G. T. Thomson. Edinburgh: T. and T. Clark, 1936.

Barth, Karl. *Offenbarung, Kirche, Theologie.* ("Theologische Existenz heute," No. 9.) Munich: Kaiser, 1934.

Barth, Karl. *Die Theologie und die Kirche.* Munich: Kaiser, 1928.

Bauhofer, Oskar. *Das Metareligiöse.* Leipzig: Hinrich, 1930, pp. 180 f.

Brightman, E. S. *A Philosophy of Religion.* New York: Prentice-Hall, Inc., 1940.

Brunner, Emil. *The Divine Imperative.* Translated by Olive Wyon. London: Lutterworth Press, 1927.

Brunner, Emil. *The Philosophy of Religion.* Translated by A. J. D. Farrer and Bertram Lee Woolf. London: Ivor Nicholson and Watson, 1937.

Case, Shirley Jackson. *The Christian Philosophy of History.* Chicago: University of Chicago Press, 1943, pp. 104–7.

Conger, G. P. *The Ideologies of Religion.* New York: Round Table Press, 1940, pp. 52, 262 n. 4.

Douglass, Paul F. *God Among the Germans.* Philadelphia: University of Pennsylvania Press, 1935, pp. 304–5.

Eisenhuth, H. E. *Der Begriff des Irrationalen als philosophisches Problem.* Göttingen: Vandenhoeck und Ruprecht, 1931.

Gunz, Johanna. *Sozialismus und Religion im Deutschland der Nachkriegszeit.* Munich and Leipzig: Dunker und Humblot, 1933.

Heimann, Eduard. *Grundriss der Sozialökonomik,* Division I: Historische und theoretische Grundlagen, Part I: Wirtschaft und Wirtschaftswissenschaft, Book I, Section A. Subsection III: System und Ideale II. 2nd ed. Tübingen: Mohr, 1924, pp. 190–94.

Heimann, Eduard. *Kapitalismus und Sozialismus.* Potsdam: Alfred Protte, 1931.

Heimann, Eduard. *Die soziale Theorie des Kapitalismus.* Tübingen: Mohr, 1929.

Heimann, Eduard. *Sozialwissenschaft und Wirklichkeit.* Tübingen: Mohr, 1932.

Hirsch, Emanuel. *Christliche Freiheit und politische Bindung; Ein Brief an Dr. Stapel und andere.* Hamburg: Hanseatische Verlagsanstalt, 1935.

Hirsch, Emanuel. *Die idealistische Philosophie und das Christentum.* Gütersloh: Bertelsmann, 1926, pp. 6 f., 95.

Karrenberg, Friedrich. *Christentum, Kapitalismus und Sozialismus.* Berlin: Junker und Dünnhaupt, 1932.

Koepp, Wilhelm. *Einführung in die evangelische Dogmatik.* Tübingen: Mohr, 1934.

Kuhlmann, Gerhardt. *Brunstäd und Tillich.* Tübingen: Mohr, 1928.

Leese, Kurt. *Philosophie und Theologie im Spätidealismus.* Berlin: Junker und Dünnhaupt, 1929.

Leese, Kurt. *Die Religion des protestantischen Menschen.* Berlin: Junker und Dünnhaupt, 1938, pp. 104–18.

Leisegang, Hans. *Religionsphilosophie der Gegenwart.* Berlin: Junker und Dünnhaupt, 1930, pp. 75–77.

Löwe, Adolf. *The Price of Liberty.* London: Hogarth, 1937. A letter addressed to Tillich on his fiftieth birthday.

Lowrie, Walter. *Our Concern with the Theology of Crisis.* Boston: Meador Publishing Company, 1932.

Macintosh, D. C. *The Problem of Religious Knowledge.* New York: Harper & Brothers, 1940, pp. 303, 327, 348–50, 354.

Marck, Siegfried. *Die Dialektik in der Philosophie der Gegenwart.* First Half-Volume. Tübingen: Mohr, 1929, pp. 112–19.

Means, Paul B. *The Things That Are Caesar's.* New York: Round Table Press, 1935, pp. 108, 120, 122, 124, 135–39, 151.

Mulert, Hermann. *Religion, Kirche, Theologie.* Giessen: Töpelmann, 1931, pp. 44 f., 137.

Nadler, Käte. *Der dialektische Widerspruch in Hegels Philosophie und das Paradoxon des Christentums.* Leipzig: Meiner, 1931.

Oepke, Albrecht. *Karl Barth und die Mystik.* Leipzig: Dörffling und Franke, 1928.

Piechowski, Paul. *Proletarischer Glaube.* Berlin: Furche, 1927, pp. 214, 216.

Piper, Otto. *Weltliches Christentum.* Tübingen: Mohr, 1924, p. 68.

Piper, Otto. *Recent Developments in German Protestantism.* London: Student Christian Movement Press, 1934, pp. 137–43.

Plachte, Kurt. *Symbol und Idol.* Berlin: Bruno Cassirer, 1931.

Przywara, Erich. *Ringen der Gegenwart.* 2 vols. Augsburg: Filser, 1929, pp. 186, 232, 352, 356 ff., 564, 691 f., 931, 946.

Rall, H. F. *Christianity.* New York: Charles Scribner's Sons, 1940, p. 318.

Schumann, F. K. *Der Gottesgedanke und der Zerfall der Moderne.* Tübingen: Mohr, 1929, pp. 208 ff.

Seillière, E. *Morales et Religions Nouvelles en Allemagne.* Paris: Payot, 1927, pp. 168–90.

Sombart, Werner. *Der proletarische Sozialismus.* 2 vols. 10th ed. Jena: Fischer, 1924.

Wieman, H. N., and Meland, B. E. *American Philosophies of Religion.* Chicago: Willett, Clark and Co., 1936, pp. 14, 37, 84, 85, 88–92, 94, 309, 338.

Wobbermin, Georg. *Richtlinien evangelischer Theologie.* Göttingen: Vandenhoeck und Ruprecht, 1929, pp. 54–61.

Wünsch, Georg. *Evangelische Wirtschaftsethik.* Tübingen: Mohr, 1927, pp. 267 f, 536.

Wünsch, Georg. *Wirklichkeitschristentum.* Tübingen: Mohr, 1932, pp. 132 f.

F. *Articles Discussing Tillich*

Allwohn, Adolph. "Das liturgische Problem," *Theologische Rundschau,* III (1931), 173–74.

Allwohn, Adolph. "Die Form der kirchlichen Verkündigung und das öffentliche Leben," *Theologische Blätter,* V (1926), 245–53.

Allwohn, Adolph. "Der Symbolbegriff in der Theologie," *Theologische Blätter,* VI (1927), 57–66.

Aubrey, E. E. "The Religious Symbol," *Journal of Liberal Religion,* II (1941), 201–2.

Bizer, Ernst. "Die Zeitschriften des deutschen religiösen Sozialismus," *Christliche Welt,* XLV (1931), 716–19.

Bockestein, M. H. "Jets over de Kairos-idee bij Paul Tillich," *Vox Theologica,* VII (1935), 39–49.

Bruhn, Wilhelm. "Zur Religionsphilosophie," *Zeitschrift für Theologie und Kirche*, VIII (1927), 75–77.

Büchsel, Friedrich. "Die Stellung der Theologie im System der Wissenschaften; Eine Auseinandersetzung mit P. Tillichs System der Wissenschaften," *Zeitschrift für systematische Theologie*, I (1923–24), 399–411.

Buschman, Harold. "Paul Tillich," *Christian Register*, CXII (1933), 791–94.

Dell, August. "Der Charakter der Theologie in Tillichs System der Wissenschaften," *Theologische Blätter*, II (1923), 235–45.

Dietrich, Heinrich. "Die Kirchenwahlen in Baden," *Christliche Welt*, XL (1926), 856.

Doerne, Martin. "Die Idee des Protestantismus bei Tillich," *Zeitschrift für Theologie und Kirche*, XI (1930), 206–25.

Eger, Martin. "Pfingsttagung in Augustusburg," *Christliche Welt*, XL (1926), 651–52.

"Ein Brief aus Amerika," *Christliche Welt*, XLVIII (1934), 1071–72.

Eisler, R. "Unbedingt," *Wörterbuch der philosophischen Begriffe*, Vol. III. 4th ed. Berlin: E. S. Mittler und Sohn, 1930.

Feigel, F. K. "Der deutsche Idealismus und das Christentum," *Christliche Welt*, XLII (1928), 403–11, especially 408.

Fuchs, Emil. "Die erste internationale Konferenz der religiösen Sozialisten," *Christliche Welt*, XXXVIII (1924), 609–14.

Fuerth, Martha. "Religiöse Gegenwartshaltung und menschliche Grenzsituation," *Christliche Welt*, XLV (1931), 109–12, especially 111.

Gerlach, Paul. "Von der Sterbensnot der Sakramente," *Christliche Welt*, XLV (1931), 149–58.

Harkness, Georgia. "The Abyss and the Given," *Christendom*, III (1938), 508–20.

Hartmann, Hans. "Zur inneren Lage des Christentums," *Christliche Welt*, XXXV (1921), 86.

Heimann, Eduard. "Socialist Christians in the Present Crisis," *Christianity and Society*, V, No. 4 (1940), 14–18.

Heimann, Eduard. "Rationalism versus Traditionalism," *Radical Religion*, IV (1939), 10–15.

Heitmann, Ludwig. "Gegenwärtige Verkündigung und symbolhaftes Denken," *Christliche Welt*, XLVI (1932), 689–94.

Herberger, Kurt. "Historismus und Kairos; Die Ueberwindung des Historismus bei Ernst Troeltsch und Paul Tillich," *Theologische Blätter*, XIV (1935), 129–41, 161–75.

Hermelink, H. "Das Kerygma des freien Protestantismus," *Christliche Welt*, XLVI (1932), 896–900.

Hermelink, H. "Ist die evangelische Kirche als rein kultische Grösse möglich," *Christliche Welt*, XLII (1928), 594–602, especially 599.

Kappes, Heinz. "Der dritte Kongress der religiösen Sozialisten Deutschlands," *Christliche Welt*, XL (1926), 910–13.

Kattenbusch, Ferdinand. "Die evangelische Theologie. Ihr jetziger Stand und ihre Aufgaben," *Christliche Welt*, XLIII (1929), 515–28, especially 517–18.

Kattenbusch, Ferdinand. "Gott erleben und an Gott glauben," *Zeitschrift für Theologie und Kirche*, IV (1923–24), 149 ff.

Kattenbusch, Ferdinand. "Das Unbedingte und der Unbegreifbare," *Theologische Studien und Kritiken*, XCIX (1926), 319–422.

Kirchner, Georg. "Religiös, fromm, Christ," *Christliche Welt*, XLVI (1932), 687–88.

Knittermeyer, Hinrich. Review of F. Kattenbusch, *Das Unbedingte und der Unbegreifbare, Theologische Literaturzeitung*, LII (1927), 595–97.

Knittermeyer, Hinrich. "Zum religiösen Sozialismus," *Zeitschrift für Theologie und Kirche*, IV (1923–24), 47–62.

Küppers, Erica. "Zur Religionsphilosophie Paul Tillichs," *Zwischen den Zeiten*, IX (1931), 123–53.

Lam, Elizabeth P. "Tillich's Reconstruction of the Concept of Ideology," *Christianity and Society*, V, No. 5 (1940), 11–15.

Leese, Kurt. "Die Geschichtsphilosophie des religiösen Sozialismus," *Christliche Welt*, XXXVII (1932), 370–85.

Leese, Kurt, "Vom religiösen Apriori," *Zeitschrift für Theologie und Kirche*, XI (1930), 95.

Leese, Kurt. "Zur Philosophie und Religionsphilosophie," *Zeitschrift für Theologie und Kirche*, XI (1930), 63–65, 71–72.

Leese, Kurt. "Zur Philosophie und Religionsphilosophie," *Zeitschrift für Theologie und Kirche*, XII (1931), 461.

Leese, Kurt. "Das System der Wissenschaften," *Christliche Welt*, XL (1926), 317–25, 371–75.

Lehmann, Kurt. "Das Wort Gottes als Aufgabe der Theologie," *Christliche Welt*, XXXIX (1925), 338–44.

Meland, Bernard E. "The Significance of Paul Tillich," *Christian Register*, CXII (1933), 797.

Mensing, Carl. "Schelling," *Christliche Welt*, XLV (1931), 266–68.

Mensing, Carl. "Vom Psychotherapeutischen Kongress in Dresden," *Christliche Welt*, XLV (1931), 719–23, especially 722.

Müller, A. Dedo. "Wünschs evangelische Wirtschaftsethik," *Zeitschrift für Theologie und Kirche*, IX (1928), 363–82.

Müller, Karl. "29. Deutscher Protestantentag in Potsdam, 5.–7. October 1926," *Christliche Welt*, XL (1926), 1136–37.

Müller, Karl. "Zum Vorschlage der kirchlichen Wirtschaftskommission," *Christliche Welt*, XL (1926), 955–59.

Nadler, Käte. "Hegel und der Angriff auf die Sinndeutung der Geschichte," *Christliche Welt*, XLVIII (1934), 819–24.

Niebuhr, Reinhold. "The Contribution of Paul Tillich," *Religion in Life*, VI (1937), 574–81.

Noack, Herman. "Recent Interpretations of Religion in German-Speaking Countries," *The Monist*, XL (1930), 42–44.

Oldham, J. H. "The God of History," *The Christian News Letter*, No. 212 (July 12, 1944), pp. 2–3.

Paulus, Rudolf. "Theologie und Religionsphilosophie," *Zeitschrift für Theologie und Kirche*, XIV (1933), 205–6.

Petersmann, Werner. "Zur deutsch-amerikanischen Verständigung," *Christliche Welt*, XLV (1931), 577–80, especially 580.

Petersmann, Werner. "Zur religiösen Krisis in Amerika," *Christliche Welt*, XLVII (1933), 551–58.

Piper, Otto. "Zur theologischen Lage der Gegenwart," *Christliche Welt*, XLI (1927), 938–45.

Piper, Otto. "Das 'Deutsche Volkstum' und der religiöse Sozialismus," *Neuwerk*, XIII (1931), 192.

Pongs, Hermann. "Tollers Dramen vom Menschen der Masse," *Christliche Welt*, XXXVIII (1924), 462–72.

Przywara, Erich. "Protestantische und katholische Ur-Einstellung," *Theologische Blätter*, VII (1928), 226–27.

Quervain, Alfred de. "Das zweite Gebot in der dogmatischen Arbeit," in *Theologische Aufsätze; Karl Barth zum 50. Geburtstag*, edited by E. Wolf. Munich: Chr. Kaiser, 1936, p. 97.

Rade, Martin. "Idealismus und Dämonie," *Christliche Welt*, XLVI (1932), 231–32.

Ruttenbeck, Walter. "Theologie und Wirklichkeit," *Theologische Rundschau*, IV (1932), 178–94.

Schafft, Hermann. "Zur 'Auflösung der Landgemeinden,'" *Neuwerk*, XIII (1931), 47–49.

Scharbau, Carl. "Die religiöse Lage der Gegenwart," *Christliche Welt*, XL (1926), 1196–97.

Schlaich, Ludwig. "Das Problem der Theodizee und die Aufgabe der Seelsorge," *Zwischen den Zeiten*, VIII (1930), 493–511.

Schmidt, E. W. "Zum Problem der Offenbarung," *Theologische Blätter*, IV (1925), 109–13.

Schowalter, August. "Die Bischofsfrage in der evangelischen Kirche," *Christliche Welt*, XL (1926), 71–78.

Schütz, Roland. "Ehrenrettung des Idealismus wider Johannes Müller," *Christliche Welt*, XLII (1928), 194–208, especially 196.

Schwarz, Rudolf. "Der Böse und das Böse," *Christliche Welt*, XLVII (1933), 6–16.

Siegfried, Theodor. "Das Unbedingte und der Undebingte," *Zeitschrift für Theologie und Kirche*, VII (1926), 323–47.

Siegfried, Theodor. "Review of Siegfried Marck, *Die Dialektik in der Philosophie der Gegenwart*," *Theologische Literaturzeitung*, LVI 1931), 403–7.

Stählin, Wilhelm. "Berneuchen," *Christliche Welt*, XLI (1927), 459–64.

Stählin, Wilhelm. "'Kirche und humanistische Gesellschaft,'" *Neuwerk*, XIII (1931), 112–17.

Steiner, Herman. "Das Rätsel des Uebels," *Christliche Welt*, XLVII (1933), 629–37.

Steinmann, Theophil. "Aus der dogmatischen Arbeit," *Zeitschrift für Theologie und Kirche*, X (1929), 63–66.

Steinmann, Theophil. "Zur Dogmatik," *Zeitschrift für Theologie und Kirche*, VII (1926), 462–65.

Stephan, Horst. "Ein neuer Schritt zum Verständnis des deutschen Idealismus," *Christliche Welt*, XLIII (1929), 693–94.

Stephan Horst. "Notizen," *Zeitschrift für Theologie und Kirche*, XI (1930), 75.

Stephan, Horst. "Das Unbedingte," *RGG*, V, 1350.

Stephan, Horst. "Die religiöse Frage—die Schicksalsfrage des deutschen Idealismus," *Zeitschrift für Theologie und Kirche*, VII (1926), 243–67.

Thomas, Wilhelm. "Noch einmal: Kirche und humanistische Gesellschaft," *Neuwerk*, XIII (1931), 139–47.

Urban, Wilbur M. "A Critique of Professor Tillich's Theory of the Religious Symbol," *Journal of Liberal Religion*, II (1940), 34–36.

Weinel, Heinrich. "'Schöpfungsordnungen,' eine neue Grundlegung der Sozialethik?" *Christliche Welt*, XLVII (1933), 242–49, 292–301.

Wieman, H. N. "Authority and the Normative Approach," *Journal of Religion*, XVI (1936), 175–202.

Williams, George H. "Priest, Prophet, and Proletariat: A Study in the Theology of Paul Tillich," *Journal of Liberal Religion*, I, No. 3 (1940), 25–37.

Winkler, Robert. "Der Erkenntniswert der religiösen Vorstellung," *Zeitschrift für Theologie und Kirche*, X, (1929), 395–96, 398–99.

Winkler, Robert. "Die Theologie des Philosophen Tillich in seinem Buch *Religiöse Verwirklichung*," *Christentum und Wissenschaft*, VI (1930), 212–20.

Wünsch, Georg. "Antikritisches zu 'Religion und Wirtschaft'; Auseinandersetzung mit Marr, Foerster, und Heimann," *Christliche Welt*, XL (1926), 482–89.

Wünsch, Georg. "Wöchentliche Chronik," *Christliche Welt*, XLV (1931), 437. Description and personnel of the six organizations of Religious Socialists in Germany.

G. *Reviews of Tillich's Books*

Mystik und Schuldbewusstsein in Schellings philosophischer Entwicklung (1912)

Cl. Kopp, *Theologische Revue*, XI (1912), 282–84.

A. S. Martin, *Review of Theology and Philosophy*, VIII (1912), 74.

L. Jacobskötter, *Theologisches Literaturblatt*, XXXIII (1912), 420–22.

A. Dorner, *Theologische Literaturzeitung*, XXXVIII (1913), 177–79.

"Ueber die Idee einer Theologie der Kultur" (1919)

E. W. Mayer, *Theologische Literaturzeitung*, XLVI (1921), 162–63.

Hans von Soden, *Zeitschrift für Theologie und Kirche*, II (1921), 468–77.

Georg Wunderle, *Theologische Revue*, XXI (1922), 237.

M. Schian, *Theologische Literaturzeitung*, XLVIII (1923), 47.

Masse und Geist (1922)

Gerhard Colm, *Archiv für Sozialwissenschaft und Sozialpolitik*, XLIX (1922), 821–22.

Das System der Wissenschaften (1923)

Friedrich Büchsel, *Zeitschrift für systematische Theologie*, I (1923–24), 399–411.

August Dell, *Theologische Blätter*, II (1931), 235–45.

August Dell, *Annalen der Philosophie und der philosophischen Kritik*, IV (1924), Bücheranzeigen, 13.

N. V. Bubnoff, *Archiv für Sozialwissenschaften und Sozialpolitik*, LIII (1925), 543–45.

Wilhelm Sauer, *Archiv für Rechts- und Wirtschaftsphilosophie*, XIX (1925–26), 316–18.

Kurt Leese, *Christliche Welt*, XL (1926), 317–25, 371–75.

Kirche und Kultur (1924)

J. E. McFadyen, *Expository Times*, XXXVI (1925), 284–85.

Carl Schneider, *Christentum und Wissenschaft*, I (1925), 128–29.

Emanuel Hirsch, *Theologische Blätter*, V (1926), 270.

"Rechtfertigung und Zweifel" (1924)

M. Meinertz, *Theologische Revue*, XXIV (1925), 328–29.

Carl Schneider, *Christentum und Wissenschaft*, I (1925), 128–29.

"Religionsphilosophie" (1925)

Emanuel Hirsch, *Theologische Literaturzeitung*, LX (1926), 97–103.

Wilhelm Bruhn, *Zeitschrift für Theologie und Kirche*, VIII (1927), 75–77.

Kairos: I (1926)
Kurt Leese, *Christliche Welt,* XL (1926), 1260–61.
Wilhelm Bruhn, *Zeitschrift für Theologie und Kirche,* VIII (1927), 75–77.
Robert Winkler, *Theologische Literaturzeitung,* LII (1927), 377–81.
Das Dämonische (1926)
Kurt Leese, *Annalen der Philosophie: Literaturberichte,* VI (1926), 119.
Hermann Mulert, *Theologische Literaturzeitung,* LIII (1928), 169–72.
Elert, *Theologisches Literaturblatt,* XLIX (1928), 130–31.
Die religiöse Lage der Gegenwart (1926)
Stange, *Theologisches Literaturblatt,* XLVIII (1927), 154–55.
Das Berneuchener Buch (1928)
Karl Müller, *Christliche Welt,* XLII (1928), 53–58.
Religiöse Verwirklichung (1929)
Käte Nadler, *Logos,* XIX (1930), 407–9.
Robert Winkler, *Christentum und Wissenschaft,* IV (1930), 212–20.
Thomas Thomassen, *Deutsches Volkstum,* June 1931.
H. W. Schmidt, *Theologisches Literaturblatt,* LIII (1932), 234–35.
G. Wehrung, *Kant-Studien,* XXXVIII (1933), 486–87.
Kairos: II (1929)
Erich Schaeder, *Theologisches Literaturblatt,* LIII (1932), 182–86.
Otto Piper, *Kant-Studien,* XXXVIII (1933), 469–71.
Protestantisches Prinzip und proletarische Situation (1931)
Ernst Bizer, *Christliche Welt,* XLVI (1932), 234–35.
Robert Winkler, *Christentum und Wissenschaft,* VIII (1932), 274.
The Religious Situation (1932)
Thomas Thomassen, *Boston Transcript,* December 24, 1932, p. 2.
Reinhold Niebuhr, *World Tomorrow,* XV (1932), 596.
E. T. Buehrer, *Christian Century,* L (1933), 155–56.
E. T. Buehrer, *Survey Graphic,* XXII (1933), 229.
Alter Brody, *New Republic,* LXXVI (1933), 315.
Alter Brody, *New York Herald Tribune* Books, January 1, 1933, p. 10.
Stewart G. Cole, *Journal of Religion,* XIII (1933), 348–49.
T. V. Smith, *Ethics,* XLIII (1933), 375–76.
P. W. Wilson, *Saturday Review of Literature,* IX (1933), 379.
A. E. Avey, *Philosophical Review,* XLIII (1934), 433.
The Interpretation of History (1936)
Reinhold Niebuhr, *Radical Religion,* II, No. 1 (1936), 41-42.
E. E. Aubrey, *Christendom,* II (1937), 299–302.
Clifford Barrett, *New York Times* Book Review, January 24, 1937, p. 6.
Harold Buschman, *Review of Religion,* I (1937), 426–33.
S. J. Case, *Journal of Religion,* XVII (1937), 213–21.
K. J. Grimm, *Lutheran Church Quarterly,* X (1937), 443-44.
R. E. E. Harkness, *Crozer Quarterly,* XIV (1937), 244.
C. E. M. Joad, *The New Statesman and Nation,* XIII (1937), 374–76.
D. D. Zuver, *The Churchman,* CLI (February 1, 1937), 19.
Charles A. Beard, *American Journal of Sociology,* XLIII (1938), 666–67.

H. *Unpublished Material on Tillich*

Lam, Elizabeth P. "The Place of Marx in Christian Thought." Unpublished Ph.D. dissertation, The Divinity School, University of Chicago, 1939. Pp. 156.

Phillips, Charles W. "Ethical Decision in Paul, Barth, Brunner and Tillich." Unpublished B.D. dissertation, The Divinity School, University of Chicago, 1941. Pp. 144.

Sabin, Raymond A. "Tillich's Concept of God." Unpublished B.D. dissertation, The Meadville Theological School, Chicago, 1944. Pp. 133.

Stiernotte, Alfred. "The Place of Marxism in Religious Thought." Unpublished B.D. dissertation, The Meadville Theological School, Chicago, 1944. Pp. 160.

Walker, E. R. "The Problem of Religious Commitment as an Object of Empirical Inquiry." Unpublished Ph.D. dissertation, The Divinity School, University of Chicago, 1939. Pp. 143.

Weston, Hugh W. "A Comparative Study of Four Modern Philosophies of History: Christopher Dawson, Benedetto Croce, Ortega y Gasset, and Paul Tillich." Unpublished B.D. dissertation, The Meadville Theological School, Chicago, 1942. Pp. 187.

Williams, George H. "Sin in the Theology of Paul Tillich." Unpublished B.D. dissertation, The Meadville Theological School, Chicago, 1939. Pp. 114.

I. *Fugitive References*

Aubrey, E. E. *Living the Christian Faith.* New York: The Macmillan Co., 1939.

Aubrey, E. E. *Man's Search for Himself.* Nashville: Cokesbury Press, 1940.

Aubrey, E. E. *Present Theological Tendencies.* New York: Harper & Brothers, 1936.

Bosley, Harold A. *The Quest for Religious Certainty.* Chicago: Willett, Clark and Co., 1939.

Demant, V. A. *The Religious Prospect.* London: Frederick Muller, Ltd., 1939.

Franken, J. C. *Kritische Philosophie und Dialektische Theologie.* Amsterdam: H. J. Paris, 1932.

Hammer, George. *Christian Realism in Contemporary American Theology.* Uppsala: A.-B. Lundequistska, 1940.

Heimann, Eduard. *Communism, Fascism, or Democracy?* New York: W. W. Norton and Co., 1938.

Horton, W. M. *Contemporary Continental Theology.* New York: Harper & Brothers, 1938.

Horton, W. M. *Realistic Theology.* New York: Harper & Brothers, 1934.

Hoyle, R. Birch. *The Teaching of Karl Barth.* New York: Charles Scribner's Sons, 1930.

Kattenbusch, F. *Die deutsche evangelische Theologie seit Schleiermacher.* 5th ed. Giessen: A. Töpelmann, 1926.

McCown, C. C. "In History or Beyond History," *Harvard Theological Review,* XXXVIII (1945), 151–75.

May, Rollo. *The Art of Counselling.* Nashville: Cokesbury Press, 1939.

May, Rollo. *The Springs of Creative Living.* New York: Abingdon-Cokesbury Press, 1940.

Müller, A. Dedo. *Ethik. Der evangelische Weg der Verwirklichung des Guten.* Berlin: A. Töpelmann, 1937.

Pauck, Wilhelm. *Karl Barth, Prophet of a New Christianity?* New York: Harper & Brothers, 1931.

Schafft, Hermann. *Vom Kampf gegen die Kirche für die Kirche.* Schlüchtern: Neuwerk, 1925.

Stephan, Horst. *Geschichte der evangelischen Theologie seit dem Deutschen Idealismus.* Berlin: Töpelmann, 1938.

Van Dusen, H. P. *God in These Times.* New York: Charles Scribner's Sons, 1935.

Whale, J. S. *Christian Docrine.* New York: The Macmillan Co., 1941.

Wieman, H. N. "The New Supernaturalism," *Christendom,* III (1938), 68–81.

Index